DYNAMICS OF POLITICAL VIOLENCE

The Mobilization Series on Social Movements, Protest, and Culture

Series Editor

Professor Hank Johnston
San Diego State University, USA

Published in conjunction with *Mobilization: An International Quarterly*, the premier research journal in the field, this series disseminates high quality new research and scholarship in the fields of social movements, protest, and contentious politics. The series is interdisciplinary in focus and publishes monographs and collections of essays by new and established scholars.

Other titles in the series

Beyond NGO-ization
The Development of Social Movements in Central and Eastern Europe
Edited by Kerstin Jacobsson and Steven Saxonberg

Violent Protest, Contentious Politics, and the Neoliberal State
Edited by Seraphim Seferiades and Hank Johnston

Student Activism and Curricular Change in Higher Education
Mikaila Mariel Lemonik Arthur

Dynamics of Political Violence
A Process-Oriented Perspective on Radicalization
and the Escalation of Political Conflict

Edited by

LORENZO BOSI
European University Institute, Italy

CHARES DEMETRIOU
Queen's University Belfast, UK

STEFAN MALTHANER
Bielefeld University, Germany

ASHGATE

© Lorenzo Bosi, Chares Demetriou, Stefan Malthaner and the contributors 2014

All rights reserved. No part of this publication may be reproduced, stored in a retrieval system or transmitted in any form or by any means, electronic, mechanical, photocopying, recording or otherwise without the prior permission of the publisher.

Lorenzo Bosi, Chares Demetriou and Stefan Malthaner have asserted their right under the Copyright, Designs and Patents Act, 1988, to be identified as the editors of this work.

Published by
Ashgate Publishing Limited
Wey Court East
Union Road
Farnham
Surrey, GU9 7PT
England

Ashgate Publishing Company
110 Cherry Street
Suite 3-1
Burlington, VT 05401-3818
USA

www.ashgate.com

British Library Cataloguing in Publication Data
A catalogue record for this book is available from the British Library

The Library of Congress has cataloged the printed edition as follows:
Bosi, Lorenzo, contributor.
  Dynamics of political violence : a process-oriented perspective on radicalization and the escalation of political conflict / by Lorenzo Bosi, Chares Demetriou and Stefan Malthaner.
      pages cm. – (The mobilization series on social movements, protest, and culture)
  Includes bibliographical references and index.
  ISBN 978-1-4094-4351-3 (hardback : alk. paper) – ISBN 978-1-4094-4352-0 (ebook) – ISBN 978-1-4724-0192-2 (epub) 1. Political violence. 2. Violence–Religious aspects. 3. Violence–Social aspects. 4. Radicalism. I. Demetriou, Chares, contributor. II. Malthaner, Stefan, contributor. III. Title.
  JC328.6.B677 2014
  303.6–dc23

2013028026

ISBN 9781409443513 (hbk)
ISBN 9781409443520 (ebk – PDF)
ISBN 9781472401922 (ebk – ePUB)

Printed in the United Kingdom by Henry Ling Limited,
at the Dorset Press, Dorchester, DT1 1HD

Contents

List of Figures and Tables	*vii*
List of Contributors	*ix*
Acknowledgements	*xi*

1   A Contentious Politics Approach to the Explanation of Radicalization   1
    Lorenzo Bosi, Chares Demetriou and Stefan Malthaner

PART I   DYNAMICS OF INTERACTION BETWEEN OPPOSITIONAL MOVEMENTS/GROUPS AND THE STATE

2   The Mechanisms of Emotion in Violent Protest   27
    Hank Johnston

3   A Typology of Backfire Mechanisms   51
    Lasse Lindekilde

4   Processes of Radicalization and De-radicalization in Western
    European Prisons (1965–1986)   71
    Christian G. De Vito

PART II   COMPETITION AND CONFLICT: DYNAMICS OF INTRA-MOVEMENT INTERACTION

5   Competitive Escalation During Protest Cycles: Comparing Left-wing
    and Religious Conflicts   93
    Donatella della Porta

6   Intra-movement Competition and Political Outbidding as
    Mechanisms of Radicalization in Northern Ireland, 1968–1969   115
    Gianluca De Fazio

7   The Limits of Radicalization: Escalation and Restraint in the
    South African Liberation Movement   137
    Devashree Gupta

PART III DYNAMICS OF MEANING FORMATION: FRAMES AND BEYOND

8   Contentious Interactions, Dynamics of Interpretations, and
Radicalization: The Islamization of Palestinian Nationalism   169
Eitan Y. Alimi and Hank Johnston

9   Radical or Righteous? Using Gender to Shape Public Perceptions
of Political Violence   189
Jocelyn Viterna

10   From National Event to Transnational Injustice Symbol:
The Three Phases of the Muhammad Cartoon Controversy   217
Thomas Olesen

PART IV DYNAMICS OF (TRANSNATIONAL) DIFFUSION

11   Radicalization from Outside: The Role of the Anarchist Diaspora
in Coordinating Armed Actions in Franco's Spain   237
Eduardo Romanos

12   Protest Diffusion and Rising Political Violence in the Turkish '68
Movement: The Arab-Israeli War, "Paris May" and The Hot
Summer of 1968   255
Emin Alper

13   The Evolution of the al-Qaeda-type Terrorism: Networks
and Beyond   275
Ekaterina Stepanova

14   Conclusion   293
Martha Crenshaw

Index   *305*

List of Figures and Tables

Figures

2.1	Fear abatement mechanism	38
2.2	Anger-spiral mechanism	42
6.1	Civil rights and loyalist protests in Northern Ireland, August 1968–December 1969	125
6.2	Network of violence, Northern Ireland, May 1968–July 1969	127
6.3	Network of violence, Northern Ireland, August 1969–December 1969	130
7.1	Intra-movement radicalization process	145
7.2	Limitations on intra-movement radicalization	155
8.1	Primary framework structure and the Jihadist rim	173

Tables

3.1	The typological grid of backfire mechanisms	55
3.2	Backfire mechanisms in the field of counterterrorism	58
6.1	Dynamics of ethnic and political outbidding	119
10.1	Al-Qaeda communiqués related to the Muhammad cartoons	225
10.2	Successful and unsuccessful/aborted attacks motivated by the cartoons	226

List of Contributors

Eitan Y. Alimi is based at The Hebrew University, Israel.

Emin Alper is based at Istanbul Technical University, Turkey.

Lorenzo Bosi is based at the European University Institute, Italy.

Martha Crenshaw is based at Stanford University, USA.

Gianluca De Fazio is based at Emory University, USA.

Christian G. De Vito is based at the Department of Historical Studies, University of Leicester, UK.

Donatella della Porta is based at the European University Institute, Italy.

Chares Demetriou is based at Queen's University Belfast, UK.

Devashree Gupta is based at Carleton College, USA.

Hank Johnston is based at San Diego State University, USA.

Lasse Lindekilde is based at Aarhus University, Denmark.

Stefan Malthaner is based at the European University Institute, Italy.

Thomas Olesen is based at Aarhus University, Denmark.

Eduardo Romanos is based at Universidad Complutense de Madrid, Spain.

Ekaterina Stepanova is based at the Institute of the World Economy and International Relations (IMEMO), Moscow.

Jocelyn Viterna is based at Harvard University, USA.

Acknowledgements

The idea for this book originated in the conference "Processes of Radicalization and De-Radicalization" hosted by the International Journal of Conflict and Violence (IJCV) in Bielefeld, Germany, in April 6–8, 2011. That conference brought together a group of scholars who shared an interest in looking beyond disciplinary boundaries and entrenched fields of regional expertise which, in turn, brought together different perspectives to search for new and broader ways of studying processes of political violence. In its theoretical outlook as well as in its broadly comparative approach, this volume owes many insights and inspirations to this encounter. Therefore, in more than one sense, this is a truly collective achievement.

We would like to thank Wilhelm Heitmeyer, editor of the IJCV, and Donatella della Porta and Gary LaFree, who acted as academic hosts of the conference and contributed important impulses for us to proceed with this ambitious project.

We also thank Teresa Koloma Beck, André Bank, and Alex Veit – our partners in organizing this conference – who helped realize an event that was remarkable not only for the quality of scholarly contributions but also for the broad diversity of participants with respect to disciplinary and regional backgrounds.

The conference was made possible by funding from the Volkswagen Foundation and could not have been organized without the excellent logistical support from the staff at the Center for Interdisciplinary Research (ZiF) and at Bielefeld University. In particular, we are grateful to Julia Marth (IJCV editorial staff) and Heiko Mata, for their efficient work and cheerful support.

We thank all authors represented in this volume for their commitment to this project and for the patience with which they submitted their contributions to several reviews, both by the editors and external reviewers.

To Hank Johnston, Editor of Ashgate's *Mobilization Series on Social Movements, Protest, and Culture*, we are grateful for his support and constructive criticism – and the balance of the two he kept – which helped us to constantly further develop and in the end complete this book. Finally, we wish to thank Jude Chilmann, Carolyn Court, Claire Jarvis and Barbara Pretty, editorial staff in charge of handling our project at Ashgate.

Lorenzo Bosi
Chares Demetriou
Stefan Malthaner

Chapter 1
A Contentious Politics Approach to the Explanation of Radicalization

Lorenzo Bosi, Chares Demetriou and Stefan Malthaner

Research on political violence is currently undergoing transformation, following a decade of increase in terms of "quantity, scope and variety" (Crenshaw 2011: X). Not only are dominant perspectives, such as the school of "terrorism studies," being challenged (see Gunning 2007; Jackson, Smyth, and Gunning 2009); fields of research on different violent phenomena and geographical areas, which were hitherto largely separated, have also started to communicate and collaborate with one another, sharing theoretical approaches and engaging in comparative projects. The most notable development in research on political violence, however, is the increasing influence of theoretical approaches developed in the study of social movements and, in particular, the *contentious politics* paradigm formulated by Doug McAdam, Sidney Tarrow, and Charles Tilly (2001; Tilly and Tarrow 2007).[1] Whereas few researchers in the field of social movement studies had until recently concerned themselves with the element of violence in political struggles—perhaps because researchers had been inclined to study groups and organizations they felt sympathetic to, which had not included violent political organizations—now a growing number of social movement scholars have turned their attention towards violent phenomena; at the same time, more and more studies on militant groups and violent conflicts have adopted a social movement perspective.[2]

---

1 For a comprehensive review of scholarly critical debate on the 'mechanism–process' research program, see: *Qualitative Sociology* 2008: 31(4); and *Mobilization* 2003: 8(3).

2 This development is represented, inter alia, by Alimi 2006; 2011; Alimi, Bosi, and Demetriou (2012); Araj (2008); Bosi (2012); Bosi and della Porta (2012); Demetriou (2007; 2012a); della Porta (1995, 2008, 2013); Goodwin (2006); Gunning (2009); Hafez (2004); Hafez and Wiktorowicz (2004); Obershall (2004); Seferiades and Johnston (2011); Steinhoff and Zwerman (2008); Snow and Byrd (2007); Tilly (2003/2005); White (1989); Wiktorowicz (2004); Zwerman and Steinhoff (2005); Zwerman,Steinhoff, and della Porta (2000). Notable is also the adoption of social-movement approaches by scholars studying civil wars and violent insurgencies; see Hegghammer (2010); Malthaner (2011); Wood (2003); Viterna (2006). Moreover, special issues as well as dialogues on political violence in *Qualitative Sociology* (vol. 31, 2008), *Mobilization* (vol. 12/no.2, 2007; vol. 17/no. 1, 2012) and *Mobilizing Ideas* (http://mobilizingideas.wordpress.com/category/essay-dialogues/is-terrorism-a-form-of-activism/) indicate increasing coordination and consolidation within this line of research.

What characterizes this emerging line of research—and the shift of perspective it represents—is, above all, an emphasis on the *contextualization of violence*. These scholars insist that political violence emerges in the context of broader social, political and cultural conflicts, which, on closer examination, is a perspective that entails the contextualization of violent actions in three respects. Firstly, it considers violence as one of several forms of confrontation within a wider *repertoire of actions and strategies*. Oppositional groups and movements adopt from the available repertoire elements that not simply match their goals and identity orientation but correspond to changing environments and actions of their opponents. Confronting over-structural macro assumptions, this reading recognizes the agency of the individuals and groups involved in radicalization. Secondly, this perspective acknowledges that militant groups are embedded within the broader field of actors involved in the conflict. This is a *relational field* that includes state-agents, counter-movements, audiences, as well as groups and organizations which belong to the same movement—all of whom shape the evolution of the conflict as they are linked by asymmetrical power relations. Finally, it recognizes that violent interactions are embedded in the wider *processes of political contention*. Such interactions are considered to be the result—and part—of temporal sequences of events and causal dynamics bounded together through their connection to the state—that is, through claims that implicate the state and through counter-positioning by the state. This perspective, in sum, emphasizes the emergent quality of political violence by locating it within broader political processes, relational fields, and repertoires of action. As the proponents of this perspective point out, violence becomes in this way de-exceptionalized and de-essentialized (see Beck 2008; Goodwin 2012; Gunning 2009; Goodwin 2012; Tilly 2003).

This volume locates itself within this field of research. Its aim is to further develop our understanding of the processes in which violence emerges, increases, and ceases, focusing on the recurring causal patterns that shape trajectories of radicalization. In general, we perceive *radicalization* to be a process forming through strategy, structure, and conjuncture, and involving the adoption and sustained use of violent means to achieve articulated political goals.[3] Each in its way, the chapters of this volume follow this approach, rejecting along the way approaches which treat violence as a *sui generis* phenomenon or as one attributable to a distinct class of people. Far from being inevitable, the process of radicalization involves in our view the adoption of long-term strategy as well as short-term tactics, each chosen from among alternative violent and non-violent options and in the service of goals which potentially evolve in the course of the process. At the same time, however, the formation of strategy is contingent on specific social, political and cultural contexts, as well as emergent events; the shift to political violence, in fact, can neither be explained in a vacuum nor in isolation from other forms of contention. While the ways in which process-dynamics shape

---

3 We acknowledge the importance of state or state-sponsored violence as an object of research, but this volume focuses mainly on non-state actors.

social movements have been explored extensively, this volume aims at providing a more systematic account of the dynamics of political violence by drawing attention to its mechanisms and conditions, based on a set of case studies that allow for a comparative perspective across forms of violence and geographical regions. We believe that the dynamic perspective, which considers processes and mechanisms to be the key units of analysis, can enhance our understanding of how and when processes of radicalization unfold as well as allow comparison among different forms of political violence (violent protest, guerrilla warfare, insurgency, terrorism, and civil wars) across time and places. The chapters cover cases ranging from the anarchist movement and left-wing militancy in European history to contemporary Islamist violence, to insurgent movements in South Africa and Latin America. These cases converge around four process-dynamics which we consider of major importance to processes of radicalization and the escalation of violence: dynamics of movement-state interaction; dynamics of intra-movement competition; dynamics of meaning formation and transformation; and dynamics of diffusion. The emphasis of this volume, thereby, is on providing rich empirical analyses which allow for precise reconstructions of process-dynamics, but which also point to complexities and particularities that enable us to critically assess and further develop the theory of radicalization process-dynamics.

When arguing for an emergent perspective within an academic field, however, there is a tendency to emphasize its "newness" and point out differences rather than continuities with previous research and other fields; yet, this should not be overdone. While locating this project within an emerging line of research on political violence and building upon elements of social movement theory, we also seek to embed our approach within the broader field of political violence research. It has to be emphasized that various (earlier and contemporary) works outside social movement studies and the contentious politics paradigm have already developed contextual and process-oriented perspectives. For one, several leading scholars in research on terrorism have consistently insisted on analyzing violence within its historical, social, and political context (e.g. Crenshaw 1995; English 2009; Horgan 2005; Rapoport 1987; Waldmann 1989, 1998), and Friedhelm Neidhardt, to single out but one scholar, has quite early stressed the role of relational dynamics in processes of radicalization and escalation (Neidhardt 1981, 1982). Moreover, research on civil wars has recently begun to take a closer look at processes of violence, producing original empirical studies and significant theoretical advances (e.g. Kalyvas 2006, Weinstein 2007, Wood 2008).

Processes of Radicalization

Examining processes of radicalization and the emergence of political violence from a contentious politics perspective entails, above all else, an emphasis on their processual dimension. At the core of this paradigm lies the notion that processes and mechanisms (or sub-processes) possess causal efficacy, which renders these categories crucial at forming causal analogies.

At the most general level, a social process is a series of happenings that unfold over time, are bounded together in some way, and produce change of some kind. One can, as various scholars have done, emphasize different aspects of this basic definition and arrive at different conceptualizations of process, the most central ones understanding social process by virtue of its bounds or by virtue of the change it entails (see Demetriou 2012b). However conceptualized, the general epistemological perspective that follows from this understanding holds that to describe the unfolding of an actual process is to explain it. This perspective resonates, at various degrees, with this volume's featured studies. Though the categories expressing processes may vary, they tend to revolve around the idea of emergence.

Relating to incremental and potentially manifold and compound change, emergence follows a model of fluid causality, as opposed to discrete, "billiard ball" causality. Emphasis is placed on the development of outcomes while accepting the likelihood that these may be affected by multiple causes at once. Qualitative data are often needed to apprehend patterns relevant to processes, but that does not mean that quantitative data and statistical methods are excluded. But it does mean, first, that the information provided by such data and methods ultimately supports process theorizing—accounting for how processes unfold—and not what Abbott (2001) calls general linear reality (for a discussion on the relationship between the analysis of covariance and processes, see Tarrow 2010). It also means that induction is unlikely to be sufficient on its own and so would need to be combined with, or even take the backseat to deduction, including reasoning through conjecture (Bunge 1997; Pettigrew 1997; Demetriou 2009).

Emergence, then, must make analytical room for conjuncture and contingency. These interrelated notions have a series of ramifications. First, they suggest that the sequence and order of happenings may be important. Indeed, the same events occurring in different order may produce drastically different processes. Secondly, and related to the above, timing can also be important. The effects of an event therefore may be different if it happens in point A in time rather than in point B, while some events may even completely lose their effect if their context changes. Finally, conjuncture may amount to turning points in a process (McAdam and Sewell 2001; Sewell 2005). Accounting for turning points is obviously very important in accounting for a process, but that does not necessarily mean that the forces generating the change need to be well understood. For example, while an event may be transformative, tracing the forces that precipitated it may be too complicated to be sorted out, while the transformation itself may be the important element in a given process and the useful thing to know in accounting for similar processes.

Processes of radicalization conform to this understanding of social processes. What characterizes them in particular is the element of violence—the outcome as well as the constitutive part of the process, shaping dynamics of interaction and transforming their conditions. However, while we aim to draw attention to radicalization as a process of violence emerging out of broader political conflict, we also seek to understand the particular implications and conditions of dynamics of political violence as well as to consider their specific effects and outcomes. We subscribe to the notion that violent strategies and actions must not be regarded as sui generis phenomena, but rather as ones that have to be explained as part of broader political struggles and through processual causal models. At the same time, we insist that political violence does not constitute a single strategic form. Rather, various forms and levels of violence exist, entailing transformations of political conflicts that are complicated as much as they are significant—hence a richness which the analysis must capture. In this volume we seek to develop this understanding of political violence by focusing on four groupings of dynamics that drive and shape processes of radicalization, namely, dynamics pertaining to state-movement interactions, intra-movement competition, meaning formation, and (transnational) diffusion. These four groupings are by no means exhaustive or comprehensive, of course. Radicalization is influenced by a multitude of mechanisms and factors—ranging from changes in opportunity structure and other macro-level factors to changes in predispositions and motives at the micro-level—which may be grouped in different ways. Yet, we maintain that the four delineations of dynamics proposed in this volume offer key gateways into insight of how political violence emerges, increases, and spreads.

Dynamics of Interaction between Oppositional Movements/Groups and the State

Most of the literature on political violence, as the school of critical studies of terrorism underlines, has provided one-sided explanations. They tend to focus prevalently on the armed groups or their militants, ignoring the several ways in which states can influence the emergence, development and decline of violence. Yet radicalization processes always take place in the context of the state and typically involve claims to the state. As Hank Johnston puts it, protest movements' "targets are usually state authorities who are in positions to make changes and reforms that answer protesters' demands. While it is possible that protesters sometimes challenge nonstate institutions, such as university administrations or religious organizations, in the twenty-first century, the vast majority of protest campaigns and social movements target the state" (2011: 1). States respond variously: they resist changes and concessions demanded by social movements, oppositional groupings, or external contenders (Amenta 2006; Amenta and Caren 2004); they attempt to physically repress these organizations by force (della Porta 1995; della Porta and Fillieu 2004; Earl 2003; Davenport 2007); they institutionalize the changes and demands or part of them (Meyer 2007; Suh 2011); or, to complicate matters further, they respond in any possible combination of the aforementioned ways.

How states respond is shaped simultaneously by multiple factors. But a central element regarding these factors is the interactive relationship existing between the state and its challengers. To borrow from Johnston again, "popular protest and the structure of the state are in a dynamic and mutually influencing relationship, each pushing and constraining the other" (2011: 16). As Bosi and Uba write "protest and repression, but also concession and co-optation, are closely inter-related via reciprocal relationship. There are not 'magic' responses able to dampen protest, as there are not specific protest strategies able to achieve social movement goals. The impact of political and institutional responses should be understood in their context" (forthcoming). In particular cases states even promote death squads (Campbell and Brenner 2002) and passively support violence from non-state actors for geopolitical reasons (Byman 2005). Therefore, any reading of how and when radicalization develops needs to pay attention on the interaction between oppositional movements/groups and the state.

This observation leads to an important question: are certain types of regimes more likely than other to experience radicalization processes? This is not the place to review the rich literature addressing this question, but some basic insight can be noted. First, democratic regimes are not immune to violent protest—one can readily find examples of violent protest taking place in the United States, Canada, Great Britain, Germany, France, or Italy. At the same time however, research also suggests that socio-revolutionary violence in particular is more prevalent in the context of regime transitions (Hegre et al. 2001), while ethno-nationalist violence is found in various regimes—from authoritarian to democratic—governing deeply divided societies (Sanchez-Cuenca and de la Calle 2009).

In Chapter 2 of this volume, Hank Johnston chooses to draw evidence from a variety of regimes in order to search for commonalities in the mode of contention. He maintains that the levels of violent protest relate to two recurrent mechanisms: fear abatement and anger spirals. This is not a reductionist thesis, for it is built on a relational-dynamic understanding of the radicalization process in which strategic interactions take place between "forces aligned with the protesters, and the various forces of social control." Indeed, in his approach Johnston challenges the idea of the image of a two-party struggle between a unified movement and a unified opponent, pointing, instead, to the complexity of actors both on the movement side and on the side of security forces. What is more, in his framework Johnston weaves together several established ideas regarding radicalization. They include the role of frustration-aggression from the classic J-curve hypothesis, the role of emotions characteristic of collective behavior theories, the emergent definition of normative protest repertoires of symbolic interactionism, and the strategic use of violence and disruption of the classic analysis by Piven and Cloward of poor people's movements.

Like Johnston, Lasse Lindekilde, in Chapter 3, advances a general thesis vis-à-vis radicalization and the state. Drawing on Vedung's policy instrument classification, Hess and Martin's ideas of backfire, and McAdamn, Tarrow and Tilly's conceptualization of processes and distinctions of types of causal mechanisms, Linkekilde develops a typology regarding the effects of counterterrorism. More specifically, he focusses on how liberal-democratic states' repressive responses in the area of counterterrorism and radicalization prevention may work contrary to intentions to produce counterproductive effects in terms of widening and intensifying societal tensions. His typology of "backfire mechanisms" cross-classifies hard counterterrorism policies and soft radicalization prevention instruments with three dimensions of dissent mobilization and behavior: strategy, interaction, and identity. This yields six sets of backfire mechanisms, each of which the author describes and illustrates through a variety of empirical evidence.

While general theses such as the ones developed by Johnston and Linkekilde are much needed, also needed are analyses of more specific institutions of state repression—armies, paramilitaries, police, courts, and prisons. The latter of these institutions, prisons, is perhaps the one least studied by the scholarship on violence and radicalization (Goldstone and Useem 1999), despite the fact that they are the state arm most invasive on the individual. Chapter 4 goes some way to correct this general oversight. Here Christian De Vito explains processes of radicalization and de-radicalization in the context of prisons. His approach, however, examines dynamics both within and outside the prison, hence the relationship between internal and external mechanisms. He therefore arrives at a dynamic understanding of prison repression which is shaped by its context (outside) and the agency of the prison authorities and of the prisoners (inside). Following research in different Western European countries at different moments (second half of the 1960s; 1972–1973; 1974–1975; the end of the 1970s and the beginning of the 1980s), De Vito is ultimately able to propose a cultural and arguably novel perspective on the question of radicalization vis-à-vis prisons.

Future research on the relation between opposing movements/groups and the state has ample work to do. Among its priorities, we maintain, must be the examination of states' response to threats and challenges, particularly the apparent puzzle of why state institutions often do not respond in sensible ways. Related to this is the question of why and how repressive responses result in success or alternatively provoke radicalization. Furthermore, we need to remember that on their part oppositional movements/groups are not passive actors in this relationship with the state. Eventually they seek to provoke the state to overreact in an indiscriminate way so to alienate the population and build key constituencies who take the side of the insurgents (Zwerman and Steinhoff. 2005). We need, then, to better study oppositional movements/groups strategic choice in relation to the state.

Competition and Conflict: Dynamics of Intra-movement Interaction

Whether perpetrated by large organizations or small underground groups, political violence often develops in the context of larger protest movements. Indeed, as Donatella della Porta notes in Chapter 5 of this volume, one of the main advantages in analyzing political violence from the perspective of social movement studies is that it enables us to locate it within the organizational fields with which they interact. Oppositional movements are composed of networks of groups and organizations which share certain goals and collaborate to engage in collective protest, but which may also diverge in their ideological and tactical preferences and compete for resources (see Curtis and Zurcher 1973; Zald and McCarthy 1979; Rucht 2004). In particular when competition triggers a process in which groups try to outbid one another in winning attention and support by taking on more radical positions or by using more militant forms of action, intra-movement interactions can entail mechanisms of radicalization that contribute to the emergence and increase of political violence.

The analytical groundwork to examining dynamics of intra-movement competition has been laid by proponents of the resource mobilization approach to the study of social movements (Zald and Ash 1966; McCarthy and Zald 1977; Zald and McCarthy 1979) and by related work on political organizations (Wilson 1974), as well as by political process-scholars (Tarrow 1998). Competitive relations between social movement organizations (SMOs) result from the fact that they depend on scarce resources to survive and to be able to engage in protest activities. The most crucial resources, thereby, are participation and approval from constituencies, supporters, and bystander publics (McCarthy and Zald 1977: 1221), which gives competition a complex, triangular dynamic: Competing movement organizations seek to outbid their rivals in winning support from a third party (supporters or audiences), whose reactions and attitudes play a critical role in the process. Consequently, competition is often the strongest when it takes place between organizations which pursue similar goals and target the same constituent groups; in such instances, competition tends to include differentiation in goals and tactics as these forms of action help the groups to distinguish themselves from each other (McCarthy and Zald 1977: 1234; Zald and McCarthy 1979). Political process-scholars have broadened this picture by taking into account the role of external actors (governments, police, counter-movements), and their strategies to encourage (or inhibit) internal splits and factionalization within oppositional movements (Tarrow 1998: 147).

While the issue continued to receive some attention in the field of social movement studies (for an overview see Clemens and Minkoff 2004; Rucht 2004; della Porta and Diani 1999), until recently only few works on political violence examined competition between oppositional and militant groups systematically (Crenshaw 1995, 2001; della Porta 1995), despite the apparent role of factionalism and intra-movement rivalries in cases such as, for example, the Republican movement in Northern Ireland or militant groups in Palestine.[4] During the past decade, however, the emerging shift in perspective towards social movement approaches in the study of political violence also entailed a growing interest in dynamics of intra-movement competition in processes of

---

4   Single case studies, such as Klein (1996) on Palestine, mentioned the role of intra-movement competition. Recently, some works in the "terrorism-studies"-field began to take processes of intra-movement competition into account; see, for example, McCauley and Moskalenko (2008).

radicalization (see Zwerman and Steinhoff 2005; Alimi 2006, Wiktorowicz 2006; Gunning 2009; Alimi/Bosi/Demetriou 2012). This research not only confirms the central role of competitive interactions in the emergence of violence. It also shows that applying this approach to the study of political violence requires further specification and differentiation with respect to forms of movements and types of violence, mechanisms of competition, and the conditions for their emergence. In other words, existing studies indicate that competition takes place in different patterns and settings, and does not always lead to radicalization; and that it is closely intertwined with the overall development of oppositional movements and their interactions with opponents, constituencies, and audiences. Moreover, to understand the dynamics of intra-movement competition in processes of political violence, we need to identify particular patterns and implications of rivalries that involve violence. Violent "outbidding," for example, entails a particular dynamic in which militant groups receive increasing attention when they escalate violent attacks, and sometimes gain approval from core-followers, but at the same time they risk to repel broader audiences and to provoke counter-attacks which hurt their constituencies. Also, conditions of underground organizations differ from those of open protest movements because they depend on different resources and take place in different arenas. The studies in this volume contribute to further developing our understanding of competitive interactions in processes of radicalization not only by specifying fundamental aspects of this dynamic, but also by specifying conditions under which they take place (or fail to do so).

In her chapter in this volume, which draws on a comparative analysis of left-wing militancy in Italy and Germany and religious movements in the Middle East, della Porta links inter-organizational competition to *cycles of protest*—that is, to the patterns in which social movements expand, radicalize (and/or institutionalize), decline, and re-stabilize (Tarrow 1998: 141–150/2011). This is relevant insofar as conditions for intra-movement interactions change over the course of protest cycles, particularly with respect to the availability of resources. During phases of declining mobilization, many activists withdraw and public attention dwindles, increasing rivalry between movement organizations which now compete for a shrinking pool of recruits. Moreover, the field of movement organizations transforms during the cycle. Phases of institutionalization or stagnation often entail centralization and the consolidation of organizations with more exclusive structures and identities (see also Tarrow 1999). Rivalries and factionalism increases in this phase, because competition is more intensive between exclusive organizations which do not permit multiple membership and place higher demands on their members (see also Zald and McCarthy 1979). Donatella della Porta also links intra-movement interactions to broader processes of political contestation in another way: by emphasizing the fact that competition is interlinked with state repression. Drawing on Tarrow's work on the Italian movement (Tarrow 1989), she argues that repressive strategies can exacerbate internal divisions and often deliberately seek to do so. Competition between movement organizations, in other words, is shown here to be part of a complex constellation of relations, in which rivals seek to influence audiences and constituent groups and at the same time interact with state-authorities and security forces.

In Chapter 6, Gianluca De Fazio examines intra-movement interactions in a case study on the civil rights movement and the following wave of ethno-nationalist mobilization in Northern Ireland in 1968–1969. His analysis further specifies mechanisms of radicalization in competitive interactions, arguing that competition only results in radicalization if it triggers a mechanism of "political outbidding," in which organizations seek to outdo one another in taking more radical positions and accusing the other to sell out or be "soft" on the movement's goals. The case of Northern Ireland, thereby, also provides insights into the role of constituencies (or supporters) in competitive interactions. As De Fazio notes, increasing frustration and the revitalization of the ethno-nationalist cleavage were crucial in preparing the ground for the dynamic of political outbidding. In other words, adopting a radical position promised to win support among constituent groups because a *demand for militancy* existed within these audiences, which was also a result of state-repression and interactions with counter-movements. Moreover, as the result in the case of Northern Ireland was the radicalization of more or less the entire movement (some groups withdrew), the case offers an important contrasting example to the left-wing social movements examined by della Porta, where only some, comparatively small parts of the movement radicalized, went underground, and isolated themselves gradually from the broader movement.

Chapter 7, Devashree Gupta's contribution, adds an important corrective perspective to this section. Analyzing a case in which radicalization would be expected but did not occur (or did not develop further)—the rivalry between the ANC (African National Congress) and PAC (Pan African Congress) in South Africa—Gupta is able to critically examine key assumptions about competitive radicalization. Her account of intra-movement competition corresponds closely to the main findings of the two previous chapters, emphasizing, similar to De Fazio, that competition leads to radicalization only where militancy is rewarded by relevant target audiences. In the case of the South African movement, Gupta argues that all these preconditions were present, but whereas the PAC adopted increasingly radical positions, and its paramilitary wing applied extreme forms of violence, the ANC did not follow suit or react competitively. Her answer to this puzzle is, firstly, that competition depends on the power balance and mutual perception of rival organizations. If the other side is not seen as a threat to an organization's position among constituent groups, a challenger's adoption of more radical means and positions does not necessarily lead to a pattern of outbidding. Secondly, an organization's membership and allies have important influence on strategic decisions which, in the case of the ANC, had a moderating effect. In other words, in addition to an organization's constituencies, its "internal audience"— its staff members and rank-and-file—represents an important reference group. Leaders have to justify their decisions and receive pressure from the rank and file, which can also be a factor intensifying, instead of moderating, radicalization, of course, when rank-and-file members involved in street protests push for militant actions to outbid rivals or in revenge for fallen "comrades." The function of internal audiences is closely related to organizational structures, such as, for example, its inclusiveness/exclusiveness and organizational boundaries which, as della Porta emphasizes in her chapter, may change over the course of protest cycles.

Dynamics of Meaning Formation: Frames and Beyond

In much of the twentieth century the relationship between meaning and radicalization was considered simple. Radical ideas were thought to lead to radical politics and to violence. In recent decades, however, this view has been deemed too simple. For not only does it overlook the interactive and constitutive nature of the meaning-radicalization relationship, it also assumes too easy a correspondence between ideas and meaning, as if ideas were understood without social mediation. Rejecting the existence of an autonomous realm of signification, therefore, most contemporary social-scientific discourse considers meaning to be part of social relations and of the varied socio-cultural configurations that form in time and space out of social interaction (Elias 1978; Giddens 1984; White 1992; Bourdieu 2000).

Given this orientation, scholars increasingly focus attention on the social underpinning of meaning (and violence), considering meaning vis-à-vis wide-raging forms of violence to be comparable. While drawing distinctions among the social underpinning of violence becomes a fruitful direction for research, it would suffice for the purposes of this introduction to merely draw some basic analytical distinctions. Hence distinctions of time and space: slow formation/transformation of meaning versus fast one, spread-out versus narrow. But one needs also to keep in mind that what may seem slow-changing and slow-spreading meaning from a macro perspective, may appear static from a meso or micro perspective. Thus whether one views meaning either as situational and emergent formation or as structure has ultimately to do with one's spatio-temporal scope. Nevertheless, it is common to expect that "structures of meaning" are entrenched and ingrained—sometimes to the point of being taken for granted—while "changing meaning" is more flimsy and shallow. The qualities of meaning pertaining to "depth" and spatio-temporal scope can therefore be taken to offer a simple way to approach empirical studies of meaning, while the "correlation" between these qualities—the more lasting and encompassing, the more entrenched—may be considered a basic working hypothesis. As it will be discussed below, this approach allows for the juxtaposition of the theses advanced in Chapters 8, 9 and 10 respectively pertaining to the first Palestinian Intifada, the El Salvador Civil War, and the Danish cartoons depicting the Prophet Muhhamad.

But if meaning is interactive and relational, adjusting for spatio-temporal scope, how do we go about studying its connection to processes of radicalization? One approach, widely utilized in the field of social movement studies, is frame analysis. Its leanings towards process analysis are evident from its origins. Stemming from the symbolic interaction tradition, Erving Goffman's seminal work on frame analysis (1974) sought to analyze the fluidity of meaning in micro-level quotidian life. Central tools for this analysis were "primary frameworks," taken by Goffman to refer to mediating principles of signification in the course of individuals' interaction with each other and with their environment. Social movement analysts, focusing as they do on emergent collective action, added meso-level organizational analysis to this approach. They have therefore explored the role of frames as organizers of experience of and through collective action, exploring in particular socio-cognitive frame mechanisms producing focus, articulation and transformation of meaning vis-à-vis collective action (for reviews of frame analysis in social movement studies, see Snow 2013 and Polleta and Ho 2006; also, Chapter 9, by Johnston and Alimi in this volume; for a critical perspective on Goffman, see Jameson 1976).

Among the frame mechanisms that have held the attention of the social movement scholarship are frame alignment and frame resonance. These are often key operations in the development and effectiveness of social movements. To take frame alignment mechanisms first, these refer to the seeming linkage between the interests of the social movement organization and the interests of their prospective supporters. Such linkages, however veritable or fictitious, can emerge through different courses, including frame bridging (the connection of previously unconnected frames) and frame transformation (changing prior frames to match the social movement organization's perspective) (Snow, Rochford, Worden, and Benford, 1986). Pointed examples of frame alignment are offered by Jocelyn Viterna in Chapter 8, in a study of the mobilization and recruitment strategies of the FMLN during El Salvador's civil war and of the FMLN's electoral campaign in the post-war period. Viterna points out that interested publics do not necessarily view violence in negative terms, but can instead deem it righteous. She finds that this was the case with regard to violence perpetrated by the FMLN, and maintains that the organization shrewdly cultivated an image of righteousness through the use of, among other means, gender frames. Hence the FMLN succeeded in bridging its own revolutionary frames with preexisting frames about the vulnerability of women by projecting itself as women's protector, which is to say, by portraying the state army as the aggressor against women and its own campaign of violence as violence in defense of women. In addition to frame bridging, moreover, the FMLN employed frame transformation. Thus, for example, by recruiting women as fighters, the organization transformed prior understandings of femininity (peace-loving, pacifist, and so on) to show that, as Viterna writes, "even women are willing to risk their lives, and the lives of their children, to support it".

Whereas frame alignment is often the result of the strategy of social movement organizations, frame resonance refers to the effects social movement organizations' messages have on audiences, which is an outcome determined by factors that relate not only to strategy but also, and to a large measure, to structure and conjuncture. Thus, while a message's resonance may depend on the message's saliency and credibility, as Snow and Benford (1988) maintain, one needs to remember that these two qualities are precipitated by accumulated history as well as particular junctures of history. Historically created belief systems, values, and identities, as well as contingent horizons of expectation, create therefore much of the conditions that make frames effective. At the same time, this does not mean that resonance operates by way of a direct congruence between structure and action; it is rather a process, an emergent condition which is situational as much as it is structural.

The chapter by Viterna points also to frame resonance mechanisms. The author argues that the FMLN's role of protecting women resonated widely in Salvadoran society, or at least among the men in this society, because political violence against women disturbed deep-seated notions about masculinity. Thus the state agents who engaged in violence against women challenged average men's customary jurisdiction over their women, while the FMLN's intervention aimed precisely at restoring the traditional, local gendered hierarchies—the novelty of women recruitment in arms notwithstanding. Viterna alludes to, though not fully explains, the operations, or mechanisms, of resonance at play. Thus the correspondence between the pre-existing masculinity significations and the FMLN's stand as, at once, defender of women and backer of masculinity operated in contexts in which the FMLN beat the government troop in gaining control of areas in Salvadorian countryside. As the arrival of government troops was looming, their infamy had already made inroads, and so the mechanisms of resonance here pertained to mechanisms of reputation formation, in which the FMLN's narratives played their role. Resonance, in other words, operated through mechanisms that were local, multiple, and underpinned by broader and deeper structures of meaning.

Even more so than Viterna, Hank Johnston and Eitan Alimi, in Chapter 9, build their thesis on frame analysis. Their central analytical tool is Goffman's notion of "keying," meaning the adjustment of primary frameworks to new situations. This notion helps the authors analyze the process through which, in the course of the first Palestinian Intifada (1987–1992), the discourse of Palestinian nationalism developed into the discourse of Islamic jihad. The primary framework of Palestinian nationalism had been, as per Johnston and Alimi, one embracing an attachment to the land and celebrating the land's defenders, while at the same time upholding Muslim identity and singling out Zionism as the main enemy. This framework shifted in key, the authors argue, along turning points in Middle Eastern political life, because these moments altered the plane field for not only action but also interpretation. The series of adjusted frames thus followed such developments as Yasser Arafat's speech at the UN in 1988, in which he expressed willingness to accept the co-existence of Palestinian and Israeli states, King Hussein's declaration in the same year to disengage the Jordanian presence from the West Bank, and the Gulf War of 1990, during which Arafat supported the Iraqi side. In all this, nationalist and Islamist narratives increasingly moved apart from each other, with the latter moving the furthest away from the pre-established primary framework of Palestinian nationalism. Thus the Islamic framework now repositioned the Palestinians within a nation of believers and framed the Jews as historically evil.

Johnston and Alimi take adjusted frames (rims) to be their topic of analysis—their explanandum—while Viterna treats frame operations as an explanans of emergent signification forms relating to the legitimacy of violence and its perpetrators. In both studies, frames are said to intertwine with the broader radicalization of political contention, though much of these relationships fall outside the scope of the two studies. In El Salvador and the West Bank, then, frames are presumed to link to complicated contexts. But how can we conceptualize such contexts beyond acknowledging their social-relational underpinnings? Can we say, for example, that frames are enveloped in narratives or discourses? In the final analysis, how does the notion of frames compare with the notion of narrative and the notion of discourse, or the notions of mentalities and ideologies?

These are probing queries and this is not the place to treat them at length. But one can side with Polletta and Ho (2006) in observing that, at least within the literature on social movements, the difference between frames, on the one hand, and discourses and ideologies, on the other, is one of specificity. Discourses are often taken to mean the sum total of talk produced in a given context, which then means that they are characterized by more diversity, inconsistency, and conflict than frames are; ideologies, too, conventionally referring to encompassing systems of belief, appear to be more complex and less specific than frames. Yet while the point about specificity holds, it would be a mistake to think of frames as ready parts of narratives or ideologies. This is because frames operate via socio-cultural mechanisms which may not mirror those operating to produce, sustain, and alter narratives or ideologies. The same can be said about the notion of narrative— which is attached to syntactical rules in addition to any sociological factors.

In Chapter 10 Thomas Olesen investigates questions pertaining to discourse and its audience, and while he does not conceptualizes his investigation in terms of frames, one could translate his findings into frame terms without much being lost in the translation. The subject of his investigation is the repercussions of the publication by a Danish newspaper in 2005 of cartoons depicting unfavorably the Prophet Muhammad. More particularly, among the varied repercussions, he focuses on the transformation of this affair into a transnational justice symbol used to justify violent activism by extreme Islamic groups. The author reflects perceptively on the national-to-transnational transformation, and in this sense he offers insight on the question of event scale-shift; it would not be unfitting, in fact, to situate this chapter within this volume's last section, covering modalities of diffusion. But Olesen's is also an analysis of the career of a symbol, hence an analysis of political culture—to use his term.

He holds that the cartoons acquired their symbolic linkage to injustice through their resonance with injustice communities, that is, audiences already predisposed to injustice frames articulating the Palestinian Cause, Western disrespect of Islam, and Western acts of violence against Muslims (in Abu Ghraib, Guantanamo, etc.). He offers, then, an understanding of signification as a relational concept. But this is a relational take not only because symbol relates to audience in a constitutive fashion, but also because this linkage happens through networks of activists where strategy and negotiation take place. As Olesen stresses, symbols are in this sense not only the result of activism but also the causes of it, hence a dialectic between action and culture.

Olesen's analysis, therefore, demonstrates some of the promise of the processual analysis of the meaning-radicalization dialectic. It also shows that frame analysis, which the work of Viterna, Johnston and Alimi variously utilizes, is not the only approach that fits the processual bill. Taking a small hint from Olesen, one could mention the sociology of Pierre Bourdieu, which takes Goffman to a different direction than social movement studies do but one which is no less processual. For marrying the analysis of mental schemes to the analysis of dispositions in fields of power, Bourdieu has devised an analytical framework capable to treat emergence. This includes the emergence of meaning, which is held to be generated through, among other things, the uses of symbolic capital (see Demetriou 2007 for a field analysis of meaning vis-à-vis violence).

Dynamics of Diffusion

The study of diffusion of political violence has been motivated by an interest on contemporary transnational terrorism since the September 11, 2001 attacks on the World Trade Center and the Pentagon (Bergesen and Lizardo 2004; Bloom 2005; Horowitz 2010; Rapoport 2004; Sedgwick 2007; Midlansky, Crenshaw, and Yoshida 1980). The major claim of these researches is that a "new terrorism," different from the previous waves of violence, has appeared at the end of the twentieth century and at the beginning of the twenty-first century, and will prevail in the near future. Central to this claim is that new contextual opportunities for violence arise from the global dimension of international political and economic governance (Crenshaw 2011; Nacos 2009). While radicalization processes were rarely isolated and independent from one another even in the past (see Romanos and Alper's chapters in this volume), this literature has nevertheless seen special reason to focus on dynamics of diffusion now. By diffusion we mean a complex multidimensional dynamic that involves the strategic spread of tactics, ideas, social and cultural practices, and so forth, across time, borders and cultures, engaging different actors, networks and mechanisms. In fact, as McAdam and Rucht note, those engaging in political contention "do not have to reinvent the wheel at each place and in each conflict ... They often find inspiration elsewhere in the ideas and tactics espoused and practiced by other activists" (McAdam and Rucht 1993: 58). In this volume we avoid "contagion type" of negative or pathological interpretations where adopters are perceived as passive recipients. We concur, rather, with those who see diffusion dynamics as being marked by innovation, political learning, strategic transmission and adaptation (Snow 2004; Givan, Roberts and Soule 2011). Such diffusion dynamics can be direct or indirect. In reference to protest diffusion, della Porta and Diani remind us that "as far as direct interaction is concerned, geographical proximity, historical interaction, and structural similarities all tend to produce language and norms which facilitate direct contacts between the activists of parallel movements. Unmediated exchanges are rendered more probable by the existence of cross-border associations, cultural exchange programs, linguistic knowledge, or even a common language" (2006: 186). As a theoretical tool, diffusion helps us to challenge the general national-centric bias still evident in most of the field, offering interesting new perspectives on the origins, forms and consequences of political violence.

The role of anarchist diasporas in France in coordinating and diffusing violent tactics among its community of origin against Franco's authoritarian regime in Spain, first in the late 1940s and then in the early 1960s, is the subject matter of Eduardo Romanos' study, in Chapter 10. Through a rich, cross-temporal comparison, it inquires as to who the transmitter was and where it was positioned, what was diffused, how diffusion was established, and in which form the actors became involved in the diffusion process. Romanos underlines those similarities (the presence of direct ties and the fact that transmitter and adopter were both active) and differences (the transmitters were differently positioned and instrumental vs. expressive types of violence) which have emerged between the case of the 1940s and the case of the 1960s. His main thesis is that in repressive regimes, such as Franco's regime in Spain, diffusion dynamics require direct interpersonal relations to emerge and develop. The strength of Romano's work is to emphasize the internal heterogeneity among the transmitters and the adopters, thus improving on a literature that tends to provide a simplified image of two homogeneous actors. While connecting with our discussion of the intra-movement competition dynamics in the second part of this volume, this study demonstrates in particular the strategic dimension of diffusion dynamics.

Emin Alper's study, in Chapter 11, challenging previous interpretations produced mainly from former activists, illustrates the importance of the global student movement for the development of the Turkish student movement and its initial radicalization process, between the late 1960s and early 1970s. The broadcasting of practices and information through media channels (mainly through newspapers) of the global student movement provided first the indirect diffusion of frames and afterwards the repertoires which were borrowed and then adapted to the local political dynamics from the Turkish student movement. Alper first stresses how the already established Turkish student movement was integrating the global student movement anti-imperialist discourses within the Turkish popular nationalist feelings (weak reference to the Vietnam War and strong reference to the Arab-Israeli War and the Cyprus crises) building a momentum for the movement. In this way he shows the role of agency in selecting the adoption of anti-imperialist demonstrations on behalf of Turkish students. Furthermore, for Alper, media reports of international student protests in 1968 (Paris, Berlin, London, Rome, etc.) reinforced a common identity of "students" between the Turkish and the Western European ones. This created "a sense of shared identification between activists" that facilitated such self-confidence among them as to make them think that their win of university regulations and administration reforms was almost inevitable.

Such developments led to local dynamics which started simultaneous chain of action-counteraction mechanisms as has happened in many western countries leading to the escalation of conflict in the Turkish case (see the first part of this volume). In short, Alper's chapter is significant in underlining that the context of the adopters shapes the content of the diffusion.

Ekaterina Stepanova's study, in Chapter 12, challenges previous interpretations of the evolution of al-Qaeda since 9/11—the al-Qaedaization approach and the regionalization approach –, proposing instead an actor-oriented approach which supports a "post-Qaeda" interpretation. The author maintains that al-Qaeda's organizational patterns go beyond the standard network form, allowing it to overcome some of the main weaknesses inherent to networks (difficulties in making strategic political–military decisions, ensuring that these decisions are followed by the main elements within the network and exercising control over the implementation). Stepanova speaks of ideology-functional networks with a segmented polycentric integrated network structure. In this configuration, each cell is hardly linked to one another in any formal way and is mostly united by the shared ideological discourse of "global jihad." Stepanova thus views organizational systems of militant-terrorist actors, along with the high mobilizing potential of their extremist ideologies, as their two key asymmetrical resources in confrontation with state actors who enjoy qualitative power and status superiority.

The contributions of Romanos, Alper, and Stepanova in this volume enrich the literature on diffusion dynamics of political violence. The field is open to more research, however, and future research can take different directions. Scholars, for one, might begin to ask how political violence adopted from certain groups may discourage certain tactics. For example, the events of 9/11, and the violence by al'Qaeda more generally, may have led different armed groups to alter their tactics. Furthermore, we need to show how diffusion dynamics relate not only to the spread of political violence, but to disengagement from violence as well. The peace process in Northern Ireland, for example, is said to be relevant for the current disengagement process of the ETA, as the end of apartheid in South Africa was relevant for Northern Ireland. Another way forward for the literature is to examine which types of diffusion dynamics are more likely to occur, and through which links; contrasting those who succeeded with those who do not is a particularly productive way to go about this (Soule 2004). Furthermore, given that diffusion dynamics depend on the contexts of the transmitter and of the adopter, research can ask why and how certain contexts are more fertile than others. Finally, we think that the agency of the transmitter and adopters should be better recognized by future explanations of how diffusion dynamics relate to political violence. In conclusion, it must be pointed that work along these research lines can be optimized if the work covers not only case studies but also comparisons across countries, movements, and time.

References

Abbott, A. 2001. "Transcending General Linear Reality," in *Time Matters: On Theory and Method*. Chicago: Chicago University Press.

Alimi, E. 2006. "Conceptualizing Political Terrorism: A Collective Action Perspective for Understanding the Tanzim." *Studies in Conflict and Terrorism* 29(3): 263–83.

Alimi, E. 2011. "Relational Dynamics in Factional Adoption of Terrorist Tactics: A Comparative Perspective." *Theory and Society* 40(1): 95–118.

Alimi, E., L. Bosi, and C. Demetriou. 2012. "Relational Dynamics and Processes of Radicalization: A Comparative Framework." *Mobilization* 17(1): 7–26.

Amenta, A. 2006. *When Movements Matter*. Princeton, NJ: Princeton University Press.

Amenta, E. and N. Caren. 2004. "The Legislative, Organizational, and Beneficiary Consequences of State Oriented Challengers." Pp. 461–89 in *The Blackwell Companion to Social Movements*, edited by D.A. Snow, S.A. Soule, and H. Kriesi. Oxford: Blackwell.

Araj, B. 2008. "Harsh State Repression as a Cause of Suicide Bombing: The Case of the Palestinian-Israeli Conflict." *Studies in Conflict and Terrorism* 31(4): 284–303.

Beck, C. 2008. "The Contribution of Social Movement Theory to Understanding Terrorism." *Sociology Compass* 2(5): 1565–81.

Bergesen, A. and O. Lizardo. 2004. "International Terrorism and the World-System." *Sociological Theory* 22(1): 38–52.

Bloom, M. 2005. *Dying to Kill: The Allure of Suicide Terrorism*. New York: Columbia University Press.

Byman, D. 2005 "Passive Sponsors of Terrorism." *Survival* 47(4): 117–44.

Bosi, L. 2012. "Explaining Pathways to Armed Activism in the Provisional IRA, 1969–1972." *Social Science History* 36(3): 347–390.

Bosi, L. and D. della Porta. 2012. "Micro-mobilization into Armed Groups: The Ideological, Instrumental and Solidaristic Paths." *Qualitative Sociology* 35: 361–83.

Bosi, L. and K. Uba. Forthcoming. "Political and Institutional Confrontation" in *Protest Cultures: A Companion*, edited by K. Fahlenbrach, M. Klimke and J. Scharloth. Oxford: Berghahn.

Bourdieu, P. 2000. *Pascalian Meditations*. Cambridge: Polity Press.

Bunge, M. 1997. "Mechanism Explanation." *Philosophy of the Social Sciences* 27(4): 410–65.

Campbell, B. and A.D. Brenner. 2002. *Death Squads in Global Perspective: Murder with Deniability*. New York: Palgrave Macmillan.

Clemens, E.S. and D.C. Minkoff. 2004. "Beyond the Iron Law: Rethinking the Place of Organizations in Social Movement Research". Pp. 155–70 in *The Blackwell Companion to Social Movements,* edited by D.A. Snow, S.A. Soule, H. Kriesi. Oxford: Blackwell Publishers.

Crenshaw, M. 1995. "Thoughts on Relating Terrorism to Historical Contexts" Pp. 3–24 in *Terrorism in Context*, edited by M. Crenshaw. Pennsylvania State University Press.

Crenshaw, M. 2001. "Theories of Terrorism: Instrumental and Organizational Approaches" Pp. 13–31 in *Inside Terrorist Organizations*, edited by D. Rappoport (2nd edn). London: Frank Cass.

Crenshaw, M. 2011. *Explaining Terrorism. Causes, Processes and Consequences*. London: Routledge.

Cuenca, I. and L. de la Calle. 2009. "Domestic Terrorism: The Hidden Side of Political Violence." *Annual Review of Political Science* 12: 31–49.

Curtis, R. and L.A. Zurcher (1973). "Stable Resources of Protest Movements: The Multi-Organizational Field." *Social Forces* 52(1): 53–61.

Davenport, C. 2007. "State Repression and Political Order." *Annual Review of Political Science* 10: 1–23.

della Porta, D. 1995. *Political Violence and the State*. Cambridge: Cambridge University Press.

della Porta, D. 2008. "Research on Social Movements and Political Violence." *Qualitative Sociology* 31: 221–30.

della Porta, D. 2013. *Clandestine Political Violence*. Cambridge: Cambridge University Press.

della Porta, D. and M. Diani. 2006. *Social Movements: an Introduction*. Oxford: Blackwell Publishers.

della Porta, D. and O. Fillieule. 2004. "Protest policing: An introduction" Pp. 217–41 in *The Blackwell companion to social movements*, edited by David A. Snow, Sarah A. Soule, Hanspeter Kriesi. Oxford: Blackwell.

Demetriou, C. 2007. "Political Violence and Legitimation: The Episode of Colonial Cyprus." *Qualitative Sociology* 30(2): 171–93.

Demetriou, C. 2009. "The Realist Approach to Explanatory Mechanisms in Social Science: More than a Heuristic?" *Philosophy of the Social Sciences* 39(3): 440–62.

Demetriou, C. 2012a. "Political Radicalization and Anti-Colonial Violence in Palestine, Ireland, and Cyprus." *Journal of Social Science History* 36(3): 391–420.

Demetriou, C. 2012b. "Processual Comparative Sociology: Building on the Approach of Charles Tilly." *Sociological Theory* 30(1): 51–65.

Earl, J. 2003. "Tanks, Tear Gas and Taxes: Toward a Theory of Movement Repression." *Sociological Theory* 21(1): 44–68.

Elias, N. 1978. *What is Sociology?* London: Hutchinson.

English, R. 2009. *Terrorism. How to Respond*. Oxford: Oxford University Press.

Giddens, A. 1984. *The Constitution of Society*. Cambridge: Polity Press.

Givan, R., K. Roberts and S. Soule. 2010. "Introduction: the Dimensions of Diffusion" Pp. 1–15 in *The Diffusion of Social Movements: Actors, Mechanisms, and Political Effects*, edited by R. Givan, K. Roberts and S. Soule. Cambridge: Cambridge University Press.

Goffman, E. 1974. *Frame Analysis: An Essay on the Organization of Experience.* New York: Harper and Row.

Goldstone, J.A. and Useem, B. 1999. "Prison Riots as Microrevolutions: An Extension of State Centered Theories of Revolutions." *American Journal of Sociology*, 67: 985–1029.

Goodwin, J. 2006. "A Theory of Categorical Terrorism." *Social Forces* 84: 2027–46.

Goodwin, J. 2012. "Introduction to a special issue on political violence and terrorism: political violence as contentious politics." *Mobilization* 17(1): 1–5.

Gunning, J. 2007. "A Case for Critical Terrorism Studies." *Government and Opposition* 42(3): 363–93.

Gunning, J. 2009. "Social Movement Theory and the Study of Terrorism" Pp. 157–77 in *Critical Terrorism Studies: A New Research Agenda*, edited by R. Jackson, M.B. Smyth and J. Gunning. London: Routledge.

Hafez, M. 2004. *Why Muslims rebel: Repression ad resistance in the Islamic world*. Boulder and London: Lynne Rienner Publishers.

Hafez, M. and Wiktorowicz Q. 2004. "Violence as Contention in the Egyptian Islamic Movement" in *Islamic activism: A social movement theory approach*, edited by Q. Wiktorowicz. Bloomington: Indiana University Press, 61–88.

Hegghammer, T. 2010. *Jihadism in Saudi Arabia*. Cambridge: Cambridge University Press.

Hegre, H., T. Ellingsen, S. Gates, and N.P. Gleditsch. 2001. "Toward a Democratic Civil Peace? Democracy, Political Change and Civil War, 1816–1992." *American Political Science Review* 95(1): 33–48.

Horgan, J. 2005. *Psychology of Terrorism*. London: Routledge.

Horowitz, D. 2010. "Nonstate Actors and the Diffusion of Innovations: The Case of Suicide Terrorism." *International Organization* 64 (Winter), 33–64.

Jackson, R., M. Breen Smyth and J. Gunning (eds.) 2009. *Critical Terrorism Studies: A New Research Agenda*. London: Routledge.

Jameson, F. 1976. "On Goffman's Frame Analysis." *Theory and Society*, 3(1): 119–33.

Johnston, H. 2011. *States and Social Movements*. Cambridge: Polity.

Kalyvas S.N. 2006. *The logic of violence in civil war*. Cambridge: Cambridge University Press.

Klein, M. 1996. "Competing Brothers: The Web of Hamas-PLO Relations." *Terrorism and Political Violence* 8(2): 111–32.

McAdam, D. and D. Rucht. 1993. "The Cross National Diffusion of Movement Ideas." *Annals of the American Academy of Political and Social Science*, 528, 36–59.

McAdam, D. and W.H. Sewell, 2001. "It's About Temporality: in the Study of Social Movements and Revolutions" Pp. 89–125 in *Silence and Voice in the Study of Contentious Politics*, edited by R. Aminzade, J. Goldstone, D. McAdam, E. Perry, W. Sewell, S. Tarrow, and C. Tilly. Cambridge: Cambridge University Press.

McAdam, D., S. Tarrow, and C. Tilly. 2001. *Dynamics of Contention.* New York: Cambridge University Press.

McCarthy, J.D. and M.N. Zald. 1977. "Resource Mobilization and Social Movements: A Partial Theory." *American Journal of Sociology* 82(6): 1212–41.

McCauley, C. and S. Moskalenko (2008). "Mechanisms of Radicalization: Pathways Toward Terrorism." *Terrorism and Political Violence* 20: 415–33.

Malthaner, S. 2011. *Mobilizing the Faithful: The Relationship between militant Islamist groups and their constituencies.* Frankfurt am Main: Campus Verlag.

Meyer, D. 2007. *The Politics of Protest: Social Movements in America.* New York: Oxford University Press.

Midlarsky, M.I., M. Crenshaw and F. Yoshida, "Why Violence Spreads: The Contagion of International Terrorism." *International Studies Quarterly*, 24(2): 262–98.

Moore, Kelly. 1999. "Political Protest and Institutional Change: The Anti Vietnam War Movement and American Science." Pp. 97–115 in *How Social Movements Matter*, edited by M. Giugni, D. McAdam, and C. Tilly. Minneapolis: University of Minnesota Press.

Nacos, B. 2009. "Revisiting the contagion hypothesis: Terrorism, news coverage, and copycat attacks." *Perspectives on Terrorism* 3/3.

Neidhardt, F. 1981. "Über Zufall, Eigendynamik und Institutionalisierbarkeit absurder Prozesse. Notizen am Bespiel der Entstehung und Einrichtung einer terroristischen Gruppe," Pp. 243–57 in *Soziologie in weltbürgerlicher Absicht*, edited by H. von Alemann, H.P. Thurn. Opladen: Westdeutscher.

Neidhardt, F. 1982. "Soziale Bedingungen terroristischen Handelns. Das Beispiel der 'Baader-Meinhof-Gruppe' (RAF)," Pp. 434–76 in *Gruppenprozesse*, edited by W. von Baeyer-Katte, D. Claessens, H. Feger and F. Neidhardt. Opladen: Westdeutscher Verlag.

Oberschall, A. 2004. "Explaining Terrorism: The Contribution of Collective Action Theory." *Sociological Theory* 22: 26–37.

Pettigrew, A. 1997. "What is A Processual Analysis?" *Scandinavian Journal of Management* 13(4): 337–48.

Polletta, F. and M.K. Ho. 2006. "Frames and Their Consequences," Pp. 187–209 in *The Oxford Handbook of Contextual Analysis*, edited by R.E. Goodin and C. Tilly. Oxford: Oxford University Press.

Rapoport, D. 2004. "Four waves of modern terrorism" Pp. 46–73 in A. Ludes and J. Cronin (eds.), *Attacking Terrorism. Elements of a Grand Strategy* in. Washington, D.C.: Georgetown University Press.

Rapoport, D. (ed.) 1987. "Inside Terrorist Organizations", Special Issue of *The Journal of Strategic Studies* 10(4).

Rucht, D. 2004. "Movement Allies, Adversaries, and Third Parties" Pp. 197–216 in *The Blackwell Companion to Social Movements*, edited by D.A. Snow, S.A. Soule and H. Kriesi. London: Blackwell Publishing.

Sedgwick, M. 2007. "Inspiration and the Origins of Global Waves of Terrorism." *Studies in Conflict and Terrorism* 30 (2): 97–112.

Seferiades, S. and H. Johnston. 2011. "The Dynamics of Violent Protest: Emotions, Repression and Disruptive Deficit" Pp. 3–18 in *Violent Protest, Contentious Politics. And the Neoliberal State, edited by* S. Seferiades and H. Johnston. Farnham: Ashgate.

Sewell, W.H. 2005. *Logics of History Social Theory and Social transformation.* Chicago: the University of Chicago Press.

Snow, D. 2013. "Framing and Social Movements" in *The Blackwell Encyclopedia of Social and Political Movements, edited by* Snow, della Porta, Klandermans, and McAdam.

Snow, D. and R. Benford. 1988. "Ideology, Frame Resonance, and Participant Mobilization." *International Social Movement Research*, 1: 197–217.

Snow, D.A., and S.C. Byrd. 2007. "Ideology, Framing Processes, and Islamic Terrorist Movements." *Mobilization* 12(2): 119–36.

Snow, D., B. Rochford, Jr., S. Worden, and R. Benford. 1986. "Frame Alignment Processes, Micromobilization, and Movement Participation." *American Sociological Review*, 51: 464–81.

Soule, S.A. 2004. "Diffusion processes within and across movements" Pp. 294–310 in *The Blackwell Companion to Social Movements*, edited by D.A. Snow, S.A. Soule and H. Kriesi. Malden, MA: Blackwell,.

Steinhoff, P. and G. Zwerman. 2008. "Introduction to the Special Issue on Political Violence." *Qualitative Sociology* 31(3): 213–20.

Suh, D. 2011. "Institutionalizing Social Movements: The Dual Strategy of the Korean Women's Movement." *The Sociological Quarterly*, 52, 442–71.

Tarrow, S. 1998. *Power in Movement*, 2nd edn. New York: Cambridge University Press.

Tarrow, S. 2010. "The Strategy of Paired Comparison: Towards a Theory of Practice." *Comparative Political Studies* 43:230–59.

Tilly, C. 1978. *From Mobilization to Revolution*. Mcgraw-Hill College: Addison-Wesley.

Tilly, C. 2003. *The Politics of Collective Violence*. Cambridge: Cambridge University Press.

Tilly, C. 2005. "Terror as Strategy and Relational Process." *International Journal of Comparative Sociology* 46(1–2): 11–32.

Tilly, C. 2006. *Regimes and Repertoires*. Chicago: University of Chicago Press.

Tilly, C. and S. Tarrow. 2007. *Contentious Politics*. Boulder, CO: Paradigm Publishers.

Viterna, J. 2006. Pulled, Pushed, and Persuaded: Explaining Women's Mobilization into Salvadoran Guerrilla Army. *American Journal of Sociology* 112: 1–45.

Waldmann, P. 1989. *Ethnischer Radikalismus: Ursachen und Folgen gewaltsamer Minderheitenkonflikte*. Opladen: Westdeutscher Verlag.

Waldmann, P. 1998. *Terrorismus: Provokation der Macht*. München: Gerling Akademie Verlag.

Weinstein, J.M. 2007. *Inside Rebellion: The Politics of Insurgent Violence*. New York: Cambridge University Press.

White, H. 1992. *Identity and Control: A Structural Theory of Social Action*. Princeton: Princeton University Press.

White, R.W. 1989. "From Peaceful Protest to Guerrilla War: Micromobilization of the Provisional Irish Republican Army." *American Journal of Sociology* 94(6): 1277–1302.

Wiktorowicz Q. 2004. "Islamic activism and social movement theory"Pp. 1–33 in *Islamic activism: A social movement theory approach*, edited by Wiktorowicz Q. Bloomington and Indianapolis, Indiana University Press.

Wilson, J.Q. 1974. *Political Organizations*. New York: Basic Books.

Wood, E.J. 2003. *Insurgent Collective Action and Civil War in El Salvador*. Cambridge: Cambridge University Press.

Wood, E.J. 2008. "The Social Processes of Civil War: The Wartime Transformation of Social Networks." *Annual Review of Political Science* 11: 539–61.

Zald, M.N. and R. Ash. 1966. "Social Movement Organizations: Growth, Decay and Change." *Social Forces* 44: 327–41.

Zald, M.N. and J.D. McCarthy. 1979. *Social Movement Industries: Competition and Cooperation among Movement Organizations*. CRSO Working Paper No. 201. University of Michigan, Center for Research on Social Organization.

Zwerman, G. and P.G. Steinhoff. 2005. "When Activists Ask for Trouble: State-Dissident Interactions and the New Left Cycle of Resistance in the United States and Japan" Pp. 85–107 in *Repression and Mobilization*, edited by C. Davenport, H. Johnston and C. Mueller. Minneapolis: University of Minnesota.

Zwerman, G., P.G. Steinhoff and D. della Porta. 2000. "Disappearing Social Movements: Clandestinity in the Cycle of New Left Protest in the US, Japan, Germany and Italy." *Mobilization* 5: 83–100.

PART I
Dynamics of Interaction between Oppositional Movements/Groups and the State

Chapter 2

The Mechanisms of Emotion in Violent Protest

Hank Johnston

The study of collective violence is a research focus that brings together in common task two major disciplines in the social sciences—sociology and political science. It has important implications for understanding democratic participation and transitions to democracy, and, as we enter the second decade of the twenty-first century, has practical political importance in two different parts of the world characterized by distinct political regimes. In Western Europe, protests against austerity measures to reduce government debt have erupted into violence—in Greece, Spain, Ireland, Italy, Portugal, and the UK. In the Middle East, the different trajectories of Arab Spring protests brought the violence of the state security apparatus to the forefront of understanding the transitions there. Developments in these two parts of the world direct our attention to recent theoretical trends in the field of social movements, which promise to deepen our understanding of how protests turn violent.

In this chapter, I will focus specifically on two distinct currents of research:

1. The renewed interest in emotional aspects of collective action which has threaded through the field for the past decade; and
2. Theoretical interest in the dynamics of collective action, specifically the quest to identify general mechanisms and processes. This too is a perspective that has coursed through the field of protest studies for the past decade.

Neither, however, would be characterized as paradigmatic, although, as I will suggest, they are both central to understanding protest violence. Drawing on a broad spectrum of empirical examples both from current events and from my own field research, I will bring them together to suggest preliminary models for two fundamental *emotional management mechanisms* in collective violence: fear abatement and anger spirals. If successful, these mechanisms will be sufficiently robust to explain how collective violence unfolds in settings as diverse as Middle Eastern authoritarian states, European liberal democracies, and state regimes that lie in between.

For example, in 2010 and 2011 protesters poured into the streets in Athens, Greece, to protest austerity measures proposed in response to the country's debt crisis. May 1 is a traditional day of mobilization for labor, but in 2010 a broad-based protest of about 17,000 marched in Athens's streets against the government. Newspaper headlines captured protesters' sentiments about proposed cuts in pensions, social security, and wages: "Fear, Rage, Hope" (Bilefsky 2010). Protests were mostly peaceful, yet the in front of the Parliament building hundreds of black-clad anarchists attacked police and threw gasoline bombs. The police responded by firing tear gas into the crowd. Four days later a general strike to protest government corruption and austerity took place throughout Greece. Again, protests were mostly peaceful. Most commerce and transportation came to a standstill. Yet, anarchist groups again escalated the confrontation, breaking away from the main protest of 100,000 they threw gasoline bombs into the Marfin Egnatia Bank in Athens, trapping many workers who had to be rescued by fire brigades. Tragically three bank employees died of smoke inhalation (Kakissis 2010).

Greece is an important case because it is a state where the prevailing strategy toward protests parallels that of other Western democracies, namely the negotiated management of protest events to permit public expression of claims and grievances. Also, there are strong parallels with antiausterity protests in Spain, Portugal, and Ireland, all democratic countries where elections are fair and open by most standards, and citizen protections guaranteed by articles in their constitutions. Still, there reigns in Greece—and in several other European countries—broad popular discontent over hardships from austerity measures aimed at reducing national debt, and anger toward the politicians who passed those measures despite popular resistance. Perceptions of political unresponsiveness are aggravated by the common view that—at the minimum—the political class pursues its self-interest at public expense, or—at the maximum—are corrupt and incorrigible bandits. In the spring and summer of 2011, protests in Greece escalated during parliamentary deliberations about cuts in social services, public salaries, and pensions, and the privatization of national industries. Attacks on riot police by masked protesters, tear gas clouds, Molotov cocktails being thrown, windows broken, and businesses set ablaze in the downtown shopping district of Athens were standard fare in nightly news. Despite the outrage evident on the part of the protesters, and in spite of numerous arrests and injuries during police-protester confrontations, only three deaths were reported. How this might have been accomplished despite aggressive and confrontational tactics by some protesters suggests an overarching normative understanding of proportionality by all social actors.

In stark contrast, and as part of the diffusion of prodemocracy movements throughout the Middle East in 2011, a deadly wave of protest and repression commenced in Syria in March of that year. The Syrian state's prevailing strategy toward protests, unlike Greece, was highly repressive. The al-Assad regime had a history of brutal repression of Sunni Islamist movements, most notably in the city of Hama where an estimated 10,000–25,000 protesters were killed by the Syrian military in 1982. As of this writing, Syrian protests have spiraled out of control into a protracted civil war that has claimed a huge toll in lives lost, and caused over 2.5 million Syrians to flee their homes.

The Syrian conflict began as a wave of protests centered in the southern city of Dara'a. Protests erupted when the police detained and tortured several youths who were accused of spraying antigovernment graffiti. Tolerating no replication of Egypt and Tunisia's regime-toppling protests, police fired on protesters, but as news of government repression spread the effect was to animate the opposition rather than to quell it. The al-Assad regime reacted with a combination of concession and repression. On the one hand, President Bahsar al-Assad reshuffled the cabinet, appointed a new prime minister, ended the emergency law that been in effect for decades, issued calls for dialogue, and even permitted opposition activists to meet in a Damascus hotel (Shadid 2011a). On the other, the regime sent security forces and the military, especially the 4th Armored Division, led by Bashar Assad's brother Maher, to cities where the opposition was strongest, with the goal of crushing the rebellion before it grew further.

As protests spread around Syria, activists estimated that about 10,000 people were arrested and about 2000 killed in March and April 2011, suggesting a systematic policy of the regime to induce fear. The regime instituted widespread arrests, military incursions, checkpoints, and occupations in the most restive cities such as Homs, Baniyas, Dara'a, Deir al-Zour, the outskirts of Damascus, and northern towns in the Idlib region near the Turkish border. The regime also made concessions, granted freedoms to the Kurdish minority, and increased salaries of government workers, but protests continued to grow. In early July, 2011, activists reported that more than 200,000 protesters amassed in both Hama and Homs—the largest protests to date—after Friday prayers, defiantly calling the actions, the "Friday of Departure" (of the al-Assad regime). Continuing the regime's strategy of fomenting fear, it was also reported that police killed 24 protesters that day (Sandals 2011).

These examples reflect vastly different modalities of repressive response—organized state violence and civil war in Syria with over 100,000 deaths (as of this writing), and only three deaths in Greece. They suggest several themes that I will be developing in the course of this chapter:

1. To begin, the Syrian case amply demonstrates the fundamental axiom of the repression-mobilization nexus, namely, that state is the main source of violence, often as a matter of policy at the national level. The worst violence during the period of initial protests was perpetrated by the military and/or police as a result to elite-level decisions. Koopmans and Kriesi (1998) have termed the general orientation of these decisions as the state's "prevailing strategy" toward social protest. Part of this may mean that state or state factions may provoke violence for their own advantages, using the military (Tilly 1995) or rogue police and vigilante groups (White and White 1995) to repress opposition and/or gain advantage over rivals. In 2010, army and police units in Kyrgyzstan initiated violence in which perhaps 2000 ethnic Uzbeks died and 400,000 fled the country. Similar patterns were seen in the Rwandan genocide, and in Bosnia and Kosovo. Ethnic cleansing is often

the result of elite-initiated decisions. When violence is overlaid upon ethnic divisions, it can become an especially hot button for emotional reactions.

2. Social movements and protest campaigns are complex phenomena, which have diverse participants and groups, some of which may be more prone to violence than others—radical Islamists in Syria and anarchist groups in Greece, for example. In general, most protest participants would like to avoid the high costs of violence, but militant minorities that are included under the broad movement umbrella are often willing to incur these costs and may spark violence within larger campaigns

3. Violent tactics get the attention of state elites. Reflecting Tilly's WUNC conditions (worthiness, unity, numbers, and commitment) for successful movement displays (Tilly and Wood 2009), property destruction and violence affirms the seriousness of protesters' claims and their dedication. Such tactics are also magnets for media attention. The strategic use of violence, then, is not without its benefits for a protest campaign.

4. Of the elements in the total repertoire of protest tactics, violent confrontation and property damage run the greatest risk of engaging emotional behaviors that impede cool and considered decision making. They hold the potential of rapidly escalating beyond strategic intent.

5. They similarly risk emotional responses on the part of the police and security forces (as opposed to considered, strategic reactions characteristic of negotiated management policing—see Soule and Davenport 2009; Earl and Soule 2006). In complex gatherings and regardless of protester militancy, the actions of the police and/or military often escalate confrontations and precipitate violent reactions by protesters if front-line policemen perceive threats or loss of control. Different policing strategies can either avoid violence or cause it.

6. Putting these last two observations together, there is a dynamic relationship between strategic planning by both protesters and police and how action actually unfolds in the streets. This makes violent and/or destructive actions, and their intensity, highly contingent on the situation, and especially how they are affected by the emotionality of protesters. One must only recall the anger that fueled youthful protests in Greece at the killing of a 15-year-old student in December 2008 to recognize the mobilizing force of emotions. Moreover, emotions are not the sole province of protesters—I have in mind police brutality and overreaction, sometimes guided by fight-or-flight responses—that can turn otherwise peaceful protests toward violent trajectories.

Taken together, these points lay out the conceptual map of my analysis. To begin, for protesters there are two choices. They may rationally plan and strategically employ either peaceful tactics or violence as a means to gain attention and publicly assert commitment. Complicating this statement, it is not uncommon that demonstrations or protest campaigns can involve different groups that have different tactical orientations on the violence-nonviolence continuum. And then, despite the best-laid plans, confrontation can occur as anger and frustration drive protesters' behaviors in the streets, taking the careful and strategically planned protest campaigns into uncharted combinations of emotional spirals.

Then, given this complexity on the protesters' side, the same array of variations hold for security forces as well. The regime may, as a matter of policy, order crushing repression or managed restraint. Also, as with protesters, in the heat of the moment, emotional responses may shape police behaviors. Commonly, there is a loss of restraint in the face of protester provocation, which can be quite threatening at times, but also there may be the opposite effect of softening the repression and even identification with protestors, as for example when conscript troops refuse to fire on protesters, which occurred in Yemini demonstrations in April 2011, or, reportedly, in early Syrian protests when troops in the Jisr al-Shoughour region refused to fire on peaceful demonstrators.

Most empirical occurrences of collective violence are a complex mix of these strategic choices, situational outcomes, multiplied by a factor based on the complexity of actors both on the movement side and on the side of security forces (local police, secret police, riot squads, military conscripts, and elite troops). In al-Assad's Syria prior to the civil war, there were no less than 16 distinct branches of security forces at work in the larger cities (Shadid 2011b). The result is that this complexity imparts strong contingency in the way that violence may occur. Both in democratic and nondemocratic regimes, there is a complex dance that unfolds among those forces aligned with the protesters, and the various forces of social control. For the analysis of collective violence, it suggests a focus on the relations between and among the variety of protesters and security forces play out. For Charles Tilly, this complexity called for a focus on recurrent mechanisms of collective violence, rather than a quest for universal theoretical models that hold across all episodes (Tilly 2003).

A Relational Perspective

Charles Tilly (2003) has put forth a novel approach to collective violence that lays stress on the complex relations among actors. His goal is to identify a "fairly small number of causal mechanisms and processes that recur throughout the whole range of collective violence—with different initial conditions, combinations, and sequences" (Tilly 2003: xi). Tilly's analysis seeks to isolate general mechanisms that work in all manifestations of collective violence, including forms a varied as cowboy brawls, gang violence, interethnic violence and genocide, insurgencies, and revolutions. It is fair to say that his approach grows out of the dynamics of contention program (McAdam, Tarrow, and Tilly 2001), which similarly seeks general and "robust" causal processes that apply beyond protest mobilization to other forms of "contentious politics." In both works, a broad range of rich and varied historical and contemporary examples is the basis of inductively arriving at a long list of generalizable "processes and mechanisms."

32   *Dynamics of Political Violence*

Tilly presents a typology of violence that varies on two dimensions:

1. Degree of coordination among violent social actors; and
2. The degree of "salience of violence to the act," which roughly refers to the degree to which violence defines the action.

Generally, more coordination among perpetrators means more destruction, injury, and death, as in civil wars and revolutions. Many of the forms of collective violence in Tilly's typology are less relevant to social movement research, such as *brawls* (street fights and sporting event free-for-alls) and—at the other end of the spectrum—*coordinated destruction* (civil wars, insurrections, organized terrorism and genocide). Violence and property destruction that occur as an outgrowth of social movement and/or protest campaign mobilization direct our attention to the two intermediate forms in his typology that occupy a middle ground in terms of size, coordination and salience.

First, a common form of protest violence is *scattered attacks*. These typically burst forth from larger, mostly nonviolent actions such as antiregime demonstrations or policy protests when participating militant groups violently make their claims or register discontent. In another episode of Greek violence, this time in 2008, anarchist groups and, to a lesser extent, small revolutionary communist cells were the primary sources of violent tactics (Kanellopolous 2011). These mobilizations, which lasted for almost the entire month of December, occurred initially in response to the death of a young student, Alexandros Grigoropoulos. He had been out with his friends, making teenage mischief, on a Saturday night and was shot by a policeman. Although the protests, which evolved over course of several weeks, were mostly nonviolent, the strategy of radical groups from the outset was to spark an uprising (given their high salience of violent action). When violence did occur, it was carried out mostly by small groups driven by revolutionary and/or anarchist ideology and not as part of coordinated efforts among many participating actors in the protests (Kanellopolous 2012). Property destruction was extensive during the Greek December (Johnston and Seferiades 2012) but personal violence was minimal. Among the militant groups, such scattered attacks are usually strategic actions, and therefore planned and rational rather than reflexive emotional responses.

A second common form of protest violence derives from *broken negotiations.* This is a common pattern of initially nonviolent protests becoming entirely violent in reaction to authorities' unresponsiveness, such as the red-shirt rebellion in Bangkok, 2010. Here, violence is a spontaneous product of claim making and not a tactic of a specific group. Underlying the category's violence is a widely shared emotional response to being ignored—generating anger that consumes protesters in its downward spiral.

Tilly offers these categories to clarify their determining role as causal mechanisms, but in practice there is considerable overlap among them. For example, the scattered attacks of a radical group of anarchists in a larger demonstration might precipitate the large-scale property destruction, which, in turn leads to police escalation and to broken negotiations among parties. On the other hand, when violence appears to be highly salient in an action, we cannot be certain that all groups are dedicated to violent tactics.

Polarization, a "widening of political and social space between claimants in a contentious episode" (Tilly 2005: 222), is a general process that is especially relevant to protest violence. This typically involves the movement of uncommitted bystanders and/or moderates to one of the two extremes. Polarization is a complex emergent process of social definition of interests, of identity, and of appropriate courses of action, but above all it is a *process of social construction*. Another process that seems relevant to collective violence is *actor constitution* (McAdam, Tarrow, and Tilly 2001), an iterative and interactional category of identity construction forged in the fire of contention for both protesters and opponents. These processes, I suggest, are important sites for future research to focus and refine through observation how interaction unfolds in the heat of conflict. Their importance is compounded because they also are sites where emotions may enter into the causal equation. Tilly's descriptions are surprisingly devoid of emotional inputs, but surely in the polarization process, anger, rage, shame, and hatred all play roles.[1] In contrast, social movement research on emotional factors often stresses a process perspective, for example, how emotions figure into mobilization for action and identity construction (for example, Bernstein 1997; Gould 2002; 2009).

Emotion-management Mechanisms

Researchers in the field of protest studies have shown renewed interest in the role of emotions. This interest is not a recycling of "moments of madness" in social movements and revolutions (Zolberg 1972), but rather reflects a rediscovery of elements that have always been present in social movements but largely neglected because of paradigmatic shifts in the field toward interest-based and structural foci over the past 30 years (Jasper 1998).

Beginning in the 1990s, a body of research on the feminist movement began to emphasize the emotional dimension of women's organizations (Taylor 1989; 1995; 1996; Taylor and Whittier 1996; Morgen 1995). Then, linked with the cultural turn in sociology, several scholars of social movements, working separately and in collaboration, began to elaborate the emotional dimensions of different social movements, ranging from the Huk rebellion in the Philippines, to animal rights protests, to the US civil rights movement (Goodwin, Jasper, and Polletta 2001; Goodwin, Jasper, and Polletta 2004; Goodwin 1997; Goodwin and Pfaff 2001; Jasper 1998; Jasper and Poulsen 1995; Polletta 1998; 2002; Aminzade and McAdam 2001; Flam and King 2005). These studies tended to focus on the

---

1 Polarization is a large-scale and complex process. Several of the mechanism Tilly discusses as relevant to breakdown of negotiations and scattered attacks are also emotion-laden: network-based escalation, signaling spirals, and selective retaliation, to name a few.

cultural construction and channeling of emotions for mobilization (Gould 2002; 2009; Flam and King 2005), and, as such, yielded insights into the mechanisms by which emotions are manifested in collective action. These studies, however, did not take up a dynamic process-and-mechanisms approach that Tilly had in mind. Nor did they generally explore the link between the emotions and collective violence. Many focused on anger, outrage, and grief, but were mute on the role of fear as an emotion, which is highly relevant to confrontations with security forces.

Drawing together the various threads of thought developed in the previous pages, I offer the proposition that the role of emotions is sufficiently widespread in protest violence that it is useful to consider identifying key mechanisms associated with their management and channeling in episodes of contention. These are mechanisms that would seem to occupy an important place in a dynamic approach to collective violence, but which were absent from Tilly's catalogue of mechanisms. While emotions are individually experienced, the mechanisms of which I speak are complex, mid-level chains of interaction. They may partly play out in real-time street confrontations, but tend to work out their fullness in the long term, especially as contentious episodes develop in the street day in and day out, as in all the examples mentioned earlier.

As a first step in such an approach, and especially relevant to protest violence, I will focus on the emotion of fear, which is a key emotion among protesters in authoritarian, nondemocratic regimes, where the army and police often violently repress protests. A second emotion particularly relevant to spirals of violent interaction between protesters and police is anger, which in the heat of the moment can turn protests that were planned as peaceful into violent confrontations, with or without police provocation. The category of broken negotiations in particular seems to ride on waves of anger. Moreover, anger and fear can sometimes mix to drive mobilization processes. Anger has been considered in movements as varied as Three-Mile Island and anti-AIDS mobilizations (Jaspers 1998; Gould 2002, 2009), but regarding fear management, one encounters mostly silence or the assumption that there is a straightforward and noncontroversial relationship between levels of fear and the rising costs of activism such that higher costs linearly reduces collective action.

Fear Abatement

Most analyses in the rational-choice perspective recognize that the perceptions of cost could change during a protest, as when additional resources of repression are brought to bear. Also from a rationalist perspective, high costs of protest participation can be offset by changing calculations of benefits. What is missing from this reasoning is that fear is an emotional state that influences cognitive processes, such as perceptions and interpretations of costs, benefits, and their relative weight. Also missing are the social construction of emotional experience and its antecedent effects on perception. Extrapolating from Jasper's analysis of Three Mile Island (1998), the emotions can change the assessments of costs and, in some circumstances, lead to their transcendence. On the one hand, fear can inflate the perceptions costs, closing down tightly opportunities of activism. But on the other, fear can be managed collectively and its effects regarding mobilization greatly reduced, even though the high costs (rationally) remain. I have suggest a mechanism of *fear abatement* that is social process both common and critical at key junctures in mobilization when costs of participation are high, especially in authoritarian regimes prone to violent repression. If fear can be transcended by certain collective mechanisms, then mobilization will occur, regardless of how high the costs may seem to detached observers and analysts. The notions of "losing your fear" or "fear being dispelled" were widely reported in media accounts of mobilizations in Tunisia, Egypt, and Syria. In authoritarian regimes, the mechanism of fear abatement would seem to be a common mechanism in protest mobilization.

Under such conditions, fear abatement seems has a two-step role in the development of protest. First, it is a sub-process highly relevant to initial mobilization because it breaks the reigning political silence that grants to the regime implied legitimacy. I have in mind Kuran's (1995) concept of *preference falsification,* which operates during periods of protest quiescence to stifle communication about regime dissatisfaction. Kuran suggests that fear of reprisals imparts a veil of silence that keeps most citizens from voicing their true attitudes about the regime and its leaders, which fosters the belief that they are alone in their grievances. This fear must be broken as a first step in mobilization. Second, fear takes on a more specific and focused influence as protesters take to the street. In these circumstances, bodily injury, arrest, and even death are immediate considerations. It is the collective perception of safety in numbers that mitigates this second dimension of fear abatement. This is then reinforced in two ways:

1. As decreased fear is collectively manifested through the persistence and support of other protesters; and
2. Confirmed by the apparent inability of the forces of social control to contain the increasing number of protesters.

Indeed, when protests grow in repressive contexts, it is common that there is a point at which fear is placed aside through collective redefinition. Researchers who have studied participation will recognize generalizability of the following statement, which was reported during my research on protests in Spain. I present a segment from an interview conducted with a nonactivist, middle-class, father, a mid-level manager, Catholic, and Socialist Party member, as an exemplary statement that helps approximate this mechanism of fear abatement. Although the events he reports are long past, his words remain relevant in their description of how he was drawn to join the protests against Spanish authoritarianism, capturing several essential elements of the fear abatement mechanism. The interview was conducted in Spanish and translated by the author.

36 *Dynamics of Political Violence*

Respondent: There were two impressive demonstrations in February of 1976. [. . .] For the first time in Barcelona, 70,000–80,000 people went into the streets, hounded by the police, still, still, struck by the police, and some detained. It was, all of Barcelona, was a battle during the entire morning for two consecutive Sundays. The police couldn't do anything! They ran around a lot and at times they'd arrive at a spot in a jeep and get down and find some isolated people.

Interviewer: Did you go out?

Respondent: Eh? Yes, yes, of course, Evidently. In these cases you have to go. You can't stop.

Interviewer: Why was that?

Respondent: Because we thought it was necessary at that time. Come on! These mobilizations, uh, come on! I couldn't have stayed in the house [laugh], evidently, nor could any of my family either.

Interviewer: But, let's say, five years earlier, would you have gone into the streets?

Respondent: Well, it's that, during the period of Franco, the things were much more serious. Then, too, we went, but with much fear, and the demonstrations were small. There was one on May 1 [1974], a small thing, but, well, with a lot of fear and much caution. But these two demonstrations [in 1976] were the first in which the people massively risked to go out into the streets, because they thought . . . the gentlemen in Madrid, saw that we were serious, that it wasn't a minority, because to send police to repress 70,000–80,000 people, you pay a high price. Because there's many more who think the same. And it was ... Come on! It was marvelous for us to be in the street. Calle Aragon, you know it, filled from one end to the other, and people came from Grand Via. In each neighborhood, there was a small gathering, which, when they arrived in the center of Barcelona, made a mass of people.

In this interview segment, one finds the two elements of my proposed model of fear abatement. The respondent describes three protest mobilizations, one in 1974 before the death of Franco, and two others in 1976, shortly after his death which drew about 70,000 participants each day. Fear limited the size of the first, as would be predicted by the high costs: "demonstrations were small," and there was "much fear," and "great caution." For researchers of authoritarian regimes, the respondent's poignant words reflect the axiomatic truth, that fear constrains participation.

Yet, in order for initial these protests to have occurred, the fear that motivated preference falsification had to be transcended. The first protests were attended by people with a higher threshold of fear, fewer in number, but who saw that voicing their discontent publicly was critical for the movement's development, despite the small circle of believers. Early protests against Francoism were not intended to send a message to "the gentlemen in Madrid . . . that we were serious," (as the larger ones did). Rather, they had as their primary audiences—and this is crucial to the mechanism—those citizens who were more timid and quiescent. The strategic goal, implicit for many but no doubt recognized by leaders, was to break preference-falsification spiral by offering affirmation that there are many who are dissatisfied with the regime and, if you are too, you are not alone.

Two years later, another dynamic was at work. He states, "You have to go," and, "In these cases you can't stop." Not that fear was absent, for he opens the statement with a description of how the police were still beating people, and that "it was a battle." Both the size of the protest and the stalwart presence of a mass of other protesters were the two key factors, I suggest, in this second step of fear abatement. At the end of the segment, his words emphasize collective presence of others, not in terms of sheer numbers but in terms of their motives: "Because there's many more who think the same." And then he expresses with emotion: "Come on! It was marvelous for us to be in the street." Here he speaks of a well-known phenomenon (but one that is hard to pin down empirically—for obvious reasons), namely, the collective joy that is palpable in some protest events. Fear is redirected into a celebration of the collectivity. The social-psychological basis of this is well-established experimentally: the experience of voice—of standing up to be heard as part of a collectivity—has the effect of raising the social basis of one's identity, which produces a shared sense of well-being and enjoyment (Tajfel 1981).

Like many other of Tilly's mechanisms (as well as others in the dynamics of contention approach, see Tarrow and Tilly 2011), fear abatement embodies ongoing collective assessments and reassessment that resituate the group vis á vis the immediate context in an ongoing and recursive social process. Presuming that the regime's option of brutal repression is constrained for the time being—more on this shortly, for fear *abatement* requires that protests are able to develop—Figure 2.1 graphically presents the mechanism in two steps. The first is precipitated by what I call early-riser activists who have a higher fear threshold (they tolerate a higher level of fear). Their actions break the reign of preference falsification that undergirds the regime, and leads to the second step of progressive larger mobilizations, again, assuming repression is not increased.

Both steps are recursive and relational regarding the forces of social control. In step one, police threats are constant factors, but early-riser groups risk the high costs of repression to stage symbolic actions. Recently, the authoritarian regime of Belarus had a difficult time stamping out such symbolic and creative but basically nonthreatening protests of students who gathered publicly and clapped or set their mobile phones to go off simultaneously. Such actions did not bring down the regime—nor were they designed to—but rather they communicated that there were citizens not willing to falsify their preferences, but rather make them known in innovative ways. In my own research on oppositions in authoritarian states, flag placements, graffiti writing, unauthorized singing at concerts, mass shredding the official newspapers, night-time pranks (e.g., putting a load of excrement in the

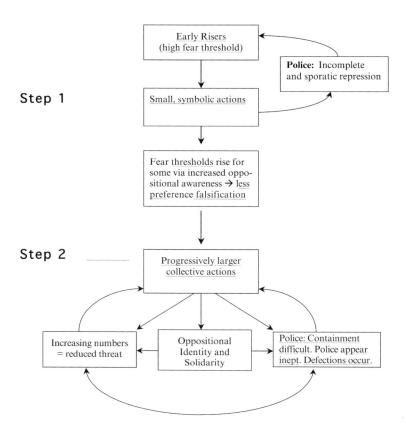

Figure 2.1 Fear abatement mechanism

outstretched hand of Lenin), internet guile (e.g., ingenious *doubles ententres* to circumvent the "great firewall" in China),[2] among many others, are the concrete actions that fill the box in Figure 2.1 of small, symbolic actions (Johnston 2005, 2006; 2011; Johnston and Mueller 2001; Johnston and Tavera Fenollosa 2010).

One way of looking at these actions is that they serve the purpose of *triggering*, a central concept in Gamson, Fireman, and Rytina's (1982) analysis of how quiescence is transformed into collective action. Triggering is a parallel concept to the classical social-psychological concept of *risky shift* (see Myers 1982 for a summary), which traces how the surface tension of group conformity can be

---

2   There is the fascinating case of Chinese internet phenomenon of the "grass mud horse" which was portrayed as a children's story but which sounds like a vulgar epithet that surely would be censored. Although fundamentally nonpolitical, it recently went viral there, providing an example of creative mischief that challenges state censorship (see Wines 2009).

broken by open discussion (as opposed to preference falsification), and often by the outspokenness of just one or two members. Gamson, Fireman and Rytina (1982) found that outspoken group members were critical to fomenting rebellion in small group settings. Applied to repressive contexts, early riser groups play a triggering role in breaking the norm of quiescence that prevails in preference falsification, which brings more participants into these kinds of early, symbolic collective actions.

Step 2 in the figure invokes several elements that have been recognized by researchers in the rational choice perspective. Increasing numbers reduce the risk of injury and arrest by spreading out the probability of harm among many and pushing calculations of cost past the tipping point for action. Then, in a related vein but often left implicit in tipping-point analyses, increasing numbers makes the policing of mass protests less certain, less efficient, and apparently more haphazard, as our Spanish respondent noted earlier, "The police couldn't do anything!" But a third element, present in step one and now beginning to get firm traction, lies outside the calculations of tipping points altogether, namely, the changing normative and emotional currents—as I said, difficult to pin down empirically—but captured in the Spaniards words, "It was marvelous to be there." I have in mind the development of solidarity and shared identity among protesters. These were obviously apparent in the huge protest gatherings in Cairo and Tunis in the past year, and well-known to anyone participating in a mass event. A propos of rationalist analyses, to interpret such statements solely as reflections of "solidarity incentives" (Olsen 1962) misses their emotional content, and the strong degree to which the immediate experience of the moment can drive the trajectory of events in the street.

Figure 2.1 also captures how the evolution of police presence in the street plays a role in fear abatement. In step one, the box on the right depicts levels of police repression characteristic of high-capacity authoritarian regimes. These are complex societies, which means that social control can never be complete and encompassing. Free spaces always exist, often creatively carved out by activists, as the seminal studies of James C. Scott have demonstrated (1985, 1990; see also Polletta 1999). For those activists with a high fear threshold, their symbolic actions of opposition are cat-and-mouse games with the police, with the police often looking foolish and incompetent and activists daring and smugly (and dangerously) overconfident. This is not to underestimate the brutality and thuggishness of the security forces, as torture, rape, and killings in Egypt, Syria, and Iran demonstrated during the recent mobilizations there. However, as a reflection of coping mechanisms in the face of danger, the *mukhabarat* and *shabiha* militiamen in those countries are often mocked and depreciated. Paradoxically (give the evil they perpetrate), it is common that they are portrayed as incompetent buffoons, unable to contain symbolic protests, and who miss the subtleties of oppositional symbolism. This is an act of social construction of the enemy that is typical in repressive regimes, and which works to raise the threshold of fear by overlaying it with fun and excitement—paralleling the way that laughter sometimes masks nervousness on the individual level.

In the second stage of fear abatement, the same practice of *perceiving incomplete repression* is still at work. As crowds get larger, protesters hold their own in clashes with the police. This is because, from the perspective of the police, numbers of participants are unexpected. Sometimes protesters win the engagements as police retreat, creating euphoria. In such critical moments, it is common that regime falters in its response, unsure of how to negotiate the "dictators dilemma" (Francisco 2007). This refers to the choice between draconian repression and the outrage it sparks versus reigning in the police and letting the protests gain momentum—a process apparent in how the al-Assad regime's response to Syrian protests in the spring and summer of 2011 has led to the spiral of violence there.

The mechanism of fear abatement is more than simply a process of social construction characteristic of framing approaches. While the recursive steps outlined here specify the development of new, collectively defined, schemas of interpretation, key elements of the mechanism also include shifts in the distribution of the population regarding fear thresholds, patterned actions of the police, and increasing magnitudes of protester presence. Also, the fear abatement mechanism is more than just a recalculation of costs and payoffs of collective action, although that too is present as a function of protest size. Significantly, cost-benefit assessments are influenced by cognitive change that comes from the reduction of the fear response. Partly, fear abatement is achieved by the surge of new emotions such as joy, excitement, and passion from the highly contexualized experience of group affirmation. Also, there is the common perception of police helplessness in containing large numbers in the second stage, which works to reinforce the progress of fear abatement.

Anger Spirals

The notion of escalating spirals of interaction was a feature of the *Dynamics of Contention's* process and mechanisms approach (McAdam, Tarrow, and Tilly 2001, e.g., opportunity-threat spirals in polarization, p. 322). Here I apply it to emotional aspects of protest events that are especially relevant to collective violence: anger and how it plays out in the heat of protester-police interaction. Fear and anger are not the same emotions, but they are closely related in the fight-or-flight response (or acute stress response), which can be triggered when protesters perceive threats to their safety from security forces. Arousal of anger is linked to such threatening situations, but anger by itself does not necessarily translate into collective violence. Again, it is useful to examine the collective mechanisms that translate perceptions of threat/anxiety to anger, and then to violent behavior, such as property destruction, Molotov cocktails, and pitched battles with the police. As with the fear-abatement mechanism, threat and anger can also be translated into violence on the part of the police and security forces. While autocracies often order the violent repression of protests, a more common occurrence in democracies is that orders for strategic management of protests do not hold and violent repression erupts from the immediate context of police-protester interaction. This too is a major factor in the downward spiral of anger that leads to collective violence.

Anger as an element of mobilization is a complex emotion because it functions in two dimensions. In the long term, anger simmers in the background as the emotional component to injustice and/or threats to interests. In this way it is highly relevant as a motivational component to protests, as we see in the 2011 mobilizations of Greek, Spanish, Chilean, British, French, and Irish youth, angry at the lack of opportunities in economies shaped by neoliberal policies. On the other end of the political spectrum, this brand of "festering anger" fuels the rise of anti-immigrant parties in Europe, especially in Scandinavia (Kulish 2011). Anger in the long term, much like resentment and hatred (Goodwin et al. 2004: 418), is not accompanied by immediate and intensely experienced physiological changes in the actors common to more reflexive emotions, such as anger, fear, and joy. Donatella della Porta (1995) suggests that long-term anger can be imbedded in ideological discourse. She found that police beatings, imprisonment, and routine brutality against Italian and German radical groups fomented an intense anger against the repressive "fascist" state, which was used to justify acts of revolutionary antistate violence. Under such conditions, long-term anger quickly becomes volatile, passion-fueled anger when taken into the streets and submitted to pressures of police confrontation and countermovement groups.

This is the second dimension of anger. It is an outgrowth of the first, activated quickly by suddenly imposed grievances, by precipitating events that reveal intolerable levels of injustice, by demagogic leaders who fuel it to encourage violence, but especially by highly contextualized confrontation with the forces of social control. The 2008 Greek riots are exemplary of how long-term anger among students—known as the "generation of 700 euros," a reflection of its limited future opportunities—can ignite reflexive anger that leads to collective violence. In this case, the police killing of a young student began an interactive chain that suspended normative cat-and-mouse tactics between the police and protesters to begin three weeks of violent confrontation and property destruction (Johnston and Seferiades 2012).

In this context, anger is what Jasper (1998) calls a reflexive emotion, one of those few involuntary and rapid responses that arise among humans given appropriate external stimuli. Paul Ekman (1972) identified six universal facial expressions that can serve as quick measures fundamental reflexive emotions—anger, fear, joy, surprise, sadness, and disgust. It makes sense that all are relevant in various ways to different kinds of social movements (Goodwin et al. 2004: 416), but regarding collective violence, reflexive anger, I suggest, takes first place on the list by far. Especially when fueled by simmering resentment that lies at its base, and spurred by ideological discourse and/or intense interaction among protesters, anger can strongly shape the flow of protest and lead to violent outbursts in protest events—especially when provoked by police.

To summarize, the anger-spiral mechanism begins with long-term anger that is brought to initial confrontations with forces of social control. Street clashes,

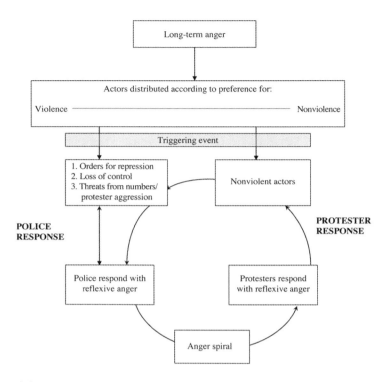

Figure 2.2 Anger-spiral mechanism

then, are the immediate loci of this mechanism. Long-term anger is a background sentiment that comprises part of the complex equation of the anger-violence nexus, but it is central, first because it often is the raison d'être of the protest event in the first place, and second, because it is the fuel, so to speak, that brings protesters who are less prone to violence into the fray as the confrontation escalates. This distribution of violence propensity is manifested through the organization of various actor groups (or mobilizing structures), as presented in Figure 2.2

Regarding propensities to violence, some groups under a social movement umbrella may strategically choose violent tactics. Piven and Cloward's (1977) classic analysis of poor peoples' mobilization in the US found that disruption (not specifically violence) had a positive effect in achieving movement goals. Similarly, Gamson (1990 [1975]) used a large historical database of "challenging groups" to find that disruptive tactics were associated with achieving movement goals. While neither of these two studies focused specifically on violence, it is plausible that if disruption gets the attention of policymakers—as Gamson reasoned—then tactical violence, within limits, may be even more effective. The key point for our analysis is that, rather than violence stemming solely from reflexive emotions, it sometimes occurs that there are actors within a broad social movement umbrella ideologically and strategically disposed to violent tactics, Black Bloc groups in the battle of Seattle, for example (Smith 2002), or anarchist groups in the 2008 Greek protests (Kanellopolous 2011). Figure 2.2 shows that such violence-prone groups—animated by their own particular collective interpretations of long-term anger—figure centrally in anger spirals in the streets.[3]

Although some militants may consciously intend to break windows, set fires, and throw stones, as Max Weber observed, the state is main repository of violent means, and more often than not protest violence comes from the state. During the summer of 2011, protests in Hama, Syria, were peaceful but the snipers fired on them from roofs in the city on orders from the al-Assad regime, spilling blood solely on the account of state action. The top box on the police response side of Figure 2.2 captures the various roles that the state can play in violent protests. It can precipitate violence either by direct orders or, perhaps more benignly, in reaction to perceived threats from protesters. Such threats would tend to originate from groups with propensities for violence, as shown by the arrow originating on the left of the continuum in the collective actor box. Earl and Soule (2006) have noted that large, unexpected numbers of protesters, perceived loss of control, perceived threat, and small scale violence initiated by protesters, such as throwing rocks and pavers, have a high likelihood of precipitating a violent response from the police. Especially when unexpectedly large numbers congregate and/or when protesters are aggressive, the police are more likely to respond with reflexive anger. The cycle of arrows at the bottom of Figure 2.2 portrays how police anger elicits protester anger, especially form those with a greater propensity toward violence at first, but then drawing in those who have a higher anger/violence threshold. Violent tactics risk turning public opinion against the movement, and may alienate bystander groups and potential allies, but when the police respond with violence out of proportion to the protests, reflexive anger can incorporate some of these bystanders into the action, compounding the intensity of the conflict as the crowd grows larger.

Discussion

As I write the final words of this chapter, current events press the urgency of its approach to emotional mechanisms:

1. In Syria, the al-Assad regime responded to early-riser protests with escalated repression, sending army units into several cities, shelling rebellious neighborhoods, and going door to door to arrest young men. After weeks of uneven and sporadic responses, the regime reverted to the military option

---

3   Elsewhere I have augured that cognitive factors among young protesters, say 16–20 years of age, increase the likelihood to violence by virtue of less developed impulse control in a (male) brain that is still growing, compounded by limited strategic experience in protest campaigns (Johnston 2011b).

44 *Dynamics of Political Violence*

to preserve its power. Figure 2.2 generically traces how mass protests and regime repression interact to increase anger and violence. Analyzing how Syria descended into civil war brings additional factors into the causal equation: the demands of taking and holding of territory, the flow of war materiel, international geopolitical stratagems, and the introduction of foreign actors and resources. A key element closely related to escalating anger and violence is the increasing number of desertions from the Syrian Army as repression passed an acceptable threshold for Sunni officers and recruits. The progression from an opposition movement to a civil warrants a new mechanism—one that goes beyond the scope of this chapter.

2. In Santiago de Chile, peaceful student demonstrations calling for increased support of education recently had erupted into violence. Protests numbered in the tens of thousands over several days, but ended in the arrest of over 900 participants, the triggering an anger spiral. Violence broke out as a militant minority of students attacked and set fire to buildings, looted stores, attacked cars and apartment buildings. The police responded with force, beginning the cycle of reflexive anger and leading to escalating violence as laid out in the previous section.[4]

3. In London too, an anger spiral was recently set off by the killing of a police suspect in the immigrant neighborhood of Tottenham. Violence spread quickly as groups of youths from poor neighborhoods were guided by social networking sites to gather in various locales throughout the city to vandalize stores, steal merchandise, and set fires. Although this episode escalated beyond protest violence to become an occasion for youthful rioting and looting, media reports poignantly noted that a key process was weak and sporadic police response. The youths saw that they "were actually taking a stance [against the police and] realized that they could get away with it" (Stobart 2011: 5). Actors with high violence propensity acted first. Police reactions then led to increased participation by those with lower propensities, but now with outlets for their long-term anger.

These examples take their place with several others alluded to in the previous pages, all which build an empirical base by which the fear management mechanisms can be tested and refined. The goal has been to specify the causal channels of how structural factors, such as levels of social control and surveillance or inequalities caused by economic policies translate, through emotional arousal, into violent protests. For students of contentious politics, emotional reactions in the heat of protest are both potent and near-ubiquitous factors. This chapter has presented

---

4 In a similar scenario occurring the end of May 2011, the largely peaceful protests M-15 anti-austerity protests in Spain erupted into violence in Barcelona, this time precipitated by police attempting to break up the youths' encampment in the downtown Plaça de Catalunya.

the first steps toward specifying the causal trajectory of how emotions shape the outbreak of violence in protest events.

I close by pointing out that the key contribution of anger-management mechanisms is how they bridge structural inputs and individual emotional arousal. This contrasts with older approaches to collective violence, such as relative deprivation and J-curve hypotheses, which took for granted the link between individually experienced frustration (from structural changes) and its social manifestation in the form of violence (Davies 1969). For the anger spiral mechanism, long-term anger, variously distributed beforehand in the quiescent population, is the emotional link between structural injustice and the causative force of immediate reflexive anger as it is manifested both in the street and in the different levels of anger intensity among various social actors. The key question emotional management mechanisms answer is how individual states are socially defined, channeled, and translated into collective action. Specifying the elements that accomplish this is the justification for emotional mechanisms in the first place.[5]

By providing the link between the structure and immediate context, the anger spiral mechanism can help answer another salient question, namely why long-term anger is manifested in violence rather than, say, a petition campaign or party politics. To more fully pursue this link empirically, in addition to organizational data or newspaper reports of the kind Tilly uses, a full research program would require on-the-ground ethnographic observation and analysis of participant accounts. This is a research methodology that is precisely attuned to shed light on processes of social construction, which are really what most of Tilly's mechanisms and processes of collective violence are. Tilly's *relational perspective*, focusing as it does on conflict, negotiation and brokerage, is thoroughly *interactional* and *constructivist,* although he does not use these terms. Many of his ideas have migrated from the earlier work, *Dynamics of Contention* (McAdam, Tarrow, and Tilly 2001: 322–33), which remains undervalued in terms of its interactional and social constructionist elements (see also Johnston and Alimi 2012). Applied to collective violence, it is through the social construction of emotion in the heat of interaction with the police and security apparatus that the causal forces behind protest violence are unleashed.

---

5   The concept of relative deprivation similarly sought to link structural changes with collective violence. It animated a great deal of research in the 1960s and 1970s, and was applied to domestic civil unrest in the US (Gurr 1970) during those years. As the theory went, perceptions of relative deprivation led to frustration, which was incorrectly suggested as the root emotional force behind urban violence. Frustration is not an emotion of action, anger is.

References

Aminzade, R.R., and D. McAdam. 2001. "Emotions and Contentious Politics. Pp. 14–50 in *Silence and Voice in the Study of Contentious Politics*, edited by R.R. Aminzade, J.A. Goldstone, D. McAdam, E.J. Perry, W.H. Sewell, Jr., S. Tarrow, and C. Tilly. New York: Cambridge University Press.

Bilefsky, D. 2010. "Greeks Take to Streets in Protest of Deep Spending Cuts." *New York Times*, May 1: A3.

Davies, J. 1969. "The J-Curve of Rising and Declining Satisfactions as Cause of Some Great Revolutions and a Contained Rebellion. Pp. 690–730 in *Violence in America,* edited by H.D. Graham and T.R. Gurr. New York: Praeger.

della Porta, D. 1995. *Social Movements, Political Violence, and the State: A Comparative Analysis of Italy and Germany*. Cambridge: Cambridge University Press.

Earl, J., and Soule, S.A. 2006. "Seeing Blue: A Police-Centered Explanation of Protest Policing." *Mobilization: An International Quarterly* 11: 145–64.

Ekman, P. 1972. *Darwin and Facial Expressions*. New York: Academic Press.

Flam, H. and King, D. eds. 2005. *Emotions and Social Movements*. New York: Routledge.

Francisco, R.A. 1995. "The Relationship between Coercion and Protest. An Empirical Evaluation in Three Coercive States." *Journal of Conflict Resolution* 39: 263–82.

Gamson, W.A., B. Fireman and S.A. Rytina. 1982. *Encounters with Unjust Autority*. Homewood, IL: Dorsey Press.

Gamson, W.A. 1990 [1975]. *The Strategy of Social Protest.* Belmont, CA: Wadsworth.

Goodwin, J. 1997. "The Libidinal Construction of a High-Risk Social Movement: Affectual Ties and Solidarity in the Huk Rebellion." *American Sociological Review* 62: 53–69.

Goodwin, J., Jasper J.M. and Polletta, F. 2001. *Passionate Politics. Emotions and Social Movements*, Chicago: University of Chicago Press.

Goodwin, J., Jasper, J.M., and Polletta, F. 2004. "Emotional Dimensions of Social Movements" in *The Blackwell Companion to Social Movements*. Pp. 413–32, edited by David Snow, Sarah Soule, and Hanspeter Kriesi. Malden, MA: Blackwell.

Goodwin, J. and S. Pfaff, 2001. "Emotion Work in High-Risk Movements: Managing Fear in the US and East German Civil Rights Movements. Pp. 282–302 in *Passionate Politics: Emotions and Social Movements,* edited by J. Goodwin, J. Jasper, and F. Polletta. Chicago: University of Chicago Press.

Gould, D. 2002. "Life during Wartime: Emotions and the Development of ACT-UP. *Mobilization* 7: 177–200.

Gould, D. 2009. *Moving Politics: Emotion and ACT UP's Fight Against AIDS*. Chicago: University of Chicago Press.

Gurr, T.R. 1970. *Why Men Rebel*. Princeton, NJ: Princeton University Press.

Jasper, J.M. 1990. *Nuclear Politics: Energy and the State in the United States, Sweden, and France.* Princeton, NJ: Princeton University Press.

Jasper, J.M. 1997. *The Art of Moral Protest.* Chicago: University of Chicago Press.

Jasper, J.M. 1998. "The Emotions of Protest: Affective and Reactive Emotions in and around Social Movements." *Sociological Forum* 13: 397–424.

Jasper, J.M. and J. Poulsen. 1995. "Recruiting Strangers and Friends: Moral Shocks and Social Networks in Animal Rights and Anti-Nuclear Protests." *Social Problems* 42: 493–512.

Johnston, H. 2005. "Talking the Walk: Speech Acts and Resistance in Authoritarian Regimes." Pp. 108–137 in *Repression and Mobilization,* edited by C. Davenport, H. Johnston, and C. Mueller. Minneapolis: University of Minnesota Press.

Johnston, H. 2006. "The Dynamics of (Small) Contention in Repressive States." *Mobilization: An International Quarterly* 11: 195–212.

Johnston, H. 2011. *States and Social Movements.* Cambridge: Polity Press.

Johnston, H. 2012. "Age Cohorts, Cognition, and Political Violence." Pp 55–80, in *Violent Protest, Contentious Politics and the Neoliberal State,* edited by S. Sepheriades and H. Johnston. Farnham: Ashgate.

Johnston, H. and A. Aarelaid-Tart. 2000. "Generations, Microchorts, and Long-Term Mobilization: the Estonian National Movement, 1940–1991. *Sociological Perspectives* 43: 671–98.

Johnston, H. and E. Alimi. 2012. "Primary Frameworks, Keying and the Dynamics of Contention in the Chechen and Palestinian National Movements." *Political Studies* 60: 603–620.

Johnston, H. and C. Mueller. 2001. "Unobtrusive Practices of Contention in Leninist Regimes." *Sociological Perspectives* 44: 351–76.

Johnston, H. and S. Seferiades. 2012. "Greek December 2008." Pp. 199–213 in *Violent Protest, Contentious Politics and the Neoliberal State,* edited by S. Sepheriades and H. Johnston. Farnham: Ashgate.

Johnston, H. and L. Taverna Fenallosa. 2010. "Silence, Voice, and Authoritarian Withdrawal: The Deep Roots of Mexican Democratization." Unpublished paper, Department of Sociology, San Diego State University.

Kakissis, J. 2010. "Rebels Hope New Austerity Rekindles Spirit of Greece's Activist Heart." *New York Times,* August 3: A4.

Kanellopolous, K. 2012. "The Accidental Eruption of an Anarchist Protest." Pp. 229–44 in *Violent Protest, Contentious Politics and the Neoliberal State,* edited by S. Sepheriades and H. Johnston. Farnham: Ashgate.

Koopmans, R. and H. Kriesi 1995. "Institutional Structures and Prevailing Strategies." Pp. 26–52 in *New Social Movements in Western Europe*, edited by H. Kriesi, R. Koopmans, J.W. Duyvendak, and M. Giugni. Minneapolis: University of Minnesota Press.

Kulish, N. 2011. "Swedish Nationalists in Struggling City See Rival Parties Steal Their Thunder." *New York Times*, August 4: A4.

Kuran, T. 1995. *Private Truths, Public Lies.* Cambridge, MA: Harvard University Press.

Morgen, S. 1995. "It was the Best of Times, It was the Worst of Times": Emotional Discourse in the Work Environment in Feminist Health Clinics." Pp. 234–47 in *Feminist Organizations: Harvest of the New Women's Movement*, edited by M. Marx Ferree and P. Yancey Martin. Philadephia: Temple University Press.

Myers, D.G. 1982. "Polarizing Effects of Social Interaction." Pp. 125–161 in *Group Decision Making*, edited by M. Brandstatter, J.H. Davis and G. Stocker-Kreichgauer. London: Academic Press.

Olson, M. 1963: *The Logic of Collective Action*. Cambridge, MA: Harvard University Press.

Piven, F. Fox, and Cloward, R. 1977. *Poor People's Movements*. New York: Pantheon.

Polletta, F. 1998. "Contending Stories: Narrative in Social Movements." *Qualitative Sociology* 21: 419–46.

Polletta, F. 1999. "Free Spaces in Collective Action." *Theory and Society* 28: 1–38.

Polletta, F. 2002. *Freedom is an Endless Meeting: Democracy in American Social Movements*. Chicago: University of Chicago Press.

Sandels, A. 2011. "Twenty-four Syrians Slain During Protests." *Los Angeles Times*, July 2: A3.

Scott, J.C. 1985. *Weapons of the Weak*. New Haven CT: Yale University Press.

Scott, J.C. 1990. *Domination and the Arts of Resistance*. New Haven, CT: Yale Press.

Shadid, A. 2011a. Syria Allows Opposition to Meet in Damascus." *New York Times*, June 28: A10.

Shadid, A. 2011b. "In a Scarred Syrian City, A Vision of a Life Free from Dicatators." *New York Times* July 20, A1–14.

Smith, J. 2002. "Globalizing Resistance: The Battle of Seattle and the Future of Social Movements" in *Globalization and Resistance: Transnational Dimensions of Social Movements*. Pp. 207–26, edited by J. Smith and H. Johnston. Lanham, MD: Rowman & Littlefield.

Soule, S.A., and Davenport, C. 2009. "Velvet Glove, Iron Fist, or Even Hand? Protest Policing in the United States 1960–1990." *Mobilization* 14: 1–22.

Stobart, J. 2011. "London Looks Inward, Lashes Out." *Los Angeles Times*, August 10: A1–5.

Tajfel, H. 1981. *Human Groups and Social Categories*. Cambridge: Cambridge University Press.

Tarrow, S. and D. McAdam. 2011. "Dynamics of Contention Ten Years On." *Mobilization: An International Quarterly* 16: 1–15.

Taylor, V. and N. Whittier. 1995. "Analytical Approaches to Social Movement Culture: The Culture of the Women's Movement." Pp. 163–87 in *Social Movements and Culture*, edited by H. Johnston and B. Klandermans. Minneapolis, MN: University of Minnesota Press.

Taylor, V. 1989. "Social Movement Continuity: The Women's Movement in Abeyance." *American Sociological Review* 54(5): 761–75.

Taylor, V. 1995. "Watching for Vibes: Bringing Emotions into the Study of Feminist Organizations." Pp. 223–33 in *Feminist Organizations: Harvest of the New Women's Movement*, edited by M. Marx Ferree and P. Yancey Martin. Philadelphia: Temple University Press.

Taylor, V. 1996. *Rock-a-by Baby: Feminism, Self-Help, and Postpartum Depression.* New York: Routledge.

Tilly, C. 1995. *Popular Contention in Great Britain, 1758–1834.* Cambridge, MA: Harvard University Press.

Tilly, C. 2003. *The Politics of Collective Violence.* New York: Cambridge University Press.

Tilly, C. and L. Wood. 2009. Social Movements 1768–2008. Boulder, CO: Paradigm.

Tilly, C., Tilly, L. and Tilly, R. 1975. *The Rebellious Century, 1830–1930.* Cambridge, MA: Harvard University Press.

Tran, M-T. and M. Magnier. 2010. "Edgy Calm in Bangkok." *Los Angeles Times* May 21: A6.

White, R.W., and White, T. Falkenberg. 1995. "Repression and the Liberal State. The Case of Northern Ireland, 1969–1972." *Journal of Conflict Resolution* 39: 330–32.

Wines, M. 2009. "A Dirty Pun Tweaks China's Online Censors." *New York Times*, March 11: A4.

Zolberg, A.R. 1972. Moments of Madness. *Politics and Society* 2: 183–207.

Chapter 3
A Typology of Backfire Mechanisms

Lasse Lindekilde

Introduction

Efficiency of counterterrorism efforts in preventing terrorist attacks and fertilizing de-radicalization processes is a central concern of counterterrorism officials and policymakers. Simply put, the question is how to obtain the most security gains from designing and implementing counterterrorist policies. Another increasingly salient concern is whether, and how, state repressive responses to terrorism may contribute to the radicalization of contention and lead to security losses rather than gains. A growing academic literature addresses this concern under headings of "perverse effects," "iatrogenic effects" or "backfire effects" (Bigo and Tsoukala 2008, Lindekilde 2012). Common to this literature is the ambition to empirically investigate under what conditions repressive counterterrorism efforts and recently also strategies of radicalization prevention may increase threats from terrorism. Following this trend in the literature, the purpose of this chapter is to develop a typology of "backfire mechanisms" in regard to hard counterterrorism policies and soft radicalization prevention instruments. The typology conceptualizes and categorizes causal mechanisms that have been shown in the literature to obscure/pervert policy intentions upon implementation in the field of counterterrorism within liberal, democratic settings. Focus is on the diverse mechanisms that link hard and soft forms of counterterrorism to unintended, counterproductive changes in target group behavior. Luckily most counterterrorism measures work according to intentions and result in processes of disengagement from terrorism and ideological de-radicalization (see Bjørgo and Horgan 2009). This chapter, however, emphasizes how such intended processes of change may under certain circumstances be substituted by backfire processes driven by backfire mechanisms.

The term "backfire" has been used most extensively in social movement studies. Here the concept has been employed in studies of the dynamics of state repression and mobilization (Davenport, Johnston and Mueller 2005) in general, and in studies of protest policing more specifically (e.g. della Porta and Reiter 1998). Especially David Hess and Brian Martin (Hess and Martin 2006, Martin 2007) have worked to conceptualize how state repression may backfire in terms of defusing dissident mobilization, and how states may try to manage backfire. In their terminology "backfire" refers to "a public reaction of outrage to an event that is publicized and perceived as unjust" (2006: 250). Focusing mostly on backfire stemming from singular repressive events their case studies comprise, among others, the Rodney King police beating, the brutal crackdown on the Gandhi-led Salt March in India, and the massacre of peaceful protestors in the East Timorese uprising in 1991. In these cases backfire stems from the outrage in the general public in reaction to the events, which increased rather than decreased dissidence and protest.

For the purpose of this chapter, I will apply a modified version of Hess and Martin's concept of backfire and focus on backfire caused by the "ongoing" implementation of counterterrorism policies rather than singular repressive events. In addition, building on McAdam, Tarrow and Tilly's work on processes and mechanisms of contentious politics (McAdam, Tarrow and Tilly 2008, Tarrow and Tilly 2007), I find it necessary to distinguish between backfire as larger scale processes of change and as constituent causal mechanisms. *Backfire processes* will in the following refer to the perversion of policy effects, so that contrary to intentions counterterrorist policies lead to increased risks of terrorist violence, increased opposition and adverse attitudes among target groups. As indicated above, backfire processes can concern at least three dimensions of target group behavior (strategy, interactions, and identity). Furthermore, backfire processes can materialize in both the short and the long run. Counterterrorist policies may produce immediate security gains, for example through stop-and-search zones, but the more long-term effects might be security losses. In the case of stop-and-search zones, Muslim citizens in Western democracies have been disproportionately targeted and Muslims perceive policies as discriminatory and stigmatizing. This is believed to be key ingredients in radicalization of many "home grown terrorists" (Olsen 2009), and the long-term effect may be one of backfire. *Backfire mechanisms* then refer to certain types of causal mechanisms, which assemble into combinations or sequences of events, which constitute larger scale backfire processes. I here build on McAdam, Tarrow and Tilly's understanding of causal mechanisms as the "delimited changes that alter relations among specified sets of elements in identical or closely similar ways over a variety of situations" (McAdam, Tarrow and Tilly 2008: 308). Thus, backfire mechanisms are the recurrent ways that different types of counterterrorist policies, events and target group reactions under different circumstances alter target groups' behavior in counterproductive ways. When I talk about "backfire" as such, I mean both backfire mechanisms and the backfire processes they help produce. As it will be clear below, the suggested typology operates with three main types of backfire mechanisms, namely environmental, relational, and cognitive backfire mechanisms, which correspond to the three dimensions of target group behavior.

Finally, it is important to specify that backfire mechanisms may concatenate into backfire processes in more or less direct ways. At times counterterrorist policies, such as increased surveillance, may change radical entrepreneurs' working environment in a direct way and produce immediate changes in, for example, recruitment practices. Here policy changes lead directly to conscious, strategic new thinking in the target group, which can be counterproductive as new recruitment practices are more covert. In other cases backfire mechanisms form part of backfire processes in a lagged manner through more indirect and less observable routes.

For backfire to play out in the area of counterterrorism a number of initial conditions must be met. I will suggest two necessary conditions, building again on Hess and Martin's understanding of backfire (2006), and two that mediate the intensity of backfire:

Necessary Conditions
1. Knowledge of counterterrorist policies is communicated and received by target groups, or the implementation of policies experienced in practice.
2. A perception develops within target groups of counterterrorist policies or specific instruments as unjust, unfair, excessive or disproportional.

Mediating Conditions
1. States' management of backfire, i.e. the degree to which states are able to cover up injustices and re-interpret repressive instruments as legitimate law enforcement.
2. Public opinion on counterterrorism instruments, i.e. the degree to which the general public shares perceptions of counterterrorism instruments as unjust, unfair, excessive or disproportional

The first necessary condition simply stipulates that in order for backfire to occur some degree of secondary knowledge of or lived experience with counterterrorist policies must circulate within target groups. Secondary knowledge can stem from the media and public debate, while practice experiences can be either first-hand or, as it is often the case, second-hand (Mythen, Walklate and Khan 2009). The second necessary condition is that this knowledge of or experience with counterterrorist policies leads to negative evaluations and perceptions of state actions. If all members of the target group, say violent Jihadists in the West, perceived counterterrorist efforts as just, fair, and balanced chances are that these instruments would work according to intentions. This is supported by a vast literature within policy implementation studies, which shows that policy effects depend partly on target groups' perception of the policies' legitimacy (Winter and Nielsen 2008). The first of the two conditions that can be said to mediate the intensity of backfire focuses on state reactions to backfire. As shown by Hess and Martin, states attempt to manage backfire using a variety of strategies which may hamper backfire (2006: 254). The last mediating condition stipulates that chances of backfire of counterterrorism instruments are larger when the general public in a given context shares target groups' perceptions of policies as unjust. This means that states' chances of managing backfire become smaller. I will return to these mediating conditions towards the end of the chapter.

In terms of methodology the chapter draws upon the approach and understanding of causation developed in "process tracing" (George and Bennet 2005). The starting point in process tracing approaches is that causal mechanisms pose important building blocks of scientific explanations of social phenomena, here the (in)efficiency of counterterrorism instruments. Causal mechanisms are understood as causal propositions that explain specific outcomes by identifying the generative process which produces them. This chapter is interested in backfire mechanisms as a variant of causal mechanisms, and investigates how counterterrorist policies alter target group strategy, interaction and identify in counterproductive ways under different circumstances. Concretely the chapter reviews existing case studies and causal narratives, across different types of counterterrorism policies and target groups, to categorize identified mechanisms of backfire into a typology. This constitutes an analytical move from specific "X follows Y stories" to the conceptualization of generalized and robust backfire mechanisms. However, empirically pinpointing and isolating backfire processes and mechanisms at work is a very difficult task (see McAdam, Tarrow and Tilly 2008: 309). The evidence of the suggested six types of backfire mechanisms is therefore of an illustrative and suggestive kind. A more substantial, empirical validation of the various types of backfire mechanisms is beyond the scope of this chapter.

Categorizing Backfire Mechanisms in the Field of Counterterrorism

The following section lays out the foundation of the proposed typology of backfire mechanisms, while the next section empirically fills out the actual cells. The typology investigates and categorizes backfire mechanisms on two dimensions. The first dimension is type of state counterterrorism instruments, distinguishing between a) "hard" regulative and sanctioning counterterrorism policies, and b) "soft" incentive- and information-based radicalization prevention policies. The distinction builds on Evert Vedung's policy instrument categorization, especially his fundamental distinction between "regulations," "economic instruments," and "information." The second dimension is types of perverse processes altering target group behavior, distinguishing between: 1) strategy processes, 2) interaction processes, and 3) identity processes. The typology suggests six logical and, as it will be argued, empirically identifiable types of backfire mechanisms, which form key constituent parts of these perverse processes. The identification of diverse types of backfire mechanisms draws conceptually on Doug McAdam, Sidney Tarrow and Charles Tilly's work on explanations and causal mechanisms in the area of contentious politics, in particular their distinction between "environmental," "relational," and "cognitive" causal mechanisms (2001: 25–6). Conceptually the six types of backfire mechanisms can now be delimited as shown in Table 3.1.

The horizontal dimension of the typology regards the distinction in counterterrorism policy instruments between what can be termed "hard counterterrorism instruments" and "soft radicalization prevention instruments." Basically, "hard counterterrorism instruments" refer to anti-terrorist legislation policies, particularly those enacted across the world in the immediate aftermath of 9/11. Characteristics of these instruments were changes to penal codes, increasing

A Typology of Backfire Mechanisms 55

Table 3.1   The typological grid of backfire mechanisms

	"Hard" counterterrorism instruments (regulation, sanctions)		"Soft" radicalization prevention instruments (material incentives, information)
Strategy processes	a.	Environmental backfire mechanisms	b.
Interaction processes	c.	Relational backfire mechanisms	d.
Identity processes	e.	Cognitive backfire mechanisms	f.

penalties for terrorist activities and outlawing support of terrorism, for example the spread of terrorist propaganda and/or financial support. A central part of these policy changes, in a number of countries, meant increased leverage for security agencies in terms of pursuing suspected terrorists. "Soft radicalization prevention instruments" refer to the kind of action plans that have spread across especially Western Europe after the Madrid and London bombings. Characteristic of these policy packages is the aim to prevent radicalization and stop radicalization processes before any terrorist activities, or other kinds of political violence, are planned/carried out. Thus, "soft" counterterrorism instruments typically address earlier phases of radicalization processes than the "hard" ones, but spread as a type of policy instrument in the area of counterterrorism at a later stage.

Building on Vedung (2007), this basic distinction between "hard" and "soft" counterterrorism instruments can be further spelled out. Vedung distinguishes between three basic forms of public policy instruments: regulation, economic instruments and information. Symbolically he talks about policies using "sticks," "carrots," or "sermons" in order to reach intended outcomes (Vedung 2007: 30). The basis of division in Vedung's threefold classificatory scheme is the authoritative force involved in government efforts, moving from a high degree of restraining force involved in "regulations," to a lower degree of incentive-based force in "economic instruments" to the lowest degree of persuasive force involved in "information" instruments. According to Vedung, *regulations* "are measures undertaken by governmental units to influence people by means of formulated rules and directives which mandate receivers to act in accordance with what is ordered in these rules and directives" (Vedung 2007: 31). Regulations are most often associated with threats of negative sanctions such as fines, imprisonment, and other types of punishment. *Economic instruments* are defined as involving "either the handing out or the taking away of material resources, be they in cash or in kind. Economic instruments make it cheaper or more expensive to pursue certain actions" (Vedung 2007: 32). It is important to notice that in contrast to regulations economic tools always give the target groups some leeway to choose to take a certain action or not. When it comes to *information*, this leeway is even bigger. Information covers "attempts at influencing people through the transfer of knowledge, the communication of reasoned argument, and persuasion" (Vedung 2007: 33). Instruments of information most often focus on prevention of wrong or stimulation of the right conduct by offering insights into consequences of certain behaviors.

Relating Vedung's classificatory scheme to counterterrorist policy instruments, I argue that what the literature often refers to as "hard" counterterrorism policies build upon varieties of regulative instruments, while "soft" radicalization prevention draws upon, and mixes, economic and/or information instruments. Hard counterterrorism policies include, for example, regulative instruments of proscribing planning of terrorist attacks, spreading of terrorist propaganda, certain organizations or what can legally be brought onto an airplane. However, regulative instruments may also be formulated in affirmative terms, for example prescribing how demonstrations, marches, and other types of protest can be carried out. A variant of these regulative instruments in the area of counterterrorism policies are the powers given to security agencies in terms of, for example, "visitation zones," preventive arrests, and increased possibilities of surveillance of individuals and localities. In the literature on counterterrorism policies it is this last line of regulation that has been problematized as encroaching on civil rights. Soft radicalization prevention policies include economic instruments designed to alter the cost-benefit calculus of certain actions, for example by offering educational opportunities, jobs, new housing, mentors and so on to individuals believed to be in the early phases of a radicalization process. Formulated in the negative such instruments may also include depriving individuals or organizations of resources or opportunities in case they do not want to cooperate with authorities in the battle against radicalization, if they do not in organizational by-laws or goal formulations distance themselves from the use of violence, embrace democracy, liberal values, and so on. In addition, soft radicalization prevention policies frequently draw heavily on instruments of information. As indicated, the basic logic of governance here is that by providing factual knowledge about certain phenomena and consequences of actions, informational instruments can help persuade individuals to administer their free choice in more productive ways, that is, in a non-radicalized direction. This is seen in a variety of measures which appeal to "common values" of liberal freedoms, democracy, and the rule of law, while de-certifying radical ideologies and means, through state subsidized booklets, leaflets, movies, campaigns, conferences, networks, education, and so on.

Now, the vertical dimension of the typology refers to distinctions in types of perverse policy effects vis-à-vis target group behavior, meaning in this context radicalized or radicalizing individuals or groups. As mentioned, I distinguish between three sets of backfire processes, which alter target groups strategy, interaction, and identity formation respectively. "Strategy processes" cover the alterations that counterterrorist policies may produce in terms of choices of protest venue, action repertoires, recruitment and framing within target groups. Counterterrorist policies are often designed to affect these elements of strategic planning by, for example blocking recruitment to terrorist organizations and radicalized milieus through increased surveillance, and promoting alternatives to violent forms of claims-making. However, as it will be further investigated below, such intentions can backfire, for example by driving recruitment further underground, and changing terrorist choices of targets/venues in new and less predictable directions. "Interaction processes" refer to changes that counterterrorism policies may lead to in terms of target groups' everyday performances and interactions—the way "radicals" present themselves, network, build alliances and interact with authorities, the public and internally. Many counterterrorism efforts aim, for example, to isolate, play out, or co-opt "radical" actors. Again, the following section will show how such intentions can be perverted upon policy implementation and lead, for example, to more desperate measures and counterproductive practices of self-surveillance. Finally, "identity processes" cover the way various counterterrorism efforts set in motion counterproductive alterations of the way radical actors perceive themselves, are perceived by others, and the way they construct categories of "us" and "them." Many soft policies of radicalization prevention more or less explicitly communicate a picture of "us," the community of ideal citizens, and at the same time create a picture of "them," the radicals and their intolerable practices, beliefs, and means. Below, it will become clear that such discourses of "good" and "bad" citizens may have perverse effects on identity formation among target groups. It is important to notice that the three types of processes need not occur simultaneously, but may do so according to the intensity of perceived injustice of a particular policy instrument. Changes along the three dimensions of behavior will often occur gradually: First radical groups will adapt their immediate strategy, which will slowly change the way radical actors socialize, interact and perform in everyday life, and finally actors' entire identity may be transformed.

As indicated by Table 3.1, the three types of backfire processes are connected to three main types of backfire mechanisms—environmental, relational, and cognitive. Conceptually I here build on McAdam, Tarrow and Tilly's (2001) definition of environmental causal mechanisms as "externally generated influences on conditions affecting social life" (2001: 25). Thus, a general environmental mechanism in the field of counterterrorism could be the resource depletion stemming from increased crackdown on financial support of terrorist groups, which alters the conditions of operation for radical actors. Relational mechanisms refer to the alteration of "connections among people, groups and interpersonal networks" (ibid. 26). A relevant example could here be the de-linking of supportive milieus and radical organizations, which is obtained by, for example, increased surveillance and repression. Finally, cognitive mechanisms are defined as operating through "alterations of individual and collective perception" (ibid. 26).

58   *Dynamics of Political Violence*

In the following, I am particularly interested in how counterterrorist policies may alter individual and collective perceptions of self and other, and, thus, identity formation.

Although Table 3.1 may give the impression of a one-to-one relationship between strategy processes and environmental mechanisms, interaction processes, and relational mechanisms, and identity processes and cognitive mechanisms this is not entirely the case. I find that it makes sense to view these pairs of types of processes and mechanisms as ideal typical relations, but also that backfire processes in practice most often are the product of interactions between environmental, relational, and cognitive backfire mechanisms. Likewise, Table 3.1 may give the impression that I am proposing only three and not six types of backfire mechanisms. However, I will argue that in order for the typology to be not just conceptually parsimonious, but also empirically exhaustive, the different versions of environmental, relational, and cognitive backfire mechanisms ignited by hard counterterrorist instruments and soft radicalization prevention instruments respectively, must be accounted for.

Six Types of Backfire Mechanisms in the Field of Counterterrorism

Below, I exemplify the six types of backfire mechanisms outlined in Table 3.1 (cells (a)–(f)), building on causal narratives presented in my own and others' empirical research. The presentation of the six types will be ordered in three sections corresponding to the three general types of backfire processes. The identified backfire mechanisms are summarized in Table 3.2.

Table 3.2   Backfire mechanisms in the field of counterterrorism

	"Hard" counterterrorism instruments (regulation, sanctions)	**"Soft" radicalization prevention instruments** (material incentives, information)
Strategy processes	Strategic venue-shopping Diffusion Re-framing	Self-silencing Re-framing
Interaction processes	Encapsulation implosion Delegitimation Dehumanization	Performing safety Self surveillance Checking Hushing
Identity processes	Boundary formation Sectarian positioning Commitment enforcement	Reactive pride Responsibilization Disenchantment

Backfire and Target Group Strategy

Regulative counterterrorist instruments, such as outlawing of support of terrorists and security agencies' increased interventions in radicalized milieus, have on several occasions been connected to backfire processes altering target groups' strategic choices (cell (a)). For example, through security agencies' crackdown on radical mosque milieus in western Europe, such as the Finsbury Park Mosque raid in London in 2003, cultivation of Jihadist beliefs and recruitment to violent Jihadist groups can be said to have shifted from relatively open (official mosques and organizations) to more closed arenas (O'Neill and McGrory 2006, Schiffauer 2009). Through mechanisms of what I call *venue shopping*, radical entrepreneurs have adapted their recruitment strategy, found new arenas for distributing their messages and planning attacks. Thus, venues have shifted from mosques to private homes, from offline to online, from the political sphere to the social sphere. Likewise, strategic choices of objects of attacks have with increased airport security seemingly shifted from airplanes to trains, and in some cases increased pursuit of particular groups has turned police and security agencies into prioritized targets (della Porta 1995: 135, Sprinzak 1990: 82). The mechanism of strategic venue shopping forms part of larger backfire processes, as the new preferred venues of radical recruitment, socialization, claims-making and attacks lend themselves less easily to security agencies' surveillance, and as the strategic changes have given radical entrepreneurs a head start in these new arenas.

The US incarceration of alleged al-Qaeda and Taliban terrorists at Guantanamo Bay, and the use of interrogation methods such as "water-boarding" serve as other examples of how hard counterterrorism efforts may have counterproductive effects. These practices have through mechanisms of *diffusion* spread negative views of US human rights observance and foreign policy, which al-Qaeda has amplified and made use of as a central part of their rhetorical recruitment strategy (Pape 2006, Bergen and Cruickshank 2007). Likewise research has shown how al-Qaeda and likeminded skillfully *re-framed* the "war on terror" from a discourse of self-defense to one of aggression, imperialism, and crusades (Hegghammer 2006). Through environmental mechanisms of diffusion and more cognitive mechanisms of reinterpretation and re-framing, the US led war on terror can be said to have backfired in terms of intensifying grievances and fertilizing recruitment to al-Qaeda on the Arab peninsula and in the West.

While the backfire processes ignited by hard, regulatory counterterrorism and counter insurgency efforts have been discussed in a number of scholarly works (e.g. Bigo and Tsoukala 2008), and constitute the core case material for Hess and Martin's conceptualization of backfire dynamics, the extent to which soft preventive instruments of changing economic incentives and information may have similar perverse effects is much less studied. Looking now at cell (b) in Table 3.1, I will argue that this is in fact the case. My own research on radicalization prevention policies in Denmark and the way they are perceived by Muslim communities (Kühle and Lindekilde 2009, Lindekilde 2012) shows that a majority of Muslims in the study perceive the Danish action plan against radicalization in general, and particular instruments, such as mentoring schemes, role model campaigns, targeted civic education and distribution of information material on citizenship, as misrecognizing Muslims. The general perception was that the Danish radicalization prevention plan in policy wording and design of policy instruments was biased towards problematizing Muslims in general, not distinguishing clearly enough between the radical few and the big majority (for similar results in other countries see Heath-Kelly 2011, Mythen, Walklate and Khan 2009). In terms of altering target group strategy at least two counterproductive effects can be identified. First, the Muslim experience of misrecognition, and being stigmatized as radicals or radicalization threatened, has been shown to cause some Muslim actors to withdraw from public debates. Faced with the risk of being labeled "radical," actors who are orthodox Muslims, but not violence prone, found it easier to shut up and not partake in public discussions on Islam, integration, and so on (Lindekilde 2012: 24). Why is this a perverse effect of radicalization prevention? Well, if radicalization prevention policies create a policy and discursive environment in which Muslims feel misrecognized and stigmatized, and this makes certain Muslim actors adapt strategically to this environment by opting out of public debates and dialogue with authorities, we risk losing contact to the Muslim actors who can make a difference in the fight against radicalization. I argue that this process of missing out on potential important allies in the battle against radicalization is a product of the mechanism of *self-silencing* (see also Ferree 2005). Self-silencing here refers to the strategic withdrawal from public debates and engagement by actors who reason that in the current public environment they are better off shutting up than speaking up.

The second way that radicalization prevention policies perceived as misrecognizing Muslims may alter target group strategic choices in a counterproductive manner, is the tendency of some radical Muslim actors to exploit and emphasize this perceived injustice in framing activities. As already indicated, al-Qaeda rhetoric has for years emphasized the injustices of the "war on terror." But also perceived injustices of soft radicalization prevention instruments are now actively being used by radical entrepreneurs in the West to legitimize actions and reinforce discourses on Muslims as suppressed victims. For example, the website of the Danish branch of Hizb ut-Tahrir devotes an entire section to the Danish radicalization prevention plan, arguing how the action plan should be seen as a part of a larger government plan to eradicate Islam from Denmark. Thus, through mechanisms of *re-framing*, actors like Hizb ut-Tahrir are turning radicalization prevention policies into tools for recruitment and radicalization.

Backfire and Interactions of Target Groups

I now turn to backfire processes evolving from the implementation of hard and soft counterterrorism instruments, which reconfigure target group interactions and everyday performances—the way "radicals" administer themselves in interactions, network, build alliances with authorities, the public, and internally. Looking first at cell (c) in Table 3.1, a good deal of research indicates how increased surveillance and pursuit of particular terrorist groups have altered not just the groups' strategic preferences, but also their fundamental modus operandi in ways that from a security perspective are counterproductive. Donatella della Porta has convincingly shown how a dramatic limitation of exchanges with the external environment among left-wing terrorist groups in Italy in the mid-1970s was partly a product of a secret service reform, which significantly increased the repressive capacity of these institutions (della Porta 1995: 114). Although the creation of new, and more effective, branches of security forces led to massive arrests of members of left-wing terrorist groups, the reforms also had more negative, unintended consequences. The increased repression isolated many groups deep underground with very few opportunities for exchanges with the surroundings in terms of recruitment, resource allocation, and ideological exchanges with supportive communities. Donatella della Porta argues that through a mechanism of *encapsulation-implosion* this isolation actually further radicalized groups (1995: 134). Encapsulation-implosion refers to the de-linking of terrorist groups from external, supportive milieus, and the following radicalization of ideology and performances in the underground. Isolated in the underground, groups become increasingly paranoid and wound up in their own lines of reasoning, making former allies part of the enemy, and legitimizing still more bloody attacks. Ehud Sprinzak has identified similar mechanisms at play with the case of the American Weather Underground. He shows how the encapsulation-implosion interacts with mechanisms of *delegitimation* of the entire political system, and *dehumanization* of perceived enemies (Sprinzak 1990: 82).

Looking at cell (d) in Table 3.1, I will exemplify how target group reactions to perceived stigmatization inherent in soft radicalization prevention policies can result in counterproductive changes in patterns of interaction and self-performance. For example, in Denmark a particular element of the radicalization prevention plan is extra inspection visits to private schools, in practice especially Muslim free schools, to ensure that they live up to obligations to educate their students to be active citizens in a democratic society (see Lindekilde 2012). It is a variant of economic policy instruments, and the idea is to create incentives for certain kinds of behavior by threatening to cut funding. However, research has shown how these "terrorist checks" have had counterproductive side effects in terms of frustrations and resource allocation (Kjærgaard and Larsen 2010). Schools selected for these visits have felt obliged to go out of their way to "put on a show" on the day of inspection, although they felt they had nothing to hide in the first place. Kjærgaard and Larsen show how schools were intensively cleaned and class decoration rearranged to give inspectors a good impression (Kjærgaard and Larsen 2010: 71). My argument is that through mechanisms of *performing safety*, schools are responding to ascribed suspicion in counterproductive ways. Other institutions, such as Muslim organizations, have also been found to perform safety, for example by excluding members or decertifying previous allies, in order to retain status as privileged dialogue partners with government bodies or

62   *Dynamics of Political Violence*

government funding (Pram-Gad 2011). On an individual level, Gabe Mythen has shown similar mechanisms at play. He describes how young Pakistani Muslims in Britain faced with disproportional stop-and-search practices carried out by police adopt practices of *self-surveillance* in order to demonstrate their safeness (Mythen 2011). In particular, Mythen talks about practices of *checking* and *hushing*. Checking refers to "behaviors where self-inspection leads to the conscious performance of self restrainment" (ibid. 13). Mechanisms of checking cover, for example, the selected use of dialect (avoiding speaking Arabic, Farsi) and alterations of physical appearance (trimming beard, avoiding traditional Muslim clothing, not carrying a backpack on public transportation) when moving in the public sphere. Hushing refers to the "moderation of religious viewpoints and the concealment of political perspectives" in public interactions (ibid. 15). Building on Mythen, my argument here is that checking and hushing are mechanisms of backfire, in which target groups react to ascription of risk flowing partly from soft forms of counterterrorism instruments, which result in counterproductive feelings of discrimination and loss of own security.

Backfire and Target Group Identity Formation

The last two categories of backfire mechanisms pertain to more cognitive changes in identity formation. As indicated, it seems reasonable to believe that counterterrorism policies' effects on collective identity formation will most often follow previous adaptations of strategy and interactive performances. Identity processes are often lagged and link more indirectly to particular instruments of counterterrorism than is the case with the other types of backfire processes. However, starting with cell (e) in Table 3.1, research has shown how intensified hard repression (arrests, surveillance, outlawing, etc.) on many accounts has been linked to the confirmation and further radicalization of those identities (see Sedgwick 2011, Davenport, Johnston and Mueller 2005) and not, as expected and hoped, the withering away of radical, collective identities. According to Quintan Wiktorowicz (2005), British authorities' crackdown on the terrorist recruitment of the Muslim organization al-Muhajiroun in the aftermath of 9/11 made it possible for the organization to position itself within the Muslim activist milieu as the "true salafists" or the "vanguards" of the Muslim uprising (Wiktorowicz 2005: 167). Exploiting the public image as "dangerous," al-Muhajiroun through mechanisms of oppositional *boundary formation* and *sectarian positioning* reinforced the brand value of the al-Muhajiroun collective identity. Likewise, Wiktorowicz and others have shown how the involvement in "high risk activism," where risk of sanctioning from authorities is severe, often leads to the establishment of intensely felt bonds of affection and comradeship—the building blocks of strong collective identities. Thus, fears of sanctioning work through mechanisms of what I will call *commitment enforcement*, to strengthen feelings of devotedness and willingness to continue fighting, making collective identification with the group even stronger.

Several research projects have pointed to the importance of collective risk taking in forming strong collective identities (Olsen 2009).

At the center of many instruments of radicalization prevention lay ambitions to change and shape identity formation among youngsters away from radical communities towards more mainstream identification with majority society. As I have argued in a Danish context, the ultimate goal of radicalization prevention policies is to create "ideal citizens" out of "radicals" (Lindekilde 2012: 17). The ideal citizen is in the Danish action plan first and foremost pro-democratic and non-violent, non-supportive/non-sympathetic vis-à-vis violent or un-democratic groups, and the ideal citizen is responsible and active (ibid.: 18). In opposition to this ideal citizen, the action plan situates "the radical," "the extremist" or the "radicalization-threatened" youngster. In many ways the "radical" is characterized by the negation of traits of the responsible, liberal citizen, and the two fundamental subject positions are understood in terms of either-or. Either you take on the liberal identity or you take on a radical identity and become the target of neo-liberal disciplining policies. Thus, large parts of the Muslim population, for example, who are not "radicals," but who are not included in the category of good, liberal citizens either, are ascribed risk and suspicion, and entire "suspect communities" are thus created (Mythen, Walklate and Khan 2009, Lindekilde 2012). Heath-Kelly talks in this connection about how groups of citizens with immigrant background, who in terms of socio-economic integration are considered "at risk," are being categorized as potentially "risky" also in terms of security (Heath-Kelly 2011: 5). However, a number of counterproductive identificational strategies have been displayed in reaction to this pressure for conformity and liberal self-identification. Looking at cell (f) in Table 3.1, at least three different identity strategies have been discussed in the literature—strategies which do not involve reinforcement of radical identities, but which do not lead to "ideal citizens" either. First, target groups faced with the subtle forms of prevention of wrong and stimulation of the right identities may react by demonstratively enforcing elements of identity building which are problematized. Through mechanisms of *reactive pride*, for example, young Muslims in the West have responded to assimilation pressures by becoming more devoted Muslims, flashing their Muslimness more openly (Modood et al. 1997) and hence not responding in the desired way. Second, target groups may react by taking up the fight for the right to be different—for example to be visibly Muslim in the public sphere (Schiffauer 2007). Building on Mythen et al. (2007: 746), I will argue that a mechanism of *responsibilization* is at play here, which refers to the desire to challenge ignorance and misunderstandings about particular identities and ideologies in the light of ascribed risk, leading individuals to take on a role as public educators of, for example Muslim culture, faith, and politics. One could argue that this type of reactive identification cannot be said to be counterproductive, as it leads to active, responsible citizenship. However, it hardly leads to the type of active citizenship envisioned. Finally, some target group members respond to the ascription of risk and suspicion with a sense of bewilderment and resignation. Through a mechanism of *disenchantment*

64   *Dynamics of Political Violence*

feelings of belonging, inclusion and community are substituted by feelings of disconnection and exclusion. Disenchantment are by some scholars said to be linked to oppositional identity formation, where disenchanted individuals seek a sense of belonging in alternative, at times "radical," milieus (Campbell 1972). But disenchantment may also lead to confusion and a sense of not belonging anywhere—a distorted and counterproductive mode of being, characterized by passive rather than active citizenship.

Management of Backfire in the Field of Counterterrorism?

In the introduction to this chapter I underlined four conditions—two necessary and two mediating—for the development of backfire processes. In the following I return to these conditions, in particular the possibility that government authorities are able to avoid or reduce backfire processes from taking pace. As shown by Hess and Martin (2006), backfire is constituted and managed through a dynamic exchange of behavior between authorities and dissidents. In the field of counterterrorism, policies of both hard and soft counterterrorism are responses to perceived threats, which, as shown in the previous section, may backfire, leading again to adaptation/ reforms of policies. For example, the extensive criticism of and indications of backfire processes at play vis-à-vis the British PREVENT strategy, has resulted in a substantial reform of the policy in 2011 (Home Office 2011). However, rather than changing policies governments may also respond to backfire by activating strategies designed to manage it. Hess and Martin talk about five strategies of backfire management—cover-up, devaluation of target groups, reinterpretation, using formal procedures to give the appearance of justice and intimidating or bribing people involved (Hess and Martin 2006: 254). In the following I will briefly investigate if and how these backfire management strategies have been used in the field of counterterrorism.

The secrecy regarding security agencies' practices and procedures is legitimized by arguments of state security. However, secrecy can also work to cover up events, decisions, and practices, which may backfire. Keeping surveillance reports confidential and pursuing terrorist convictions in closed court trials, where evidence and charges are kept from the general public, has the advantage of keeping criticism of discriminatory practices, questionable evidences and large administrative discretion at bay. For example, the practice of the German Verfassungschutz of administrative expulsions and annulations of residence permits based on accusations of terrorism against individuals affiliated with organizations or milieus that are not prohibited by law, but considered dangerous by the Verfassungschutz, was for long hidden from public scrutiny (Schiffauer 2009). The practices were later found to be unconstitutional by the German constitutional court. In Denmark, the administrative expulsion of two Tunisian citizens charged with planning to kill the cartoonist Kurt Westergaard in 2008 was later annulled and the use of "secret evidence" in the court trial criticized by the Supreme Court.

An example of more deliberative cover-up by authorities is the publication of a book by a former Danish elite soldier in Afghanistan, which the Danish Ministry of Defense first tried to stop, arguing that its content would jeopardize Danish soldiers' mission in Afghanistan. A few days after the publication of the book an Arabic version of the book circulated on the internet, seemingly proving the point of the Ministry of Defense that the book's content would be highly valuable to enemy forces in Afghanistan and elsewhere. However, despite cover-up attempts, it soon became clear that the Arabic translation of the book originated within the Danish Ministry of Defense.

The second and third strategy of backfire management—devaluation of target groups and re-interpretations—often go hand in hand. In general, I would claim that to the extent that authorities are involved in the ongoing discursive battles in public debates about who is a "terrorist," "radical" or "extremist" and who is, for example, a "freedom fighter," they are involved in strategies of devaluation and re-interpretation meant to manage backfire and legitimize repression. Re-interpretations can take many forms, but references to state security and state of emergency are typical in the realm of hard counterterrorism efforts (Agamben 2005, Høilund 2010). With regard to soft radicalization prevention, responsible politicians and authorities involved with implementation of the preventive strategy have tried to legitimize and control backfire by referring to discourses of "failed multiculturalism," "muscular liberalism," and "misunderstood toleration" (see Lindekilde 2012). Common to these discursive strategies is the way they legitimize assimilation pressure and the attempts to actively form good, liberal citizens.

The fourth strategy of backfire management—making use of official channels to give an impression of justice—can also be found in counterterrorism. For example, the British government's first response to the criticism of its PREVENT strategy was to commission Lord Carlile to review the program and give recommendations. Likewise, in the case of the above mentioned Danish book scandal the Ministry of Defense first responded by putting together an internal auditor commission to investigate the affair. In terms of backfire management, these initiatives show that criticism is taken seriously and justice will prevail. More generally, it can be seen how counterterrorism efforts are constantly being justified by authorities by references to academic research and experiences from other countries, underscoring the necessity of measures taken and their effectiveness. This ongoing official work to legitimize counterterrorism efforts can be seen as a form of preventive backfire management.

Finally, authorities can try to intimidate or bribe people to manage backfire. One version of this strategy that has been at work in the field of counterterrorism is to pressure individuals who are seen as responsible for backfiring events or practices to quit their jobs. For example, a couple of central bureaucrats chose to quit their jobs in the Danish Ministry of Defense when the book scandal started to roll. Likewise, the American army tried to manage the backfire from the Abu Ghraib scandal by weeding out what was presented as a "few bad seeds."

Theoretical Implications and Conclusions

The purpose of this chapter has been, first, to build a conceptual foundation for the theoretization of the relationship between types of counterterrorism policies and backfire processes. Drawing on Vedung's policy instrument classification, Hess and Martin's ideas of backfire and McAdam, Tarrow and Tilly's conceptualization of processes and distinctions of types of causal mechanisms, I have proposed a typology of backfire mechanisms in the field of counterterrorism. The typology distinguishes between six sets of backfire mechanisms, which work in different ways to connect either hard (regulation) or soft (economic instruments, information) forms of counterterrorism policies to counterproductive changes in target groups' strategic choices, interactions or identity formation. By way of exemplification it was secondly the purpose of the chapter to show the empirical validity and theoretical productivity of the proposed typology. The backfire mechanisms in Table 3.2 were identified drawing on empirical case studies from different contexts and regarding different target groups. I will therefore argue that the identified mechanisms are relatively robust, meaning that they are recurrent ways by which counterterrorism efforts and target group reactions may concatenate into processes of backfire. However, I will also argue that although the six types of backfire mechanisms can seem to overlap at times, the distinctions are both empirically valid and theoretically important. Thus, if we want to study backfire mechanisms in the field of counterterrorism, and potentially avoid backfire processes, we need to pay attention to all forms of backfire mechanisms. The last purpose of the chapter was to discuss strategies of backfire management as identified by Hess and Martin and apply them to the field of counterterrorism. This exercise showed that the proposed backfire management strategies were well suited to study the dynamic development of policies and backfire processes in the field of counterterrorism.

As concluding remarks I would like to suggest some theoretical implications and points for further research based on the proposed typology. I will mention three points. A first question, which presents itself, and which needs further investigation, is what kind of hypotheses about backfire processes can be derived from the typology. At least three general hypotheses follow the typology's structure:

1. Backfire processes can be rooted in both soft and hard forms of counterterrorism policies;
2. Backfire processes can concern target group strategy, interactions, and identity; and
3. Backfire processes can have as their key driving element either environmental, interactional or cognitive mechanisms.

It follows from this that backfire processes can materialize both in the short and the long run. Furthermore, it can be hypothesized that only counterterrorism policies that live up to the two necessary conditions of backfire (knowledge and negative perception in target group) will potentially have perverse effects, while the policies that met also the two mediating conditions (public agreement and lack of backfire management) will have the largest risk of producing backfire effects. However, further research is needed to better specify concrete hypotheses and test them empirically.

Secondly, further research is needed to better validate and describe the identified backfire mechanisms in the typology cells. For example, mechanisms of performing safety, self-surveillance, hushing, and checking seem an important area of research as far as understanding potential negative impacts of soft radicalization prevention. However, these mechanisms are still understudied, and more attention should be paid to, for example the importance of target groups being part of the majority ethnic group or an ethnic minority for the functioning of such mechanisms. Likewise, better understanding of the mechanisms of reactive pride and responsibilization could prove valuable from a government perspective, in terms of turning the involved activation of citizenship into an advantage rather than a problem.

Finally, turning to the perspective of government strategies of backfire management in the field of counterterrorism, a few general points can be made following the above discussion. The possibilities of backfire processes are increasingly taken seriously by security agencies and other authorities involved in counterterrorism. Without necessarily using the terminology of backfire, authorities are focusing more and more on a "balanced" or "nuanced" counterterrorism approach. Examples are official titles of seminars/conferences on counterterrorism, and policy revisions. Likewise, security agencies in many West European countries are in these years beefing up public relations budgets in order to prevent and manage backfire. However, we still know little about authorities' capacity and skills in managing backfire processes in the field of counterterrorism, and to what extent failed attempts at backfire management may boost backfire processes. Although it is difficult to carry out research in this area, it is, as shown by Hess, Martin, and others, not impossible.

It is my belief that further research in these directions is a must if we want to avoid that counterterrorism efforts backfire. I hope that the proposed typology can serve as a conceptual tool and map for this endeavor.

References

Agamben, G. 2005. *State of Exception*. Chicago: University of Chicago Press.
Bergen, P. and Cruickshank, P. 2007. "The Iraq effect": The Iraq war and its impact on the war on terrorism. *Mother Jones Magazine*, March 1.
Bigo, D. and Tsoukala, A. 2008. *Terror, Insecurity and Liberty*. New York: Routledge.
Bjørgo, T and Horgan J., eds. 2009. *Leaving Terrorism Behind. Individual and Collective Disengagement*. London: Routledge.

Campbell, C. 1972. "The cult, the cultic milieu and secularization." *A Sociological Yearbook of Religion in Britain*, 5, 13–25.

Davenport, C., Johnston, H. and Mueller C., eds. 2005. *Repression and Mobilization*. Minneapolis: University of Minnesota Press.

della Porta, D. 1995. "Left-wing terrorism in Italy," in *Terrorism in Context*, edited by M. Crenshaw. University Park, PA: Pennsylvania State University Press, 105–60.

della Porta, D. and Reiter H. 1998. *Policing Protest. The Control of Mass Demonstrations in Western Democracies*. Minneapolis: University of Minnesota Press.

Ferree, M.M. 2005. "Soft repression: ridicule, stigma and silencing in gender-based movements," in *Repression and Mobilization*, edited by C. Davenport, H. Johnston and C. Mueller. Minneapolis: University of Minnesota Press.

George, A.L. and Bennet, A. 2005. *Case Studies and Theory Development in the Social Sciences*. Cambridge: MIT Press.

Heath-Kelly, C. 2011. *State of Exception, State of Prevention; Radicalized British Counterterrorism Policy in the War on Terror*. IJCV conference, Bielefeld, April 6–8, 2011.

Hegghammer, T. 2006. "Terrorist recruitment and radicalization in Saudi Arabia." *Middle East Policy*, 13(4), 39–60.

Hess, D. and Martin, B. 2006. "Repression, backfire and the theory of transformative events." *Mobilization: The International Journal of Research on Social Movements, Protest and Collective Behavior Mobilization*, 11, 249–67.

Høilund, P. 2010. *Frygtens ret*. Copenhagen: Hans Reitzel Publishers.

Home Office. 2011. *Prevent Strategy 2011*, online: http://www.homeoffice.gov. uk/publications/counter-terrorism/prevent/prevent-strategy/

Kjærgaard, K. and Larsen, M.Ø. 2010. *På vej mod en fælles og tryg fremtid? Et governmentality-perspektiv på anti-radikalisering*. Unpublished masters dissertation from the Department of Political Science, Aarhus University.

Kühle, L. and Lindkilde, L. 2009. *Radicalization among Young Muslims in Aarhus*. Research report. Aarhus: CIR.

Lindekilde, L. 2012. "Neo-liberal governing of 'radicals': Danish radicalization prevention policies and potential iatrogenic effects." *International Journal of Conflict and Violence*, 5(2), 109–25.

McAdam, D., Tarrow, S. and Tilly, C. 2001. *Dynamics of Contention*. Cambridge University Press.

McAdam, D., Tarrow, S. and Tilly, C. 2008. "Methods for measuring mechanisms of contention." *Qualitative Sociology*, 31(4), 307–31.

Martin, B. 2007. *Justice Ignited*. Lanham, MD: Rowman & Littlefield Publishers.

Modood, Tariq et al. 1997. *Ethnic Minorities in Britain: Diversity and Disadvantage*. London: Policy Studies Institute.

Mythen, G. 2011. *Why Should We Have to Prove We're Alright? Risk, Suspect Communities and Contingent Securities*, Radicalization Prevention and the Limits of Tolerance, international conference at Aarhus University, May 26–7, 2011.

Mythen, G., Walklate S. and Khan, F. 2009. "I'm a Muslim, but I'm not a terrorist: victimization, risky identities and the performance of safety." *British Journal of Criminology*, 49(6), 736–54.

O'Neill, S. and McGrory, D. 2006. *The Suicide Factory. Abu Hamza and the Finsbury Park Mosque*. Harper Collins Publishers.

Olsen, J.A. 2009. *Roads to Militant Radicalization—Interviews with Five Former Perpetrators of Politically Motivated Organized Violence*, DIIS Report 2009: 12, 21–40.

Pape, R. A. 2006. *Dying to Win: The Strategic Logic of Suicide Terrorism*. New York: Random House Trade Paperbacks.

Pram-Gad, U. 2011. *Self-securitizing Narratives on Radicalization Prevention through Dialogue*, Radicalization Prevention and the Limits of Tolerance, international conference at Aarhus University, May 26–7, 2011.

Schiffauer, W. 2007. "From exile to diaspora: the development of transnational Islam in Europe," in *Islam in Europe. Diversity, Identity and Influence*, edited by A. Al-Azmed and E. Fokas. Cambridge: Cambridge University Press, 68–95.

Schiffauer, W. 2009. "Suspect subjects. Muslim migrants and the security agencies in Germany," in *The Social Life of Anti-Terrorism Laws*, edited by J. Eckert. Bielefeld: Transcript Verlag, 55–79.

Sedgwick, M. 2011. *Radicalization Prevention within the Limits of Tolerance: Focusing on Key Security Concerns*, Radicalization Prevention and the Limits of Tolerance, international conference at Aarhus University, May 26–27, 2011.

Sprinzak, E. 1990. "The psychopolitical formation of extreme left terrorism in a democracy: The case of the Weathermen," in *Origins of Terrorism*, edited by W. Reich. Baltimore, MD: The Johns Hopkins University Press, 65–86.

Tarrow, S. and Tilly, C. 2007. *Contentious Politics*. Boulder: Paradigm Publishers.

Vedung, E. 2007. "Policy instruments: typologies and theories," in *Carrots, Sticks and Sermons. Policy Instruments and their Evaluation*, edited by M-L Bemelsmans-Vidic, R.C. Rist and E. Vedung. New Brunswick: Transaction Publishers, 21–58.

Wiktorowicz, Q. 2005. *Radical Islam Rising. Muslim Extremism in the West*. Lanham, MD: Rowman & Littlefield Publishers.

Winter, S. and Nielsen, V.L. 2008. *Implementering af politik*. Copenhagen: Academica.

Chapter 4

Processes of Radicalization and De-radicalization in Western European Prisons (1965–1986)

Christian G. De Vito

Preliminary Remarks on the Study of Radicalization/De-radicalization in Prison Context

By focusing on Western European prisons from 1965 to 1986, this chapter seeks to contribute to the general debate on the processes of radicalization and de-radicalization in three distinguished ways, presented in this section.

Redefining Radicalization and De-radicalization

We are first concerned with the definition of radicalization and de-radicalization themselves. As recent publications on the topic (della Porta and LaFree 2012, Alimi, Bosi and Demetriou, 2012) and the editors' introduction to this volume show, social sciences scholars tend to understand the processes of radicalization and de-radicalization in terms of a shift to political violence. That is to say, from an epistemological perspective, they objectivize the qualitative and/or quantitative characteristic of changes in the form of contention by defining the processes of radicalization and de-radicalization by their outcome and by equating this outcome with political violence.

Yet, this assumption is highly problematic. Theoretically, because political violence is only one of the possible outcomes of processes of radicalization within social movements, as much as it is just "one form among others that contentious politics sometimes takes" (Goodwin 2012: 1). Historically, because processes of radicalization and de-radicalization have both included or excluded shifts to political violence. Indeed, historians have investigated them in relation to areas of research as different as medieval, early modern and modern messianic movements, nineteenth-century French freemasonry, US labour movement during the Great depression and grass-roots communities within the Brazilian Catholic church in the 1960s.

We look for a definition of the processes of radicalization/de-radicalization freed from the teleological equation between them and political violence. A definition that recognizes that radicalization might imply a shift to violent forms and contents, but this is not the only case when radicalization takes place. One that acknowledges that the investigation of the shift to violent forms and contents of contention does not require different theoretical frameworks than those used in research on processes of radicalization and de-radicalization in general.

Neither historians nor social sciences understanding political violence as *one* form of contention have provided such a definition. We propose the following: a shift in the contents and/or forms of contention that, in relation to previous contents and/or forms of contention, is perceived as an escalation by (some) historical agents and/or by external observers.[1]

By this definition, we point to one major theoretical issue. Because no single reference—such as political violence—exists that allows to "objectify" the qualitative and/or quantitative characteristic of changes in contention, the process and the concept of radicalization have to be understood in radically relative terms. That is, we should acknowledged that they are no objective phenomena, but are constructed by historical agents and/or by external observers (including the researcher) *in relation to* their perception of previous forms and contents of contention and through their mutual connections and exchanges. This further implies that: a) these constructions are always time-, space- and scale-bound; b) since the perception of this shift might refer to forms *and/or* contents, recourse to violent forms of contention might actually imply a de-radicalization in its contents, and viceversa; c) the perception of radicalization varies for each (individual and collective) actor. In the most extreme—but historically by far the most common— situation, some actors may see radicalization where others do not.

Making Sense of Radicalization and De-radicalization

How can we study such a relative process without essentializing it? Or, to state it differently: How can we study the processes of radicalization and de-radicalization in a way that makes them comparable across time, space and scales, while at the same time recognizing their variations through time, space and scales and the subjectivity involved in their definition?

In a recent article, Alimi, Bosi and Demetriou (2012) have provided a useful framework for addressing these issues, building especially on, and proposing specific adjustments to, McAdam, Tarrow and Tilly (2001).[2] As far as this chapter is concerned, three statements contained in their article matches with our understanding:

---

1 Accordingly, we define de-radicalization as a shift in the contents and/or forms of contention that, in relation to previous contents and/or forms of contention, is perceived as a de-escalation by (some) historical agents and/or by external observers. A similar definition for radicalization and de-radicalization by state actors might be: "A shift in the forms and/ or contents of policy ... "

2 For a theoretical discussion of Tilly's approach: Demitriou 2012.

1. "Factors affecting radicalization are context-sensitive and interactive" (p. 7);
2. "The most robust explanations stem from the examination of the interplay among a variety of relational mechanisms" (p. 8); and
3. "Looking at dissimilarity in similarity … fosters a research program that sensibly aims at the middle road between reductionism and thick description" (p. 8).

Moreover, the authors identify four interrelated "arenas of interactions"—movement/political environment; intramovement; movement/security forces; and movement/countermovement—four related general relational mechanisms—respectively: opportunity-threat spirals; competition for power; outbidding; and object shift—and a number of submechanisms.

This chapter accepts this framework of analysis, because it is apt to recognize the comparability of the effects/mechanisms across time, space and scale as well as the differentiation/dissimilarities of and within factors and processes conducive to them. In the following section therefore we will use some of its key-concepts as a guide in the description of the processes of radicalization and de-radicalization in the prison(ers') movement in Western Europe in the "long 1970s."

However, coherently with our definition, we suggest that the scope of this framework should be modified or expanded in three key-areas. Firstly, while Alimi, Bosi and Demetriou exclusively use the framework to analyze the shift to political violence, we extend it to the shifts taking place both among violent and non-violent forms and contents of contention. Consequently, we point to the fact that the very concepts of radicalization and de-radicalization are socially constructed both by historical actors and observers (including scholars) operating in other times and spaces. In the concluding section we address the deep implications of these changes for the study of the related processes. Secondly, we stress the importance of temporality in the study of processes of radicalization and de-radicalization. Therefore, in the next section we propose a detailed chronology of prison(ers') movements and seek to show how the form and content of the mechanisms involved in radicalization and de-radicalization change across even a short time. Thirdly, whereas social scientists tend to consider the context of radicalization merely in terms of "political environment," this chapter highlights the significance of social, economic and cultural factors as well.

"Inside" and "Outside" the Prisons

This chapter points to the need for a dialectical understanding of the relationship between the "inside" and the "outside" of the prison as the key-area of study for the processes of radicalization and de-radicalization in the prison context. This approach will be presented in the next section and its implications will be discussed in the final section. What is important to anticipate here is that, by defining our field of research in the intersection of the "inside" and the "outside," we take distance from three concurrent frameworks.

74   *Dynamics of Political Violence*

Firstly, we object to those theories that conceive prisons as separated institutions ruled exclusively by special mechanisms and relationships. As has been convincingly argued also for mental hospitals (e.g. M. Gijswijt-Hofstra, H. Oosterhuis, J. Vijselaar and Hugh Freeman 2005, Ernst and Mueller 2010), the "total institution" approach (Goffman 1961) is productive only insofar as it does not describe the internal mechanisms in isolation from those of the society as a whole.

Secondly, the opposite denial of any specificity of the prison context is equally avoided in this chapter. Especially J.A. Goldstone and B. Useem (Goldstone and Useem 1999, Useem and Goldstone 2002) have proposed a "fractal approach" (Goldstone 1991)—the idea that "the principles of social organization repeat themselves on different *scales*" (Goldstone and Useem 1999: 986)—and have consequently applied their state-centered theories to the phenomena of prison riots. Considered as a particular "microcosm," prison becomes a mere "laboratory" where the macro-mechanisms and structures of the overall society are directly reproduced and can therefore be observed. The postulated "great similarity between the sociopolitical structures of prisons and of early modern monarchical/ imperial states" (Goldstone and Useem 1999: 987) and the equation of prison riots with "microrevolutions" reveal the formalistic nature of this perspective, its scarce contextualization and its denial of the agency of the historical actors.

Thirdly, once the "inside-outside" relationship is considered, it cannot be looked at through an exclusively formal juridical perspective. This is particularly the case of some sholars working on the history of law and of those historians of the prison (e.g. Franke 1990) who are inspired by a oversimplified version of Norbert Elias' "civilized sensibilities" perspective (Elias 1939) and whose narratives present prison "modernity" as a consequence of a linear juridical process. On the contrary, we share the viewpoint of that part of the literature on the history of prison (Salvatore and Aguirre 1996, Bernault 1999, Dikötter and Brown 2007, Johnston 2008) that has shown the systematic gap between the official—juridical, administrative, media—representations of the prison and the everyday reality within penal institutions and has stressed the need for a more comprehensive approach embracing both the internal and the external mechanisms and their mutual connections.

From this perspective, prison is conceived as a two-fold repressive institution: on the one hand, as a terminal of a larger process of social control which does not imply a mere exclusion from society, but also a "productive" symbolic role of penal justice and prisons in defining both deviancy and normality; on the other hand as an institution where the potentially total control prison authorities have over inmates takes the form of minute disciplinary techniques (Foucault, 1975, 1994) including both further punishment and concessions and leaving space for prisoners' agency (Clemmer 1940, Sykes 1958, Mathiesen 1965, Jacobs 1977). Prison repression shows then a high level of flexibility, which does not correspond to a one-way authorities/prisoners relationship inside the penal institutions, but is rather shaped by overall socio-economic processes, disciplining discourses and practices, cultural factors and the agency of prisoners and other actors in general and within each prison.

This has one major implication for this chapter. If the intrinsic repressive nature of prison is not a static "fact" but lies in a process comprising actors and factors on both sides of the prison walls, the processes of radicalization and de-radicalization too cannot be looked at esclusively inside nor exclusively outside the walls of the penal institutions, but need to be understood at the intersection of internal and external factors and both on the side of the social movements and on the side of the State. Indeed even the categories of "inside" and "outside" do not refer to a prison/society divide, but to the need for the researcher to fully address the peculiarity of the relationship betweeen the society "inside" and the society "outside" the prison walls.

Historical Episodes of Radicalization and De-radicalization in Prison Context

This section aims to ground the conceptual approaches presented above in a concrete historical context. In particular, it investigates prison(ers') movements in some Western European countries during the "long 1970s."

We present a synthesis of the findings of the historical research we have conducted on Western European prison systems, on 1970s prisoners' movements, on terrorism and antiterrorism in the 1970s and on the role of technicians and intellectuals in the social movements of the 1960s and 1970s (De Vito and Vaiani 2008; De Vito 2008, 2009, 2010, 2011, 2012). Unpublished archival sources from various Western European countries form the core of the section, together with historical and social science literature.[3] The latter appears to have largely ignored or underestimated the perspective of prisons in the analysis of the processes of radicalization and de-radicalization in the 1960s and 1970s. Indeed, the whole prison history remains marginal in the literature as far as the post-1945 period is concerned, nothwithstanding the fundamental role prisons have played in some key moments of the recent European history, for instance the Second World War, deportation towards the concentration camps and social movements in the 1960s and 1970s. Even in the case of the research on terrorism and antiterrorism, where

---

3 The main archival collections consulted for the above mentioned research are held at the following archives. Public archives: Archivio Centrale dello Stato (Rome); Archivi dello Stato (Bari, Florence, Perugia, Turin); Archives Nationales (Paris); National Archives (London); Archivio Marco Pezzi (Bologna); Istituto Cattaneo (Bologna); Istituto Gramsci Toscano (Firenze); Bibliothèque de documentation internationale contemporaine (BDIC—Nanterre). Archives of the Prison Administrations: Rome, Paris. Archives of organizations: KROM (Oslo); European group for the study of deviance and social control (London). Private archives: Irene Invernizzi; Joe Sim; Mick Ryan; Sante Notarnicola; Mauro Palma; Davide Melodia; Ruggero Cipolla.

76　　　　　　　　　　　　　*Dynamics of Political Violence*

multiple connections with the prison history might seem self-evident, scarse attention has been devoted to them both in the "classic" studies by Donatella della Porta (della Porta and Pasquino 1983, della Porta 1984, 1990) and in more recent studies (Sommier 2009, Graaf, 2010, Hof 2011). In this respect, then, this chapter aims to start filling this gap.

In order to investigate the complex interaction of mechanisms in the processes of radicalization and de-radicalization, we make explicit reference here to Alimi, Bosi and Demetriou's framework discussed in the previous section, and address them through four different moments/perspectives of the "long 1970s":

1. The origins of the prisoners movements in the second half of the 1960s;
2. The peak of the prisoners' movements in 1972–73;
3. The repression and reforms of the 1974–75; and
4. Prisons and terrorism/antiterrorism in the second half of the 1970s and the beginning of the 1980s.

This chronological division is mirrored by the structure of the section.

The Revolts of 1967–69

If we exclude some isolated protests which took place in specific institutions during the 1950s, and the early 1960s hunger strikes of the Algerian inmates in the French prisons (Petit, Faugeron and Pierre 2002, Delbaere 2002), prisoners' resistance rarely took the form of collective protests inside the Western European prisons after the late 1940s. Then, suddenly, in the late 1960s a series of violent, spontaneous revolts took place at some major prisons. Among others: at Paris-*La Santé* in 1967; at Turin-*Le Nuove* in April 1968 and then again in April 1969; at Parkhurst, October 1969. Similar outbursts took place in the Swedish, Norwegian and West German prisons in the same months (Ricci and Salierno 1971, Stratton 1973, Invernizzi 1973, Livrozet 1973, Mathiesen 1974, Fitzgerald 1977, Verde 2002).

If we are to look at the process of radicalization, it is this common timing which first requires explanation. Why did those outbursts take place in the late 1960s, when prison conditions were not significantly worse than in the previous decades of silence? Why did they take place almost simultaneously, notwithstanding the differences in the political cultures and in the material conditions of the prisons?

Because in the late 1960s neither prisoners' movements nor their connections with the "outside" were yet fully structured in the countries we are considering, the arenas of interactions within the movement and between the movement and countermovement played no role in the processes of radicalization. By contrast, the mechanisms of opportunity/threat spirals and outbidding had a major influence on them. Their combined impact is revealed by three sets of factors, mainly pointing to structural equivalences within different national contexts, as direct links between the protests seem scarsely relevant for this early period (apart from the circulation of infomation through the media).

Firstly, the attitude of State authorities played an important role in at least two ways. In the long run, the late 1960s witnessed the crisis of the top-down attitude of politicians and prison administrators towards prison reform. Both in the case of retributive and rehabilitative perspectives, the individual and collective role of prisoners had been completely ruled out: state authorities had tried to impose a strictly repressive relationship with "their" prisoners. On the eve of the outbursts, this repressive attitude became even more evident. While minor concessions were made and reform debates advanced at low pace, a violent intervention took place. Massive use of legal and illegal disciplinary punishment followed each and every revolt, in the long term producing two undesired outcomes: a substantial legitimation of the prisoners' claims among political activists, public opinion and some lawyers, magistrates and prison officials; a further diffusion of the protest to other prisons, particularly through the uncontrolled practice of punitive transfers of inmates involved in the revolts.

In many cases, such as in France and Italy, one of the main concern of the State was that of separating common-law and political prisoners in order to stop the protests. In its most visible form this took place through the concession of amnesties for social and political conflict-related prisoners, such as in Italy in 1970, and special status to the latter, in the French case following a well establishing practice already in used with the FLN prisoners.

This tendency implicitly reveals a second factor of radicalization, belonging to the arena of interaction between the movement and the social and political environment, that is, the relation between the prisoners' movement and the "1968" movement. Notwithstanding the efforts of the prison authorities to keep them separate, imprisoned activists did play an important role in breaking the isolation of the "common-law" prisoners, enforced through limited relatives-inmates contacts and the censorship on correspondance. Besides exchanging information with the other inmates, once they left the prison they fostered the (very low) awareness of the prison situation among their fellow comrades.

By the way, it would be wrong to assume that the activists had a direct role in the organization of the early prison revolts and protests. The short term sentences they eventually served didn't give them the very time either to master the complexity of the prison and to connect with a sufficient number of inmates. Moreover, their often recently acquired political experience simply didn't match the prison reality, where no assemblies and public speeches were possible, but only illegal "kites" and clandestine meetings in the yards.

The relatively growing awareness of (a part of) the external movements and the process of prisoners' politicization thus proceded along fairly separated paths, influencing each other through a precarious flow of information and illegal correspondance rather than through direct contacts. Indeed, this separation was to remain a major source of weakness for the prisoners' movements during their whole existence, affecting both the uneven interest of external political movements on prisons and the actual level of prisoners' politicization. From a different perspective, however, this separation also underlines the prisoners' agency, not least because their continuous transition from prison to "society" and viceversa was another channel of information on both prison protests and social movements at large.

This points to the need to pay attention also to the transformation of the composition of the prison population during the previous years, in connection with general societal transformations. According to some Italian studies (e.g., Quadrelli 2004), this transformation might represent a third factor of radicalization, pointing to mechanisms operating at the crossroads of the arenas of interaction between the movement and the social and political environment and within the movement itself. For although prisoners continued to be selected largely from the most excluded sections of society, by the late 1960s this exclusion was synonym for a precarious relationship with an expanding labour market rather than that of a complete social marginalization. Moreover, albeit often materially excluded from it, prisoners now shared the consumerist mentality linked with urban society: most of them lived in the main cities, had a higher level of education that their predecessors, and often had a recent experience of migration from rural to industrial contexts such as Turin, Genoa and Milan, which eventually turned to be also the settings for the most important prison revolts of the 1968–69 period. By the way, much more research is needed to clarify this point. In particular, comparative studies are needed to understand whether these trends can be generalized beyond the Italian case or they relate to the peculiar, accelerated transition known as the Italian "economic miracle" and to its social consequences.

1972–73: The Peak of the Prisoners' Movements

Not only the timing of the original outburst of the prisoners' movements, but also its subsequent developments, proceeded in parallel in the Western European countries we are considering. Thus, after the substantial downturn of 1970–71, the following two years were marked by a new process of radicalization. Importantly, this did not generally lead to political violence, but rather to a higher level of organization than in the late 1960s and to a relatively more structured connection between groups of prisoners on the "inside" and specific organization on the "outside."

This process of radicalization was located in the arena of interaction between the movement and the social and political context. In particular, an opportunity spiral was at work here, one that fostered the inside-outside relations as well as the solidarity among prison movements across different countries. Central in the construction of this network was a diffuse marxist analysis of the social function of prison. For activists started conceptualizing it in connection with the ups and downs of the capitalist economy; and, contradicting some specific comments Marx wrote on the lumpenproletarians but remaining within a marxian analysis of the relationship between capital and labour, they saw prisoners as part of the proletariat, if not because productive labourers themselves, certainly as members of the "industrial reserve army."

This marxist framework legitimized prisoners' contention in their own eyes, from the perspective of the external activists and, up to a certain point, in the view of some sectors of society as a whole. It also pushed external activists to respond positively to the prisoners' struggles and to (try to) establish connection with them. And it allowed prison movements in different Western European countries to develop almost simultaneously and to communicate with each other. For although the European group of deviance and social control created in 1973 never resembled the "prisoners' International" some activists had hoped to create (Bianchi, Simondi and Taylor 1975), a sustained exchange of information and contacts at various levels did take place, for instance, between the Scandinavian and the British groups and between the French and the Italian ones, and more episodically between the Swedish and the French movements. All Western European prison groups, moreover, looked at the contemporary prison struggles in the USA and found sources of inspiration in the writing of the Black Panthers, the prison diaries of George Jackson and the revolt of Attica and the international campaign for the liberation of Angela Davis. These transnational networks altogether constituted a significant factor of radicalization, particularly because they promoted a sense of legitimation within the prison(ers') movements.

Underlining the common characteristics of the prison(ers') movements thus proves useful to single out some important mechanisms of radicalization in the early 1970s. Other significant mechanisms can be identified by proceding in the opposite direction, that is, by investigating the differences. These are, again, mainly located in the arena of interaction between the movement and the social and political environment and operate through the same process of opportunity and solidarity. Yet, diversity between the experiences of the Italian movement (and partly the French one), on the one hand, and of the Scandinavian and British ones on the other, suggests the work of other submechanisms of radicalization.

In Italy an "extraparliamentary model" prevailed, with a key role being played by the most important extraparliamentary group, *Lotta continua* (Lotta continua 1972, 1973, Invernizzi 1973, Bobbio 1988, Cazzullo 1998, Petricola 2002). By the end of 1971 this organized a national (but unstable) "Prisoners' committee," whose militants established illegal correspondence contacts with a certain number of prisoners leaders or "internal vanguards." In turn, the latter formed some (unstable) *nuclei* inside the prisons of Porto Azzurro, Perugia, Lecce, Brescia, Turin and Milan: these mainly served as places of political education and discussion, fostering a transition from the alleged individualistic mentality of the petty offender to the alleged collective approach of the militant and from individualistic forms of resistance (self-harm, escapes, violence, revolts) to organized collective protests aimed at better conditions of imprisonment, prisoners' rights and general political reforms.

In Scandinavia and in Britain, by contrast, a "union model" prevailed inside the prisons (Stratton 1973, Mathiesen 1974, Fitzgerald 1977, Scraton, Sim and Skidmore 1991), revealing more pragmatic aims of the prisoners within prison systems where convict labour had a much more significant role than in Italy. The most important prisoners' organizations—the Swedish FFCO, the Norwegian FFF and Preservation of the Rights of Prisoners (PROP) in Britain—used strike as their

80   *Dynamics of Political Violence*

main form of action and tried to gain free workers' rights for the prisoners and to establish themselves as fully recognized unions, although they were rarely able to reach these goals.

The external forms of organizations corresponded to these aims of the prisoners. These were no extraparliamentary organizations, but rather eterogeneous groupings of criminologists, sociologists, students, social workers and psychologists, some eventually working inside the prisons themselves. Within the Swedish KRUM, the Norwegian KROM and the National Deviancy Conference (NDC) and the Radical Alternatives to Prison (RAP) group in Britain, the general radicalization of the professionals intertwined with the process of radicalization in and around the prison (Di Vittorio 1999, Reisch and Andrews 2002), for the professionals questioned their own social role and their professional knowledge in order to allow the "prisoners' voices" to be finally heard.

Radical professionals' organizations thus became a fundamental external resource for the inmates, particularly in the above mentioned countries, but also in West Germany (Mathiesen, 1979) with the *Arbeitskreis Junger Kriminologen* (AJK) and even more clearly with the French *Groupe d'informations sur les prisons* (GIP), where Michel Foucault played a key-role (Livrozet 1973, Delbaere 2002, Artières, Quéro and Zancarini-Fourmel 2003). Critical criminologists also played an important role in Italy, albeit in more conventional academic forms (Melossi and Pavarini 1977), but professionals were substantially absent in the prison movements. However, common to all these countries was the fact that the engagement of professionals, intellectuals and activists on the side of the prisoners mirrored and, in turn, influenced a more general crisis of legitimation of the prison, which in itself represents a major factor of radicalization. In place of the traditional hold of the penal ideology, a contradictory and yet diffused series of critiques against it were levied through academic books and popular songs, films and the informed articles of some prison officers and magistrates.

1974–75: Repression, Reform

The arena of interaction between the movement and the social and political environment continued to be central in this period, but the opportunity-threat mechanism now produced diffused de-radicalization in the common-law prisoners' movements. Moreover, its different combinations with mechanisms operating in the arenas of interactions between the movement and, respectively, security service and countermovements, led to strong dissimilarities in different contexts.

Since 1974, as the international economic crisis and its social and political consequences impacted on all countries, a wind of "law and order" started blowing over most of the Western European countries, bringing increasing limitations to the prisoners' rights and to their mobilizations. The loosening of direct and indirect connections between the prison(ers') movements and between the "inside" and the "outside" followed, but the effects of these changings on the processes of radicalization and de-radicalization related to prison were contradictory.

De-radicalization was reached in the Scandinavian countries through prison reform (Mathiesen, 1990), that led to the co-optation of the prisoners' groups and made external organizations disappear (KRUM) or undergo a process of internal transformation (KROM). Conversely, state repression hit particularly hard on France (Delbaere 2002),[4] where the new wave of prisoners' struggles that erupted on 18 July 1974 was met by the authorities with deadly violence in the following months and with the creation of the *quartiers à sècurité renforcée* (QHS) in ten prisons the next year. The process operating here can hardly be labelled as outbidding, since the shift to violence that occurred in the strategy of the security forces was not paralleled by a similar shift in the prisoners' movement. Rather than an interactive spiral leading to increasing political violence, what we observe here is therefore simply the end of the French prisoners' movement that had started in 1970, or at least its forced de-radicalization. As a matter of fact, after 1974 no relevant mobilization took place in the French prison, and the focus of subsequent discussions and actions of intellectuals and prisoners became the denounciation of prison isolation and the much abused category of "dangerousness" for high security prisoners.

The situation in Italy was in many regards similar to the French one and 1974 witnessed two main episodes of deadly repression in the prisons of Florence (23 February) and Alessandria (9 May). Systematic violence by the authorities followed, supported by the claims of the existence of an organization called *Arancia Meccanica* [Clockwork Orange]—which never really existed but turned to be a very useful invention. Under the assault of repression, the Italian prisoners' movement started declining and showed its huge weaknesses, while *Lotta continua* decided in June 1974 to terminate any political intervention on prisons.

Repression thus severed the existing links between the "inside" and the "outside." However, differently from the French situation this did not lead to an outright end of the prisoners' movement in Italy. A reason for this lies in the fact that the important 1975 reform in Italy had no substantial impact in the earlier years, because of limited budget and for the constraints imposed by old buildings and personnel (Melodia 1976, Magistratura democratica 1979). Prison reform in this context, therefore, did not favour de-radicalization, but its opposite, through the cumulative joint influence of mechanisms located in various arenas of interactions. For the movement internally polarized between non-violent organizations such as the Lega non-violenta dei detenuti and a prison-based clandestine group, the *Nuclei armati proletari* (NAP), with fierce competition for power at work in this area. This polarization was further radicalized by violent State repression, that was legitimated with the need to fight the rising "terrorist" threat outside the prisons and, in turn, legitimized the use of violence by prison(ers') movements, thus marginalizing non-violent groups. Finally, the emergence of armed groups outside the prisons gave former "internal vanguards" the chance to rebuild an "inside-

---

4   For the effects of the repression against the prisoners' strikes coordinated by PROP in 1972 see Fitzgerald 1977.

82   *Dynamics of Political Violence*

outside" connections. As a matter of fact, as early as 1976 NAP members had already joined the Brigate rosse (BR [Red Brigades]) (Silj 1977, Ferrigno 2008, Lucarelli 2010).

A fundamental shift thus took place in this period in Italy, from common-law prisoners' movements—that virtually ceased to exist around 1977—to political prisoners' movements. This process can be found elsewhere, with more or less similar features.

In the Federal Republic of Germany, for instance, the attempt the sociologist Karl Schumann and other activists made in 1979 to rebuild an external support for the common-law prisoners' movement found no more space available between the polarized situation of terrorist violence and state repression (Mathiesen 1979).

In Spain common-law prisoners had made their voice heard though a series of revolts in 1972–74 and had founded the *Coordinadora de los presos españoles en lucha* (COPEL [Coordination of the struggling Spanish prisoners]) in Barcelona in 1975, after the new regime had excluded them from an amnesty granted to political prisoners (Rubio 2006, Forero Cuéllar 2010). During the Spanish political transition the movement expanded, but then came to a sudden end in 1978–79, when the external support ended and the State repression raised after the murder of the general director of the prisons by an anarchist armed group, this in turn being a response to the death of an anarchist prisoner held at the Madrid prison.

An even more extreme case in the exclusive relation between political and common prisoners' movements after the mid-1970s is that of Northern Ireland. Here the permanent centrality of imprisoned members of the armed organizations has till recently completely marginalized the specific issues of the common prisoners, thus operating as a factor of preventive de-radicalization (McKeown 2001).

Terrorism and Antiterrorism in the Prisons

By the late 1970s and the beginning of the following decade, prisoners' movements were virtually limited to political prisoners belonging to armed organizations in the Federal Republic of Germany, Italy and Northern Ireland. Their monopoly of the prisoners' movement went so far in marginalizing the common-law prisoners, that they actually operated as countermovements, through a mechanism of object shift. Briefly said, there was no more possibility for a common-law prisoner and for an external activist to engage into a prison movement without clashing with the political prisoners' movement, its discourses and practices and its representation in the media and in the policy.

In this new situation, the "inside-outside" relation came to coincide with the links between free and imprisoned members of the armed groups themselves. The repertoire of action and the forms of organization also changed: they focus no more on the creation of internal solidarity networks with common-law prisoners, but mainly aimed at escapes and violent actions linked with the external "campaigns" elaborated by the organizations. In this context, intramovement competition for power, movement/security forces outbidding mechanisms and intra-security forces competition for power took central stage, because the processes of radicalization and de-radicalization in prison context came to depend exclusively on the internal logic of the armed organization, on the one hand, and of the antiterrorist forces, on the other. Consequently, the performative power of some aspects of the antiterrorist strategies (Graaf 2010) related to the prison context favoured radicalization.

For instance, deaths in custody—such as those of the leader of the Baader-Meinhof group at Stammheim prison—and the use of torture—such as was the case in Italy, particularly after the Dozier kidnapping in 1982—generally had an escalating effect, becoming a *leitmotiv* in the legitimizing discourse of the clandestine militants. More generally, the lack of transparency on the side of the authorities, particularly when coupled with a broad visibility of their antiterrorist operations, generated critiques on the latter; this holds expecially true for antiterrorist strategies involving the prison, because of its material isolation and structural closeness. Not surprising then, the creation of maximum security prisons represented one of the most sensitive aspects in both the antiterrorist strategies and the terrorists' discourse. One only has to think about the symbolic importance the H-blocks and the prison of Stammheim and Asinara respectively assumed on a transnational scale (Coogan 1980, Prette 2006, Graaf 2010, Hof 2011).

Equally important is the way the differentiation of political prisoners in general was managed within antiterrorism. For this clearly had contradictory effects in terms of radicalization/de-radicalization in different places and time.

In Italy during the late 1970s, Dalla Chiesa used prison differentiation as part of his strategy to polarize the terrorists' field between *pentiti* [collaborators] and *irriducibili* [indomitables]—eventually introducing further differentiation within the maximum security prisons themselves—and accelerate the political conflicts among the tens of armed groups that populated the Italian late 1970s. Similarly in Northern Ireland, the refuse of the British authorities to recognize the political status of the republican prisoners became a major factor of radicalization, as it induced a prolonged prisoners' response. By the way, the hunger strike of 1980 which concluded that phase of confrontation held a double and contradictory meaning: on the one hand it created a long-lasting "myth" and clearly became a point of reference for any republican armed militant in the following years; on the other hand, through the election of Bobby Sands, it inaugurated the republicans' electoral strategy which proved decisive for starting the peace process in the area (Beresford 1987).

As these events show, prison systems are not only passive fields for antiterrorist strategy, but shape anti-terrorism themselves. Indeed, the single most effective deradicalizing strategy in Italy was developed by the prison administration together with a part of the political prisoners rather than by the antiterrorist forces (Segio 2006). The political proposal of the *dissociati*—political prisoners mainly belonging to the group Prima linea, who openly and collectively refused the use of political violence in June 1983—emerged through their systematic contacts with the general director of the prisons, Niccolò Amato; later on it was further developed, on the "inside," through the institutions of special *aree omogenee* [homogeneous wings] for the "dissociati," and, on the "outside," through an extented network of individuals and associations, in order to find an appropriate legislative way-out from the "terrorist emergence" and to prepare the social inclusion of the former terrorists at the end of their sentence.

The process of *dissociazione* was thus situated at the cross-roads of mechanisms of opportunity-threat spirals, competition for power—both within the movement and within anti-terrorism—and outbidding. Moreover, the mechanism of object shift influenced the process de-radicalization since the early 1980s. The role of the countermovement here was not played by the neo-fascist armed organizations, as these proved incapable to oppose the prisoners' movements and the influence left-wing extraparliamentary groups had on them. It was rather the rise of confrontations within organized crime—and particularly the *camorra*—and the intervention of the State in that field that introduced a new powerful actor on the social and prison scene. This contributed to transform the situation, as a shift from the "terrorist emergency" to the "mafia emergency" was perceived both by policy-makers and in the Italian society as a whole. The extension of typical tools of anti-terrorist policy (maximum security prisons and the *pentitismo*) to the anti-mafia policy and Dalla Chiesa's transition from head of anti-terrorism to prefect of Palermo in 1982 visualized this shift.

Concluding Remarks

Building on the theoretical discussion in the first section and on the historical overview in the second one, in this final section we present some areas in which our study of the processes of radicalization and de-radicalization in prison context contributes to the understanding of processes of radicalization and de-radicalization in general.

In the first place, we have stressed the need to study the processes of radicalization and de-radicalization in prison context at the crossroads of the "inside/outside" relations, instead of isolating the prison or, conversely, denying its specificities. Spontaneous revolts and armed actions, as well as what we named the "union model" and the "extraparliamentary model" of organization thus emerged from our account as the result of influences on both sides of the prison walls.

More generally, we have understood political violence as one of the many forms of contentious politics. Therefore, in the previous section we have addressed the whole cycle of the prison(ers') movements in Western Europe in the long 1970s, and not just that part of it marked by the emergence of armed organizations. From a theoretical perspective, this implies that the arenas of interaction, the mechanisms and the sub-mechanisms by which Alimi, Bosi and Demetriou have explained shifts towards political violence, operate for all shifts in the forms and/or contents of contention that entails escalation, whether involving the use of political violence or not. For instance, opportunity/threat spirals played a role both in the expansion of "unionization" among common-law prisoners in Britain in the early 1970s and in the growing use of violence in France and Italy in the mid-1970s. Furthermore, we have stressed that no single mechanism, but their combinations, account for radicalization and de-radicalization. Again, this holds true for the mix of opportunity spirals and outbidding leading to the emergence of the non-violent *nuclei* inside the Italian prisons, for the intertwining of (lack of) opportunity spirals, outbidding and competition for power leading to the emergence of the NAP, and for the interactions leading to the "dissociazione."

However, if political violence is not the exclusive parameter by which processes of radicalization and de-radicalization can be defined, the very epistemological foundations of the framework provided by Alimi, Bosi and Demetriou and in the introduction to this volume have to be revisited. The definition of radicalization we have provided in the first section is not based on any "objective" reference— such as the shift to political violence—but rather stresses the relativity of this process *vis-à-vis* multiple contexts, temporalities, spaces and interactions and the multiple perceptions by the historical actors and by external observers. In this context, adopting a "model of fluid causality"—as suggested in the introduction to this volume—entails acknowledging that the concepts of radicalization and de-radicalization, as well as the mechanisms and submechanisms proposed in Alimi, Bosi and Demetriou, are useful not because they indicate "facts," but in so far as they frame fundamentally different processes together in a way that recognizes historical and subjective polysemy.

What is "radicalization" for whom? What is "legitimation" for whom? What is "polarization" for whom? What is "political violence" for whom? The irreducible complexity that lies behind these questions is not only visible on a macro-scale, e.g. in the differences between prisoners' movements in various nations. Common-law prisoners held in the same wings of the same prison interacted differently with the social and political environment, the state security forces, movements and countermovements. And one prisoner or group of prisoners focused on the on-going "radicalization" in state repression, another on the shift to violence promoted by some fellow-prisoners, while others considered "terrorism" as a more radical *form*, but a less radical *content vis-à-vis* the mass common-law prisoners' movement of the early 1970s. The same holds true for external activists, and for all other actors on the social scene, including state agents such as "common" policemen and top-antiterrorism generals and individual prison governors.

These social constructions, the very words by which they were defined and the way they were communicated to other actors shaped fundamentally different images of "radicalization." To call a process "radicalization" or "politicization," or to call its effect "terrorism," "armed struggle" or "liberation movement," produced different (understanding of those) events. In addition to this, different frames used by different actors reveal some features of a movement, while they hide others. In our case, for instance, violent discourses and practices were far more visible than the non-violent ones, and both of them were over-represented in comparison to the ideas and practices of those who did not join the prisoners' movements at all.

Similarly, by framing historical events through the concept of radicalization (or any other related concept) scholars themselves create an image of that phenomenon, no matter how complex their theoretical framework. This is, of course, not to say that all conceptualizations should be avoided. We rather wish to stress the need to avoid any essentialization of concepts and mechanisms, through self-reflexivity on their socially-constructed nature. This means, for instance, that research on these issues should be independent from ideologically biased approaches that seek not just to understand radicalization, but also to address "how it can be prevented, and how it can be contained" (della Porta and LaFree 2012), thus essentializing it and prejudicially taking side.

Stemming from the same need to acknowledge the relativeness of the process and concept of radicalization/de-radicalization, this chapter also suggests modifications to the framework provided by Alimi, Bosi and Demetriou. It expands the concept of political environment to include social, cultural, and economic features. Therefore, we have addressed the changing social composition of the prison population and the role played by welfare professionals in Northern Europe.

Moreover, this chapter calls for attention to the temporality of the processes of radicalization and de-radicalization. The timing of both process changes rapidly and in a nonlinear way, in each phase leading to a reshuffling of the mechanisms and sub-mechanisms involved, as well as of their interactions. Therefore, in the previous section we have introduced a historical approach and detailed chronologies in order to avoid generalizations, or, at least, to become more aware of the relativity of the comparisons we were drawing.

Finally, we stress the need to focus on the spatial dimension of radicalization. Different forms and contents of contentious politics entail a different "spatial division of radicalization,"[5] and the shift that radicalization and de-radicalization imply changes across time. In our study we have observed consistent spatial shifts at different scales: at continental level, since countries involved in radicalization and de-radicalization were different in different periods; within the national level, the late 1960s revolts were mainly located in big prisons in major cities, common-law prisoners' radicalization in the 1973/74 period took place in more multifaceted settings, while the spatial configuration of the political prisoners' movements in the late 1970s and early 1980s was forcibly dependant on the geography of the maximum security prisons and wings where they were imprisoned.

Different time and spaces also construct radicalization differently. The radicalization of common-law prisoners in a big city-prison in the early 1970s and that of political prisoners in a maximum security prison on a peripheral island, for instance, entailed fundamentally different power relations, created different imaginaries outside the prisons and were communicated to different audiences in different ways.

To state that the arenas of interaction, the mechanisms and the submechanisms involved in the shift to political violence are not qualitatively different than those

---

5   For this approach on space: Massey 1994.

leading to forms of radicalization that did not include political violence, does not mean that no specificities can be observed in the contents of radicalization that did involve political violence. The findings in the previous section provide significant insights in this respect. By using the same framework of analysis for non-violent and violent prison(ers') movements we were actually able to observe that the emergence and then the hegemony of armed groups inside and outside the prisons did mark a fundamental break with previous prisoners' movement.

For instance, the *political* environment proved much more important for the radicalization of armed organizations inside and outside the prisons than for the one of the common-law prisoners' movements and the extraparliamentary groups of the early 1970s. The latter were able to, and willing to, interact with the social, cultural and economic context as well. Consequently, political prisoners were more prone to enter into threat spirals and outbidding mechanisms with, respectively, the State and the security forces, whereas common-law prisoners disposed of a broader arrays of alternatives and benefited from broader social transformations. For the same reason, however, armed groups were more prepared to resist State strategies of repression and co-optation.

The use of violence by some groups, both inside and outside the prison, also made inter-movement competition for power much more influencial as a mechanism for radicalization. It reduced the chances for solidarity and cooperation among groups with heterogeneous ideological background—a feature that, conversely, had played a major role in the diffusion and radicalization of the prisoners' movements across Western Europe in the early 1970s. In this context, violent political prisoners' movements tended to act more or less explicitly as countermovements *vis-à-vis* the common-law prisoners' movements.

References

Adams, R. 1992. *Prison Riots in Britain and the USA*. Houndsmills: MacMillan.
Alimi, E.Y., Bosi and L., Demetriou, C. 2012. Relational dynamics and processes of radicalization: a comparative framework. *Mobilization: An International Journal*, 17(1), 7–26.
Artiéres, P., Quéro and L., Zancarini-Fourmel, M. 2003. *Le Groupe d'Information sur les Prisons Archives d'une lutte, 1970–1972*. Paris: Editions de l'IMEC.
Babini, V.P. 2009, *Liberi tutti. Manicomi e psichiatri in Italia: una storia del Novecento*. Bologna: Il Mulino.
Beresford, D., 1987. *Ten Men Dead. The Story of the 1981 Irish Hunger Strike*. Hammersmith: Harper Collins Publishers.
Bernault, F. 1999. *Enfermement, prison et chatiments en Afrique du 19ème siècle à nos jours*. Paris: Karthala.
Bianchi, H., Simondi, M. and Taylor, I. (eds.) 1975, *Deviance and Control in Europe*. London-New York-Sydney-Toronto: John Wiley & Sons Ltd.
Bobbio, L. 1988. *Storia di Lotta Continua*. Milano: Feltrinelli.

Cazzullo, A. 1998. *I ragazzi che volevano fare la rivoluzione. 1968–1978 Storia di Lotta Continua*. Milano: Mondadori.

Clemmer, D. 1940. *The Prison Community*. Boston: The Christopher Publishing House.

Coogan, T.P. 1980. *On The Blanket. The H-Block Story*. Dublin: Ward River Press.

De Vito, C.G. 2008. Tecnici e intellettuali dei 'saperi speciali' nei movimenti degli anni settanta a Reggio Emilia, in *Tempi di conflitti, tempi di crisi. Contesti e pratiche del conflitto sociale a Reggio Emilia nei "lunghi anni Settanta,"* edited by L. Baldissara. Napoli-Roma: l'ancora del mediterraneo, 387–426.

De Vito, C.G. 2009. *Camosci e girachiavi. Storia del carcere in Italia 1943–2007*. Roma-Bari: Laterza.

De Vito, C.G. 2010. L'uomo a due dimensioni. I tecnici nell'Autunno caldo, tra identità professionale e lotte sociali, in *Il 1969 e dintorni. Analisi, riflessioni e giudizi a quarant'anni dall' "autunno caldo,"* edited by P. Causarano, L. Falossi and P. Giovannini. Roma: Ediesse, 161–81.

De Vito, C.G. 2011. *I luoghi della psichiatria*. Firenze: Polistampa.

De Vito, C.G. 2012. La lotta armata e la 'questione delle carceri,' in *Violenza politica e lotta armata*, edited by S. Neri Serneri and M. Maccaferri. Bologna: Il Mulino, 285–303.

De Vito, C.G. and Vaiani, S. 2008. Ci siamo presi la libertà di lottare. Movimenti dei detenuti in Europa Occidentale. *Zapruder*, 16 (May–August), 8–22.

Delbaere, L. 2002. *Le système pénitentiaire à travers les luttes des détenus de 1970 à 1987*. Available at: http://prison.eu.org/spip.php?article9315 [accessed: July 25, 2011].

della Porta, D. 1990. *Il terrorismo di sinistra*. Bologna: Il Mulino.

della Porta, D. (ed.) 1984. *Terrorismi in Italia*. Bologna: Il Mulino.

della Porta, D. and LaFree G. 2012. Guest Editorial: Processes of Radicalization and De-Radicalization. *International Journal of Conflict and Violence*, 6(1), 4–10.

della Porta, D. and Pasquino G. (eds) 1983. *Terrorismo e violenza politica. Tre casi a confronto: Stati Uniti, Germania e Giappone*. Bologna: Il Mulino.

Demetriou, C. 2012. Processual Comparative Sociology: Building on the Approch of Charles Tilly. *Sociological Theory*, 30(1), 51–65.

Di Vittorio, P. 1999: *Foucault e Basaglia. L'incontro tra genealogie e movimenti di base*. Verona: ombre corte.

Dikotter, F. and Brown I. (eds.) 2007. *Cultures of Confinement: A History of the Prison in Africa, Asia and Latin America*. London: Hurst & Company.

Elias, N. 1939. *Über den Prozess der Zivilisation. Soziogenetische und Psychogenetische Untersuchungen*. Basel: Haus zum Falken.

Ernst, W. and Mueller, T. (eds.) 2010. *Transnational Psychiatries: Social and Cultural Histories of Psychiatry in Comparative Perspective, c. 1800–2000*, Newcastle upon Tyne: Cambridge Scholars Publishing.

Ferrigno, R. 2008. *Nuclei Armati Proletari—Carceri, protesta, lotta armata*. Napoli: Edizioni La Città del Sole.

Fitzgerald, M. 1977. *Prisoners in Revolt*. Middlesex: Penguin.

Forero Cuéllar, A. 2010. *Prison Movement in Spain: The Experience of the Coordinadora of Spanish Prisoners in Struggle (COPEL)*. Paper presented at the 13th ICOPA. Belfast, 23 June 2010.

Foucault, M. 1975: *Surveiller et punir. Naissance de la prison*. Paris: Gallimard.

Franke, H. 1990. *Tweee eeuwen gevangen. Misdaad en straf in Nederland*. Utrecht: Aula.

Gijswijt-Hofstra, M., Oosterhuis, H., Vijselaar, J. and Freeman, H. (eds.) 2005. *Psychiatric Cultures Compared. Psychiatry and Mental Health Care in the Twentieth Century*. Amsterdam: Amsterdam University Press.

Goffman, E. 1961. *Asylums. Essays on the Social Situation of Mental Patients and Other Inmates*. New York: Anchor.

Goldstone, J.A., Useem, B., 1999. Prison Riots as Microrevolutions: An Extension of State-Centered Theories of Revolutions. *American Journal of Sociology*, 67, 985–1029.

Goodwin, J. 2012. Introduction to a special issue on political violence and terrorism: political violence as contentious politics, *Mobilization: An International Journal*, 17(1), 1–5.

Graaf, B. de 2010. *Evaluating Counterterrorist Performance: A Comparative Study*. Abingdon: Routledge/Francis & Taylor.

Hof, T. 2011. *Staat und Terrorismus in Italien 1969–1982*. München: Oldenbourg Verlag.

Invernizzi, I. 1973. *Il carcere come scuola di rivoluzione*. Torino: Einaudi.

Jacobs, J.B. 1977. *Stateville. The Penitentiary in Mass Society*. Chicago and London: Chicago University Press.

Johnston, H. (ed.) 2008: *Punishment and Control in Historical Perspective*. Houndmills: Palgrave MacMillan.

Livrozet, S. 1973. *De la prison à la révolte*. Paris: Mercure de France.

Lotta Continua 1972. *Liberare tutti i dannati della terra*. Roma: Edizioni Lotta Continua.

Lotta Continua 1973. *Ci siamo presi la libertà di lottare. Il movimento di massa dei detenuti da gennaio a settembre '73*. Roma: Edizioni Lotta Continua.

Lucarelli, V. 2010. *"Vorrei che il futuro fosse oggi." Nap: ribellione, rivolta e lotta armata*. Napoli: L'ancora del mediterraneo.

McAdam, D., Tarrow, S. and Tilly, C. 2001. *Dynamics of Contention*. New York: Cambridge University Press.

McKeown, L. 2001. *Out of Time: Irish Republican Prisoners, Long Kesh, 1972–2000*. Belfast: Beyond the Pale.

Magistratura Democratica 1979. *Il carcere dopo le riforme*. Milano: Feltrinelli.

Massey 1994. *Space, Place, and Gender*. Minneapolis: University of Minnesota Press.

Mathiesen, T. 1965, *The Defences of the Weak. A Sociological Study of a Norwegian Correctional Institution*. London: Tavistock Publications.

Mathiesen, T. 1974. *The Politics of Abolition*. London: Martin Robertson.

Mathiesen, T. 1979, *Uberwindet die Mauern! Dis Skandinavische Gefangenenbewegung als Modell politischer Randgruppenarbeit*. Neuwied-Darmstadt: Luchterhand Verlag.

Melodia, D. 1976. *Carceri: riforma fantasma*. Milano: SugarCo.

Melossi, D. and Pavarini, M. 1977, *Carcere e fabbrica: alle origini del sistema penitenziario 16–19 secolo*. Bologna: Il Mulino.

Petricola, E. 2002. *I diritti degli esclusi nelle lotte degli anni Settanta. Lotta Continua*. Roma: Edizioni Associate.

Prette, M.R. (ed.) 2006. *Il carcere speciale*. Dogliani: Sensibili alle Foglie.

Quadrelli, E. 2004. *Andare ai resti. Banditi, rapinatori, guerriglieri nell'Italia degli anni* settanta. Roma: DeriveApprodi.

Reisch, M. and Andrews, J. 2002. *The Road Not Taken. A History of Radical Social Work in the United States*. New York: Brunner-Routledge.

Ricci, A., Salierno, G. 1971. *Il carcere in Italia. Inchiesta sui carcerati, i carcerieri e l'ideologia carceraria*. Torino: Einaudi.

Rubio, C.L. 2006. COPEL La revuelta de los comunes, Available at: http://antonionietogalindo.wordpress.com/la-revuelta-de-los-comunes-el-movimiento-de-presos-sociales-durante-la-transicion/ [accessed: July 25, 2011].

Salvatore, R.D. and Aguirre C. (eds.) 1996. *The birth of the penitentiary in Latin America: essays on criminology, prison reform and social control, 1830–1940*. Austin: University of Texas Press.

Scraton, P., Sim., J. and Skidmore, P. 1991. *Prison Under Protest*. Buckingham: Open University Press.

Segio, S. 2006, *Una vita in prima linea*. Milano: Rizzoli.

Silj, A. 1977. *"Mai più senza fucile!" Alle origini dei NAP e delle BR*. Firenze: Vallecchi.

Sommier, I. 2009. *La violenza rivoluzionaria. Le esperienze di lotta armata in Francia, Germania, Giappone, Italia e Stati Uniti*. Roma: Derive Approdi.

Stratton, B. 1973. *Who Guard the Guards*. London: PROP North London Group.

Sykes, G.M. 1958. *The Society of Captives. A Study of a Maximum Security Prison*. Princeton: Princeton University Press.

Useem, B., Goldstone, J.A. 2002. Forging Social Order and Its Break-Down: Riot and Reform in US Prisons. *American Sociological Review*, 67, 499–525.

Verde, S. 2002. *Massima sicurezza. Dal carcere speciale allo Stato penale*. Roma: Odradek.

PART II
Competition and Conflict: Dynamics of Intra-movement Interaction

Chapter 5

Competitive Escalation During Protest Cycles: Comparing Left-wing and Religious Conflicts

Donatella della Porta[1]

Violence in Context: Competitive Escalation During Protest Cycles

While violence has rarely been addressed within social movement studies, that have concentrated instead on contentious, but peaceful forms of protest, social science research on violence has tended to isolate it from broader context, considering it as pathological and illegitimate. As I'm going to suggest in this chapter, one of the main analytical advantages in using social movement studies to understand political violence is in their capacity to locate it within broader conflicts, in which violence is only one form. Additionally, social movement studies allow us to locate radical organizations within the complex networks—or organizational fields—with which they interact. A main observation coming from social movement studies is that causal mechanisms for radicalization are activated by interactions between movement activists and opponents, but also by competition inside social movement families during cycles of protest—that is, moments of intensified protest mobilized by many and different actors. In what follows, I shall discuss how the concept of protest cycle helps in overcoming some of the limitations of a static analysis of causes and effects, by singling out some common contextual causal mechanisms in the various forms of clandestine political violence. I shall look in particular at the *competitive interactions* developing during cycles of protest. This will also help me to introduce references to the social movements in which violence developed.

Research on protest cycles indicates that violence is driven less by strategic concerns than by relational dynamics developing during moments of intense mobilization. The concepts of cycles, waves, or campaigns all attempt to describe and explain periods of intensified protest. The analysis of protest cycles is particularly useful for an understanding of the development of political violence,

---

1 This chapter has drawn upon material from within Donatella della Porta 2013. *Clandestine Political Violence*, Cambridge University Press, reproduced with permission. The author is grateful to the European Research Council that has financed her project on Mobilizing for democracy

frequently one (though neither the only nor the most important) of the protest's outcomes. Tarrow has defined cycles of protest as "a phase of heightened conflict across the social system, with rapid diffusion of collective action from more mobilized to less mobilized sectors, a rapid pace of innovation in the forms of contention employed, the creation of new or transformed collective action frames, a combination of organized and unorganized participation, and sequences of intensified information flow and interaction between challengers and authorities" (2011: 199). As in culture and the economy, he has in fact identified a recurrent dynamic of ebb and flow in collective mobilization which proceeds "from institutional conflict to enthusiastic peak to ultimate collapse" (1994: 168).

Cycles have their own dynamics. The cycle evolves through different stages: expansion through diffusion, radicalization/institutionalization, exhaustion, and restabilization (Tarrow 2011). Diffusion happens at the beginning of a cycle, as the first movements to emerge lower the cost of collective action for other actors, by demonstrating the vulnerability of the authorities. In addition, the victories of the early risers undermine the previous order of things, provoking counter-mobilization. Civil rights coalitions emerge to push for increasing recognition of the right to demonstrate. Repeatedly, spin-off movements contribute to the mobilization of other groups, inventing new forms of action, enlarging the protest claims and winning some concessions, but also pushing elites and counter-movements to form law-and-order coalitions (della Porta 1998). When elites reorganize, often adopting a mix of repression and concessions, mass protest tends to decline in intensity: radicalization, but also institutionalization might ensue.

During cycles, in fact, the repertoires of collective action tend to change. In the initial stages of protest the most disruptive forms often come to the fore (della Porta and Tarrow 1986). New actors invent new tactics as emerging collective identities require radical action (Pizzorno 1978). As the cycle of protest extends, the reaction of the authorities produces a proportional increase in radical forms of action, but also a simultaneous moderation of protest forms, with a reduction of disruptive action. Both processes, for different reasons, bring about the demise of the cycle.

Radicalization is in fact activated by *competition* between movement activists and opponents, especially in the form of escalating policing (see next chapter), but also of competitive escalation within the social movement sector, as well as within social movement families. Competitive dynamics tend to intensify during cycles of protest, as social movement organizations split over the best strategies to adopt, some of them choosing more radical ones. Looking at violence as an escalation of protest repertoire during cycles of protest points at the fluid borders between different strategies, as well as the reciprocal adaptation and learning processes between social movements and external actors, mainly police and other adversaries. However, social movements are also often divided on which tactics to pursue. In this sense, different groups not only adapt to environmental conditions, but also exercise agency: they discuss strategies, experiment with them, divide over them. As Alimi recently observed (2011: 99):

> One of the most basic features of opposition movements is that they consist of various actors and groups who, based on common interest and beliefs, interact informally with one another and mutually affect each other's strategy. These actors do not necessarily hold the same ideology, strategy, or preferable modes of action and goals. The mechanism "competition for power" between movement actors is about how challengers sometimes complement and sometimes undercut each other's strategies. This occurs as they struggle over whose strategy and tactics will dominate the goals, resource flow, translation of the struggle to specific gains, and the support of yet uncommitted adherents and allies.

In these various steps, in fact, various organizations, movements, and counter-movements interact, gaining and losing weight and power in intense relations of cooperation and competition. Protest tends to develop from splinter groups coming from within traditional actors. The peak of contention sees the mobilization of social movement organizations that actively sponsor the diffusion of protest. When the momentum is over, political parties and other more traditional actors regain control, taking advantage of the disruption of previous assets and negotiating new agreements. Radicalization is also produced by the *different pace of demobilization*. While those at the periphery, who are also more moderate, tend to drop out earlier, the more core activists, who are also more radical, tend to remain mobilized. So, "Unequal rates of defection between the center and the periphery shift the balance from moderate to radical claims and from peaceful to violent protest" (Tarrow 2011: 206).

The development of political violence during cycle of protest has been observed first of all in the analysis of political conflicts mobilized by a left-wing social movement family. In particular, in the late 1960s and early 1970s, Italy experienced a most turbulent wave of protest, in what was defined, referring to the wave of strikes started in the Fall of 1969, as a "long Autumn." The next part will indeed address this historical case, summarizing the results of existing research. To which extent is, however, the process of radicalization of (part of) the Italian Left in the 1970s historically unique? In order to address this question, I shall—within a most different research design and based upon secondary analysis of existing literature—single out similar dynamics in the escalation of Islamic fundamentalism. Without implying that specific historical circumstances do play a role in the evolution of political violence, this type of "global comparison" helps in fact to "de-essentialize"—to use a fashionable term—recent forms of violence, singling out the similarities, not in root causes, but rather in causal mechanisms (della Porta 2012).

Competitive Escalation and Left-wing Violence

In the Italian cycle of protest, violence developed from the intensity of the conflict: the forms of action were initially disruptive but peaceful, and the aims were moderate, mainly claims for the reform of existing institutions. Although remaining mainly non-violent, protest repertoires radicalized at the margins, especially during street battles with adversaries and the police. In particular, escalating police strategies contributed to radicalization. In a very long process, students and workers paved the way for the mobilization of other actors. New collective identities were formed on issues of gender equality or urban structures, while groupings of different sizes, forms, and ideas enriched the left-libertarian social movement family, combining Old Left social rights concerns with emerging visions of liberty.

In his analysis of the Italian case, Tarrow (1989) observed that the forms of political violence used tend to vary according to the stages of the cycle. At the outset of protest, violent action was usually limited in its presence, small in scope and unplanned. Typically, violence in this phase was an unforeseen result of direct action such as sit-ins or occupations. As protest developed, violent forms of action initially spread more slowly than non-violent forms, frequently taking the shape of clashes between demonstrators and police or counter-demonstrators. Starting out as occasional and unplanned outbursts, such episodes nonetheless tended to be repeated and to take on a ritual quality. During this evolution small groups began to specialize in increasingly extreme tactics, built up an armory for such action, and occasionally went underground. Their very presence accelerated the moderate exodus from the movement, contributing to demobilization.

Generalizing from the Italian case, Tarrow suggested that the final stages of a cycle of protest tend to see both a process of institutionalization and a growing number of violent actions:

> When disruptive forms are first employed, they frighten antagonists with their potential cost, shock onlookers and worry elites concerned with public order. But newspapers gradually begin to give less and less space to protests that would have merited banner headlines when they first appeared on the streets. Repeating the same form of collective action over and over reduces uncertainty and is greeted with a smile or a yawn. Participants, at first enthused and invigorated by their solidarity and ability to challenge authorities, become jaded or disillusioned. Authorities, instead of calling out the troops or allowing the police to wade into a crowd, infiltrate dissenting groups and separate leaders from followers. Routinisation follows hard upon disruption (1994: 112).

The analysis of the evolution of violent forms of action during that cycle has in fact shown the specific relations between cycles of protest and violence. In a joint article, this author and Sidney Tarrow concluded:

> The incidence of political violence is strictly connected with collective action in at least two ways. First, it grew in total numbers during the whole cycle. Second, its percentage weight was average in the beginning, low during the upswing, and high in the declining period of the protest wave. Violent forms were, therefore,

part of the protest repertoire from the very beginning and their presence tended to grow in total numbers during the whole cycle. But it was when the wave of collective action declined that their percentage distribution increased (della Porta and Tarrow 1986: 616).

The type of violence also changed during the cycle:

> Violence tends to appear from the very beginning of a protest cycle. In this phase, it is usually represented by less purposive forms of action and it is used by large groups of protesters. Clashes with adversaries or police during mass actions are the more widely diffused types of political violence during the height of the cycle and decline at its end. In the last phase, aggression carried out by small groups of militants and direct attacks on persons become more frequent. The more dramatic form of violence rise when the mass phase of the protest cycle declines. To put it differently, as mass mobilization winds down, political violence rises in magnitude and intensity (ibid.: 620).

In his analysis of the Italian cycle of protest, Tarrow pointed at the role of internal competition in its evolution:

> During the upward curve of the cycle, as mass participation increases, there is creative experimentation and a testing of the limits of mass participation. As established groups, such as trade unions, parties and interest associations, enter the movement sectors, they monopolize conventional mass forms of action, producing incentives for others to use more disruptive forms of mass action to outflank them. But as participation declines later in the cycle, the mass base for both moderate and confrontational mass actions begins to shrink. New groups who try to enter the movement sector can only gain space there by adopting more radical forms of action that do not depend on a mass base. Through this essentially political process, the social movements sector evolves, divides internally, incites repression and eventually declines. This differentiation, competition and radicalization of the social movement sector is the central process that give the cycle a dynamic character (1989: 19).

The spread of protest was triggered by a demonstration effect: early risers showed the possibility and potential success of contention. There was, however, also competition: within a social movement sector, victories by those mobilizing challenged existing rights and interests, and within a social movement family, organizations competed on the best strategies to adopt. As Tarrow observed, "competition may arise from ideological conflict, from competition for space in a static organizational sphere, or from personal conflicts for power between leaders. Whatever its source, a common outcome of competition is radicalization: a shift of ideological commitments toward the extremes and/or the adoption of more disruptive and violent forms of contention" (2011: 207).

98   *Dynamics of Political Violence*

Competition increased with the very pace of mobilization as large number of social movement organizations were created during the protest—in fact, "the growth in popular participation in the upward phase of the cycle invites organizational proliferation, and these new organizations compete for space with each other and with earlier risers" (ibid.: 208). Competition interacted with repression as "when elites sense that the mass base for the collective action is in decline, they can re-knit the fabric of hegemony by repression, by press campaigns against violence, as well as by selective reform" (Tarrow 1989: 343). In this way, state responses contributed—often consciously, sometimes not—to divide the movement into good and bad activists, trying to co-opt the former and repress the latter.

In fact, radicalization developed in dense organizational fields, from intense interactions between various organizations that cooperated and conflicted with each other (among other issues) on the use of violence. My own research has shown that underground organizations have evolved within and then broken away from larger, non-violent social movement organizations. In the late 1960s, the decline of the student mobilization, and the consequent reduction in available resources, increased competition among the several (formal and informal) networks that constituted the left-libertarian families. After having created semi-clandestine marshal bodies, the organizations then tended to split on the issue of violence (della Porta 1995: ch. 4). Exploiting environmental conditions conducive to militancy, these splinter groups underwent further radicalization and eventually created new resources and opportunities for violence.

During the cycle of protest of the late 1960s–early 1970s, a myriad of new groups emerged at the school, university, or factory level. Most developed from, but also challenged, previously existing social movement organizations such as main trade unions, student unions, catholic organizations, and left-wing political parties. With the evolution of protest, various sites of coordination developed, at first often territorial and issue based, but also some with a strong political and ideological basis. Competition and cooperation gave rise to the foundation, in 1968 and 1969, of the main organizations of the Italian New Left: the Union of the Italian Communists (Marxist-Leninist) (Unione dei Comunisti Italiani-ml); Workers' Vanguard (Avanguardia Operaia, AO); Worker's Power (Potere Operaio, PO); Il Manifesto; the Student Movement (Movimento Studentesco, MS); Continuous Struggle (Lotta Continua, LC). The coordination of local protests, often with weekly meetings of representatives of different organizations, was, for instance, the basis of LC, at first just a group of comrades that mobilized around the strikes in the large factories in Northern Italy, often through *Assemblee operai studenti* (workers' and students' assemblies). In this dense environment, various groups, including LC, formed, with internal ideological differences that reflected past organizational and strategic debates on the Left. For instance, in the beginning, LC was not much more than an "umbrella term for a loose coalition of extreme left groups and radical workers who met everyday in the bar" (Tarrow 1989: 268).

In time, the groups that emerged for the coordination of the thousands of small collectives that operated at the local level not only became more centralized at the national level, but also acquired a more exclusive structure, moving from a movement identity to a strong organizational identity. In 1972, with about 150 chapters all around the country, LC discussed overcoming the limits of spontaneity and "return to the patrimony of militancy, discipline, and seriousness typical of the working class" (Bobbio 1988: 129). From this, the assumption developed that "There are not only many groups ... there are many political lines. Among them, *only one is correct*, because it contributes to unifying and strengthening the working class; the others are wrong because they weaken the working class" (quoted in Bobbio 1988: 97).

Typical of most of the mentioned groups of the New Left was the creation of specialized semi-military units to provide "self-defense" for movement activities and militant actions, sometimes even in physical fights with each other. In addition, the groups that would later give birth to underground organizations developed through a gradual process, beginning with the use of forms of action that were illegal but not very different from those tolerated—or even overtly advocated—by other social movement organizations.

Experiences of daily fights developed into the creation of marshal bodies. A member of a left-wing underground group recalls that: "Thanks to the activities in the marshal, I had no trouble in adapting myself to the more dramatic techniques of the armed struggle. ... It was all familiar to me. One could say that I had substituted the gun for the monkey-wrench [a widespread 'arm' in the marshal bodies]" (in Tranfaglia and Novelli 1988: 247). An activist remembers, "Our milieu is the one of the marshal body of Lotta Continua, the youth circles" (39); "we lived in a very fluid relations, the most continuous, with our network of militants or legal sympathizers" (40); "I remember some of them, they drove us crazy, because they run away to see their mom, their girlfriend" (46). The 1977 protest was "a very violent movement that sediments through the bad network of the previous stories and political class" (41). It then produced a disaggregation in their milieu, with the development of some activists into robbers and drug dealers.

Justification for violence developed in action, especially during conflicts with political opponents. It also came from the experience of physical fights with opponents, in a sort of community polarization (for a review, see Zald and Useem 1987). On the Left, daily experiences of defense and offense with radical right activists are recalled to justify violence. An Italian left-wing militant recalls, for instance, that "at school, there was a very small group of fascists, a daily source of fights. They were few, but evil. Moreover, they had the external support of a military group, the Alpha Group, based in a residence hall ten meters away from my school. They were fanatics, really threatening; many of them ended by bombing trains. They came to the entrance of the school and made revenge attacks, they even knifed people" (Life history no. 12: 9). In 1970, as a defense against the neo-Fascists, his collective organized a marshal group, which he "joined with excitement, very glad to have been chosen" (Life history no. 12: 9); its activities "consisted of the fact that we met at six o'clock, or at very dreadful hours, and we patrolled all around the school with iron bars, to check if any fascist was there.

Then, we garrisoned at the entrance, to be sure that all the students could enter the school quietly. After that, we went to class—at the second hour, of course, because we were members of the marshal group, and this was appreciated even by our professors" (Life history no. 12: 10). In these struggles, violence became more and more brutal, with a reciprocal adaptation to increasingly dangerous weapons, from stones and sticks to "monkey-wrenches," heavy chains, and guns. In the Italian radical Left, "[since] the physical struggle with the political counterpart, I mean with the fascists, was a matter of almost every single day … it was therefore inevitable that we would start to equip ourselves in a military way" (Life history no. 13: 29). These continuous battles justified violence as a needed defense—as an Italian militant recalled, as "the problem of the fascist in Rome was big and then, there was little to ethically reflect upon: you needed to defend yourself" (Lapponi 1995: 197).

In the second half of the 1970s, recruitment to the underground developed inside the "autonomous" collectives: "squads of the underground organizations were built inside a legal collective. A militant of the organization got involved in the collective and convinced those who he thought were more conscious to start an intermediary structure" (Life history no. 12: 31). Marco's life history testifies of this escalation in the experiences with and justification of violence. He remembers the splits in the Movimento studentesco in 1973–74 as starting "this thing that I always hated, of the internal divisions on streams of different degrees of radicalism" (ibid.: 334). With the Autonomous groups, in 1974, he participated in burning the car of a school director and in a hold-up in the house of an arms trader, where—he recalled—a sick girl was sleeping.

In the second half of the 1970s, experiences with violent forms of protest spread, up to their peak in the so-called "77 movement." According to a left-wing militant, "In these years, between 1974 and 1977, the radical autonomous collectives grew enormously; month after month, they multiplied their presence in the city, their bases, their guns" (Life history no. 12: 25). In the second half of the seventies, "From a 'trot' phase, in Milan the armed struggle started to ride at full gallop. There were armed actions every day, at every march, at every deadline, at every strike" (Life history no. 12: 23). The acceptance of illegal forms of action was so widespread that "there were periods in which we intervened in a general meeting of the movement and, in front of 200, 300 or 500 people, we almost openly supported the strategy of the armed struggle" (Life history no. 12: 33). In fact, "guns in the streets had become as common as the sticks of the flags some time before, and guerrilla attacks that started with marches and then reverted to marches were an everyday practice" (cited in Novelli and Tranfaglia 1988: 294). As a future Italian left-wing militant recalled, when he became responsible for the marshal body of PO in Rome: "I started to study the problems, how to say?, political-military, that is, I started to read all what was available. I think I have read everything: Lussu, Marx himself, that Polish there, von Clausewitz: I have read all was available" (Lapponi 1995: 192). In fact, he spoke of "two levels. One was the marshal body: there they taught us little: Molotov cocktails, the use of explosives …

And then there was the school of Valerio … I was his pupil for those two or three years. And I have learned everything he knew" (196).

Spirals of revenge developed in the fights between movements and countermovements. On the left-wing side, there was "an atmosphere [that encouraged the] lynching of fascists. 'If you see black, shoot at once,' this was the slogan, … there was a man-hunt, without any pity, it was a hunt against the fascists that then had repercussions for us, because there was a spiral of revenge" (Life history no. 6: 29). As many left-wingers remembered, "Milan had a large bunch of funerals that were a continuous plea, over the deaths, those killed by the fascist, an continuous plea to revenge, and then when you take revenge, well it is not traumatic" (interview Baglioni: 65).

Although extremely violent, the '77 movement was very critical of the Red Brigades. While the BR were considered as "compagni che sbagliano [comrades who make mistakes], with their concept of a strategic use of the armed struggle," the new radicals aimed at "Linking the use of force, forms of struggle, mass practice and realization of the objectives" (Piero: 263). In the mid-1970s, one of them remembers the "splitting in the group, and the spreading of the thousands of forms, also spontaneous, also not organized. You started to see what was going to take a definite form in 1976" (ibid.: 264). This is seen as a testimony of "the possibility of a mass practice of violence, subversive and antagonist, that was going to be the 1977" (ibid.: 264). The BR are instead considered to be "hostile to the movement. In '77 the BR did not exist, the '77 movement outlawed them. They were put at the margins by a armed and illegal practice that has a mass dimension and therefore exclude the formations such as the BR" (ibid.: 265). And an activist remembers that "most of the Autonomia was against the kidnapping of Aldo Moro" (the president of the Christian democratic party, kidnapped and killed by the RB). In this moment, "the project was to revitalize the elements of the movement that were dispersed" (ibid.: 269). Similarly, Marco remembered that at an assembly after the kidnapping of Aldo Moro, 90 per cent were against it: "For us, the Moro kidnapping, as it was developed and ended, is a clamorous failure from the political point of view. There is a restriction of the spaces we had opened in society and, at the human level, it was an imagine of violence, cold, that creates many problems" (ibid.: 355).

The second largest and longer-lasting clandestine organization in Italy, Prima Linea (PL—Front Line) emerged, at the end of 1976, via a split within the Comitati Comunisti per il Potere Operaio (CCPO) when some members of the group faced legal prosecution after carrying out their first assassination. While one wing condemned illegal actions, the "military structure" (which included a former member of BR) opted for organizational "compartmentalization" and the use of increasingly violent forms of action.

Similarly, in 1977, a third, relatively large clandestine organization, the Fighting Communist Formation (Formazioni Comuniste Combattenti, FCC), emerged from a split in the collective that published the magazine *Rosso*. The FCC was founded by militants of the Communist Brigades, a kind of marshal body

102   *Dynamics of Political Violence*

formed from the various groups close to *Rosso*. After a gradual increase in the use of violent forms of action, the May 1977 assassination of a policeman during a public march organized by the more radical groups in Milan produced a split, with the majority in favor of pursuing mass actions and retaining legal structures and the Communist Brigades instead choosing to go underground.

Research on various cases has observed that the repertoire of action has radicalized in much the same forms and according to much the same timing during cycles of protest involving different political and social actors. Ruud Koopman looked at similar developments in two German waves of protest, at the end of the 1960s and at the beginning of the 1980s; in both cases "the action repertoire was relatively radical in the initial periods of rapid expansions, around 1968 and 1981. Subsequently, these radical forms declined, while the number of demonstrative actions continued to increase, reaching their peak in, respectively, 1972 and 1983. After this period of moderation, the number of demonstrative actions decreased, and simultaneously radical actions made a come-back, although in both waves they did not reach the level of the first peak of disruption" (Koopman 1992: 141). Protest cycles started with symbolically innovative tactics and then shifted to mass action, which sometimes escalated into violence. When mass mobilization declined, many movement activists returned to more institutional forms, while small groups resorted to more radical action.

As is always the case, however, comparative analyses contributed not only to confirm, but also to challenge and specify the various components of this picture. For instance, my comparison of the Italian and the German cases showed similar dynamics, but also relevant differences (della Porta 1995). In both countries, there was some radicalization of the student protest, with a shift from defensive to organized violence. This radicalization involved only small groups within much broader non-violent movement milieus, and was fuelled by conflicts with the police and political opponents. In both countries, while the protest spread to various social groups, semi-military violence was criticized within the movement but contributed to the spread of some radical symbolic violence in small and loosely coordinated autonomous groups. The presence of clandestine organizations contributed to radicalize protest forms. Later on, in the 1980s, in both countries, the mobilization of the peace movement against the deployment of NATO missiles helped to spread non-violent repertoires.

A main difference emerged, however, in the spread of violence. While in Germany a consensual culture and neo-corporatist agreements, together with the Left in government, tended to facilitate moderation, in Italy violence escalated during longer lasting and more intense protests (see also next chapter). In particular, developing from the crisis of the New Left organizations, the Italian radical "autonomous" groups had a much broader base and were more highly structured than their German counterparts. The more exclusive attitudes of the Italian state towards challengers and the presence of a violent, neo-fascist countermovement, interacting with a larger acceptance for radical frames and forms of action in the

Competitive Escalation and Religious Violence

In repressive milieus, social movements developed within mosques as well as Islamic NGOs, including hospitals, schools, and cultural centers. Professional organizations or student associations represent important networks for both reformist and radical Islamist groups. In general, the importance of religious places in facilitating mobilization in repressive regimes is related with their capacity to provide mobilized networks. Religious networks are often safe spaces for activism against dictators, given institutional legitimacy, or at least tolerance (Aminzade and Perry 2001: 159ss.). Religious spaces work as (relatively) free spaces, and this is one of the reasons why "religious groups have a unique institutional legitimacy that gives them distinctive advantages; it is harder to repress them; and they feel 'safer' to confront and discuss issues that no one else can" (Aminzade and Perry 2001: 159, in ibid.: 152). In the Middle East, if the authoritarian nature of several regimes jeopardized political mobilization, "the Mosque was the one institution the state had the most difficulty dominating or controlling. Religion, mosques and mullahs became a rallying point when there was no space allowed for any other" (Esposito 2006: 147).

Moreover, far from using only terror, several Islamist organizations in the Middle East have developed charity activities. In his economic approach to violence, Berman suggests that religious prohibitions are productive for the community because they "increase the availability of members for collective activities such as mutual aid, an essential part of what makes radical religious communities cohesive" (2009: 81). In this sense, "Radical religious groups, or sects, operate as economic clubs. They collectively provide both spiritual services and an entire array of concrete social services through mutual aid systems" (118). He recalls, in fact, that "charity is a pillar of mainstream Islam and that radical Islamist groups like the Muslim Brotherhood are famous for running religious schools, orphanages, soup kitchens, clinics, hospitals, and even youth centers and soccer clubs, all operated as charities" (Berman 2009: 77). The importance of these social services increased with the declining capacity of Arabic states in the provision of welfare (Ahmed 2005). In a similar way, Islamic student associations are said to have provided the space for the formation of informal nets.

These informal networks facilitated the spread of Islamic organizations. Recruitment in Islamic groups occurred through activities such as "attending religious lessons at a nearby mosque, joining an informal study groups, or accompanying a friend of neighbor to special prayer services in observance of an Islamic holy day" (Rosefsky Wickham 2004: 232). The legitimacy of those institutions reduced the perception of risks as "Islamic lessons, seminars, and prayer meetings offered some of the few socially sanctioned venues for graduates of both sexes to congregate outside the home" (ibid.: 233). Socially embedded Islamic groups also allowed for different degrees and forms of involvement, and therefore for a gradual integration into the organization. Additionally, "most residents had a brother, cousin, friend or neighbor involved in Islamic prayer circles or study groups, and Islamist participants frequently maintain close relations with non-activist peers" (ibid.).

Often considered a product of fanaticism or frustration, Islamic fundamentalism is also located within broader cycles of protest in which religious claims are intertwined with socioeconomic and nationalist ones. The nationalist dimension of religious clandestine violence has been indeed stressed. According to Esposito (2006: 146), "Political Islam is in many ways the successor of failed nationalist ideologies and projects in the 1950s and 1960s, from Arab nationalism and socialism of North Africa and the Middle East to the Muslim nationalism of post-independence Pakistan." Bin Laden's message has been defined as primarily political (Esposito 2006). Suicide terrorism itself has been presented as a strategy of nationalists fighting against occupation by democratic regimes, motivated by expectations of success, when other means are lacking. Additionally, research has pointed at the role of social, especially class conflicts in the development of Islamism (for example, Gunning 2007; Ritter 2010). This means that the evolution of radical Islamist organizations has to be located not only within the dynamics of competition within Islamic movements, which always involved nonviolent components as well, but also in waves of protest in which different types of organizations—religious, but also nationalist and class-oriented—interacted.

That religious, nationalist, and class motivations tend to interact is no new discovery. Under some conditions, the search for national independence takes a religious tone: "under the circumstances of a foreign occupation, the relative importance of religious and linguistic differences normally reverses and religious difference can influence nationalist sentiments in ways that encourage mass support for martyrdom and suicide terrorism" (Pape 2005: 88). From this perspective, political violence is more likely when "the presence of a religious difference reduces room for compromise between the occupying power and the occupied community, because the conflict is seen as a zero sum game" (ibid.: 89). Examining al-Qaeda's pool of suicide terrorists (ibid.: 71), Pape observes that the presence of American military forces for combat operations on homeland territory has a stronger explanatory capacity than (Salafi) Islamic fundamentalism (ibid.: 103).

In order to understand the development of radical Islamism it is therefore important to look at forms of internal competition. As Sadowski correctly reminded us, Muslims have internally diverse values, and this is also true of the so-called political Islam: "studies of political Islam commonly begin from two faulty assumptions, guaranteeing that whatever questions are asked will generate misleading answers. The first assumption is that Muslims around the world share a common, relatively homogenous body of doctrine on a wide array of religious, social, and political matters. The second is that this doctrine is actually the primary determinant of Muslim behavior" (2006: 216). Not only are there doctrinal differences between Sunni and Shia Muslims, but rural-urban cleavages as well as cleavages related with specific national declination of Islam (ibid.: 218). In addition, Islamic movements are divided over strategies, with pietistic movements aiming at personal transformation and political ones sharing a belief in the importance of political power.

Even political Islam is internally split: traditionalist groups tend to focus on local tradition and privilege informal networks; while fundamentalist groups aim to purify Islam from local practices, often coalescing around clerics. Islamist groups, in turn, emerged from a critique of fundamentalism. As Sadowski (2006: 221–2) summarized:

> The Islamists, with their cosmopolitan backgrounds, introduced various tools they had borrowed from the West into their organizational arsenal. Ideologically, they drew on anti-modernist philosophies that embodied Western dissatisfaction with the consequences of industrialization and positivism: Spengler, Althusser, and Feyerabend supplied some of their favorite texts. They rearticulated Islam as a modern ideology in which control of a totalistic Islamic state would permit the transformation of society in a manner that promoted not only piety but progress. Recruiting from the same intellectual groups through which Marxism penetrated the Muslim world—and often doing jail time in the same prisons as persecuted communists—they quickly learned the advantages of organizing into parties of disciplined cadres, organized into discrete cells, that could work to lay the foundations for revolution among wider groups.

Conflicts between, but also within these different versions of Islamism heavily influenced the evolution of Islamist clandestine organizations. Again according to Sadowski (2006: 228), "relations between Muslim communities have grown dramatically worse since the 1990s. Neo-fundamentalist groups such as the Salafis [Wahhabis who reject the authority of the traditional Saudi clerics] in Algeria and Syria, the Taliban in Afghanistan, the Jama`at-i Ulema-i Islam in Pakistan, and the Jaysh-i Muhammad in Kashmir are strikingly less tolerant than older Islamic movements." In part a reaction to the increasing relevance of Shia in Iran and in Lebanon (through the Hezbollah), some Sunni Salafi groups have even denied that Shia belong to Islam, attacking Shia minority groups in Pakistan and Afghanistan, as well as the Iraqi security forces, which are dominated by Shia Muslims. In 2005, for instance, in the document "Why do we Fight and Whom do we Fight," the Islamic legal committee of AQ in Iraq stated that they wanted to "restore their rightly guided caliphate" and "reject rule by the Shia … who have betrayed Muslims" (in Hafez 2007: 73).

In fact, contextualized analyses of specific cases of radicalization during cycles of protest in the Middle East point at the importance, during cycles of protest, of internal competition between social movements and social movement organizations, often with interactions of, and competition between, class, nationalist, and religiously oriented narratives. This is, for instance, the case in

Egypt, where a socialist project was linked to a nationalist one, and then entered in competition with a religious vision.[2]

Founded at the end of the 1970s, the Egyptian radical groups *al-Jamaa al-Islamiyya* (The Islamic Group) and *Tanzim al-Jihad* ("Jihad Organization") have grown inside a broader Islamist movement which—as Malthaner wrote (2011: 25)—"had radicalized in political confrontation with the government of Anwar al-Sadat." Although both belonged to the radical Islamist wing, these two organizations differed from and competed with each other, investing much energy in internal fights. Al-Jihad developed as a small and secret group, al-Jamaa al-Islamiyya instead as a large organization with a double organizational structure, including a grassroots level. Allied in the assassination of President Sadat in 1981, both groups suffered the heavy repression that followed, but then reemerged during a wave of (also violent) protests in 1988 and 1989. While violence initially took the form of clashes with the police, it radicalized in 1991, "including attacks against police officers, politicians, intellectuals, Coptic Christians, and the tourist industry in Upper Egypt and Cairo." While al-Jamaa participated in the protests, eventually being defeated by the Egyptian security forces, until its unilateral disbanding in 1998 al-Jihad was responsible for a few attacks between 1992 and 1993, renouncing action in Egypt, and instead joining the al-Qaeda network (ibid.).

The history of both groups can only be understood if we take into account their development within, and later competition with, the Muslim Brotherhood (MB) during broader waves of protest. Founded in 1928, MB initially focused on educational and charitable activities at the local level as a way to form pious Muslims who could then create a new Islamic nation (ibid.: 62). Politicization evolved during confrontations with the Egyptian authorities, but initially addressed especially opposition to the influence of foreign powers, in particular of Great Britain (which, even after Egypt became an independent state in 1936, still had troops on the Suez Canal)—as well as against the Israeli state.

In addition, the later evolution of the MB was determined by competition with non-religious nationalists. After some cooperation with Nasser's government, which came to power after a coup d'état in 1952, strong tensions emerged, leading to repression and ensuing radicalization two years later. Islamist reorganized in the beginning of the 1970s, especially within the university system, which had been expanded by Nasser. While left-wing and national groups had been dominant in the late 1960s, addressing especially social and economic policy issues, Islamic student groups had initially focused on religious activities, slowly extending their concerns to address political questions. Thus a student activist described this process, in an interview with Stefan Malthaner:

---

2 In reconstructing the role of competitive escalation during cycles of protest in this type of political violence, referring especially to the work of Stefan Malthaner (2011) on Islamic groups in Egypt.

Competitive Escalation During Protest Cycles 107

> I think, first, the activity was mainly religious activity and did not focus on some political demand or quest. But through the activity increased the interest in political issues. [...] And the political issues then increased over time and it is also a symbol for the whole group, it is the disaster of 1967, this big defeat in the history of Egypt, that made up our minds that we are going in the wrong direction and we must have a new start and bring back the Islamic traditions [...]. But as students we were part of a big movement. [...] There was a big return at that time to Islamic prayers, Islamic regulations (ibid.: 57).

The Islamist students thus came to perceive themselves as the vanguard of a broader movement, or a broad Islamic Awakening: "They identified with the Muslim population and emphasized their strong bonds with their families, who approved of Islamic traditions and supported their struggle, rejecting notions of self-separation or challenging their parents' values 'because our religion makes this harmony in our life between what is right for a family and what is right for a person'" (ibid.: 61). The Islamic student groups expanded rapidly: by the mid-1970s they covered all main universities with their several thousand members (Kepel 1985: 144, cit. in ibid.). Initially concerned mainly with providing services (such as lectures and teaching materials, or even clothes), they then started to put pressure on the administration to prohibit what they considered as anti-Islamic activities (such as concerts) (ibid.: 66–7). On these issues they even engaged in physical fights with other students and the university administration, as well as Sadat's government.

By the late 1970s the conflict had quickly escalated, involving different organizations and factions which then split over their reactions to repression. In fact, "the Islamists rejected Sadat's policy of economic openness towards the West, and when the president began direct negotiations with Israel in 1979 and offered refuge to Shah Pahlavi after the Islamic revolution in Iran, campuses were blocked in protest and students clashed with the police. In reaction, police arrested numerous Islamic activists, the national student union was dissolved, and student activity was severely restricted" (ibid.: 62). While in Cairo and Northern Egypt some groups chose more moderate forms and claims, in Upper Egypt others—which later formed al-Jamaa al-Islamiyya—thought that an Islamist society had to be reached through a violent jihad that included attacks on property.

Radicalization in Egypt spiraled in 1981, after violence erupted in Cairo in June, with ensuing repression (including 1,500 arrests and the dissolution of 13 organizations) and the assassination of President Sadat in October by a member of al-Jihad, the brother of an arrested al-Jamaa activist. In the following wave of repression under the presidency of Hosni Mubarak, most radical Islamist leaders were arrested and four of them executed, while the moderate Muslim Brothers wing grew under the unfavorable economic conditions determined by the declining oil price, which increased unemployment also among university graduates and brought many migrants back from the Gulf states (ibid.: 73). While the moderate Islamist movement expanded,

108 *Dynamics of Political Violence*

> the Muslim Brotherhood, reinvigorated by the influx of former student activists, became the most important oppositional political force, took over the leadership of most professional associations, and began to forge a coalition with other oppositional parties, such as the Labor Party. On the local level, a broad spectrum of religious associations spread 'the call' and provided social services. Large Islamic charitable organizations operated hospitals and schools and, together with Islamic economic enterprises, formed a "parallel Islamic sector" rivaling or replacing the state as a provider of public services (ibid.: 105).

In the competition with nationalist and Communist organizations, the Islamists could exploit the increasing religiosity that was noted in the broader public, providing a basis of support for the activists. As Malthaner noted, "The militant Islamist groups emerged as the violent offspring, or the radical fringe, of a broader, oppositional but nonviolent, Islamist movement, and the Muslim Brotherhood and other (non-violent) Islamist groups remained al-Jamaa's main competitors. The conflict between the broader Islamist movement and the Egyptian state not only formed the origin of the militant groups, but also part of the environment within which they operated ... Protests, demonstrations, mass arrests, and police crackdowns were a regular occurrence in the late 1970s as well as during the 1980s" (ibid.: 115). In the words of one of his interviewees, "there was already a change on the religious level of the people here, as many women wore the scarf, and many frequented the mosque to do their prayers. And also because of the harsh atmosphere of living, because of the rise of prices, the people found no shelter to protect them from the hard life but to get closer to God. [...] And they admired their bravery to voice something that the government doesn't want" (ibid.: 132).

In radical Islam, internal competition favored fractionalism. In fact, "The alliance between al-Jamaa al-Islamiyya and al-Jihad, forged to kill Sadat, collapsed after the arrests of 1981. The two groups split over an argument about leadership as well as over strategic issues and re-organized separately. Al-Jamaa al-Islamiyya re-emerged in the mid-1980s as an open movement on the local level, but confrontations escalated into a nation-wide conflict in the 1990s. Al-Jihad, on the other hand, after re-organizing abroad, planned to attack targets in Egypt. After their failure, they gradually joined the global terrorist project of al-Qaeda" (ibid.: 74–5).

In the mid-1980s, al-Jamaa re-emerged as small groups active in universities and neighborhoods, becoming gradually more centralized and with a functional differentiation with separate branches, for example, for open political work and proselytism, for logistics and media, and for military operations. Leadership was in the hands of al-Jamaa's "governing council" (*maglis alshura*), comprising about 8–10 people, which was until 1993 allegedly headed by Omar Adel Rahman, a blind al-Azhar sheikh who was also the group's "spiritual guide" (Malthaner 2011: 70). Gradually, however, decision making moved towards the military command, while the political leader was in exile. In the mid-1990s, a new wave of repression brought about a new decentralization.

As for al-Jihad, it increasingly went underground:

> After a failed attempt by the imprisoned Jihad-leader Abud al-Zumur to reorganize the group, Ayman al-Zawahiri, in 1987, established an organization based partly in Egypt and partly abroad, which took the name and the remaining members of al-Jihad. Zawahiri, who had been only marginally involved in the 1981 attack, was released in 1984, left for Saudi Arabia, and later went to Pakistan, where he was involved in preparing volunteers for the Afghan jihad. He recruited from among the Egyptian Islamists in Peshawar and in Afghan training camps and together with Sayyed Imam founded a new organization called "al-Jihad organization" (*tanzim al-jihad*). Around 1986, Zawahiri came into contact with Usama bin Laden, and it was from their base in Afghanistan that al-Jihad began to establish a branch in Cairo (Al-Zayyat 2004: 33) (Malthaner 2011, 74).

The two organizations cooperated but, especially, competed with each other:

> Initially, the relationship between al-Jamaa al-Islamiyya and al-Jihad in Afghanistan was friendly, but became strained, not only due to personal animosities but also because of political and strategic differences, particularly in regard to their approach to the Muslim population. According to a former al-Jamaa leader who spent several years in Pakistan and Afghanistan in the early 1990s, his group regarded al-Jihad as isolated from the people and as "cowards," because they were reluctant to engage in a confrontation with the Egyptian government. At the same time, Zawahiri's group regarded al-Jamaa as "naive students" and accused them of rushing into confrontations with the Egyptian government without proper planning and thus "wasting" many of their young members in a hopeless war against a superior enemy. Al-Jihad, in contrast, favored an approach concentrating on carefully educating and training their members and forming a base of committed cadres. Al-Jihad's strategy of secretly preparing a coup d'etat—while refraining from direct involvement with the "masses"—certainly indicated a certain detachment from their constituencies and mistrust in popular support ("realism," in their words). In spite of that, it seems improbable that they considered the Muslim population unbelievers (ibid.: 75).

The conflicts escalated again in the second half of the 1980s, after members of al-Jamaa al-Islamiyya were released from prison and mobilized again for the implementation of the *sharia* in an Islamic state, violently clashing with police (ibid.). In 1988, police interventions against mosques and Islamists produced a wave of riots in Ayn Shams, with five people killed and hundreds wounded in August, the assassination of a policeman in December, and further rioting, deaths of activists, arrests, alleged torture of prisoners and a curfew, which further polarized and radicalized the residents. These developments increased support to

110 *Dynamics of Political Violence*

the organized Islamists, in what started to be perceived as an attack against the community.

In 1990, the assassination of the speaker of parliament followed the death of an al-Jamaa leader, triggering a wave of massive violence that lasted for eight years, along with attacks against policemen, government officials, and intellectuals. At the same time, sectarian tensions between Christian and Muslim communities increased, with spirals of reciprocal (physical and symbolic) attacks (ibid.: 113–14).

Also in the 1990s, repression interacted with competitive escalation, as it increased support for (even violent) resistance to what was perceived as unjust behavior by the authorities.

Competitive Escalation: Some Conclusions

Explanations of political violence have often looked at structural causes, considering the economic, social, political, and cultural conditions that are more conducive to radicalization and addressing both deeply rooted causes and more contingent precipitating events. Attempts to formulate a general explanation for political violence have been frustrated, however, due to the challenges created by the differences among phenomena considered as forms of political violence—and, therefore, conceptual stretching.

I have considered the embedding of political violence within broader social and political conflicts as a most important contribution from social movement studies to the understanding of the causes of violence. In particular, I have referred to the concept of protest cycle as a main analytical contribution for the understanding of political violence. I have suggested that political violence has to be understood as one of the outcomes of intense interactions developing during moments of heightened conflict. The concept of cycle of protest also allows us to see the multiplicity of actors and forms of action at work in these moments.

In Tarrow's theorization, which built upon the analysis of the Italian case, different forms of violence were linked to different stages in the cycle. Further research in part confirmed the general value of those observations, but also pointed at cases in which cycles of protest had not produced violence. While more systematic research is necessary in order to identify under which conditions protest cycles end in radicalization and in which cases they do not, my aim in this chapter has been to contribute to answering the question from the point of view of the operation of a specific mechanism or radicalization: competitive escalation. In particular, in all four, most different cases, political violence developed from competition between and within social movement families.

In the Italian case, competition between social movement families had mainly involved right-wing counter-movements, which revived long-lasting hostilities and built upon a tradition of harsh conflicts. In the Middle East, religious-oriented competed with groups oriented towards nationalist and/or classidentity, with some general trends and events favoring the religious groups. The religious awakening, together with some moment of regime liberalization contributed to the strengthening of the traditional MBs, but also to more radical groups, which often emerged from criticism of the MB's moderation. Authoritarian regimes contributed to the escalation (della Porta forthcoming).

While the protest cycles intensified the production of social movement organizations, the radicalization of repertoires of action was, in some moments, a competitive asset in this inter-movement relation. Even within the same social movement family, however, different organizations competed for followers, adopting different frames and repertoires of action. In organizationally dense environments, different groups specialized in different tactics, but they also influenced each other, with processes of imitation and "outbidding." Especially when repression hit hard, and the community solidarized, the most radical tactics spread from one organization to the next.

During protest cycles, as moment of intense relations, practices of violence develop, and activists are socialized to them. Proletarian expropriation, armed marches, burning cars, and break-ins belonged to the experiences of many social movement activists even before they entered clandestine organizations. In fact, in emergent processes, violence emerges from violence, in periods of "thickened history" (Beissinger 2002).

References

Ahamed, I.H. 2005. "Palestinean resistance and 'suicide bombers." in *Root Causes of Terrorism. Myths, Reality and Ways Forward*, edited by Tore Bjorgo. London: Routledge: 87–102.

Al-Berry, K. 2002. *La terre est plus belle que le paradis*. Paris: JC Lattes.

Alimi, E.Y. 2011. "Relational dynamics in factional adoption of terrorist tactics: a comparative perspective." *Theory and Society* 40: 95–118.

Aminzade, R.R. and E.J. Perry. 2001. "The Sacred, Religious and Secular in Contentious Politics: Blurring the Boundaries." in *Silence and Voice in the Study of Contentious Politics*, edited by R. Aminzade, J. Goldstone, D. McAdam, E. Perry, W.H. Sewell Jr., S. Tarrow, and C. Tilly. Cambridge: Cambridge University Press.

Beissinger, M.R. 2002. *Nationalist Mobilization and the Collapse of the Soviet State*, Cambridge: Cambridge University Press.

Berman, E. 2009. *Radical, Religious, and Violent. The New Economy of Terrorism*, Cambridge Mass: MIT Press.

Bianconi, G. 1992. *A mano armata. Vita violenta di Giusva Fioravanti*. Milano: Baldini e Castoldi.

Bobbio, L. 1988. *Storia di Lotta Continua*. Milano: Feltrinelli.

Caselli, G. and D. della Porta. 1984. "La storia delle Brigate Rosse: Strutture organizzative e strategie d'azione." in *Terrorismi in Italia*, edited by D. della Porta. Bologna: Il Mulino: 153–221.

Catanzaro, R. 1990. "Il sentito e il vissuto. La violenza nel racconto dei protagonisti." In Raimondo C., ed. *Ideologia, Movimenti, Terrorismi*. Bologna: Il Mulino: 203–44.

Catanzaro, R. and L. Manconi.1995. *Storie di lotta armata*. Bologna: Il Mulino.

della Porta, D. 1990. *Il terrorismo di sinistra*. Bologna: Il Mulino.

della Porta, D. 1993. "State Responses to Terrorism: The Italian Case." in *Western Responses to Terrorism*, edited by R.D. Crelinston and A.P. Schmidt. London: Frank Cass: 151–70.

della Porta, D. 1995. *Social Movements, Political Violence and the State*, Cambridge: Cambridge University Press.

della Porta, D. 2008a. *"Research on Social Movements and Political Violence"* Qualitative Sociology 31(3): 221–30.

della Porta, D. 2008b. "Leaving left-wing terrorism in Italy: a Sociological Analysis." in *Leaving Terrorism Behind*, edited by T. Bjorgo and J. Horgan. London: Routledge: 49–65.

della Porta, D. 2010. *L'intervista qualitativa*. Bari-Roma: Laterza.

della Porta, D. forthcoming. *Mobilizing for Democracy*. Oxford, Oxford University Press.

della Porta, D. and M. Diani. 2006. *Social Movements: An Introduction*. Oxford, Blackwell.

della Porta, D. and M. Rossi, 1984. *Cifre crudeli. Bilancio dei terrorismi italiani*. Bologna: Istituto Cattaneo.

della Porta, D. and S. Tarrow. 1986. "Unwanted Children. Political Violence and the Cycle of Protest in Italy, 1966–1973." *European Journal of Political Research* 14: 607–32.

della Porta, D. and S. Tarrow. 2012. "Double Diffusion: Police and protestors in transnational contention." *Comparative Political Studies*, 20: 1–34.

Esposito, J.L. 2002. *Unholy War: Terror in the Name of Islam*. New York: Oxford University Press.

Esposito, J.L. 2006. "Terrorism and the Rise of Political Islam" in *The Roots of Terrorism*, edited by L. Richardson. London: Routledge: 145–58.

Fasanella, G. and A. Franceschini. 2004. *Che cosa sono le BR*. Milano: Bur.

Franceschini, E. (with P. Buffa and F. Giustolisi). 1988. *Mara, Renato e io. Storia dei fondatori delle Brigate Rosse*. Milano: Mondadori.

Galante, S. 1981. "Alle origini del partito armato." *Il Mulino* 275: 44–7.

Galleni, M. 1981. *Rapporto sul terrorismo. Le stragi, gli agguati, i sequestri, le sigle. 1969–1980*. Milan: Rizzoli.

Gallinari, P. 2006. *Un contadino nella metropolis. Ricordi di un militante delle Brigate Rosse*. Milano: Bompiani.

Goodwin, J. 1997. *No Other Way Out*. Cambridge: Cambridge University Press.

Gunning, J. 2007. *Hamas in Politics. Democracy, Religion, Violence*. London: Hurst and Company.

Gunning, J. 2009. "Social Movement Theory and the Study of Terrorism" in *Critical Terrorism Studies. A New Research Agenda*, edited by R. Jackson, M. Breen Smyth and J. Gunning. London: Routledge: 156–77.

Hafez, M. 2006. "Political Repression and Violent Rebellion in the Muslim World" in *The Making of a Terrorist: Recruitment, Training and Root Causes*, edited by J. Forest. Westport, Connecticut-London: Praeger Security International, Vol.3: 74–91.

Hafez, M.M. and Q. Wiktorowicz. 2004. "Violence as Contention in the Egyptian Islamic Movement." in *Islamic Activism. A Social Movement Theory Approach*, edited by Q. Wiktorowicz. Bloomington: Indiana University Press: 61–88.

Kepel, G. 1985. *Muslim Extremism in Egypt: The Prophet and Pharaoh.* London: Saqi.

Kepel, G. 2002. *Jihad: The Trail of Political Islam.* Cambridge, MA, Belknap Press of Harvard University Press.

McAdam, D. 1983. "Tactical Innovation and the Pace of Insurgency." *American Sociological Review* 48: 735–54.

McAdam, D, S. Tarrow and C. Tilly. 2001. *Dynamics of Contention*. Cambridge: Cambridge University Press.

Malthaner, S. 2010. *Mobilizing the Faithful*. Frankfurt am Main/New York: Campus.

Novelli, D. and N. Tranfaglia. 1988. *Vite sospese. Le generazioni del terrorismo*. Milan: Garzanti.

Pape, R.A. 2005. *Dying to Win. The Strategic Logic of Suicide Terrorism*. New York: Random House.

Pizzorno, A. 1978. "Political Exchange and Collective Identity in Industrial Conflict." in *The Resurgence of Class Conflict in Western Europe*, edited by C. Crouch and A. Pizzorno. New York: Holmes & Meier: 277–98.

Raswan, D. 2009. "The Renounciation of Violence by Egyptian Jihadi Organizations." in *Leaving Terrorism Behind*, edited by T. Bjorgo and J. Horgan. London: Routledge: 113–32.

Ritter, D. 2010. "Why the Iranian Revolution was Non-violent: Internationalized Social Change and the Iron Cage of Liberalism," PhD Thesis, The University of Texas at Austin.

Rosefsky Wickham C. 2004. "Interests, Ideas, and Islamist Outreach in Egypt." in *Islamic Activism. A Social Movement Theory Approach*, edited by Q. Wiktorowicz. Bloomington: Indiana University Press: 231–49.

Sadowski, Y. 2006. "Political Islam: Asking the Wrong Questions?" *Annual Review of Political Science* 9: 215–40.

Singerman, D. 2004. "The Networked World of Islamist Social Movements." in *Islamic Activism. A Social Movement Theory Approach*, edited by Q. Wiktorowicz. Bloomington: Indiana University Press: 143–63.

Tarrow, S. 1989. *Democracy and Disorder. Protest and Politics in Italy, 1965–1975*. Oxford/New York: Oxford University Press.

Tarrow, S. 1994. *Power in Movement. Social Movements, Collective Action and Politics*. New York/Cambridge: Cambridge University Press.

Tarrow, S. 2011. *Power in Movement. Social Movements, Collective Action and Politics*. New York/Cambridge: Cambridge University Press, 3rd expanded edn.

Tilly, C. 2003. *The Politics of Collective Violence*. Cambridge: Cambridge University Press.

Wiktorowicz, Q. 2004. *Islamic Activism in social Movement Theory*, in *Islamic Activism: A Social Movement Theory Approach*. Bloomington: Indiana University Press, 1–33.

Zald, Mayer N. and R. Ash. 1966. "Social Movement Organizations: Growth, Decay, and Change." *Social Forces* 44: 327–41.

Zald, Mayer N. and J. McCarthy. 1987. *Social Movements in an Organizational Society*. New Brunswick, NJ: Transaction.

Zald, Mayer N. and B. Useem. 1987. "Movement and Countermovement Interaction: Mobilization, Tactics, and State Involvement." in *Social Movements in an Organizational Society*, edited by M.N. Zald and J.D. McCarthy. New Brunswick: Transaction Books, 247–72.

Chapter 6
Intra-movement Competition and Political Outbidding as Mechanisms of Radicalization in Northern Ireland, 1968–1969

Gianluca De Fazio

In the late 1960s, the Civil Rights Movement (CRM) in Northern Ireland mobilized the Irish-Catholic minority to challenge institutionalized discrimination of the Unionist regime. Since the foundation of Northern Ireland in 1920, the Unionist regime had, *de facto*, set up "a Protestant state for Protestant people" (Farrell 1980) loyal to the British Crown, barring the Catholic minority from participating to the political process. The CRM took to the streets in 1968 to secure the political inclusion of the Catholic community within the Northern Ireland polity; its requests comprised full enfranchisement ("one man, one vote"), the end of discriminatory practices in the housing and job markets, and the abolition of draconian police powers. Even though this gradualist approach entailed significant policy and symbolic changes for the Unionist regime, these would have hardly jeopardized the existence of the Northern Ireland state. Nonetheless, the Unionist government, the police and a sizeable portion of the Protestant majority reacted vehemently against these demands, staging hostile counter-mobilization and outright repression of civil rights demonstrations.

In a typical spiral of mobilization and repression (Goldstone and Tilly 2001), the conflict between protesters, counter-protesters and police escalated to the point that in August 1969 the British Army had to step in to halt an incipient civil war. The initial civil rights struggle was gradually replaced with an ethno-nationalist insurgent campaign to overthrow the Northern Ireland state and get rid of the British presence from Irish soil (Bosi 2006). The new goal of political contention was a United Republic of Ireland, rather than a reformed Northern Ireland. Paramilitary organizations till then dormant and in disarray like the Irish Republican Army (IRA), reemerged, peaceful protest leaving the main stage to urban riots, armed insurgency and counter-insurgency. The ensuing conflict between paramilitary groups and security forces—the so-called "Troubles"—turned out to be one of the deadliest ethnic conflicts in the history of modern Europe, as it claimed the lives of more than 3,600 people in 35 years of violent contention.

Why do activists engage in political violence? Why do social movements adopt radical contention? How can we explain the *radicalization* of social movements? In this chapter I use a contentious politics approach (McAdam, Tarrow and

Tilly 2001; Tilly and Tarrow 2006) to address some of these issues. Focusing on the internal dynamics of social movements, I will argue that *intra-movement competition* and *political outbidding* are two key mechanisms conducive to radical contention. To illustrate their empirical relevance, I investigate the trajectory of contention of the CRM in Northern Ireland between 1968 and 1969, when the movement shifted its political agenda and strategy towards radicalism. Relying on both archival evidence and quantitative data on collective events of contention *and* the actors participating to those events, I reconstruct how centrifugal competitive dynamics occurring inside the CRM contributed to its radicalization and eventually to the outbreak of the Troubles.

Social Movements, Political Violence and Terrorism

Social movement research is increasingly applying its analytical tools to examine various aspects of violent radicalization and terrorism (e.g., della Porta 1995; Oberschall 2004; Wiktorowicz 2004; Bergesen 2007), such as the framing activities of militants, the development of their collective identities, the political opportunities and constraints available for violent mobilization (for a review, see Beck 2008). Within this literature, the contentious politics approach has been particularly active in exploring the dynamics of violent radicalization (e.g., Alimi 2011; Alimi, Bosi and Demetriou 2012). According to this perspective, political violence does not emerge from individuals' dispositions or grievances, nor is it the necessary outcome of structural and cultural forces. While these factors shape the context of contention, they cannot explain or predict the *timing* of violent radicalization. Political violence and terrorism are instead conceived of as a *strategy* involving the interaction of various political actors, and, as such, it has to be analyzed as part of the political process (Tilly 2005: 21). Social movement radicalization is the outcome of relational dynamics of contention (Tilly 2003), as it arises from the ongoing interactions between contentious groups (allied or antagonistic), police forces, governments, parties, and transnational actors. The research agenda of a contentious politics approach does not entail the search for "root causes" of radicalization and terrorism, instead it seeks "to identify crucial causal mechanisms that recur in a wide variety of contention, but produce different aggregate outcomes depending on the initial conditions, combinations, and sequences in which they occur" (McAdam, et al. 2001: 37; Alimi 2011: 96). In this chapter, I embrace this analytical strategy and focus on some of the social and political mechanisms whose combination may lead to social movement radicalization.

Mechanisms of Social Movement Radicalization

We can distinguish between internal and external mechanisms facilitating movement trajectories toward radical contention. In this chapter, I argue that intra-movement competition and political outbidding represent two key *internal* mechanisms leading to radicalization. As internal and external mechanisms are critically intertwined in the process of social movement radicalization, I will also show here how these dynamics interacted to generate extreme contention in Northern Ireland.

Intra-movement Competition

Movement organizations usually work together to buttress the activities of the larger movement they belong to, even though they may differ in ideological orientation, targeted constituencies or preferred strategies of action, often engaging in competitive struggles, if not sheer open conflict (e.g., Ansell 2001). Since moderate and radical components normally cohabit within most political groups, "competition may arise from ideological conflict, from competition for space in a static organizational sphere, or from personal conflicts for power between leaders" (Tarrow 2011: 207).

Intra-movement competition refers to activists and groups vying for the allocation of material and symbolic resources which are typically scarce in a social movement. These resources include external funding, allies among the political elite, recruits (Rucht 2007: 204–6), but also positive media coverage and legitimacy in the political process ('certification': McAdam et al. 2001: 316; Furuyama and Meyer 2011). Insofar as internal conflicts are common within social movements, a certain degree of intra-movement competition is also expected. Competition may be valuable for the efficient functioning of a movement, as it can assist in acquiring new resources, targeting new constituencies and fostering commitment among supporters (della Porta 1995: 110). However, competition for increasingly scarce resources can escalate into conflict and eventually organizational radicalization: "whatever its source, a common outcome of competition is radicalization: a shift of ideological commitments toward the extremes and/or the adoption of more disruptive and violent forms of contention" (Tarrow 2011: 207). Clearly, internal competition does *not* always lead to radicalism, as conflicts can be managed and channeled toward more positive outcomes, internal solidarity often offsetting detrimental dynamics of disintegration (Rucht 2007: 205). My argument is that when intra-movement competition combines with another mechanism I call *political outbidding*, a social movement is more likely to radicalize.

Political Outbidding

The concept of outbidding intuitively refers to the attempts of one player to bid higher than other competitors, and it has been used to decipher various phenomena, from suicide terrorism (e.g., Bloom 2004, 2005) to ethnic conflict (e.g., Rabushka and Shepsle 1972; Chandra 2005; Kaufman 1996). Scholars of ethnic party systems have developed the concept of *ethnic outbidding* to indicate a process that may develop:

> in a context of competitive electoral politics when two or more parties identified with the same ethnic group compete for support, neither (in particular electoral configurations) having an incentive to cultivate voters of other ethnicities, each seeking to demonstrate to their constituencies that it is more nationalistic than the other, and each seeking to protect itself from the other's charges that it is 'soft' on ethnic issues. The outbidding can 'o'erleap itself' into violent confrontations, dismantling the very democratic institutions that gave rise to the outbidding. This is a powerful mechanism (and a general one, not confined to *ethnic* outbidding). (Brubaker and Laitin 1998: 434; emphasis in original)

Following Brubaker and Laitin's insight, I identify *political outbidding* as a general mechanism which may occur across a variety of political contexts, thus not being limited to ethnically divided societies and party systems. In other words, while ethnic outbidding exclusively refers to the arena of electoral competition in ethnic party systems, I argue that its underlying dynamic can be used to analyze radicalization and the emergence of political violence among different contentious groups and situations, including social movements (see Alimi and Bosi 2008). Thus, *ethnic* outbidding would be a specific variant of the more general dynamic of *political* outbidding.

Table 6.1 summarizes the main differences between ethnic and political outbidding. First, political outbidding may apply to virtually any political formation, from loosely organized activists' networks to highly structured political parties or trade unions, while ethnic outbidding pertains only to ethnic-based parties. Second, instead of trying to secure electoral support in an ethnic party system, political groups would more generally collide over the expansion of political support, trying to draw media attention and recruits within their own 'bloc.'[1] Third, the boundaries of the constituency can be broadly based upon ethnicity, class, gender, race, sexual orientation, political or religious affiliation, and so on, rather than being limited to ethnic or ethno-national groups. As a consequence, and fourth, political outbidders may claim to 'defend the vital interests' of their political constituency (or social base) broadly defined, instead of a narrow ethnic or (ethno-national) community.

Political outbidding ignites when more radical factions of a political group use extreme claims to protect their 'people' and interests, and formulate accusations of treachery against more moderate components (Mitchell, Evans and O'Leary 2009: 400). Moderate groups with a reformist agenda will have to contend with the hard-liners trumpeting more uncompromising goals. To avoid losing ground

---

1   Competitive dynamics are based on a mix of similarities and differences among groups. Thus, while they share *broadly similar* political goals, vie for the same resources and target the same *broad* constituency, they also differ in the *specific* ways to achieve those goals and the *particular* sections of the constituency they seek out.

Table 6.1 Dynamics of ethnic and political outbidding

	Ethnic Outbidding	Political Outbidding
Type of group	Ethnic party	Any political organization
Competition over	Electoral support	Political support (recruits, media coverage, resources)
Boundaries	Ethnic/ethno-national	Class, ethnic, gender, racial, religious, and so on
Defend vital interests of	Ethnic community	Political constituency

against their more radical competitors, moderates have to modulate their positions and tactics. Otherwise, they risk being perceived (or depicted) as betrayers of their group's cause before their activists, sympathizers and the general public. Thus, in a situation of political outbidding, moderates have few strategic maneuvers (sometimes without even the possibility) to sustain a gradualist platform of action, as it might drive them into political irrelevance. Ultimately, if an organization is to survive from hard-liners' accusations of treachery, chasing the rallying cry of radicalism is almost an inevitable course of action (see Horowitz 1985: 349–60).

The combination of the mechanisms of intra-movement competition and political outbidding is propitious for the organizational radicalization of social movements. The outcome of their mutually reinforcing interaction is to legitimize radical action and goals in the eyes of movement organizations and activists. Claims and goals previously considered as extreme, are later perceived as the ones truly acting in defense of a group's interests, values, identities and, eventually, physical or cultural 'survival' (on the legitimation of violence, see Demetriou 2007). Likewise, an increasingly transgressive repertoire of action progressively acquires the status of a rightful 'weapon' to preserve and put forward the movement's agenda (Alimi et al. 2012). As a result, a social movement *as a whole* embarks on the course of radicalization. During this process of transformation, the activists and groups composing the social movement are constantly evolving. Thus, while some followers will disengage from 'radical activism' and/or activism altogether, more radical sympathizers will join the movement, reinforcing its radicalizing path.

The two mechanisms proposed are not uniquely related to the Northern Irish context, but can be found in several other episodes of contention. One of the theoretical goals of the contentious politics research agenda is indeed to detect causal mechanisms applicable across disparate cases; however, their combination with other mechanisms and political structures may lead to different outcomes. Whether or not radicalization is 'successful' (i.e., moderates are compelled to chase radicals) is thus contingent upon the existing political opportunities and threats in a political system. Contentious interactions with counter-movements and state authorities are especially important in shaping the structure of opportunities

120 *Dynamics of Political Violence*

and threats for radical contention (e.g., della Porta 1995; Alimi 2011: 99–100; Alimi et al. 2012; De Fazio 2013).

External Dynamics

Successful mobilization efforts and sympathetic media coverage of a movement's goals may invite opposite groups threatened by those goals to organize collective action and spur a process of counter-mobilization (e.g., Meyer and Staggenborg 1996). The mere presence of a *hostile counter-movement* may sometimes unleash the radicalization of both a movement and its opponents (e.g., Franzosi 1999: 137–41). This is especially the case when opposing movements engage in antagonistic strategies of contention and repeatedly collide in the public space of protest, thus triggering opportunities for collective violence. Recurring violent clashes between protesters and counter-protesters polarize the political game and facilitate the propagation of extremism (della Porta 1995). Rather than pragmatic policy disputes, opposing movements clash over worldviews, physical integrity and control of territory, inter-movement conflict becoming increasingly non-negotiable (Tarrow 1989, 2011). When movements' claims and strategies of action are more and more geared toward rallying their own constituency to counteract the mobilization of their opponents, radical tactics are more likely to prevail (Collins 2001: 40).

State repression is perhaps the most important factor affecting the opportunities and threats available to contentious actors (e.g., Tilly 1978; Alimi 2011), representing a central ingredient in social movement radicalization. The link between repression, mobilization and political violence has been extensively examined in social movement research, even though with highly contradictory results (see Earl 2011). For what concerns its relationship with radical contention, Koopmans (1997) has emphasized how situational repression (i.e., brutal policing of protest) was more likely to escalate the conflict and elicit extreme forms of contention than institutional repression (e.g., ban on organizations). Heavy-handed police tactics expose protesters to symbolic and physical violence, multiplying occasions for collective violence (Tilly 2003: 26–54). Some of the activists initiated to political violence may become "specialists in violence" (Tilly 2003: 35–6) for self-defense as well as for proactive tactics. Through repeated violent interactions between challengers and state authorities, movements may end up including radical tactics as part of their legitimate repertoire of contention (White 1989, 1993).

Data and Methods

To study violent radicalization in Northern Ireland, I employ a methodological approach that blends quantitative and qualitative research methods. In particular, I draw on both archival sources and a catalogue of contentious events to investigate the internal dynamics which led to the radicalization of the CRM in Northern Ireland in the late 1960s.

For the quantitative component of this project, I used Quantitative Narrative Analysis (QNA; Franzosi 2004, 2010) to collect a large body of narrative data on contentious events. Linguists have identified the sequence Subject (S)—Action (A)—Object (O), and respective modifiers, as the most basic narrative structure accessible in a text (Propp 1968; Greimas 1966; Labov and Waletzky 1967). The SAO sequence, also known as *semantic triplet*, forms the relational structure of a *story grammar*: "the set of rules that provides the categories into which the various invariant elements of a story fall (e.g., actor, action, time, space), the nature of each category (e.g., a text, a number, a date; allowed to occur one or multiple times), and their reciprocal relationships" (Franzosi 2010: 23). Taking advantage of the structural properties of narrative, Franzosi (1997) adopted highly formalized and computerized story grammars as QNA's key tool of data collection.

The organization of a story grammar is formally represented by a set of rewrite rules (Franzosi 2010: 23–4), which are symbolized by a right-pointing arrow (→). A rewrite rule indicates how an element to the left of the symbol can be rewritten in terms of the elements to its right. For example, consider this brief story grammar:[2]

Macro-event	→ { < event > }
< event >	→ { < semantic triplet > }
< semantic triplet >	→ { < subject > } { < action > } [{ < object > }]

The grammar above aims at organizing the spatially and temporally situated actions of the social actors involved in a particular semantic triplet into an event; moreover, it also arranges the events into a higher level of aggregation, in this case a macro-event. The elements of the semantic triplet can be rewritten according to their properties and attributes. A < subject > can be rewritten as actor and its modifiers (e.g., number of actors, type, organization), < action > can be rewritten according to action and their modifiers (e.g., time, space and type of action), and so on (Franzosi 1997: 278). Most importantly, story grammars allow the analytic disaggregation of contentious events into the actors participating in them, their characteristics and the types of the relation linking them. In line with Tilly's (2008: 27) methodological lessons on the study of contentious events, QNA is capable "to move from individualistic analyses to treatments of connections among contentious actors." As the unit of analysis of QNA is the semantic triplet, it generates relational data (Scott 2000: 3) on actors and their interactions that can be fruitfully analyzed through network models (see Franzosi 1999; Franzosi, De Fazio and Vicari 2012).

---

2   In story grammars notation, angular brackets < > denote elements that can be further rewritten into other elements. Conversely, 'terminal elements'—the words or linguistic expressions found in the text—have no < >. Curly brackets { } indicate items that can occur more than one time, while square brackets [ ] denote optional elements.

122   *Dynamics of Political Violence*

For this project, the narratives come from a three-volume chronology of events (Deutsch and Magowan 1973, 1974, 1975) which details all the contentious episodes that occurred in Northern Ireland from 1968 to 1974. For each chronology entry referring to the 1968–1972 years, I employed PC-ACE[3] to record in detail 'who did what, when, where, why and how,' the basic information needed to carry out an actor-based explanation of radicalization (see Tilly and Tarrow 2006: 201–10). In addition, I consulted Sutton's Index of Deaths (1994) to verify the accuracy of the entries narrating killing events, and I complemented or amended possible missing or incorrect information. Drawing on the coding of 2,097 entries, the final database contains 6,035 semantic triplets, grouped into 2,323 events of contention. Processes of mobilization, counter-mobilization, repression and violent radicalization are tracked down through counts of actors' interactions with each other, according to different spheres of actions (violence, control, protest, etc.), and are graphically displayed through sequential network models.

Qualitative data are used to trace the mechanisms of political outbidding and intra-movement competition. In 2009, I conducted archival research in Belfast, Northern Ireland, where I consulted sources at the Newspaper Library at the Belfast Central Library and the Northern Ireland Political Collection at the Linenhall Library. The Collection holds over a quarter of a million items, from pamphlets and correspondence to minutes of meetings, recording the activities of the actors who participated to the Troubles since the 1960s; it also contains the CRM's semi-official archive with more than 35 boxes of ephemera of the various civil rights organizations. From this large amount of archival material, I examined the publications, transcripts of meetings and newspaper accounts of the activities of the CRM, its organizations and their political claims, for the 1968–1969 years. These archival data unveil the growing conflict and competition occurring among the different components of the movement, and the attempts by more radical organizations to politically outbid the moderates. The inspection of official press releases and propaganda materials of other political actors participating in the Troubles (loyalists, police, governments, etc.) details their perspectives and maneuvers, highlighting their role in the escalation of the conflict in Northern Ireland. In sum, the analysis of archival data will reveal how internal dynamics fostered the radicalization of the CRM, clarifying the trajectories of contention of the main contentious actors of the Troubles.

Social Movement Radicalization in Northern Ireland

From the brief sketch of the events which opened this chapter, it is easy to detect the shift in the requests advanced by the Civil Rights Movement, as it exacted more

---

3   PC-ACE (Program for Computer-Assisted Coding of Events) is a free software Franzosi developed to carry out QNA for large scale socio-historical research projects (http://www.sociology.emory.edu/rfranzosi/pc-ace/).

Intra-movement Competition and Political Outbidding 123

and more drastic transformation in the Northern Irish political system. What had started as an appeal for full British citizenship ("British Rights for British Citizens," as one slogan claimed in the early days of civil rights demonstrations), ended up in a bloody confrontation reclaiming the breakup of the United Kingdom altogether ("Brits out!"; Bosi 2011: 136). I now examine the internal dynamics of the CRM, detailing how the initial efforts of cooperation among its various organizations transmuted into intra-movement competition and conflict over strategies and resources. Responding to the changing political situation in Northern Ireland, and the shifting threats and opportunities associated with it (Goldstone and Tilly 2001), the more radical components of the CRM attempted to politically outbid the moderates in the movement. In an effort to keep up with a hostile environment—i.e., state and police repression, loyalist counter-protest, ethnic antagonism—and the accusation of not being effective defenders of the Irish-Catholic community, moderates in the CRM had to adapt and embrace more radical contention and claim-making. The political and social terrain for the outbreak of the Troubles was set.

The Formation of the CRM

In January 1967, the Northern Ireland Civil Rights Association (NICRA) was founded as a loose coalition of anti-unionist activists to challenge the Northern Ireland government and its discriminatory practices through a civil rights campaign (Purdie 1990: 132–3). This ideologically heterogeneous network of activists and associations aimed:

1. To defend the basic freedom of all citizens;
2. To protect the rights of the individual;
3. To highlight all the possible abuses of power;
4. To demand guarantees for freedom of speech, assembly and association; and
5. To inform the public of their lawful rights (NICRA 1978: 20).

During the first 18 months of its existence, the NICRA consciously molded its rhetoric and tactics after the National Council for Civil Liberties, the main civil rights organization in the UK, unsuccessfully supporting legal-institutional tactics to further civil rights in Northern Ireland (Purdie 1990: 133–4). Facing a botched institutional approach and inspired by the American struggle for civil rights of the 1960s (De Fazio 2009: 164–5), in the second half of 1968 NICRA finally reverted to direct political action and protest.

On August 24, 1968, about 2,000 civil rights activists marched from Coalisland to Dungannon, deliberately crossing both Protestant and Catholic areas to validate their anti-sectarian claims.[4] While the march met some opposition by loyalist

---

4 One core mission of the CRM was indeed to denounce and combat sectarianism (Mulholland 2000: 244).

124   *Dynamics of Political Violence*

counter-demonstrators and was re-routed by the Royal Ulster Constabulary (RUC), it went by relatively quietly. The second civil rights march, due to take place in Derry on October 5, was banned by the Unionist government on the ground of security concerns. When a few hundred protesters decided to go on with the march, the RUC enforced the ban with violence, using baton charges and water cannons to disperse the peaceful marchers. The televised images of police violence rapidly spread throughout the British Isles and across the world, prompting a wave of mass civil rights mobilization in the following months.

Three main civil rights organizations were at the core of the CRM: the aforementioned NICRA, People's Democracy (PD), a radical student group formed as a reaction to the police mistreatment of civil rights protesters (Arthur 1974: 30), and the moderate Derry Citizens' Action Committee (DCAC; see Ó Dochartaigh 2005). These organizations targeted different segments of the Irish-Catholic community in Northern Ireland: NICRA represented the more moderate and middle-class element of the CRM, People's Democracy was mainly based at Queen's University, Belfast and recruited students, faculty members and leftists, while DCAC was mostly concentrated in the Derry area (Cinalli 2002: 93). Notwithstanding their cleavages in terms of class, locale, age and political ideologies, civil rights organizations and activists fully cooperated in their initial efforts to challenge the Unionist government. At this stage, their shared political agenda included electoral reform ("one man, one vote" and the end of gerrymandering), anti-discrimination legislation and police reform. This phase of cooperation, though, was not fated to last very long.

Intra-movement Competition

Since the outset of the civil rights mobilization, occasions of tension between the more radical PD and the rest of the CRM surfaced. Modeled on the Selma-Montgomery marches, PD leaders organized a "long march" from Belfast to Derry in January 1969, crossing several loyalist strongholds in the Northern Irish countryside. This march ostensibly violated a "truce" settled in December by the CRM and the Northern Ireland government to let the Parliament approve a package of civil rights reforms (NICRA 1978), many moderate civil rights leaders opposing the march (Bosi 2011: 134). The intended purpose of the march was to expose the repressive nature of the Northern Irish government, as well as to embarrass the more moderate elements in the CRM (McCann 1974; Farrell 1988).[5] The Cameron Report (1969: 47) on the 1969 disturbances in Northern Ireland labeled the tactic as "calculated martyrdom," as the march came under violent

---

    5   According to Purdie (1990: 217), the PD march "was essentially an oppositional tactic, against what was seen as [Northern Ireland Prime Minister] O'Neill's fake reformism, against the truce in civil rights activities, and against the leaderships of the civil rights movement and the Catholic community."

loyalist attacks, multiple times. Near Burntollet Bridge, in the outskirts of Derry, loyalist supporters in collusion with off-duty policemen ambushed the marchers with stones and clubs, injuring several marchers (Cameron 1969: para 177), NICRA and DCAC immediately lent their support to the PD marchers and welcomed them at their arrival in Derry.

Loyalist and police violence against PD marchers had temporarily reinforced the solidarity among the different components of the CRM. However, the long march "established PD's separate existence within the civil rights movement, giving it a sense of self-importance and helping to create a division between itself and the more moderate groups" (Arthur 1974: 43). That division would become evident during the elections for the Northern Ireland Parliament in February 1969, in which three civil rights leaders (two from NICRA, one from DCAC) were elected. The elections "marked a turning point in the inter-organizational relationships" (Cinalli 2002: 93) within the CRM. In fact, as anti-Catholic violence reappeared in the streets and civil rights activists were given an institutional voice in the political process, mobilization dwindled, causing fierce intra-movement competition for grassroots support and activists.

In Figure 6.1, I chart civil rights and loyalist protests, from August 1968 till December 1969. We can notice two hiatuses in civil rights mobilization: the first one in December 1968, due to the truce with Stormont; the second one in February 1969, due instead to the elections. Many activists in the CRM were involved with the organization of the electoral campaigns of their leaders, temporarily setting aside transgressive contention. During the election, People's Democracy activists set up branches in different towns throughout the province, including

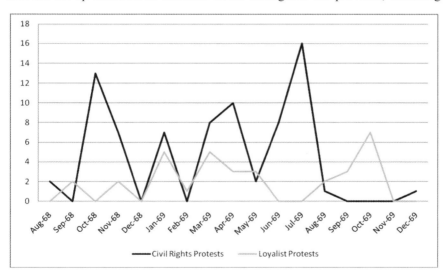

Figure 6.1 **Civil rights and loyalist protests in Northern Ireland, August 1968–December 1969**

Newry, Armagh, Enniskillen and Belfast: "this caused friction since it meant that the PD was organising in direct competition with NICRA and it also hastened the PD's leftward drift. Since it was no longer a purely student body and was competing for the same supporters as NICRA, it emphasised the characteristics which distinguished it most clearly from the association—its greater militancy and radicalism" (Purdie 1990: 223). In other words, an external political opportunity (local elections) highlighted the different strategic positions of the various civil rights organizations, fomenting intra-movement competition over scarce resources like funding, militants, political support and the leadership of the movement's broad constituency: the Irish Catholic minority.

The results of the elections for the Northern Ireland Parliament signaled an essential shift in the political system, as it registered a significant increase in the "ethnic vote" (Elliott 1973). The traditional constitutional issue of Partition, until that moment never invoked by the CRM, was thus revitalized (Bosi 2006: 93), as ethno-national identities became more salient. The ideological rift between 'moderates' and 'radicals' inside the movement intensified, as "the inclusive, anti-sectarian, and polycentric collective identity of the CRM's first stage was now gradually replaced by an exclusive communal identity" (Bosi 2011: 135). The radical wing of the CRM tried to take control of the direction of the entire movement, as it displayed antagonistic tactics and more wide-ranging requests of political change. On March 14, 1969, four prominent members of NICRA resigned from its executive due to its support to a PD march planned to go across a hostile unionist area on March 29.[6] Several other resignations, both within NICRA and DCAC, ensued, as moderate activists felt that the CRM was "being undermined by extremist movements for whose actions we cannot hold ourselves responsible."[7] Eventually, PD cancelled its march and all civil rights organizations held a protest march in Derry on March 29. Nonetheless, in the first months of 1969, NICRA and DCAC had to adapt to the changing political conditions; in order to retain support and activists, moderates had to chase PD in the terrain of risky contention and far-reaching political goals. As political violence in Northern Ireland was starting to flare, many moderates dropped out from the CRM and activism (Bosi 2006: 94), and the composition of the protesters in the street changed too (Bosi 2011: 135). With the revitalization of the ethno-national divide, youngsters from the working class Irish-Catholic "ghettos" (McCann 1974) were now actively taking part to street protests; unlike earlier participants to the civil rights demonstrations, though, they were animated by strong anti-police resentment rather than reformism (Ó Dochartaigh 2005).

Figure 6.2 portrays the network of violent interactions that occurred in Northern Ireland from May 1968 to July 1969.[8] This was the period when the CRM was

---

6   *Belfast Telegraph*, March 15, 1969.

7   *Irish News*, March 17, 1969.

8   In network analysis terminology, the actors in the graph are called *nodes* and the links connecting them *ties*. For the sake of clarity, I will use the more familiar term *lines*

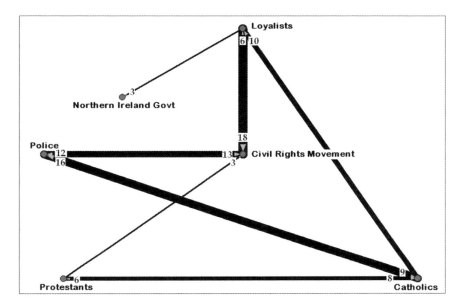

Figure 6.2   Network of violence, Northern Ireland, May 1968–July 1969

most actively pursuing its strategy of direct action to further the civil rights cause, immediately meeting the aggressive response from the Protestant majority and state authorities. The thick lines which link the CRM with police and loyalists show how these actors frequently engaged in violence, as street demonstrations were often conducive to civil disturbances. Most of the political violence which occurred in this period thus concerned street confrontations among protesters, counter-protesters and police. The bi-directional line connecting Protestants and Catholics[9] at the bottom of the graph points to a budding violent antagonism

---

instead of *ties*. The width of the *lines* is proportional to the number of violent interactions linking two actors; the arrow heads indicate the direction of the action, and the numbers near each node indicate how many times that node/actor has been the recipient of a violent action by another node/actor.

9   Under the labels 'Catholics' and 'Protestants' I have aggregated individuals or unorganized crowds belonging to those communities or residing in areas traditionally associated with them (e.g., 'Bogsiders'). These actors differ from social movement actors like the 'CRM' and 'Loyalists,' as the latter labels refer to organized groups (e.g. 'NICRA' or 'PD') or leaders (e.g., Reverend Ian Paisley) actively mobilizing in support of the larger ethno-national communities. Even though the distinction between, say, 'Protestants' and 'Loyalists' is partially an artificial one, it is crucial to maintain the analytical distinction between members of a community and *organized collective actors* originating from that community to better comprehend the dynamics of radicalization (on the issue of data aggregation in QNA, see Franzosi 2010: 92–7).

128   *Dynamics of Political Violence*

between the two communities, even though the Catholic community had also to endure a good deal of police harassment (to which it eagerly replied back).

Up until July 1969, protest-related clashes and attacks on the Catholic community prompted intra-movement competition for support and activists among the main civil rights organizations in Northern Ireland. The frustration caused by the stalled political situation and the incapacity of moderate civil rights leaders to obtain tangible results, together with the revitalization of the ethno-nationalist cleavage prepared the ground for political outbidding to unfold in the following months. As moderate political positions were losing ground and grassroots support, radical groups like PD sought to acquire prominence and leadership within the CRM and control on its strategies of contention.

Political Outbidding

Incipient ethnic animosity, coupled with a fierce competition among social movement organizations, rendered political outbidding a tempting and viable option for radical groups in the second half of 1969. The mechanisms of intra-movement competition and political outbidding unfolded in close relationship with the contentious dynamics occurring outside of the CRM. In particular, hostile counter-mobilization and state repression played a decisive role in radicalizing the CRM and, more generally, the ethno-national conflict (De Fazio 2013).

The Cameron Report (1969: 91) claimed that "fears and apprehensions among Protestants of a threat to Unionist domination and control of Government by increase of Catholic population and powers, inflamed in particular by the activities of [loyalist organizations], provoked strong hostile reaction to civil rights claims […] which was readily translated into physical violence against Civil Rights demonstrators." Loyalist mobilization, though, was not a merely reactive phenomenon, as protests in defense of the Protestant nature of the Northern Ireland state preceded the civil rights mobilization (Bruce 2007: 90–93; O'Callaghan and O'Donnell 2006). In 1966, loyalist leader Rev. Ian Paisley organized several demonstrations against the decision of the Unionist government to allow nationalists to commemorate the 50th anniversary of the Easter Rising (O'Callaghan and O'Donnell 2006: 207). The usual enemies—disloyal Catholics and the IRA—were this time flanked by the Unionist government and its attempt to modernize and secularize Northern Ireland (Bruce 2007: 92). When the CRM rose at the center of the political arena, Reverend Paisley could already rely on a plethora of loyalist organizations (Farrington 2008: 529) to counteract its mass demonstrations. Police control of civil rights protest in Northern Ireland was notoriously harsh, as the overwhelmingly Protestant RUC perceived the CRM as both an operational (Ellison and Smyth 2000: 62) and political threat, and interpreted its role as a staunch defender of the Northern Ireland state and its Unionist government (De Fazio 2007: 80). The CRM resolution to defy the ministerial bans to march often resulted in street disturbances among civil rights protesters, loyalist counter-demonstrators and the police, thus creating multiple opportunities for violent confrontations. These had momentous effects on civil rights activists and the activation of political outbidding inside the CRM.

On the one hand, the frequent clashes with loyalist counter-demonstrators, police repression and the outburst of sectarian antagonism socialized civil rights protesters to political violence, an important aspect of their radicalization. On the other hand, loyalist and police violence against civil rights demonstrations helped to displace the initial reformist agenda of the CRM. As the movement had to deal with a new wave of ethnic antagonism and violence, as well as the reinvigorated question of Partition, radical organizations like PD tried to seize the direction of the civil rights agenda and impose its confrontational attitude against the state. In a clear attempt to politically outbid the moderates within the CRM, in the last months of 1969 PD launched—through its weekly publication "*Free Citizen*"— ferocious verbal assaults against NICRA and its allegedly too moderate stances (Cinalli 2002: 101; for a detailed discussion of PD's attacks against other civil rights organizations and 'moderates,' see Arthur 1974: 75–80), accusing some of its leaders of treachery and 'selling out.' At the PD conference on October 12, 1969, its most prominent leader, Michael Farrell, presented this motion: "The People's Democracy, which has been active in the struggle for civil rights, for more jobs and houses, and against Toryism, North and South, believes that its objectives can only be obtained by the ousting of both Tory governments and the establishment of an Irish Socialist Republic." By the second half of 1969, PD had thus abandoned the goal of civil rights reform in favor of a Socialist and Anti-Partionist platform to counter British imperialism and the "threat of Orange Fascism." According to Arthur (1974: 106), the relationship between PD and NICRA "was an unhappy one because as a potential revolutionary organisation it did not want to be concerned with reformist demands; and equally the NICRA was embarrassed by its unwanted radical offshoot."

The outcome of this political outbidding was to swing of the fulcrum of the political arena in the direction of more extreme ethno-national claim-making, as these polarizing contentions gained widespread support in both communities (Farrington 2008). The severity of the sectarian violence which occurred in August 1969 detonated the ethno-national conflict and marked a defining moment of Northern Irish history. After almost a year of tense inter-community relationships, the annual Orange parade in Derry in August 1969 unleashed several days of fierce rioting and sectarian attacks on Catholic districts all over Northern Ireland. The British government sent the Army in support of the exhausted local police forces to halt an embryonic civil war and reinstate public order in the streets.

Figure 6.3 forcefully unveils the shift in the nature of the violent interactions that occurred in the second half of 1969, after the intervention of the British Army. In contrast to the previous pattern of protest-related violent disturbances, the graph above depicts the ignition of a violent ethno-national conflict in which the two ethnic communities bore the brunt of radical contention. Street protests and disorders gave way to ethnic riots and sectarian attacks (see the width of the

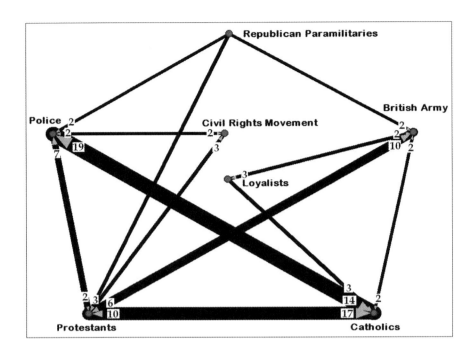

Figure 6.3 Network of violence, Northern Ireland, August 1969–December 1969

line connecting Protestants and Catholics). Moreover, while the CRM became a lesser target of police repression, the Catholic community as a whole engaged in a violent conflict with the state and its security apparatus (see especially the line linking Catholics with police).

The CRM and its unprecedented direct action challenge to the Unionist regime generated a hostile and at time violent response from the authorities and loyalists, in turn inciting ethnic antagonism and the polarization of the polity. As the British Army took charge of public order, the issue of the constitutional position of Northern Ireland became *the* issue for the Irish minority. At that point, the CRM found itself unprepared to handle the extremely volatile situation in the streets it had contributed to create. Faced with daily lethal violence and clashes with security forces, even the radicalized CRM had to retreat and leave the control of the Catholic minority to traditional Republican organizations. In the words of Fergus O'Hare, at the time a young radical activist from West Belfast:

> when police started to attack people's homes it was no longer a question of sitting down peacefully, the question of defending your homes became a major issue for the movement. And then the question of defence of areas arose. When the police were using guns against people, the issue of military defence, and in

the Irish context the issue of the IRA, came on the agenda. So the nature of the conflict and of the struggle began to change, the forces of the State became more hostile, more militarized and more directed on people's homes and the issue of defence and that sort of activity came onto the agenda. That's when IRA started reforming. (Bosi 2011: 135–16)

The Troubles had started.

Conclusion

In the late 1960s, the CRM in Northern Ireland shifted from a gradualist approach of peaceful protest to reform the state, towards radical contention, contributing to the ignition of a violent ethno-national conflict. In this chapter, I investigated how two internal relational mechanisms—intra-movement competition and political outbidding—combined to push the CRM toward its radicalization. To be sure, external factors like national elections, ethnic antagonism, hostile counter-mobilization and repression altered the political conditions under which the CRM was operating. Eventually, these shifting conditions promoted the internal dynamics of radicalization discussed here. Competition for scarce resources and attempts to outbid moderates had their own internal logic and dynamic; yet, the external environment affected the political opportunities and constraints activating these mechanisms. For instance, the internal conflict on the strategic and ideological direction of the CRM was intrinsically related to its initial heterogeneity, yet, the February 1969 elections decisively exacerbated the competition over supporters and recruits. Likewise, sectarian violence and the failure of the Unionist government to deliver a package of reforms weakened the credibility of the moderates in the CRM as advocates of the minority's interests, thus prompting political outbidding.

Deadly sectarianism and the intervention of the British Army in the summer of 1969 altered forever the rules of the political game in Northern Ireland, dictating the marginalization of the CRM at the edges of the political arena. In the final months of 1969, civil rights mobilization almost disappeared (see Figure 6.1), and the distance between radical and moderates further widened. PD kept its radicalizing trend in the direction of revolutionary politics, eventually embracing Socialist Republicanism as its ultimate goal. By 1972, PD would deem "basic Provisional [IRA's] demands as being the absolute minimum to ensure peace" (Arthur 1974: 114). NICRA and moderate activists, instead, gradually abandoned transgressive contention in favor of institutional and electoral politics. This path of institutionalization culminated in August 1970, when former civil rights leaders John Hume and Ivan Cooper, together with others MPs, co-founded the Social Democratic and Labour Party (SDLP) to advance civil rights and the re-unification of Ireland by constitutional means.

132 *Dynamics of Political Violence*

As Conor Cruise O'Brien (1972: 186) pointed out, "(a)fter August, 1969, the radical orators had in fact nothing further to offer to the Catholic population; they never had had anything to offer to the Protestants. […] The fear of the Catholic community […] did not call for more oratory or marches, or appeals to a non-existent class solidarity, or a resolution of the hopelessly divided working class. It called for guns to defend Catholic homes. […] The stage was set for the return of the Irish Republican Army." The radicalization of the CRM's tactics and claims helped to polarize the political system and deteriorate public order in the streets, contributing to the outbreak of the Troubles. Confrontations over civil rights and discrimination were thus gradually replaced by a violent ethno-national conflict fueled by paramilitary organizations and counter-insurgency. As the opportunities for the CRM to reform Northern Ireland through street politics waned, other actors took the center stage of radical contention, ultimately determining the end of the very brief 'civil rights era' in Northern Ireland.

References

Alimi, E. 2011. Relational Dynamics in Factional Adoption of Terrorist Tactics: a Comparative Perspective. *Theory and Society,* 40(1), 95–118.

Alimi, E., and Bosi, L. 2008. A Comparative Historical Analysis of the Processes of Radicalization of the Weather Underground and of the Provisional Irish Republican Army. *Ricerche di Storia Politica,* (3), 273–92.

Alimi, E., Bosi, L., and Demetriou, C. 2012. "Relational Dynamics and Processes of Radicalization: A Comparative Framework." *Mobilization* 17(1), 7–26.

Ansell, C. 2001. *Schism and Solidarity in Social Movements: The Politics of Labor in the French Third Republic*. Cambridge: Cambridge University Press.

Arthur, P. 1974. *The People's Democracy, 1968–1973*. Belfast: Blackstaff Press.

Beck, C. 2008. The Contribution of Social Movement Theory to Understanding Terrorism. *Sociological Compass,* 2(5), 1565–81.

Bergesen, A. 2007. Three-Step Model of Terrorist Violence. *Mobilization, 12*(2), 111–18.

Bloom, M. 2004. Palestinian Suicide Bombing: Public Support, Market Share, and Outbidding. *Political Science Quarterly,* 119(1), 61–88.

Bloom, M. 2005. *Dying to Kill: the Allure of Suicide Terror*. New York: Columbia University Press.

Bosi, L. 2006. The Dynamics of Social Movement Development: Northern Ireland's Civil Rights Movement in the 1960s. *Mobilization,* 11(1), 81–100.

Bosi, L. 2011. From "British Rights" to "British Out": the Northern Ireland Civil Rights Movement Between the 1960s and Early 1970s, in *Re-visiting Protests: New Approaches to Social Mobilization in Europe Since 1945*, edited by H. Kouki and E. Romanos. London: Berghahn.

Brubaker, R., and Laitin, D. 1998. Ethnic and Nationalist Violence. *Annual Review of Sociology,* 24, 423–52.

Bruce, S. 2007. *Paisley: Religion and Politics in Northern Ireland*. Oxford: Oxford University Press.

Cameron, J. 1969. *Disturbances in Northern Ireland: Report of the Commission Appointed by the Governor of Northern Ireland*. Belfast: HMSO.

Chandra, K. 2005. Ethnic Parties and Democratic Stability. *Perspectives on Politics*, 3(2), 235–52.

Cinalli, M. 2002. *Social Movements, Networks and National Cleavages in Northern Ireland*. Unpublished PhD Dissertation, Queen's University, Belfast.

Collins, R. 2001. Social Movements and the Focus of Emotional Attention, in *Passionate Politics: Emotions and Social Movements*, edited by J. Goodwin, J. Jasper and F. Polletta. Chicago: University of Chicago Press, 27–44.

De Fazio, G. 2007. Police Knowledge Revised: Insights from the Policing of the Civil Rights Movement in Northern Ireland. *Research in Social Movements, Conflicts and Change*, 27, 63–87.

De Fazio, G. 2009. Civil Rights Mobilization and Repression in Northern Ireland: a Comparison with the US Deep South. *The Sixties: A Journal of History, Politics and Culture*, 2(2), 163–85.

De Fazio, G. 2013. The Radicalization of Contention in Northern Ireland, 1968–1972: A Relational Perspective. *Mobilization*, 18(4), 489–513.

della Porta, D. 1995. *Social Movements, Political Violence, and the State. A Comparative Analysis of Italy and Germany*. Cambridge: Cambridge University Press.

Demetriou, C. 2007. Political Violence and Legitimation: the Episode of Colonial Cyprus. *Qualitative Sociology* 30(2), 171–93.

Deutsch, R., and Magowan, V. 1973. *Northern Ireland 1968–73. A Chronology of Events. Volume 1 1968–1971*. Belfast: Blackstaff Press.

Deutsch, R., and Magowan, V. 1974. *Northern Ireland 1968–73. A Chronology of Events. Volume 2 1972–1973*. Belfast: Blackstaff Press.

Deutsch, R., and Magowan, V. 1975. *Northern Ireland 1968–73. A Chronology of Events. Volume 3 1974*. Belfast: Blackstaff Press.

Earl, J. 2011. Political Repression: Iron Fists, Velvet Gloves, and Diffuse Control. *Annual Review of Sociology* 37, 261–84.

Elliott, S. 1973. *Northern Ireland Parliamentary Election Results, 1921–1972*. Chichester: Political Reference Publications.

Ellison, G., and Smyth, J. 2000. *The Crowned Harp: Policing Northern Ireland*. Belfast: Pluto Press.

Farrell, M. 1980. *Northern Ireland: The Orange State*. Belfast: Pluto Press.

Farrell, M. 1988. *Twenty Years On*. Dingle: Brandon.

Farrington, C. 2008. Mobilisation, State Crisis and Counter-Mobilisation: Ulster Unionist Politics and the Outbreak of the Troubles. *Irish Political Studies*, 23(4), 513–32.

Franzosi, R. 1997. Mobilization and Counter-Mobilization Processes: From the "Red Years" (1919–20) to the "Black Years" (1921–22) in Italy. *Theory and Society*, 26(2–3), 275–304.

Franzosi, R. 1999. The Return of The Actor. Interaction Networks Among Social Actors During Periods of High Mobilization (Italy, 1919–1922). *Mobilization,* 4(2), 131–49.

Franzosi, R. 2004. *From Words to Numbers. Narrative, Data, and Social Science.* Cambridge: Cambridge University Press.

Franzosi, R. 2010. *Quantitative Narrative Analysis.* Los Angeles: Sage Publications.

Franzosi, R., De Fazio, G., and Vicari, S. 2012. Ways of Measuring Agency: An Application of Quantitative Narrative Analysis to Lynchings in Georgia (1875–1930). *Sociological Methodology,* 42(1), 1-41.

Furuyama, K., and Meyer, D. 2011. Sources of Certification and Civil Rights Advocacy Organizations: The JACL, The NAACP, and Crises of Legitimacy. *Mobilization,* 16(1), 101–16.

Goldstone, J., and Tilly, C. 2001. Threat (and Opportunity): Popular Action and State Response in the Dynamics of Contentious Action, in *Silence and Voice in the Study of Contentious Politics*, edited by R. Aminzade et al. Cambridge: Cambridge University Press, 179–94.

Greimas, A. 1966. *Semantique Structurelle.* Paris: Larousse.

Horowitz, D. 1985. *Ethnic Groups in Conflict.* Berkeley, CA: University of California Press.

Kaufman, S. 1996. Spiraling to Ethnic War: Elites, Masses, and Moscow in Moldova's Civil War. *International Security,* 21(2), 108–38.

Koopmans, R. 1997. Dynamics of Repression and Mobilization: The German Extreme Right in the 1990s. *Mobilization* 2(2), 149–64.

Labov, W., and Waletzky, J. 1967. Narrative Analysis, in *Essays on the Verbal and Visual Arts*, edited by J. Helm. Seattle: University of Washington Press, 12–44.

McAdam, D., Tarrow, S., and Tilly, C. 2001. *Dynamics of Contention.* Cambridge: Cambridge University Press.

McCann, E. 1974. *War and an Irish Town.* London: Penguin.

Meyer, D., and Staggenborg, S. 1996. Movements, Countermovements, and the Structure of Political Opportunity. *American Journal of Sociology* 101(6): 1628–60.

Mitchell, P., Evans, G., and O'Leary, B. 2009. Extremist Outbidding in Ethnic Party Systems is Not Inevitable: Tribune Parties in Northern Ireland. *Political Studies,* 57(2), 397–421.

Mulholland, M. 2000. *Northern Ireland at the Crossroads: Ulster Unionism in the O'Neill years, 1960–9.* London: Basingstoke.

NICRA. 1978. *"We Shall Overcome" ... . The History of the Struggle for Civil Rights in Northern Ireland 1968–1978.* Belfast: NICRA.

Ó Dochartaigh, N. 2005. *From Civil Rights to Armalites: Derry and the Birth of the Irish Troubles.* 2nd edn. New York: Palgrave Macmillan.

Oberschall, A. 2004. Explaining Terrorism: The Contribution of Collective Action Theory. *Sociological Theory,* 22(1), 26–37.

O'Brien, C. 1972. *States of Ireland.* New York: Pantheon Books.

O'Callaghan, M., and O'Donnell, C. 2006. The Northern Ireland Government, the "Paisleyite Movement" and Ulster Unionism in 1966. *Irish Political Studies,* 21(2), 203–22.

Propp, V. 1968. *Morphology of the Folktale*. Austin: University of Texas Press.

Purdie, B. 1990. *Politics in the Streets: Origins of the Civil Rights Movement in Northern Ireland*. Belfast: Blackstaff Press.

Rabushka, A., and Shepsle, K. 1972. *Politics in Plural Societies: A Theory of Democratic Instability*. Columbus: Merrill.

Rucht, D. 2007. Movement Allies, Adversaries and Third Parties, in *The Blackwell Companion to Social Movements*, edited by D. Snow, S. Soule and H. Kriesi. Oxford: Wiley-Blackwell, 197–216.

Scott, J. P. 2000. *Social Network Analysis: A Handbook*. London: Sage.

Sutton, M. 1994. *Bear in Mind These Dead: Index of Deaths from the Conflict in Ireland, 1969–93*. Belfast: Beyond the Pale Publications.

Tarrow, S. 1989. *Democracy and Disorder: Protest and Politics in Italy, 1965–1975*. Oxford: Clarendon Press.

Tarrow, S. 2011. *Power in Movement: Social Movements and Contentious Politics*. 3rd edn. Cambridge: Cambridge University Press.

Tilly, C. 1978. *From Mobilization to Revolution*. Reading: Addison.

Tilly, C. 2003. *The Politics of Collective Violence*. Cambridge: Cambridge University Press.

Tilly, C. 2005. Terror as Strategy and Relational Process. *International Journal of Comparative Sociology,* 46(1–2), 11–32.

Tilly, C. 2008. *Contentious Performances*. Cambridge: Cambridge University Press.

Tilly, C., and Tarrow, S. 2006. *Contentious Politics*. New York: Paradigm Publishers.

White, R. W. 1989. From Peaceful Protest to Guerrilla War: Micromobilization of the Provisional Irish Republican Army. *The American Journal of Sociology,* 94(6), 1277–1302.

White, R. W. 1993. *Provisional Irish Republicans: An Oral and Interpretive History*. Westport, CT: Greenwood.

Wiktorowicz, Q. 2004. *Islamic Activism: a Social Movement Theory Approach*. Bloomington, IN: Indiana University Press.

Chapter 7

The Limits of Radicalization: Escalation and Restraint in the South African Liberation Movement

Devashree Gupta

Introduction

On 21 March 1960 several thousand men, women, and children assembled in front of the police station in Sharpeville, an African township about 70 km south of Johannesburg, in order to engage in a nationwide act of civil disobedience against apartheid. In Sharpeville, as in dozens of other locations across South Africa, protestors were instructed to leave behind their passbooks—hated instruments of coercion and control that black South Africans were required to carry at all times—and present themselves to the police for arrest. The Pan Africanist Congress (PAC), which had organized the protest, believed that if enough people defied the law and were arrested, "it would bring the country to a halt" and with sufficient critical mass, "the effect … would be to clog the legal machinery … [and] in an indirect way, to bring industry to a halt" (Lodge 2011: 62).

While most of the day's protests unfolded peacefully and without incident, in Sharpeville, things took a disruptive turn as an unexpectedly large crowd—estimated between 5,000 and 20,000—clashed with a skittish and over-reactive police force (Reeves 1961). The violence that ensued left 69 people dead and hundreds more wounded, many of whom were shot in the back as they fled the area (Frankel 2001: 140–50). The incident immediately triggered further unrest both locally and more broadly. In the days following the massacre, riots, killings, and destruction of property in Sharpeville and neighboring townships led to a mounting death toll and between R13–50 million (approximately \$18–70 million in 2010 USD) in damages (Parker and Mokhesi-Parker 1998: 12). Beyond the region, Sharpeville touched off riots, marches, protests, and strikes in other cities and townships across the country.

The government's swift and harsh response to this unrest proved to be a critical turning point for the anti-apartheid movement. Within two weeks, authorities had declared a general state of emergency making it possible to detain people secretly and without warrants. It prohibited public assemblies, suppressed subversive publications, criminalized strikes and stayaways, banned key liberation groups including the PAC and the African National Congress (ANC), arrested thousands of activists including many in leadership positions, and all but eradicated domestic space for public organizing and protest. In response to this sudden increase in repression, the ANC and PAC both determined that the time had come to abandon what had been wholly non-violent movement tactics and turn instead to a mixed approach involving armed struggle (Magubane et al. 2004). The lesson both organizations took away from Sharpeville was that non-violence had limited effect against the government, and since such appeals not only seemed destined to fall on deaf ears but invited even more harsh reprisals, they "concluded they had no choice but to establish armed wings" (Seidman 2000: 164). Resistance against the apartheid state did not stop, even after such a highly coercive response, but it did assume a different, more strident form (Lichbach 1995, Francisco 2004).

So far, this is a fairly conventional illustration of how movements might radicalize. It highlights how relational factors—in this case, the interactions between movement groups and the state—concatenate and contribute to the iterative escalation of tactics, goals, and/or rhetoric in a dynamic and contingent way (della Porta 1995, Alimi 2011: 100, Alimi, Bosi, and Demetriou 2012). Neither the PAC nor the ANC were destined to take up violence. It was only after the South African state made alternative political options less viable and changed "the movement's strategic position vis-à-vis the political environment and the subsequent influence on its ability to exert political leverage" (Alimi, Bosi, and Demetriou 2012: 10) that these two organizations embraced armed struggle; even then, neither abandoned non-violence but merely supplemented it with more transgressive tactics (Zunes 1999).

But while the events surrounding Sharpeville can be understood using relational models of radicalization, what happens next is not as easy to explain: after the initial escalation from non-violence to armed struggle, the radicalization process dwindles, even though pressures and incentives to radicalize do not disappear or weaken. In the case of the ANC and PAC, both groups chose to move from non-violence to armed struggle at the same time and in response to the same state-movement stimuli. But once both organizations made that transition, the PAC adopted a more intransigent stance that the ANC refused to counter despite seemingly strong incentives to do so. The relational dynamics within the liberation movement—particularly the amount of intra-movement competition that existed between these two groups—would lead us to predict increasing radicalization, not a downgraded dynamic (McCauley and Moskalenko 2008: 425–26). Consequently, the unwillingness of the ANC to follow the PAC into increasingly radical repertoires requires further scrutiny.

The first step to untangling this puzzle is to acknowledge that radicalization is not a process of infinite regress. Once set in motion, it does not continue in perpetuity, even if the initial conditions that triggered the process remain constant. Just as it is important to unpack what the dynamics of radicalization are—those processes and mechanisms that lead to an escalation of rhetoric, goals, and actions—it is equally important to investigate the mechanisms that slow or stop those processes. This is not the same thing as investigating de-radicalization or non-radicalization. De-radicalization implies movement away from radical stances and reversing earlier escalations; but neither the PAC nor the ANC reversed their choice to escalate into armed struggle. Non-radicalization implies that the radicalization process never started at all; the PAC and ANC, on the other hand deliberately chose to adopt more transgressive methods after Sharpeville. Rather than these alternatives, the South African case gives us an opportunity to investigate *stalled* or *limited* radicalization—cases in which radicalization takes place but where that process is (perhaps unexpectedly) curtailed in some way.

The answer for this divergence cannot be merely that "the ANC is not as radical as the PAC" or that "PAC members are more militant." Such statements fail to capture the way in which interactions shape actions and simply essentialize organizations as either "radical" or "not radical." Instead, it is important to understand how the interactions and relations within and among groups in the movement come to shape and constrain tactical repertoires. But relational mechanisms cannot be applied mechanistically, and even though mechanisms in themselves may be modular and largely invariant from one social setting to another (McAdam, Tarrow, and Tilly 2001: 27, Tarrow 2010), the effect that relational mechanisms have is contingent not only on the context in which they operate but also on the particular identities of the actors that are being connected. *Who* is connected in these relationships matters as much as the nature of the connection itself. As a result, the same radicalizing mechanism applied to two organizations in the same movement at the same time can have very different results; it can lead to one group staking out radical territory while others choose not to adopt radical methods or rhetoric.

Drawing on a combination of original and secondary sources,[1] I argue that in the case of the South African liberation movement, the impetus to radicalize after Sharpeville is blunted by three countervailing forces. First, organizations factor in whether their rivals represent a credible threat to their own position or power when determining whether outbidding and radicalization are strategically savvy moves. Organizations that feel secure or who believe rival groups present little threat are less likely to radicalize; only those groups that feel threatened by competing

---

1 This analysis utilizes information from a combination of secondary sources and original data collection, including oral histories of movement participants collected by the South African Democracy Education Trust; new interviews with 34 current and former members of the liberation movement, government, and NGOs conducted between October 19, 2004-March 9, 2005 in Cape Town, Johannesburg, and Durban; and analysis of internal memos, correspondence, policy statements, manifestos, press releases, and speeches from liberation movement organizations archived at the University of Cape Town manuscript and archives collection, the Mayibuye Archives at the University of the Western Cape, the South African History Archive at the University of the Witwatersrand, the National Archives, and the South Africa political materials collection, Institute of Commonwealth Studies at the University of London. Additional material came from ANC and PAC journals that were circulated to members and supporters, which have subsequently been digitized and archived by Digital Innovation South Africa, University of KwaZulu Natal (http://www.disa.ukzn.ac.za/).

groups will be likely to rise to the bait of an outbidding ploy. This assessment of threat, in turn, can depend on any number of organizational attributes, including the rival group's membership size, level of external support, and capacity to carry out strategic goals. Second, an organization's own identity conditions whether it feels pressure to differentiate itself from its main rivals via outbidding. Organizations that lack a distinct identity, historical legacy, or favorable reputation are more likely to turn to radical claims as a method of distinguishing themselves from their more well-known competitors. Groups that are secure in their identity, on the other hand, have less incentive to take up extreme stances to stand out from rivals and, therefore, are less likely to become enmeshed in a spiral of radicalization. These two factors taken together create a dynamic that actively constrains further radicalization by associating extreme positions with weak, non-threatening, and fringe actors and framing radical tactics as little more than desperation ploys. Radical strategies, when wielded by such organizations, therefore, are more likely to discredit the strategies themselves than make them more appealing to others in the movement.

Finally, choices about radicalization must be filtered through organizational structures where the demands of a group's members and allies have to be weighed against the strategic merits of radicalization. While an organization's members may clamor for more intransigent policies and create an "echo chamber" that encourages more extreme stances, this internal support for radicalization is hardly a given. Even when outbidding might make strategic sense and make a group more competitive with its rivals, if such a change in policy or practice alienates rank-and-file members, it can stall the momentum for radicalization by raising the possibility of factionalism and loss of support within the organization. In the case of the South African liberation movement, all three factors help explain why the PAC took up a more intransigent position after Sharpeville but why the ANC chose not to follow the PAC down a more radical path despite conditions that might otherwise encourage it to do so.

Radicalization Pressures and Mechanisms

Radicalization is a deceptively simple concept. Broadly speaking, it involves a process where "the expansion of collective action frames [leads] to more extreme agendas and the adoption of more transgressive forms of contention" (McAdam, Tarrow, and Tilly 2001: 69). This definition is fairly general and does not attempt to specify what counts as an "extreme" agenda or a "transgressive" tactic. I start from an assumption that extremism and transgressiveness are subjective since two individuals might categorize the same behavior differently; a person's identities, interests, and location in social structures shape whether she decides if a goal or tactic is reasonable or radical, proportional or excessive. Extremism and transgressiveness are also relational because what counts as transgressive in one setting may not be considered transgressive in another, and the same behavior might appear more or less extreme depending on what other reference points exist for comparison, the social context, and the meaning that actors attach to various strategies. After all, a non-violent public demonstration or rally can seem absolutely banal in Paris, but dangerously revolutionary in Pyongyang. As a result, what (or who) counts as "radical" is context-dependent, not an objective marker or trait.

While we conventionally refer to "a" radicalization dynamic, radicalization is not a singular, uniform process that unfolds in the same way, in the same sequence, and with the same starting and ending points in each case. Instead, radicalization is *equifinal* insofar as many different pathways can all lead to the same outcome (for example, see Beach 1977). We might observe radicalization that is induced by changes in how groups perceive the opportunities and threats inherent in their environment; emerging out of competition with rivals within the same movement; prompted by their interactions with state actors, targets, or countermovements; triggered by a larger protest cycle; or complex combinations of these factors (Tarrow 1998, McCauley and Moskalenko 2008, Alimi 2011, Borum 2011, Alimi, Bosi, and Demetriou 2012). Moreover, while the overall process of radicalization is equifinal, the mechanisms that can trigger that process are each themselves *multifinal* because the same trigger does not inevitably cause the same outcome in some deterministic way. Rather, a trigger can produce different results based on the context and the actors who are involved.

While radicalization pressures exist in a wide variety of movement sectors, and any one movement could feature multiple radicalizing mechanisms, the South African liberation movement provides a particularly useful laboratory to investigate the role that intra-movement competition plays in these processes. Though movement-state interactions (and their impact on groups' assessment of threat and opportunity) were central to both the ANC and PAC initially embracing the armed struggle, this particular relational nexus, I argue, recedes in importance as a primary trigger after 1960 primarily because state-movement interactions become more indirect. Following their banning, neither the ANC nor the PAC were truly able to operate within South Africa. Both groups had their key leaders either in prison or in exile and their grassroots organizational structures had deteriorated sharply in the 1960s and 1970s (Houston and Magubane 2004a, ka Plaatjie 2004a). As a result, these groups had less direct contact with the South African state in the post-Sharpeville period than before the massacre. And while the state's coercive power weighed heavily on ordinary citizens, many of the individuals in the liberation movement who could influence goals and tactics and shape organizational strategies had more direct contact with government officials in Europe, or Lusaka, or Moscow than functionaries in Pretoria.[2] I do not suggest that the state and its interactions with the liberation movement were irrelevant in the 1960s and 1970s—only that this particular relationship becomes comparatively less important as a potential trigger for radicalization.

---

2   Author's interview with former UDF member, Cape Town, November 22, 2004.

Intra-movement Competition, Differentiation, and Audience Support

Social movement groups operate in an environment of scarcity. Nothing that a movement needs to be successful—material resources, access to sympathetic elites, public exposure, and dedicated activists—comes with an endless supply. Even in the most prosperous of societies with vigorous protections for social protest and dissent, movement groups operate in something of a zero-sum environment: if one group takes up space on the airwaves or attracts donor funds, there is comparatively less to go around for everyone else. This fact holds true in general, but this scramble for scarce movement goods is particularly critical for organizations that exist within the same movement industry (Zald and McCarthy 1987). While public support for an environmental group may not (greatly) diminish the amount of public support that is available to a human rights group (assuming that members of the public can sympathize with and do support multiple issues and organizations), it is more likely that support for one environmental group will reduce the support available to other environmental groups. This is not an iron-clad rule, but a reasonable assumption given that individuals are likely to prioritize where to allocate their own finite amounts of time, energy, and/or resources rather than spread them thinly over a large number of groups. While movement groups can potentially lessen this competition by staking out specialized niches catering to different and non-overlapping constituencies, in practice, it is unlikely that a niche strategy will cancel out the zero-sum logic of competition entirely (McPherson 1983, Stern 1999).

In this competitive environment, movement organizations hoping to draw the attention of potential supporters, activists, and donors must make themselves noticeable and, perhaps even more importantly, make themselves distinguishable in order to attract needed resources. Especially in movements with many contending organizations, differentiating one's own group from a rival group can mean the difference between being able to acquire the resources necessary to operate successfully and not being able to operate at all. Hence, movement organizations that see themselves as competitors have a vested interest in creating and then policing clear boundaries between themselves and their rivals in order to make it easier for those outside the movement to tell groups apart.[3] Such boundary maintenance is a core component of intra-movement competition (Alimi, Bosi, and Demetriou 2012: 10–11) and can be organized around a number of different traits: tactical choices, policy preferences, underlying ideology, membership demographics, past successes, and so on. What matters is not the content of the border that is drawn, but that it is drawn clearly and subsequently maintained.

---

3   There are plausible, strategic reasons why movement groups may not always want to demarcate organizational identities so clearly, including riding a more successful group's coattails or discrediting a rival group by generating bad publicity and blaming the rival. Therefore, this pressure to differentiate should be understood as generally, but not inevitably true.

In the liberation movement, for example, the PAC and ANC differentiated themselves based on their dissimilar approaches to coalition building across different racial groups (the PAC promoted an "Africa for Africans" philosophy while the ANC embraced multi-racialism); by their ideological sympathies (the ANC partnered with the South African Communist Party (SACP), advocated socialist economic policies, and counted Moscow as a patron while the PAC initially rejected communism outright to win the support of the United States and then later modified its anti-communist stance in order to receive financial backing from China).[4] Tactically, the PAC self-identified as more aggressive and willing to employ revolutionary methods than the ANC did. These differences reduced any potential confusion about the groups' ideologies, goals, and strategic orientation.

At the same time, strong and clear boundaries and sharply differentiated organizational identities are not, in themselves, sufficient to win over the hearts and minds of the public and potential supporters. Organizations may succeed in creating distinct identities for themselves, but if that identity is based on goals or tactics that do not resonate with the target audience, clarity becomes irrelevant. As a result, organizations must carefully attend to the general preferences and values of their audience and how they frame their ideas to ensure compatibility with those preferences and values (Snow et al. 1986, Snow and Benford 1988, Benford and Snow 2000, Croteau and Hicks 2003). After all, social movements of all stripes feature organizations that are distinct and different—and marginal—because, in part, the message or goal they put forward is out of step with what their intended audience will accept or understand.

Even if organizations frame their messages so that they resonate with the public and create/maintain clear boundaries between themselves and potential rivals, radicalization is not inevitable. All of the above actions can be taken without groups adopting extreme stances. If, in fact, the audience is fairly moderate and a group's potential supporters likely to respond to incremental, as opposed to revolutionary strategies, then radicalization would be an irrational choice from a purely strategic point of view. It is true that in many social movements, the distribution of public preferences will skew to extremes depending in part on the intensity of grievances and how willing the state appears to be to address those grievances. But as Elise Giuliano argues with respect to ethnic mobilization in Tatarstan, public preferences about tactics, goals, and remedies are not set in stone but socially constructed and, therefore, fluid (Giuliano 2000).

---

4 The amounts that liberation groups received from external patrons varied tremendously. The Organization of African Unity, for example, allocated the PAC only £1,752 and gave the ANC £2,750 in 1971–1972 (Ndlovu 2004: 645). The United Nations Educational and Cultural Organization (UNESCO), on the other hand, allocated over $460,000 to the PAC in 1982 to fund a variety of educational programs, including training teachers for the PAC training center in Tanzania and providing scholarships for PAC-sponsored exiles (UNESCO 1987).

144   *Dynamics of Political Violence*

Consequently, competition among groups may exist in a movement, and may even be ferocious. But intra-movement competition is not sufficient in itself to spur radicalization; that only occurs when competition takes place in a context where moving to more extreme points on the tactical or ideological spectrum increases the likelihood of being rewarded by the audience. If a movement is located in such an environment—for example, where high levels of government repression have fueled intense grievances—then whichever organization occupies the most extreme position stands to increase its relative power in the movement. Such positioning, in turn, creates incentives for its rivals to outflank it in order to claim they are more devoted to the cause and better guardians of the community's interest. Left unchecked, such outbidding processes can polarize the political space and leave the moderate middle ground—the space where bargaining and compromise is most likely—significantly weakened (White 1989, Saxton 2005).

For most movements, finding that ideal competitive spot on the tactical and ideological spectrum is an imperfect, inexact process of continual adjustment. Movements rarely have precise information about public preferences and where the movement equivalent of the "median voter" might be located. The fact that the movement's median audience member is not fixed but can change her own preferences in response to her interactions with the state, movement groups, potential supporters, bystanders, and critics further complicates the matter; what the audience wants and will reward is a moving target. There is also the danger of overestimating the audience's appetite for extremism and taking up a position so radical that it alienates or scares away potential supporters (McCauley and Moskalenko 2008: 424). Miscalculation is costly, but in addition, it creates a larger dampening effect on overall movement radicalization via demonstration effect: the failure of one group to win over supporters via an outbidding ploy defines the outer perimeter of acceptable positions to observant rivals who benefit from that knowledge at the expense of the unsuccessful group. Finally, assuming that movement activists are not purely instrumental power-maximizers and actually have sincere ideological commitments of their own that inform their activism, they may not be particularly enthusiastic about adjusting their own priorities or tactics just to appeal to the public.

The above discussion underscores a few critical points. First, resource scarcity makes intra-movement competition a common feature of movement life. With the exception of groups that only appeal to mutually exclusive niche audiences, movement organizations must be prepared to figuratively throw some elbows to acquire the resources they need. Second, competition requires movement groups to differentiate themselves from their rivals; failure to do so can limit an organization's strength and, worst-case scenario, threaten its ability to function at all. Third, the identities that organizations create for themselves via boundary maintenance must be calibrated to resonate with the potential audience. And finally, it is only when the potential audience itself holds views that are sympathetic to radical positions that this sequence of intra-movement competition will trigger a larger radicalization process. These connections are summarized in Figure 7.1.

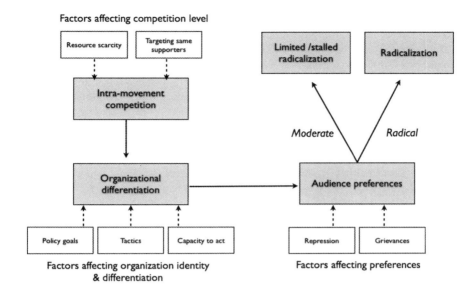

Figure 7.1   Intra-movement radicalization process

Radicalization, therefore, is not inevitable but highly contingent on the interactions that connect movements, the public, and the state. When it comes to intra-movement interaction, it is only when there is strong competition due to scarcity, clear organizational differentiation, *and* a preference on the part of the audience to reward radical stances that a radicalization spiral will ensue; absent any of these factors, radicalization will be limited.

Understanding the dynamics between the ANC and PAC, therefore, requires us first to scrutinize if their interactions would lead us to expect a radicalization spiral in the first place; if these above criteria are not fulfilled, then it is not particularly puzzling that radicalization does not continue past the initial turn to armed struggle.[5] If, however, these conditions are met, then we can explore how and why the outcome deviates from our expectations.

Internal Competition in the South African Liberation Movement

From the very beginning, the liberation movement was internally fragmented, with organizations representing different ethnic communities, regions, occupational, and economic groups. Towering over all of these groups, however, was the

---

   5   The initial radicalization process does not need to conform to the above conditions because it stems from a different triggering mechanism that comes from movement/state interactions. Consequently, it would have its own internal logic and requirements.

146   *Dynamics of Political Violence*

African National Congress, which had opposed the state's racial policies since 1912—longer than any other organization, save for the Natal Indian Congress. While originally formed to represent the interests of the black population, by mid-century the ANC aligned itself with the principles of the Freedom Charter, which explicitly sought to unite different parts of the liberation movement together and articulate an inclusive, multiracial agenda that would appeal to many different constituencies. As Nelson Mandela wrote of the Congress and the Charter, "[f]or the first time in the history of our country the democratic forces irrespective of race, ideological conviction, party affiliation or religious belief have renounced and discarded racialism in all its ramification … and united in a common programme of action" (Mandela 1956: 5). For the ANC, there was strength to be found in diversity.

But the multiracial Charter and the ANC's willingness to work with white, Indian, and Coloured groups was not universally supported. Dissidents within the ANC argued that liberation had to come from Africans themselves in order to be meaningful, and rejected cooperation across the color lines, particularly (though not exclusively) with the Indian community and the (largely white) South African Communist Party. Though who exactly was classified as "African" turned out to be something of a moving target, these dissidents defined their core audience more narrowly than groups that subscribed to the Freedom Charter (Adam and Moodley 1993). In 1959, this faction broke away from the ANC and formed the Pan Africanist Congress, which not only adopted the more uncompromising language of the Black Consciousness movement and more militant policy goals, but also called for more aggressive forms of direct action that could awaken the masses and mobilize them against the state. Though also non-violent in its initial orientation, the PAC believed that the ANC was too moderate to achieve any meaningful change and that it was the PAC, with its revolutionary political orientation that would transform the political landscape (Mayekiso 1968).

Prior to Sharpeville, both the ANC and PAC thought of themselves as primarily non-violent organizations. Though there was discussion within each group about the merits of more transgressive methods, at most, they participated in limited forms of direct action (Magubane et al. 2004). It was only with the 1952 Defiance Campaign, for example, that the ANC moved decisively away from the more conservative and institutionalized forms of opposition that had characterized its early years and engaged more systematically in small acts of civil disobedience—for instance, sitting on whites-only benches, entering post offices and railway stations through entrances reserved for Europeans, moving into and around urban areas without the necessary passes, and violating curfew (Bonner, Marks, and Rathbone 1982, Reddy 1987). The PAC, too, emphasized its commitment to peaceful methods. Speaking on the eve of the Sharpeville protests, for example, Robert Sobukwe, the group's founder and president, instructed his followers that "our people must be taught now and continuously that in this campaign, we are going to observe absolute nonviolence" (Mwakikagile 2008: 50).

This common approach, however, masked a sometimes-acrimonious relationship in which each organization saw the other as a potential rival for power, resources, public support, and the spotlight. In his autobiography, Nelson Mandela described the relationship between the two as more "competitive than cooperative" and characterized by "long and often bitter differences" (Mandela 2003: 162). For instance, Victor Mayekiso, a writer for the PAC journal *Africanist News and Views*, railed that "[f]or half-a-century, the African people led by this ANC leadership, expended their energy uselessly and futilely. Actuated by insatiable love for glorified positions, this leadership led the African people into abandoning the basic principles of their revolutionary motivation … " (Mayekiso 1968: 2). On the ANC side, some described the PAC as "a cancer," and worried how its early successes could prove to be quite costly: "they were attracting very interesting young people, and educated people, high school people, intellectuals, and so on, and they were getting the people we weren't getting," which was potentially problematic insofar as "an organization that did not have the support of youth could not survive" (Magubane et al. 2004: 67).

This competition and general mistrust meant that each organization attempted to improve its position vis-à-vis the other. The anti-passbook protest that led to the Sharpeville massacre is a classic example: one week after the ANC approved an anti-passbook campaign at its annual conference, the PAC decided it would upstage the ANC by scheduling its own campaign one week earlier. After the Sharpeville crackdown, the competitive stakes increased even more. Media coverage of the massacre put the PAC in the spotlight and brought it international attention. When its leaders went to other countries to drum up support, particularly other sub-Saharan countries, their Africanist views resonated more than the ANC's broad, multiracial ideology, and represented a potential threat to the ANC's overseas alliance-building and fundraising efforts (Esterhuyse and Nel 1990: 27–8, Gerhart and Karis 1991: 321, Ndlovu 2004). Arianna Lissoni suggests that by 1962 the PAC represented enough of a threat that, while touring other African states, Mandela "was taken aback on discovering how much support the PAC had gained abroad" and suggested the ANC needed to reposition itself strategically to be able to compete with the PAC and "be clearly seen as the leader, especially on issues directly affecting Africans" (Lissoni 2009: 291–92, 2010: 60). This competition continued in exile, as both vied with each other to attract financial backers and foot soldiers, especially able-bodied individuals willing to uproot themselves and join the armed struggle (Mphahlele 2002: 55).

Thus, the interactions between the ANC and PAC in this period suggest a competitive relationship and attempts at differentiation that could easily lead to radicalization. But in order for radicalization to occur, the intra-movement competition mechanism also requires a context where the target audience rewards outbidding and extreme positions. While the preferences of the broad public are hard to pinpoint in a setting like apartheid South Africa, by the early 1960s, the black population seemed to be growing increasingly restless and open to more radical ways of resistance. They were spurred in part by increasingly coercive government policies that tried to reverse a growing concentration of non-whites near urban centers by implementing residential segregation throughout the country. Policies like the Group Areas Act and the Pass Laws restricted population movement and forcibly relocated hundreds of thousands of individuals from their homes, touching off waves of protest in urban areas and activating new constituencies who had not been substantially involved in protest before (Mabin 1992, Smith and Mabin 1992, Wells 1993). The government's policies also helped radicalize rural areas via policies like the Bantu Administration Act, which created nominally independent Bantustans, or "homelands" ruled by tribal elders who were no more than puppets of the state. This rural discontent, in turn, sparked widespread revolts in Mpondoland and Thembuland (Mabin 1991, Matoti and Ntsebeza 2004). University students, teachers, and intellectuals also turned increasingly to Africanist theories of cognitive liberation that were emerging throughout Africa. These different populations, for their own reasons, were less inclined to support the kind of incremental, moderate tactics historically associated with the ANC and thus, created a real possibility that radical strategies would be given a sympathetic hearing and potentially rewarded. As Lodge notes, the PAC's hardline stance "evoked a profound response from men who had been forced off the land, whose families were being subjugated to every form of official harassment, as well as economic deprivation, who perceived every relationship with authority in terms of conflict" (Lodge 1986: 182). In such a climate, groups that failed to match the public mood would risk being perceived as irrelevant or out of touch (Mathabatha 2004: 306).

Moreover, there was reason to suspect that a more intransigent, radical vision would also be beneficial for lining up external allies and funders, especially in other African states where an Africanist philosophy would be familiar. The ANC was also fully aware of this point, as Mandela noted in his autobiography:

> I reported in detail the reservations I had encountered about the ANC's cooperation with whites, Indians, and particularly communists. Still ringing in my ears was my final meeting with the Zambian leaders, who told me … they understood the PAC's pure African nationalism but were bewildered by the ANC's non-racialism and communist ties. (Mandela 2003: 384–85).

Some in the ANC leadership feared that without calibrating their own policies to make them resonate with the frames that potential allies already held, they risked the PAC getting the bulk of the support and turning into a more significant threat (Magubane et al. 2004: 133). This competition for the attention and support of sympathetic allies, therefore, would have acted as a potentially powerful signal for the moderate ANC to shift policies and match (or exceed) the more intransigent PAC.

Thus, in multiple ways, both the PAC and ANC competed with each other for power and position and their relations were largely antagonistic. Moreover, this competition was grounded in careful boundary maintenance that emphasized, among other things, the Africanist vs. multiracial analysis of the two groups. And

The Limits of Radicalization   149

there was reason to believe that potential allies—both inside and outside of the country—might initially be more accepting of (and inclined to reward) the PAC's more intransigent Africanist stance over the ANC's approach. Such conditions would seem favorable to radicalization. I turn next to an examination of whether such radicalization actually unfolded.

Radicalism in the Liberation Movement

When the ANC and PAC were still allowed to operate above ground in South Africa, they both embraced non-violence as their dominant method of protest. Rhetorically, however, the two groups tried to create and maintain some kind of boundary to differentiate themselves by focusing on *who* should be part of the movement and *how effective* each group was likely to be. The PAC juxtaposed its vitality and commitment to direct action against the ANC's historically tentative and incremental approach (Gerhart 1979: 222). And it contrasted its own commitment to the idea that Africans should be the agents of their own liberation with the ANC, which "was presented as being both conservative and the instrument of Communists, whites and Indian merchants" (Dadoo 1962, Coetzee, Gilfillan, and Hulec 2002: 42). The ANC's leaders countered by dismissing the PAC as "compromised and opportunistic," and emphasized the Africanists' lack of power and influence. Walter Sisulu characterized the PAC as full of "young chaps who were not important, who had no influence whatsoever"; and Joe Slovo memorably described the PAC and its pre-Sharpeville activism as the "dampest of squibs"[6] which, as far as accusations of ineffectiveness go, is both evocative and damning (Magubane et al. 2004: 66).

After Sharpeville, the two groups drifted further apart, not just in terms of their rhetorical claims but in terms of actual tactics. When both organizations embraced armed struggle, their differences became more self-evident. The ANC and PAC's paramilitary wings—respectively, Umkhonto we Sizwe (MK), meaning "spear of the nation," and Poqo,[7] meaning "pure" or "alone"—developed operating philosophies that sharply differed from one another. In setting up MK, the ANC instructed Nelson Mandela to focus the group's activities on sabotage and avoid harming individuals at all costs, in part so that any post-conflict reconciliation in a future democratic South Africa easier might be easier to achieve (Maaba 2004: 258, Magubane et al. 2004: 89, Lodge 2011: 216). Though deaths did occur, MK's targets tended to involve economic and government targets: attacks on the security forces, explosions in official buildings, damaging railway lines, fuel depots, and power stations, and so on (Lodge 1987: 3, 2011: 216).

Poqo did not exercise the same moderation but pursued a far more radical vision from the start. In a departure from MK, Poqo deliberately intended to

---

6   A squib is a very small firecracker or explosive device.

7   Poqo was later renamed/succeeded by APLA, the Azanian People's Liberation Army, in 1968. For clarity, I refer to the organization as Poqo throughout this discussion.

kill those it associated with the continued oppression of Africans, and defined the membership of this group expansively. In its submission to the Truth and Reconciliation Commission, the PAC explained that "the enemy of the liberation movement ... and of its people was always the settler Colonial regime of South Africa" which was supported not only by the security forces but *all* white South Africans who propped up an illegitimate order. The PAC concluded, therefore, that "[i]t would ... be a fallacy in the context of white South Africa to talk about innocent civilians" (APLA 1997). Thus, any white citizen of the country—be it a government official, representative of the security forces, or ordinary civilian— was considered a legitimate target. It was Poqo that sought to "drive the settlers into the sea" and, in another incarnation of the same idea, promised "one settler, one bullet" and that "[t]he Whites will suffer—the African people will rule. Freedom comes after bloodshed. Poqo has started" (*Rand Daily Mail*, March 23, 1963).

Creating a full inventory of Poqo attacks is a nearly impossible task; not only is the reporting and press coverage of such incidents incomplete, but in official reports, Poqo attacks involving seizures of land or resources from white farmers and businesses may have been classified as robberies rather than part of the liberation struggle and therefore, not necessarily linked to the organization at all (Gerhart and Glaser 2010: 154). Even so, it is not hard to get a flavor of the kinds of tactics that Poqo employed: hacking shopkeepers to death with axes; stabbing and beating to death three women who, against Poqo rules, had been smuggled into a male hostel for a party; beating, setting on fire, and even decapitating suspected informants; and in one headline-grabbing case, killing and mutilating two white members of a road crew as well as one man's wife and his 16-year old and 11-year old daughters (Maaba 2004). Poqo's campaigns included targeting members of the police, assassinations of Bantustan leaders (who were viewed as collaborators and traitors), and indiscriminate killings of whites to instill terror into the population. In their TRC submission, the organization noted that it did not make a distinction between "hard" and "soft" targets, and that it viewed "every white citizen [as] a member of the security establishment" (APLA 2007).

When it came to civilians, Poqo militants showed little inclination towards restraint. One of Poqo's most notorious campaigns took place in Paarl, a town 60 km northeast of Cape Town. On November 22, 1962—the "Night of the Long Knives"—a group of between 200–250 men assembled around 2:30 am and set off to attack the police station. Forewarned, the police were prepared for the mob and drove them away, at which point the group

> split into smaller groups and attacked shops, petrol stations, houses and cars at random. One group moved into the white suburbs and attacked the residents of various houses. Rencia Vermeulen (17) and Frans Richards (21) were hacked and beaten to death, while others were injured. Property damage was estimated at R37,250 [approximately $371,500 in 2010 USD]. (Lodge 1982, Maaba 2004: 272–73).

Such episodic bursts of violence by Poqo cells at the local level were also accompanied by plans for a coordinated, nationwide uprising that would involve attacking the police, government offices, and taking control of communication networks. This plan also explicitly set aside four hours to kill members of the white population (Lodge 2011: 201).

MK was far more restrained than Poqo, which staked out an extreme and uncompromising position on how violence should be wielded in the liberation movement. MK leaders focused mostly on symbolic targets of the apartheid state, using armed struggle more as a dramatic form of propaganda to increase the ANC's reputation and standing rather than to terrorize the public; it tried to avoid targeting civilians entirely (Ellis 1991, Lodge 2011: 223). In the first three years of its operations, it carried out nearly 200 acts of sabotage with no deaths or injuries, though the details needed to parse out these earlier events more precisely are unavailable (Lodge 1987; ANC 1997). In the 1960s and 1970s, when many of its top leaders, including Nelson Mandela, were imprisoned, MK attacks mostly ceased (ANC 1997), and the organization used this period of dormancy to build up its organizational structures, create training camps outside the country, reach out to external allies, and plan for future operations within the country, rather than engage in the indiscriminate killings of civilians (Barrell 1990a, Houston and Magubane 2004a, 2004b, Lissoni 2009).

It was only after 1976, when MK was revitalized by new recruits streaming out of South Africa in the wake of the student-led uprisings in Soweto and elsewhere, that the organization resumed a steady stream of armed attacks. It was at this point that MK's list of targets expanded to include the police and South African defense forces as well as state officials and those who cooperated with them (ANC 1997). Unlike the PAC, collaborators were defined more narrowly, and consisted of mostly informants, black officials, and security personnel who explicitly had ties to the state. Like Poqo, MK's activities also resulted in fatalities, though many of the civilian casualties were inadvertent rather than deliberate. According to the ANC's Truth and Reconciliation Commission submission, between 1977–1989, MK operations resulted in the deaths of 129 police and security personnel, government officials, and those with ties to the state, 139 MK operatives, and 55 civilians. In a sense, MK inflicted more harm than Poqo by sheer volume,[8] though Poqo certainly *intended* to inflict more harm and a higher body count than MK. Even as late as 1997, three years after the democratic transition, Letlapa Mphahlele, the PAC Director of Operations, claimed that "there was no regret and no apology offered" for the civilian victims in this period (TRC 2003).

---

8   The PAC's Amnesty Application to the TRC listed 204 attacks, most of which were concentrated in a four-year period (1990–1994), and which resulted in 109 deaths, 24 of whom were civilians. The data reported here and for MK actions are only illustrative. The time periods are not directly comparable since MK had largely scaled down operations by the early 1990s and PAC/Poqo submissions to the TRC did not include pre-1990 actions (TRC 2003).

152   *Dynamics of Political Violence*

It is also worth nothing that MK's human targeting and resulting death rate is also not constant across this post-1976 period. According to the ANC's submission to the TRC, there were low levels of human casualties between 1977 and 1984 with most of the violence against people occurring between 1985 and 1988; the South African Institute for Race Relations and the Institute for Strategic Studies at the University of Pretoria report a 209 per cent increase in the number of MK attacks from 1984 to 1985 and a 69 per cent increase from 1985 to 1986 (reported in ANC 1997). After 1988, when the state released a number of political prisoners and the new government of F.W. de Klerk indicated a willingness to consider reform, the number of MK attacks dwindled sharply. Poqo, however, continued its operations through this period.

Thus, while MK's operations did result in fatalities, the timing of when these fatalities occurred suggests that it did not seem overly pressured to move towards a more extreme targeting philosophy simply because one of its main rivals occupied a more intransigent position. Had intra-movement radicalization been present, MK's turn to a more extreme targeting philosophy would have been more in lockstep with Poqo's timeline of activities. Yet MK did not respond to Poqo's headline-grabbing attacks in the early 1960s, and it wound down its operations after 1988 while Poqo continued to use violence. In fact, in an interview with Howard Barrell, ANC National Executive Committee member Ronnie Kasrils specifically noted that due to Poqo's indiscriminate targeting, the ANC and MK took greater pains to stress the need for disciplined and organized operations among its cadres. Rather than outbidding Poqo, Kasrils suggests the very opposite occurred: that there was a concerted effort to *not* follow Poqo's lead (Barrell 1990b).

Instead, the shift in MK targeting that took place between 1984 and 1988 was more a response to heightened conflict with South African security forces and an overall increase in state repression rather than dynamics within the liberation movement itself. In this period, there was increased unrest throughout the country, especially in the townships, which erupted in protest over, among other things, tariff increases for municipal services, price hikes for bus fares, and the recently convened Tricameral parliament, a regime "reform" intended to co-opt Indian and Coloured populations and detach them from the liberation movement (Simpson 2009). As the turmoil continued, the government imposed a state of emergency in 1985 and stepped up its repression and surveillance as well. Reintroducing the idea of equifinality, therefore, the timing of MK's more radical (and deadly) tactical turn is more easily explained by movement-state radicalization processes and not intra-movement radicalization.

So how can we characterize the relationship between the PAC and ANC, their armed wings, and their relative strategic positions? I argue that the evidence supports a fairly unambiguous distinction between the PAC and Poqo's radicalism and the ANC and MK's relative moderation. In terms of their rhetoric, the kinds of targets they acknowledged as legitimate, and the actual operations they carried out, Poqo consistently took up a position on the ANC's flanks. It called for, and carried out more destructive acts, perhaps not in sheer quantity, but in intent and psychological devastation. Had the organization achieved a similar scale to MK in terms of membership numbers and organization, it seems very likely that it would have outstripped MK in total deaths; the members of Poqo would have no doubt wished for that very thing. Poqo set out to terrorize South Africans and committed atrocities to do so. MK, on the other hand, was more selective about how it employed armed struggle and its resulting destructiveness. Its broader reach meant it did inflict more damage and death in absolute terms, but again, there is a confounding issue of organizational scale that is relevant here.

Ultimately, because "radicalness" is a relative term, the chief question is not whether MK's approach represents an objectively moderate course of activity. Within the liberation movement, there were groups that never chose violence as a tactic. Compared to these groups, MK is certainly more radical. But is MK radical compared to Poqo? In intent, in action, in focus, it is not. Moreover, there is no evidence that MK adjusted its strategy to match Poqo's more intransigent stance. It remained committed to a multiracial philosophy, it did not explicitly set out to target civilians more broadly, it focused on symbols and agents of the apartheid state, and did not change any of these core elements of its approach during its existence. In other words, despite there being a radical competitor on its flank, and despite that competitor having some appeal to a population that could conceivably reward and respond to it, the ANC did not take the bait. Having initially adopted the armed struggle in response to the *state's* actions, it did not subsequently adopt a more radical vision of armed struggle in response to the *PAC's* activities, even though radicalization mechanisms based on intra-movement competition might lead us to expect that it would have done just this. In the next section, I explore why this might be the case.

Countervailing Dynamics and Processes

The above discussion underscores the basic point that intra-movement rivalry is not sufficient for radicalization. In the South African example, each of the necessary components of the larger radicalization dynamic was present in some form—competition to win over new supporters, incentive to differentiate, and an audience that seemed primed to support a more extreme and uncompromising stance. But, I argue, each of these components had an opposing dynamic that blunted the radicalization spiral. Competition can be undermined if the actors involved do not see each other as equals or credible threats. Differentiation matters more for some groups, especially those lacking a distinct organizational identity. Consequently, not all organizations care equally about using outbidding as a way of setting themselves apart from their movement rivals. And while all groups must pay attention to how their frames resonate with the public, the public is not the only group that matters; a group's internal audience—its own members— also must support any strategic shift and, unlike the public, have more power to prevent undesirable shifts from taking place. If a group's members do not support outbidding, it is less likely to occur. These countervailing pressures, which I describe in greater detail below, are depicted in Figure 7.2.

Assessment of Threat and Capacity of Rivals

As noted before, intra-movement competition is an endemic feature of social movements, but the mere existence of competition is not sufficient in itself to change the behaviors of those doing the competing; what is required specifically is *threat* (Williamson 1983). It is only when competition is so threatening that doing nothing would be unwise that competition could potentially trigger radicalization. Threat, in turn, is pegged to an opponent's perceived capacity for action: only rivals that can plausibly make good on their threats are worth taking seriously. Therefore, it is only when competition reaches threatening levels and pits capable rivals against each other that we would expect to see strategic shifts of the kind that radicalization dynamics envisage. Rivals that are not threatening, on the other hand, are not only unlikely to trigger strategic shifts, their weakness may in fact discredit the strategies they do employ, limiting the pressure on their rivals even further. This logic is not unique to social movements. In party politics, candidates running for elected office tend to focus their attention on their main party rivals but generally not to fringe candidates. The 2012 US presidential election, for example, included several candidates from minor parties, but the attention of the two main parties was squarely focused on each other, not on the Green Party, Constitution Party, or Libertarian Party, whose combined campaign spending equaled .57 per cent of what the Republican Party spent and an even more miniscule .35 per cent of what the Democratic Party spent. Together, their collective votes represented 1.45 per cent of the total ballots cast. It is clear why they were not considered threats, and, in turn, why their competitive presence probably did not create the slightest ripple in the strategies of the Romney and Obama campaigns.

In the liberation movement, a similar dynamic emerges. Even though the PAC started out as a potentially serious threat to the ANC because its policies resonated with a potentially critical section of the population, it quickly became apparent that in terms of its operations and structures, the PAC had limited power to challenge the ANC. PAC leaders argued that Africans could be encouraged to rise up in a spontaneous revolution that would overturn the apartheid state and usher in majority rule; the hard and tedious work of creating organizational structures seemed a diversion from the real task of mobilizing the masses and accorded little importance.[9] As a result, not only were their organizational networks underdeveloped and far more informal than the ANC's, they were concentrated in only a few areas, like the Western Cape and the Vaal Triangle (Muller 1981: 498–9, TRC 2003), whereas the ANC had a more national presence (Maaba 2004, Mathabatha 2004). Tellingly, the PAC's stronger presence in the Western Cape meant that in that particular area, it *did* pose more of a credible risk to the

---

9 Author's interview, former PAC member, Cape Town, February 4, 2005.

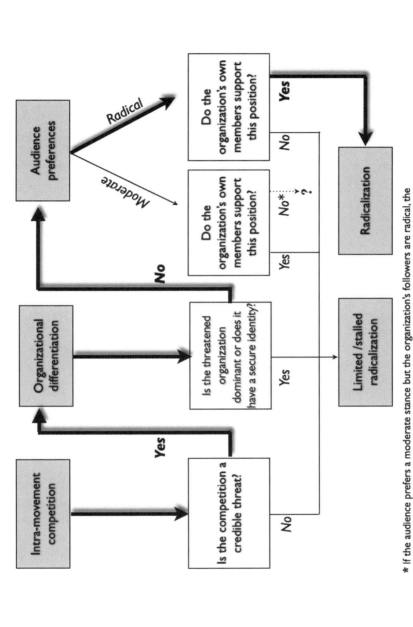

Figure 7.2 Limitations on intra-movement radicalization

* If the audience prefers a moderate stance but the organization's followers are radical, the organization may or may not radicalize; the outcome in this instance is uncertain.

ANC, and, consistent with my argument, it is in the Western Cape that the ANC's local branches and PAC members competed with each other more overtly—and violently (Magubane et al. 2004: 98). As Lissoni notes, it was areas near Paarl and Cape Town (that is, the Western Cape), that "emerged as the most dynamic centers of activity" (Lissoni 2010: 56), and the place where the PAC's violent tendencies emerged the earliest (Lodge 1985, 1986: 183).

The ANC not only had a national presence, it was far better organized, with clearly delineated reporting structures, rules, and procedures. ANC constitutional documents, for example, outlined in detail the relationship between branches, the regional conferences for each state, and the national conference. Each office holder, from the President-General to individual branch members, had their responsibilities spelled out, along with disciplinary procedures and penalties (for example, "reprimand, suspension, expulsion, payment of compensation, the performance of useful tasks, [and] demotion").[10]

The PAC, by contrast, was constantly mired in internecine struggles for leadership, discontent among the rank-and-file members about the lack of democratic process and transparency in the organization, and breathtaking strategic missteps that further weakened the group (Lodge 1984). In 1963, for example, police intercepted coded messages sent from PAC offices in Maseru, Lesotho to operatives in South Africa. The messages, which contained information and instructions about a planned national uprising, also contained the names and addresses of many local activists, who were promptly arrested. Shortly after this blow, the PAC leader, Potlako Leballo, held a press conference in Maseru where he boasted that the group had over 150,000 followers just waiting for his signal to begin the final insurrection against the South African government. This statement swiftly led to a raid on PAC offices, and netted extensive organizational records, information about the PAC's underground network, maps of arms caches, lists of supporters, and other compromising information (Lodge 1986, Lissoni 2010). The organization limped along after this raid, but continued to grapple with internal disputes and mismanagement, all of which attenuated its ability to function effectively and undermined its credibility as a serious contender for movement leadership. Ultimately, the PAC's rhetoric and potential appeal—and thus, the threat it posed—was limited by its inability to fully realize that potential and, in practical terms, its inability to compete effectively with the ANC for support and resources (ka Plaatjie 2004a, 2004b).

Even the two organizations' armed wings reflected this difference in operational competence, with MK focused on creating an organization that had strong internal reporting structures, a well-trained and disciplined cadre of activists, and well-established systems of communications, order, and control. Many of the ANC's internal documents from this time focus on the importance of creating a resilient organization, highly trained, disciplined, and capable of acting in a purposeful

---

10 ANC Interim Constitutional Framework, no date, University of Cape Town archives, BC 1081 (P25.4).

manner because, as Jack Simons, an MK political commissar in the training camps, noted, "organizational strength will determine our political fate."[11] The conditions in Poqo camps, on the other hand reflected "ramshackle logistical systems, inadequate food, poor training facilities and inhabitability which led to poor health of inmates, death and disease" (Lodge 1985: 308), which in turn undermined the group's ability to mount or sustain effective action. These differences became even more marked after the Soweto uprisings in 1976, which re-awakened mass militancy inside the country and sent hundreds of highly politicized youth into the arms of the PAC and ANC. The ANC was prepared to handle this rush of bodies and raw enthusiasm, and converted newly arrived recruits into trained cadres of activists far more effectively than the PAC, which, due to organizational inefficiencies and underdeveloped recruiting and training structures, failed to capitalize on the moment. It squandered that influx of new human capital, leaving it even further behind its main rival (Simpson 2009).

Had the PAC managed to pull off a string of tactical victories, like the national uprising it had planned in the early-1960s, perhaps these organizational failings would have mattered less as its capacity to mobilize and challenge the state would not be in question. But absent any meaningful strategic success, its organizational weaknesses raised serious doubts about the PAC's ability to lead the movement. Without a proven and sustained track record, the PAC was in danger of being viewed as a mostly toothless organization, more bluster than business compared to the ANC (Darracq 2008). Its organizational weaknesses not only harmed its own reputation, but the PAC's inability to mount a credible opposition to the ANC also spilled over to taint its strategies more broadly, linking its radical program to its operational blunders and making such tactics even less appealing for other groups who might have been tempted to follow them down such a path. Therefore, while competitive pressure existed between the ANC and the PAC on an ideological and political level, it became clear that the PAC's operational blunders and organizational weaknesses diminished it as a real threat to the power and position of the ANC.

Incentives to Differentiate from Rivals

Intra-movement competition rests on the assumption that organizational rivals have incentives to differentiate and distinguish themselves from each other, creating and then policing boundaries that telegraph information about their respective goals, priorities, and values (Melucci 1995). But insisting on difference is not a symmetrically distributed priority. Some groups come into competitive situations with organizational histories and well-established identities that require less careful cultivation and tending than newer groups that lack a track record or reputation on which to build. The desire to differentiate oneself from one's

---

11 Jack Simons, "Internal Position," undated handwritten notes. In the Simons Collection, University of Cape Town Archives, BC 1081/P8.

rivals also rests in part on the relative balance of power that exists: groups that are dominant players in a movement are less likely to care about finding ways to differentiate themselves from competitors. Rather, it is the groups that are in challenging or weak positions that have more to gain by pointing out their differences in approach. After all, if the goal of intra-movement competition is to improve your own group's power and prestige to draw more supporters, the burden of proof for why an existing hegemonic organization is unsuited or unequal to the challenge rests with the challenger. Dominant organizations, on the other hand, do not face the same burden. It is only when such a group feels weak or vulnerable, or when a challenger's actions threaten to potentially tarnish the reputation of a dominant group (Haines 1984, 1988) that a dominant group will take a more active interest in policing that boundary.

The PAC, as a newer organization without an established "brand" to call its own was therefore more concerned than the ANC about distinguishing itself in order to justify the split from its parent group, both in terms of policies and tactics. Hence, the PAC spent more care and time denigrating the ANC's conservative approach, positioning it as stuck in its ways and its leadership old and out of touch, and critiquing its multiracial approach as flawed. The ANC on the other hand could draw on a very rich and known brand. It had a long history of opposing the apartheid state. Its leaders, like Nelson Mandela and Walter Sisulu, were more well known than PAC leaders like Potlako Leballo. And their efforts to challenge apartheid were part of public consciousness thanks to high-profile acts of resistance like the 1952 Defiance Campaign and the 1956 Treason Trials, both of which were covered extensively by the press. True, there was a period of time after Sharpeville when the PAC's star seemed to be rising and that made some ANC leaders fearful of this threat, which is consistent with my claim that dominant-but-insecure organizations will want to differentiate themselves. The ANC responded to this threat and emphasized the differences with the PAC, but because it had a strong organizational legacy on which to draw and a track record it could highlight, it tended to focus more on matters of capacity and competence rather than distinctions in policy and tactical approach as the key differences between the two groups. A 1968 statement by the ANC to the Organization of African Unity (OAU) argued, for example:

> The Pan Africanist Congress has a long and sordid history of attempting to subvert the struggle for liberation in South Africa. One of the aims of the "leadership" of this organization (if it can be called that at all) was to collect for themselves as much money as possible. In the course of fighting over their loot the "organization" has broken up into numerous factions. There have been expulsions and counter-expulsions, accusations and recriminations ...

[t]here is overwhelming evidence that what is called the PAC does not exist as a cohesive organization.[12]

The statement went on to argue that the OAU should withdraw its financial support of the PAC because it was unable to function effectively and, therefore, was only squandering its OAU funding. As a well-established organization, emphasizing the PAC's organizational ineptitude reflected well on the ANC's more robust and mature structures and implied that the OAU's money would be better off in the ANC's coffers. These arguments eventually succeeded: in recognition of MK's military successes, the OAU's Liberation Committee passed a resolution in 1983 recognizing the ANC as the vanguard of the South African liberation movement (Ndlovu 2004: 657).

Superior organizational strategy is hardly the kind of difference that encourages outbidding. Tactics and goals and rhetoric can become progressively more extreme as rivals claim their stance is more valid or better suited to serving the needs of the audience. Criticism that focuses on *implementation* and *execution* of goals is much harder to appropriate and radicalize. After all, what does it even mean to adopt an "extremist" position when it comes to policy implementation or strengthening organizational capabilities? Arguing that the ANC could actually carry out its plans planted doubts about whether the PAC ever could, which was arguably more effective than simple outbidding would have been. The ANC's prominent position within the movement made it possible for it to shift the debate away from content and policy positions to competence and efficacy—an orientation that does not reward (or even invoke the idea of) militancy and dampens radicalization.

Organizational Constraints from Members

A final reason why the expected radicalization dynamic did not materialize involves the challenges that every movement and movement group faces in balancing what their own members want with what would help it advance their goals against the state or increase its support among the general public. Negotiating these different audiences is akin to a multi-level game where the choices and actions that occur at one level have consequences for the choices and actions at another (for example, see Gupta 2007). Groups that disregard the interlocking nature of these levels risk making serious strategic missteps that can constrain future activity in negative ways.

In the case of the radicalization process, one of the core steps entails calibrating organizational repertoires to the public's preferences; strategies should resonate with the public if the public is to be won over. But even if a movement group is able to correctly identify the "median audience member's" preferred strategy, it may still find itself constrained and unable to simply adopt that stance. Doing so

---

12 African National Congress, "The Pan African Congress Exists to Subvert the South African Liberation Struggle," 1968. In the Simons Collection, University of Cape Town Archives, BC 1081/P10.2.

160   *Dynamics of Political Violence*

requires persuading one's own members that such a change is both warranted and wise. Organizations with strong internal cultures, that have norms of democratic decisionmaking, or that simply have a diverse membership are likely to discover that major tactical shifts need to be sold to the rank-and-file who may or may not accept such a change. Movement groups, like any social aggregate, are not unified actors and can voice dissent. For organizational leaders, navigating this multi-level field can be treacherous: on one hand, the group may need to take on a different menu of tactics in order to remain externally competitive with its rivals, but may not be able to persuade its own members that these new tactics are desirable. Ultimately, a group's internal structures and characteristics may prevent radicalization from happening even if all the other pieces are in place. The opposite dynamic could also hold: a group might radicalize to appease its own members even when moderation might be a strategically wise move in the larger political context, though this outcome is less certain.

In the case of the ANC, the membership composition and preferences certainly played a key role in keeping it on a more moderate footing. Even if some portion of the leadership had been tempted to abandon the principles of the Freedom Charter and follow the PAC down the rabbit hole of chauvinistic African nationalism, the very membership structure of the ANC made that unlikely to be a winning proposition within the organization itself. For starters, the ANC included a number of white members, many of whom came to the organization via the SACP. The ANC also emphasized its alliances with other groups, like the Transvaal Indian Congress, and worked with the Coloured and Indian communities at the time that the Sharpeville massacre took place. The 1956 Treason Trial, for example, underscored the point that the defendants represented all the different communities in South Africa. By sitting in alphabetical order rather than separately by racial group, the defendants visually represented the interconnections between them and their common commitment to opposing apartheid (Bernstein 1999). This kind of diversity made moving to a more intransigent, anti-settler (and anti-white) position, or accepting the validity of attacks against non-white civilians simply unthinkable. The ANC's desire to forge a broad coalition created an organizational culture and membership that exerted a moderating influence on its strategic choices and goals. Even had the ANC leadership been so inclined, it would have been hard, and perhaps simply impossible, to take up radicalism in the PAC style without fracturing the ANC itself.

Conclusions

Explaining a non-event is, by nature, more complicated than trying to account for something that occurred. The fact that intra-movement competition did *not* produce a spiral of radicalization in the case of the ANC and PAC in the South African liberation movement is only puzzling if we expect such a dynamic should occur. In the above discussion, I argue that the interactions between these two groups do indeed fulfill the three basic scope conditions for intra-movement radicalization: competition (sometimes bitter), creation of distinct organizational identities, and an audience that is reasonably likely to reward radicalism more than moderation. All were present in post-1960 South Africa. And yet, the ANC did not try to outbid the PAC in its radicalism because of several countervailing pressures.

What the South African case underscores is that intra-movement competition is not sufficient in itself to produce a spiral of radicalization. Rather, the outcomes of competition vary depending on *who* the actors are who are connected in that competitive relationship, and the *context* in which they are embedded. Though the radicalization mechanism itself might follow a modular logic and can be transported and applied to a number of different movement setting, the impact that the mechanism has is contingent and not uniform. To say that mechanisms do not produce deterministic outcomes but instead concatenate with structural, organizational, and individual-level factors is not a new claim, but such interactions and their outcomes need to be more clearly specified in general.

The South African case illustrates that when we focus more closely on how intra-movement competition affects radicalization, we can get a clearer picture of how those processes unfold and appreciate how, when it comes to intra-movement competition, the pressure to radicalize is mitigated (or intensified) depending on the incentives that the respective organizations have to differentiate themselves, their assessment of the threat posed by their rivals, and the constraints placed on radical (or moderate) strategies by their own supporters. Moreover, the interaction of these various strategic and structural aspects suggests that radicalization dynamics are fundamentally influenced by factors that often are not privileged as relevant or important in analyses of radicalization processes but that nonetheless play a fundamental role in explaining why some organizations may display tactical restraint even when it seems like it the strategic incentives point in a different direction. Finally, and perhaps most fundamentally, the dynamics explored in this case point to the notion that radicalization is hardly automatic. Instead, radicalization comes about only after prior necessary conditions have been met, which suggests that intra-movement competition will only lead to radicalization under restrictive circumstances. By attending to these sometimes-overlooked dimensions of a dynamic relational process like radicalization, we can emerge with a better appreciation not only for why radicalization happens when and where it does, but sometimes, why it fails to materialize at all.

References

Adam, H. and Moodley, K. 1993. *The Opening of the Apartheid Mind: Options for the New South Africa.* Berkeley: University of California Press.
Alimi, E. 2011. Relational dynamics in factional adoption of terrorist tactics: a comparative perspective. *Theory and Society,* 40(1), 95–118.

162   *Dynamics of Political Violence*

Alimi, E., Bosi, L., and Demetriou, C. 2012. Relational dynamics and processes of radicalization: a comparative framework. *Mobilization*, 17(1), 7–26.

ANC. 1997. *Second Submission to the Truth and Reconciliation Commission, South Africa, Appendix 4: MK List of Operations.* Cape Town: South African Truth and Reconciliation Commission. [Online]. Available at: http://www.justice. gov.za/trc/hrvtrans/submit/anc2.htm#Appendix 4 [accessed: December 21, 2012].

APLA. 1997. *The Azanian People's Liberation Army Submission to the Truth and Reconciliation Commission, South Africa.* Cape Town: South African Truth and Reconciliation Commission. [Online]. Available at: http://www.justice. gov.za/trc/hrvtrans/submit/apla.htm [accessed: December 19, 2012].

Barrell, H. 1990a. *MK: The ANC's Armed Struggle.* London: Penguin Forum Series.

Barrell, H. 1990b. Interview with Ronnie Kasrils, O'Malley Archives, Nelson Mandela Centre of Memory. [Online]. Available at http://www.nelsonmandela. org/omalley/cis/omalley/OMalleyWeb/03lv03445/04lv04015/05lv04154/06lv 04159/07lv04173.htm. [accessed: February 12, 2013].

Beach, S.W. 1977. Social movement radicalization: the case of the People's Democracy in Northern Ireland. *The Sociological Quarterly*, 18(3), 305–18.

Benford, R.D. and Snow, D.A. 2000. Framing processes and social movements: an overview and assessment. *Annual Review of Sociology*, 26, 611–39.

Bernstein, R. 1999. *Memory Against Forgetting: Memoirs of a Life in South African Politics, 1938–1964.* London: Viking.

Bonner, P., Marks, S., and Rathbone, R. 1982. The Transvaal Native Congress, 1917–1920: the radicalization of the black petty bourgeoisie on the Rand, in *Industrialization and Social Change in South Africa: African Class Formation, Culture, and Consciousness, 1870–1930*, edited by S. Marks and R. Rathbone. New York: Longman, 270–313.

Borum, R. 2011. Radicalization into violent extremism I: a review of social science theories. *Journal of Strategic Security*, 4(4), 7–36.

Coetzee, J.K., Gilfillan, L., and Hulec, O. 2002. *Fallen Walls: Prisoners of Conscience in South Africa and Czechoslovakia.* New Brunswick, NJ: Transaction Publishers.

Croteau, D. and Hicks, L. 2003. Coalition framing and the challenge of a consonant frame pyramid: the case of a collaborative response to homelessness. *Social Problems*, 50, 251–72.

Dadoo, Y.M. 1962. Why the United Front failed: disruptive role of the PAC. *New Age*, 29 March.

Darracq, V. 2008. The African National Congress (ANC) organization at the grassroots. *African Affairs*, 107(429), 589–609.

della Porta, D. 1995. *Political Violence and the State.* Cambridge, UK: Cambridge University Press.

Ellis, S. 1991. The ANC in exile. *African Affairs*, 90(360), 439–47.

Esterhuyse, W. and Nel, P. eds. 1990. *The ANC and Its Leaders.* Cape Town: Tafelberg.

Francisco, R.A. 2004. After the massacre: mobilization in the wake of harsh repression. *Mobilization*, 9(2), 107–26.

Frankel, P.H. 2001. *An Ordinary Atrocity: Sharpeville and Its Massacre*. New Haven: Yale University Press.

Gerhart, G.M. 1979. *Black Power in South Africa: The Evolution of an Ideology*. London: University of California Press.

Gerhart, G.M. and Glaser, C.L. 2010. *From Protest to Challenge: A Documentary History of African Politics in South Africa, 1882–1990. Challenge and Victory, 1980–1990*. Bloomington, IN: Indiana University Press.

Gerhart, G.M. and Karis, T. 1991. *Challenge and Violence: 1953–1964*. Palo Alto, CA: Hoover Institution Press.

Giuliano, E. 2000. Who determines the self in the politics of self-determination? Identity and preference formation in Tatarstan's nationalist mobilization. *Comparative Politics*, 32(3), 295–316.

Gupta, Devashree. 2007. Selective engagement and its consequences for social movement organizations: lessons from British policy in Northern Ireland. *Comparative Politics*, 39(3), 331–51.

Haines, H. 1984. Black radicalization and the funding of civil rights: 1957–1970. *Social Problems*, 32(1), 31–43.

Haines, H. 1988. *Black Radicals and the Civil Rights Mainstream, 1954–1970*. Knoxville, TN: University of Tennessee Press.

Houston, G.F. and Magubane, B. 2004a. The ANC political underground in the 1970s, in *The Road to Democracy in South Africa: 1970–1980*, edited by the South African Democracy Education Trust. Pretoria: Unisa Press, 371–452.

Houston, G.F. and Magubane, B. 2004b. The ANC's armed struggle in the 1970s, in *The Road to Democracy in South Africa: 1970–1980*, edited by the South African Democracy Education Trust. Pretoria: Unisa Press, 453–530.

ka Plaatjie, T. 2004a. The PAC's internal underground activities, 1960–1980, in *The Road to Democracy in South Africa: 1970–1980*, edited by the South African Democracy Education Trust. Pretoria: Unisa Press, 669–702.

ka Plaatjie, T. 2004b. The PAC in exile, in *The Road to Democracy in South Africa: 1970–1980*, edited by the South African Democracy Education Trust. Pretoria: Unisa Press, 703–48.

Lichbach, M.I. 1995. *The Rebel's Dilemma*. Ann Arbor, MI: University of Michigan Press.

Lissoni, A. 2009. Transformations in the ANC external mission and Umkhonto We Sizwe, c. 1960–1969. *Journal of Southern African Studies*, 35(2), 287–301.

Lissoni, A. 2010. The PAC in Basutoland, c. 1962–1965. *South African Historical Journal*, 62(1), 54–77.

Lodge, T. 1982. The Paarl insurrection: a South African uprising. *African Studies Review*, 25(4), 95–116.

Lodge, T. 1984. The Pan-Africanist Congress, 1959–1990, in *The Long March: The Story of the Struggle for Liberation in South Africa*, edited by I. Liebenberg, et al. Pretoria: HAUM Press, 104–24.

Lodge, T. 1985. *Black Politics in South Africa Since 1945*. Braamfontein, South Africa: Ravan.

Lodge, T. 1986. The Poqo insurrection, in *Resistance and Ideology in Settler Societies*, edited by T. Lodge. Johannesburg: Ravan, 179–222.

Lodge, T. 1987. State of exile: the African National Congress of South Africa, 1976–86. *Third World Quarterly*, 9(1), 1–27.

Lodge, T. 2011. *Sharpeville: An Apartheid Massacre and Its Consequences*. Oxford, UK and New York: Oxford University Press.

Maaba, B.B. 2004. The PAC's war against the state, 1960–1963, in *The Road to Democracy in South Africa: 1960–1970*, edited by the South African Democracy Education Trust. Pretoria: Unisa Press, 257–98.

Mabin, A. 1991. The impact of apartheid on rural areas of South Africa. *Antipode*, 23(1), 33–46.

Mabin, A. 1992. Comprehensive segregation: the origins of the Group Areas Act and its planning apparatuses. *Journal of Southern African Studies*, 18(2), 405–29.

McAdam, D., Tarrow, S.G., and Tilly, C. 2001. *Dynamics of Contention*. Cambridge, UK: Cambridge University Press.

McCauley, C. and Moskalenko, S. 2008. Mechanisms of political radicalization: pathways toward terrorism. *Terrorism and Political Violence*, 20(3), 415–33.

McPherson, M. 1983. An ecology of affiliation. *American Sociological Review*, 48(4), 519–32.

Magubane, B., Bonner, P., Sithole, J., Delius, P., Cherry, J., Gibbs, P., and April, T. 2004. The turn to armed struggle, in *The Road to Democracy in South Africa: 1960–1970*, edited by the South African Democracy Education Trust. Pretoria: Unisa Press, 53–146.

Mandela, N. 1956. Freedom in our lifetime, *Liberation*, June.

Mandela, N. 2003. *Long Walk to Freedom, Vol. 2, 1962–1994*. London: Abacus.

Mathabatha, S. 2004. The PAC and Poqo in Pretoria, 1958–1964, in *The Road to Democracy in South Africa: 1960–1970*, edited by the South African Democracy Education Trust. Pretoria: Unisa Press, 299–318.

Matoti, S. and Ntsebeza, L. 2004. Rural resistance in Mpondoland and Thembuland, 1960–1963, in *The Road to Democracy in South Africa: 1960–1970*, edited by the South African Democracy Education Trust. Pretoria: Unisa Press, 177–208.

Mayekiso, V.L. 1968. PAC is the revolution, *Africanist News and Views*, September.

Melucci, A. 1995. The process of collective identity, in *Social Movements and Culture*, edited by H. Johnston and B. Klandermans. Abingdon, UK: Routledge, 41–63.

Mphahlele, L. 2002. *Child of This Soil: My Life as a Freedom Fighter*. Cape Town: Kwela.

Muller, C.F.J., ed. 1981. *Five Hundred Years: A History of South Africa*. Pretoria: Academica.

Mwakikagile, G. 2008. *South Africa in Contemporary Times*. Pretoria, South Africa: New Press.

Ndlovu, S.M. 2004. The ANC's diplomacy and international relations, in *The Road to Democracy in South Africa: 1970–1980*, edited by the South African Democracy Education Trust. Pretoria: Unisa Press, 615–668.

Parker, P. and Mokhesi-Parker, J. 1998. *In the Shadow of Sharpeville: Apartheid and Criminal Justice*. New York: New York University Press.

Reddy, E.S. 1987. Defiance campaign in South Africa recalled. *Asian Times* (London), June.

Reeves, A. 1961. *Shooting at Sharpeville*. New York: Houghton Mifflin.

Saxton, G.D. 2005. Repression, grievances, mobilization, and rebellion: a new test of Gurr's model of ethnopolitical rebellion. *International Interactions*, 31, 1–30.

Seidman, G. 2000. Blurred lines: nonviolence in South Africa, *PS: Political Science and Politics*, 3(2), 161–7.

Simpson, T. 2009. 'Umkhonto We Sizwe, we are waiting for you': the ANC and the township uprising, September 1984–September 1985. *South African Historical Journal*, 61(1), 158–77.

Smith, D. and Mabin, A. 1992. Dispossession, exploitation and struggle: an historical overview of South African urbanization, in *The Apartheid City and Beyond: Urbanization and Social Change in South Africa*, edited by D. Smith and A. Mabin. London: Routledge, 13–24.

Snow, D.A. and Benford, R.D. 1988. Ideology, frame resonance, and participant mobilization. *International Social Movement Research*, 1, 197–217.

Snow, D.A., Rochford, E.B., Worden, S.K., and Benford, R.D. 1986. Frame alignment processes, micromobilization, and movement participation. *American Sociological Review*, 51(4), 464–81.

Stern, C. 1999. The evolution of social-movement organizations: niche competition in social space. *European Sociological Review*, 15(1), 91–105.

Tarrow, S.G. 1998. *Power in Movement: Social Movements and Contentious Politics*. Cambridge, UK and New York: Cambridge University Press.

Tarrow, S.G. 2010. Dynamics of diffusion: mechanisms, institutions, and scale shift, in *The Diffusion of Social Movements: Actors, Mechanisms, and Political Effects*, edited by R. K. Givan, K.M. Roberts, and S.A. Soule. Cambridge, UK: Cambridge University Press, 204–20.

TRC. 2003. *The Pan Africanist Congress: Summary and Analysis of Amnesty Application.* Cape Town: South African Truth and Reconciliation Commission. [Online]. Available at: http://www.info.gov.za/otherdocs/2003/trc/3_4.pdf [accessed: February 4, 2013].

UNESCO. 1987. Educational assistance to the Pan-Africanist Congress of Azania (PAC): Project findings and recommendations. [Online]. Available at http://unesdoc.unesco.org/images/0007/000747/074783eb.pdf. [accessed: March 1, 2013].

Wells, J.C. 1993. *We Now Demand! The History of Women's Resistance to Pass Laws in South Africa*. Johannesburg: Witwatersrand University Press.

White, R.W. 1989. From peaceful protest to guerilla war: micromobilization of the Provisional Irish Republican Army. *American Journal of Sociology*, 94(6), 1277–1302.

Williamson, O.E. 1983. Credible commitments: using hostages to support exchange. *The American Economic Review*, 73(4), 519–40.

Zald, M.N. and McCarthy, J.D. 1987. Social movement industries: competition and conflict among SMOs, in *Social Movements in an Organizational Society*, edited by M.N. Zald and J.D. McCarthy. New Brunswick, NJ: Transaction.

Zunes, S. 1999. The role of non-violent action in the downfall of apartheid. *The Journal of Modern African Studies*, 37(1), 137–69.

PART III
Dynamics of Meaning Formation:
Frames and Beyond

Chapter 8

Contentious Interactions, Dynamics of Interpretations, and Radicalization: The Islamization of Palestinian Nationalism[1]

Eitan Y. Alimi and Hank Johnston

The study of social movements recently has been reinvigorated by a shift towards a relational approach to "episodes of contention." This change of perspective was spurred by McAdam, Tarrow, and Tilly's *Dynamics of Contention* (2001), a book that intended to refocus the field in two ways. First, the authors called for a shift in the temporal framing of contentious phenomena to analyze claim making and challenges to the state and occurring over the long term—episodes of contention of *la longue durée.* Second, a new and overarching explanatory goal was introduced, namely, to identify and refine causal mechanisms that are generalizable across these contentious episodes in different national contexts. Because the authors' past studies were founded primarily on political process analysis, it was somewhat unexpected that their book accorded cultural and interpretative processes a central role. Mechanisms such as social appropriation, attribution of threat/opportunity, and identity shift, among others, strongly relied on processes of collective definition and interpretation.

In McAdam, Tarrow and Tilly's treatment of these concepts, cultural influences are broadened beyond traditional framing concepts to include "interactive construction of disputes among challengers, opponents, the state, and the media" (2001: 44). This is the view of culture and framing that we will pursue in this chapter. Deconstructed, it stresses three key foci:

1. The ongoing discursive practice of forging new collective identities;
2. New repertoires of action, predicated in part upon; and
3. Definitions and redefinitions of opportunity and threat.

This last element is closely related to changing perceptions of the opponents in the conflict. According to this distillation, cultural elements of the *Dynamics of*

---

1 This study relies in part on previous comparative work on dynamics of contention in Chechnya and Israel/Palestine, published in *Political Studies* (Johnston and Alimi 2012). It also represents a first attempt at developing a dynamics of interpretations framework, which we pursue further in a forthcoming publication in *Mobilization* (Johnston and Alimi 2013).

Contention can be thought of as anchored in the ongoing definition and redefinition of the *subject*, its actions (the *verb*), and the target of its actions (the *object*). All three are cultural-interpretative processes, which together give rise to a leitmotif that runs through the book: the *dynamics of interpretation*. Identifying the <subject>, <verb>, and <object>, a grammatical structure that echoes Franzosi's "story grammars" of a conflict proposed for analyzing protest events (1999, 2004), represents a fundamental parsing of the social world into the bare-bones structure of our experience. On a cognitive level, they are basic elements of how interpretation is accomplished.

This chapter employs this basic grammar approach to think systematically about the interplay among enduring patterns of culture and dynamic political processes and mechanisms, using the Islamization of Palestinian nationalism as a process of radicalization.[2] Building on McAdam, Tarrow, and Tilly's interpretive approach that applies a dynamic, mechanism-process approach to framing, we focus attention on the definition and redefinition of identities, action repertoires, and targets against the backdrop of "primary frameworks"—Erving Goffman's original label for primordial cultural frames upon which shared cultural experiences are built (1974: 21–6). These are the basic cognitive schemata that orient everyday activities and come to be widely shared through social experience.

We argue that knowing a group's primary frameworks, just as it helps understanding group behavior, also helps in understanding the ongoing interpretative processes of political contention, but it is only a starting point. By themselves, primary frameworks may suggest a strong cultural determinism, but Goffman holds that they are merely the groundwork of ongoing interpretation, extended and modified by what he calls the "keying processes." The idea is that primary frameworks can be changed, or "played in a different key" (ibid.: 44) resulting in the interpretation of what is going on being altered, perhaps slightly, but sometimes drastically. The basic structure stays, but elaborations on the "rims" of primary frameworks change the meaning that is conveyed, as they are the most recent and most accessible elements of interpretation. As social experience progresses, new layers, or "frame rims" (ibid.: 82) are extended on primary frameworks, an odd term that rarely finds its way into discussions of culture and interpretation, but which captures both the primary-framework basis of framing processes and, in political contention, how they are transformed into something new as the dynamics of the conflict unfolds, adding new layers of meaning.

Regarding the analysis of collective action frames, our point is that, much as certain molecules cannot combine with others to form new compounds unless there are appropriate receptors, one cannot impose just any social construction

---

2   Radicalization of course could also be treated as the shift from nonviolent tactics to violent ones. In most cases the attitudinal and behavioral aspects of the process interact and influence one another. While focusing on the former aspect, we nevertheless rely on existing works on the case under study to make occasional references to shift in actual forms of contention.

(frame rim) upon a primary framework. Such a notion is implicitly captured by the concepts of "cultural resonance," "master frame" or "frame alignment" as important aspects of successful collective action frames (Snow et al. 1986; Snow and Benford 1988; Snow and Benford 1992), but without sufficient recognition of the layering process and what lies at its base. It would be fair to argue that the notion of primary frameworks as representing a kind of deep cultural stock, fundamental and widely shared, is deemphasized in favor of strategic actions by leaders and organizations or the ongoing framing battles taking place in the heat of social movement contention (for a similar observation see: Morris 2000).

By building on a dynamic approach, we maintain that these primary frameworks can be both available as a resource to be strategically used and a constraint on the breadth of strategic decisions, depending on the unfolding of contentious dynamics. Tracing their operation in the context of contentious interactions adds an important dimension to the dialogic of discursive fields (Steinberg 1999), thereby promising to increase our understanding of ideational dynamics of contention. We offer our analysis as a first step towards rethinking how primary cultural patterns may be relevant in the ongoing dynamics of interpretation in protest trajectories—specifically as constitutive elements in a trajectory of radicalization. There are three basic questions that we pose: First, given that primary frameworks are operative at numerous levels of social life, can we identify the ones that are invoked in cases of contentious collective action? Second, although Goffman does not specify their structure, can we approximate a basic schematic to permit a systematic way of analyzing if primary frameworks have a role in political contention? Third, with regard to the movement under study, can a focus on primary cultural elements and on the ways they are "keyed" or elaborated in the heat of contention by two main Palestinian actors offer a nuanced and systematic approach to the radicalization of the Palestinian movement. Can it offer a more detailed perspective on the framing battles that were part of the movement's radicalization?

To demonstrate our approach, we draw on historical evidence from the national struggle of the Palestinian national movement, primarily the first Palestinian Intifada as the first major cycle of popular mobilization, which consolidated during the second half of 1987. Given the theoretical objective of this chapter, we do not attempt to analyze the entire historical narrative, which is still an ongoing matter. Rather, we proceed by analyzing the episode of contention according to the primary cultural elements, focusing on how they are played out across varying political contexts and in different arenas of interactions.

Primary Frameworks and Text Structure

A starting point for approximating primary framework structures is the basic tripartite relation of subject-action-target mentioned earlier. Together they can identify the basic "story grammars" of a conflict, a concept proposed by Roberto Franzosi as a way to analyze protest events (1999, 2004). His idea is based on the fact that all action follows a simple grammatical structure comprising <subject> <verb> <object>, and that additional modifiers then give shape and substance to descriptions of collective action. The modifiers would be type, number, structure, or character for the <subject> and <object>, and time, space, or type for the <action>. Franzosi calls this structure a "semantic triplet." He proposes its use as an analytical method to capture the essential ingredients of collective action: the collective "we" of the acting subject, the action of contention, and the object of the contentious act. It is a system whose simplicity and parsimony recommends itself as a way to navigate the complex layerings of cultural work among diverse groups.

Although Franzosi is interested in coding protest events based on subject-verb-object triplets, thereby keeping the coding close to "the inherent properties of the text itself," we propose that the basic semantic triplet structure captures relevant relations of framing processes in contentious episodes, "where subjects are related to their actions, actors and actions to their modifiers, and subjects and objects (both social actors) related on one another via their actions" (Franzosi 1999: 133). Although Franzosi employed his method in a highly quantitative way, we apply it historically to analyze the patterns of action underlying and circumscribing innovation and strategy.[3] Franzosi's semantic triplets present one way that a movement's challenge can be thought of textually by specifying the fundamental subject-verb-object grammar that comprises a primary framework. The analyst can then trace its applications and permutations in evolving political contexts. This is the strategy we will follow in this chapter.

We assume that there is a wide variety of primary frameworks in Palestinian society, as in any culture with deep historical traditions. These guide social, political, and economic life by giving rise to shared predispositions that are available for application in social action. Insofar as we are interested in political contention, the fundamental triplet will take the generic form of <collective we> <challenges, makes a claim, resists, or mobilizes against> <target or opponent>. Regarding the case under study, the skeletal structures take the form <Palestinians> <make claims against> <Israelis>.

Drawing on secondary and primary sources (primarily the series of serialized leaflets published by the different Palestinian actors throughout the uprising[4]), the tasks at hand are, first, to elaborate this skeletal structure based on the collective history, shared symbols, and cultural images relevant, to suggest a primary framework of contention (see Figure 8.1). Second, the analysis will trace

---

3   Another historically nuanced approach to the interplay between <verb> and <object>, yet without and explicit recognition and treatment of primary frameworks and their keying, is Tilly and Wood's (2003) analysis of contentious connections in Great Britain between 1828 and 1834.

4   The entire collection of the original leaflets is available at the National and University Library, Jerusalem. For their role as a "written leadership" of the movement and a central means of communication with the population to express opinions and give guidance and directives for action, see Mishal with Aharoni (1989).

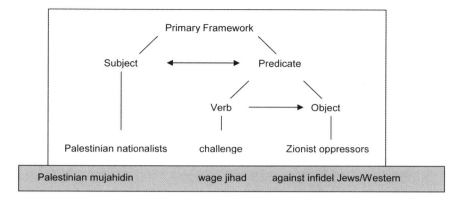

Figure 8.1   Primary framework structure and the Jihadist rim

how some transformations of the primary framework are permitted and others limited, such that, as the movement develops, battles over the immediate political manifestations of, say, what it means to be a Palestinian, or what the strategy of contention will be, guide the movement's trajectory. This is the keying process whereby different groups within the movement seek to add new frame rims that reflect their own interests, but emphasize distinct transformations of the basic cultural stock. Different rims will appear to predominate at different points in the movement's trajectory. As political opportunities and threats unfold, the process of keying primary frameworks produces a complex episode of collective action.

In the case of Palestinian contention, it eventually took the form of <heroic mujahidin> <wage jihad against> <Zionist-Western oppressor>, that is, a powerful shared definition of the Palestinian people, defined as Allah's warriors, waging a holy war against Israel in the context of the international struggle of Islam against the West. Israel was defined in binary opposition as non-Arab, nonbelieving infidels, and Zionist oppressors. In different episodes of Palestinian mobilization there were alternative texts available, more secular and pragmatic, with a less absolutist perception of the movements' object and goals. But, as we will see, the final form of fundamentalist Islamic Palestinian people waging Islamic-based holy war against Israelis was a product of political and organizational contexts that gradually privileged the eventual dominance of the Islamic-based elements of the primary framework.

We see this same process in other movements, when activists combine the raw materials of different cultural texts, oppositional and hegemonic, in creative ways. Noonan's specification of a "maternal master frame" (1997) among women in Chile revitalized feminism and the democratic movement during the Pinochet era. Zuo and Benford (1995) discuss how nationalism and communism were blended with deep-seated Confucianism in the Chinese student movement. And, Wright (2007) shows how unfolding upward spirals of political threat/opportunity between US state and police authorities and patriot organizations, pushed militant factions to engage in

174   *Dynamics of Political Violence*

"warfare framing" that drew on deep cultural elements about the constitutional right to bear arms and the American Revolution against tyranny. But the task at hand is to offer a systematic way of thinking about the basic interpretative frameworks and their differential application as contentious episodes unfold.

Following Goffman, we assume that primary frameworks are social constructs that become widely shared through cultural reproduction, kinship networks, primary socialization, and daily discursive practices. To begin, we will describe the historical emergence of the <subject>, but it is beyond the scope of this chapter to trace the Palestinian case in detail. We will do the same for the predicate, combining analysis of the <verb> and <object>, for as we shall see, they are in a close and dynamic relationship (see also Tilly and Wood 2003).

The Subject: The Dynamics of "Who We Are"

At the core of Palestine collective identity is a connectedness to the land, which came to be represented in the Palestinian motherland, in which the Arab people of Palestine—of whom over 90 per cent are Sunni Muslims and the majority of whom are peasants—have been living since the seventh century. This bond to the land, the product of continuing occupation and re-occupation by foreign forces, underlies the current struggle with the state of Israel, and historically has generated three self-images, all rooted in the Islamic tradition. The first and most central self-image is the *Sahmed,* the Palestinian peasant, the survivor who steadfastly clings to his land notwithstanding pressures of occupation and expropriation (Shehadeh 1982). Second is the *Fida'y*, the holy warrior who throws himself into battle, willing to sacrifice his life in the struggle. Third, the *Shahid,* (witness) is a young man who fights against all odds and offers the collective good, a reflection of his unwavering Islamic faith (Kimmerling and Migdal 1999). These two self images evolved after the first.

With the surge of Zionist migration to Palestine, the 1948 national catastrophe (i.e., *al-Nakba*) and, in 1967, the occupation of the territories by Israel, a gradual keying of these three primary images began as part of a new rim for the subject's definition, namely Palestinian nationalism. The fact of occupation gradually made the nationalist rim of identity much more central compared with the other Islamic and Arab ones. True, long before the Zionist migration to Palestine there existed a distinct and widely shared Palestinian collective memory with several overlapping ways of thinking of themselves as a people (Doumani 1992; Khalidi 1997). Palestinians perceived themselves, for example, as part of the Ottoman world, Arab world and part of the Islamic world. However, Palestinians inside the occupied territories were first and foremost an occupied people. They were, according to Daqqaq (1983), a nationalist public figure in the territories, the people *on* the land, who experienced in body and mind an ongoing hardship. Thus, throughout the 1980s and into the first Intifada (1988), a Palestinian nationalism closely linked with the land enjoyed widespread support by most Palestinians inside the occupied territories and synchronized closely with the Palestinian situation inside the West Bank and Gaza Strip.

On the eve of the Intifada, the PLO-led nationalist camp enjoyed widespread popularity. It articulated a definition of "who we are" by drawing upon these elements but steering clear of ideological rigidity in order to embrace various factions within one organizational framework. Nationalism was developed into an umbrella ideology that consisted of various elements of identity, including religious ones. It provided a first keying of the primary framework within which any Palestinian, regardless of his personal ideological commitment (e.g., Marxism or Islam) or personal socioeconomic situation, could identify with. By not rejecting Islam, establishing an infrastructure of collaboration with Islamic groups,[5] acknowledging the merits of leftist ideologies, glorifying the role and status of the *fellahin* (peasants), and promoting the distinctly traditional Palestinian identity, PLO's nationalism strongly linked with the primary frameworks of Palestinian identity (Swedenburg 1990).

The idea of Palestinian self-determination meant a promise of belonging within one's own national territory, ownership of property, a measure of control over their lives, and the ability to participate and design their own destiny—all of which rested on an authentic interpretation of the Palestinian primary framework. But another contender to define Palestinian identity was the Islamic Jihad, which promoted an identity based on Islam as a faith of liberation, and thus embedded within the occupied land (Hatina 2001). Yet, at this time, the Islamic Jihad's rim was problematic on two grounds: (1) it called for a total, uncompromising transformation of the self; and (2) a mode of action (i.e., terrorist activity) that entailed great sacrifice and risk. While both aspects of identity built upon the *Fida'y* and *Shahid* elements of the primary framework, it required a degree of commitment that had limited appeal.

Yet another contender was the Muslim Brotherhood (MB), which offered transnational identity, the nation of Islam, which could have been attractive, had the Palestinians not been occupied and displaced from their land. Even after the formation of Hamas, as the political arm of the MB, there was no immediate attempt to embrace a distinct Palestinian identity. The result was that MB/Hamas refrained from openly opposing the nationalist forces, and tended to accept a *modus vivendi* with them, namely, a tacit understanding to avoid confrontation and lessen ideological disagreements.[6]

---

5 Such was the case, for example, with collaboration between Fatah and Islamic Jihad activists. First signs were already present in the early 1980s when two joint social working committees—Islamic Youth Association—were formed in Eastern Jerusalem. Later on a Jihad religious faction was formed inside Fatah named "Islamic Jihad Squad."

6 Forming Hamas in January 1988 reflected MB leaders' need to preserve their sociopolitical power, especially in light of the active involvement of the Islamic Jihad and its growing popularity (Jaradat, 1992; Litvak, 1991), in addition to MB activists' participation in the increasing clashes with nationalist activists.

176   *Dynamics of Political Violence*

This truce began to disintegrate as a result of King Hussein's declaration of Jordan's disengagement from the West Bank and recognition of the PLO as the sole, legitimate representative of the Palestinian people, coupled with the decision at the Arab Summit of June, 1988 in Algeria, to allocate funds for the PLO. The recognition of the nationalists as the sole and legitimate representative of the Palestinian people immediately led to the publication of Hamas Charter on August 18, 1988. The Charter was, essentially, a public declaration of the MB/Hamas as both a political power having a distinct Palestinian-Islamic agenda and competing with the PLO over the issue of who represents the Palestinian people (Alimi 2007). Prior to the Disengagement Speech of early August 1988, Hamas's leaflets tended to emphasize the Islamic features of the struggle stating, for example, "The Islamic resistance movement praises all of our Muslim people ... Our struggle is Jihad for Allah until victory or shahid" (leaflet # 26, July 19, 1988). Slightly more than two weeks after the King Hussein's Speech, a much clearer and concrete layer of Palestinian identity surfaced, carrying with it a subtle yet unequivocal warning to the nationalist forces. As a leaflet accompanying the publication of the Charter, circulated on August 18, 1988 reads:

> An Islamic Palestine from the river to the sea! ... Bless Allah who valorizes the worshipers. ... Our people, the unwearied, the debate over who will get Palestine and who will handle its affairs will become meaningful only after the enemy is forced out. ... What we shall say to the *shuhada* who have fought for liberating Palestine for years ... when we sign on the presence of settlements among us? ... A Palestinian state is not a high-flown phrase but an achievement of a persistent struggle.

In the next year, Islamic elements of "who we are" promoted by MB/Hamas intensified, primarily due to the decline in the political and public status of Arafat throughout late 1989 and 1990. Arafat's status was seriously damaged domestically and internationally during the build-up of the Gulf crisis. First, this derived partly from a series of proposals for a political solution of the Palestinian question proposed by Egypt, the US, and Israel between mid-1989 and early 1990, all of which included no recognition of the PLO. Second, PLO-US dialogue was suspended in June 1990, triggered by PLO terrorism against Israel on May 30. Third, Arafat's unconditional support for Saddam Hussein's invasion of a Sunni Muslim state in August 1990 played a role. Together, these factors decreased significantly the flow of money from the Gulf States to the nationalists, caused domestic and international criticism, and led to a heavier Israeli crackdown.

All this contributed to the growing popularity of Hamas among Palestinians and its keying of an Islam-based <subject> (Mishal and Sela 1999). During this time, the religious ardor of the struggle gradually increased, which was observable on both sides to the conflict. The Rishon Le'Zion massacre occurred on May 20, 1990, in which Israeli citizen, Ami Popper, dressed as a soldier, shot to death seven and injured 11 Palestinian workers waiting for their daily labor. And later, the bloody confrontation at the Haram al-Shareef of October 8, 1990 in which 17 Palestinian worshipers were killed and 150 injured, and 11 Israelis were injured.

The PLO's waning popularity led to the September 1990 agreement with Hamas aimed at lessening the tension so as to avert deterioration into an all-out internal war. Yet, the agreement did not end the struggle for legitimacy and power. What practically rebalanced the situation for nationalists was the intense Israeli crackdown on MB/Hamas as a result of Hamas's terrorist actions. Israel, fully aware of the potential danger from Hamas, engaged in a systematic oppression of the MB organizational network. Israel's familiarity with the Hamas leaders, the result of traditional fostering of the MB's activities and operations throughout the early 1980s in hope they would counterbalance the nationalist camp, facilitated the crackdown. Throughout 1990, the arrest of most activists and of the MB's spiritual leader, Ahmed Yassin, brought about a significant decrease in the movement's strength.

Things became more intense and lethal with the commencement of a Palestinian self-rule in 1992, the Oslo Accords and the subsequent formation of the Palestinian Authority in 1994. Already during the self-rule elections in the territories in 1992 numerous deadly confrontations broke out between the parties. The challenge posed by Hamas to the Fatah-led Palestinian Authority was translated into systematic attempts at undermining the Oslo Accords through the use of numerous suicide bombings against Israel, which resulted in dozens of Israeli deaths and hundreds of injuries between early 1994 and 1996. As Arafat's difficulties to deliver the promise of Oslo increased (difficulties for which Hamas was partly responsible) Hamas's power increased significantly. The gradually faltering Oslo agreement, as a result, made Hamas's alternative keying of Palestinian identity increasingly attractive.

Additionally, the Palestinian Authority became the target of widespread criticism mounted not only by the Islamists but also by considerable segments of the Palestinian population and the grassroots forces that actually made the Intifada yet were pushed aside by the "old-guard" PLO members, who were contemptuously referred to as the "Tunisians," those who were outsiders and did not represent the Palestinian people. How this undermined the nationalists' secular definition of identity is readily apparent. In response, Arafat made systematic attempts to appease the Islamic forces, for example, by making references to religious symbols in his public speeches, frequently portraying himself as the leader of an army of *Shaheed* marching to liberate the holy city as did Salah al-Din, and occasionally consulting with Islamic leaders. Yet this was too little and too late, and an Islamic-based rim seems to have been firmly layered upon the primary framework of Palestinian identity. During 2000 a new, this time Islamic-driven cycle of contention consolidated, guided by both nationalist and Islamist groups, with Arafat having little if any control over the dynamics of contention.

As with the <subject>, there will be competing rims for the predicate as the movement develops, political contexts change, and various parties engage over tactics, strategies, and goals. For some groups whose <subject> had a strong Islamic rim, the predicate will also be keyed in terms of Islamic-based struggle, meaning that: (1) the <verb> of action will incorporate Islamic definitions of "what to do;" and (2) the <object> will tend toward definitions of a non-Muslim, Western, and infidel enemy.

As with the <subject>, how the battle is actually played out will be contingent on political context, generating tension and discord over issues over tactics and strategy. But, as we will demonstrate, an additional factor is that the <object> is not passive but rather an active player, whose actions affect how the challenger sees it and what its strategies are towards it. Thus, the movement's action repertoire becomes doubly contingent, first on its keying of the <subject> and, second, on its keying of the <object>—which in part is shaped by the object's own actions.

The Predicate: Dynamics of What to Do

Another central element in the Palestinian historical narrative is heroic opposition against foreign occupation by historical figures in Islamic tradition, which shapes the definition of the <verb>. For example, the willingness of the young Palestinian Muslim—the *Fida'y*—to throw himself onto the battlefield in defense of his motherland merges faith, heroism, and nation. Iconic figures in Palestinian culture are frequently mentioned in both nationalist and Islamic discourses: Salah al-Din, who vanquished the Crusader Kingdom of Jerusalem in the battle of Hattin in 1187; Sheik Izz al-Din al-Qassam, a preacher from Haifa who fought against the British Mandate forces during the 1930s; and, Jafer Ibn abu-Taleb, a *Shaheed*, or warrior, who in a battle against the Byzantine Army in 629, mythically kept fighting to his death even after his two arms were severed (Mishal with Aharoni 1989: 39). Even the *Sahmed* of the olive tree can also be said to have its roots in the Islamic tradition, representing the steadfastness of Muhammad himself in keeping with his conquest campaign even after his defeat in the battle of *Uhud* in 625.

But, as noted, the <verb> and <object> are in close and dynamic relationship. An element that touches almost every Palestinian family and defines the <object> in stark terms is the establishment of the state of Israel in 1948. The atrocities of the war inflicted by Israeli military forces and the mass exodus of Palestinians from their homes to the West Bank, Gaza Strip, and neighboring Arab states for fear of Israeli vengeance came to be known as *al-Nakbah*—the Palestinian national catastrophe (Morris 1987; Ghanem 2001; Sa'di 2002).

The refugee problem was further aggravated by the Six-Day War in June 1967, during which many other Palestinians residing inside the Israeli state, were displaced and relocated mostly in refugee camps inside the West Bank. The war turned Israel into the primary and most immediate <object> as it occupied most of Mandate Palestine, including East Jerusalem (where Israeli law was implemented in 1968). Israel dominated the occupied territories via martial law, a military government that was immediately imposed and maintained order through force and violence (e.g., deportations, demolitions and sealing of Palestinian houses,

The Islamization of Palestinian Nationalism   179

detentions, town arrests, harsh restrictions on traveling, publishing, and even on prayer procedures on the *Haram al-Shareef*, Arabic for Temple Mount). Also, immediately following the occupation, Israel began to settle the territories via the construction of new Jewish settlements and the expansion of existing ones. This "marching cancer" settlement policy (Said 1986) represented two facets to the conflict: one between an Israeli state and an occupied Palestinian minority, and the other between the Jewish and Muslim communities (Benvenisti 1989, 1992).

During the run-up to the 1987 Intifada the nationalist forces set the pace and tone of the struggle and managed to form and sustain a considerable level of coordination and a united front in terms of action strategy (Pearlman 2011). This was expressed in a systematic collective effort to discipline and coordinate activities as part of the "restricted violence" approach (JMCC 1991; Kaufman 1990), which was successfully promoted by the nationalist-led United National Command of the Uprising (UNCU). This is not to say that deadly violence did not occur, but rather that nationalist activists perceived the Intifada as national defiance against an unjust authority and an effort to *shake off* (hence Intifada) the occupation through civil disobedience, and that limiting violence would serve better their goals as well as facilitate broad participation.

Not all PLO factions fully agreed with this line of reasoning and a considerable portion of the Palestinian public was willing to employ more militant tactics (Khalidi 1988: 504). Nevertheless, the UNCU was consistently the central leadership throughout most of the Intifada. To secure broad participation, it designated specific roles and activities, all rooted in the Palestinian primary frameworks: to women, the "creators of warriors" and to witness and defuse rites of violence (Peteet 1994); to children, the "children of the stones" or "sons of the *Fida'yyin*"; and to insurgents in general, the "sons of *Fida'yyin*. Also, it avoided extreme demands that would overburden the population and reduce its ability to endure the struggle. The UNCU also made judicious efforts to equally glorify a variety of modes of actions (e.g., *Sahmed* and *Fida'y*). Referring to the children, Kuttab denotes, "To throw a stone is to be 'one of the guys'; to hit an Israeli car is to become a hero; and to be arrested and not confess to having done anything is to be a man" (1988: 15). Here too, for male youths, taking risks and coping with beatings and detentions were elements of masculinity embedded in the primary framework of the <subject>, expressions of fearlessness and assertiveness which were part of rites of passage to manhood (Peteet 1994: 34).

While coordination between the nationalist movement and the Islamic Jihad was relatively successful, the result of past collaboration and Fatah's support of Jihad's operation (Robinson 1997), coupled with the fact the latter was relatively small in size and resource-poor (Frisch 1992), similar attempts with the Muslim Brotherhood were far more complex. Throughout most of 1988, Hamas did not openly oppose the UNCU, despite its criticisms of the nationalists' tactics. Its leaflets emphasized different styles, values, and modes of action, but consistently there were calls for unity to maintain the momentum of the Intifada. Moreover, even though the relative portion of violent calls in Hamas's leaflets during the first

180 *Dynamics of Political Violence*

year of the Intifada was larger than that of the UNCU (Mishal with Aharoni 1989), this was most apparent only towards the end of 1988.

Things began to change in the second half of 1988: first, with the publication of the Hamas Charter in August; second, with the Palestinian declaration of independence in November; and, third and most distinctly, with Arafat's subsequent speech in the UN expressing his willingness to accept a two-state solution. Several weeks before the UN speech, Hamas was still calling for a united Palestinian front. For example, a leaflet from November 25, 1988 (leaflet # 32) appealed for "Full vigilance regarding the Jews' repeated attempts to split the unified Palestinian ranks. ... Let us deny them the opportunity and work together, and stand as one in the face of the common enemy." Several days following the UN speech we nonetheless trace meaningful shifts in both the <verb> and <object>. In a leaflet published on December 23, 1988 (leaflet # 33), Hamas leaders conjured up the historical exemplar of the 1947 jihad battalions and portrayed the nationalists as henchmen of the infidels. As it reads:

> A year has passed which was a new dawn in a situation [previously] fraught with despair ... and in their place the principles of self-sacrifice and martyrdom have arisen. In December of 1947 the battalions of the sacred jihad were established by the hero Abd al-Qadir al-Husseini, as a concrete reaction to the Partition Resolution, No. 181. ... Struggle and confrontation on Sunday ... to mark the anniversary of the founding of the sacred jihad battalions on the soil of Palestine. ... Praise to God, who gives victory to the believers and defeat the infidels and their henchmen, the enemy of religion.

We can see these fissures demonstrated in different images used in the leaflets. While UNCU's leaflets portrayed the insurgents as the sons of *fida'yyin*, as the descendants of the national uprising of 1936, or as *Salah al-Din,* who vanquished the Crusaders, Hamas's leaflets stressed the religious character of the uprising, referring to the story of Haybar[7] and calling insurgents *mujahidin* or *murabitun.*[8] All these references were part of the primary frameworks of <subject> and <verb> but their differential appropriation reflected the growing differences in emphasis and intensity of Islamic keying of "what to do."

Israel, anxious over Hamas's growing role the in the uprising (and its Islamic keying), reacted by arresting several Hamas leaders. Ironically, the heavier and more sophisticated Israeli crackdown against the nationalist forces created an

---

7 A Jewish settlement on the Arabian Peninsula, which was attacked and conquered in the year 628, after Muhammad accused its inhabitants of treachery against Muslims. The remaining Jews were allowed to hold on to their land in condition that half of their crops would be given to the Muslims.

8 Inhabitants of Ribat, settlers in the frontiers of the Muslim world during the initial period of Muslim conquests who were seen as fulfilling the religious precept of defending the kingdom of Islam.

opportunity for Hamas in the first place, legitimizing its own particular keying of action. While at first the "restricted violence" strategy was perceived successful in promoting the struggle vis-à-vis outside third parties (e.g., the international community and Israeli public), growing signs that the Intifada was about to spillover to other arenas (notably inside Israel and Jordan) brought about a harsh Israeli policy aimed at suppressing the uprising by using brute force and live ammunition. Moreover, the hope that "restricted violence" would influence the Israeli public was shattered as the 1988 national elections in Israel resulted in yet another "unity government", but with a stronger right-wing orientation than the former.[9] Thus, the <object> in this case played a central role in influencing the keying of the <verb>. Defense Minister Rabin's policy of massive military presence, extensive arrests, threats of mass deportation, administrative detention, and extensive use of live ammunition only fueled the uprising further. It also led to international media portrayals of Israel as an inhumane occupier and a UN Security Council Resolution N. 605 condemning Israel's "merciless policy" for controlling the Intifada.

In the face of still high numbers of deaths and injuries and consequent harsher international criticism, Israel looked for ways to lower the profile of repression and minimize physical contact with the population (i.e., heavier reliance on collective punishment such as impositions of curfews, closures, sieges, etc.). The new policy for controlling the Intifada involved a systematic attempt by military forces to keep away from main streets and population centers, and to rely more on the use of covert modes of repressive measures (JMCC 1991: 31). This meant increased reliance on intelligence and undercover squads for tracing Palestinian individuals suspected to be the key activists responsible for sustaining the momentum of the uprising.

The new policy proved successful in significantly lowering the Palestinian death toll. It succeeded also in creating confusion and distrust among Palestinians and increased the shootings of alleged collaborators with Israel. All this, plus the rise of a right-wing government in Israel, and a series of brutal attacks on Palestinians (e.g., the Rishon Le'Zion massacre), led to growing frustration and anger among the nationalists and infuriated the population. PLO hard-liners (DFLP and PFLP activists) began to collaborate with Hamas, issuing joint leaflets calling for the use of deadly weapons and appealing for raids on Israel from Arab states. The action frame of "shaking off" the occupation and "restricted violence" shifted to "burning the ground under the feet of the occupation's army . . . until the troops of the occupation are killed in the streets," as a UNCU leaflet issued following the massacre stated (Litvak 1991: 259).

While our analysis focuses on the first Intifada, during the 1990s and towards the run-up to the 2000 Intifada, the action frame was gradually rekeyed by both

---

9   Unlike the "unity government" of 1984–88 during which Shamir and Peres acted as prime minister each for a period of two years (a rotation agreement), this time no such rotation took place and Shamir acted as prime minister throughout the administration.

182 *Dynamics of Political Violence*

nationalist and Islamist activists to Islamic-based jihad. Arafat appeased the Islamist forces (e.g., releasing Hamas activists from prison) and stated repeatedly that he would march into Jerusalem with an army of *Shaheed*. We can begin to understand this process with reference to several factors in the ongoing keying of "what to do." On the <object's> side, we have the massacre at the Cave of the Patriarchs in Hebron on February 25, 1994 perpetrated by extreme right-wing zealot Baruch Goldstein, the repressive and provocative policy of Netanyahu-led right-wing coalition, the provocative visit of Sharon to the Temple Mount, the Mohamed a-Dura incident in September 30, 2000, and the barbaric lynching of two Israeli reserve soldiers in Ramallah on October 12, 2000. But we also have the deepening polarization and animosity between the Palestinian Authority and the local grassroots forces, developing in reaction to the Authority's misjudgment, corruption, and nepotism as well as to its harsh repressive measures. This process closely combined with developments on the <subject's> side, reflected in meaningful convergence between nationalist and Islamic grassroots forces. The convergence between the forces took shape in the form of the Nationalist and Islamist Front, formed in late 2000, and practically set the pace and tone of a more lethal and deadly cycle of contention labeled *al-Aqsa* Intifada. In striking contrast to the "first" Intifada, with its nationalist-oriented, restricted violence features, the al-Aqsa Intifada label denoted the religious aspect of the struggle against the Israeli-Jewish enemy, with rapidly developing anarchy and warlords, increasing use of terrorist bombings and calls for jihad, supported by flow of money and guidance of Islamic organizations from outside the territories, and an eventual Hamas's taking over of the Gaza Strip.

Conclusion

It is fair to say that the theoretical discourse in the field of protest studies has undervalued the primacy that McAdam, Tarrow, and Tilly place on cultural processes in *Dynamics of Contention*. One of their intentions is an analysis of protest episodes that is "more nuanced than a generation of culturally influenced scholarship" (2001:225), meaning, on the one hand, moving beyond the mechanistic and strategically focused application of framing theory, and, on the other, breaking the descriptive bubble that surrounds narrative and discursive approaches to social movements. We have followed their lead by tracing the temporal sequence of how cultural and interpretative processes work through the major players in Palestinian nationalism. In unfolding contention, culture and agency went hand in hand as primary frameworks were invoked yet variably applied and strategically modified, affecting perceptions of opportunity, threat, and forms of contention as political contexts shifted and collective interests changed among the players. As we have tried to demonstrate, the shift from Palestinian's strategy of national liberation to Islamic jihad was not simply a reflection of a group's ideology (Oliver and Johnston 2000), as some argue with respect to Islamic movements such as Hamas

(Levitt 2006; Litvak 1998; Tamimi 2007). Rather, this shift, as also manifested in the case of the nationalist forces within the broad movement, was an emergent process, the result of:

1. Each group's relative position of power and influence within the movement;
2. Changes in the overall political context that threaten a given group's strategic position; and
3. Repressive measures by the state—all of which combined to influence each group's preferred mode of contention.

In this respect, it is not only that our analysis supports those who warn against settling for an essentialist conception of Islamic activism as inherently violent (Gunning 2008; Wiktorowicz 2004), but it is also that our framework can be utilized to further the analysis of the social and political dynamics of the process of Islamization.

We have endeavored to elaborate the culture-agency nexus, starting with seminal work on framing theory and going back to the original frame-analysis canon. Our approach has reintroduced Goffman's concepts of primary frameworks and keying. Recognizing the cognitive foundation of primary frameworks helps capture how deep cultural patterns can influence the ongoing definition and redefinition of collective action. Additionally, we have introduced the <subject> <verb> <object> distinctions into our analysis, based on the idea that interpretative processes profitably can be analyzed in terms of a basic story grammar of action. This analytical strategy is based on the noncontroversial—in our judgment— assumption that all primary frameworks of contention will minimally have each of these elements in some basic way. Traditional framing theory also captures these elements in concepts such as "collective identity frames" (Hunt, Benford, and Snow 1994), which recognizes that defining the <subject> is an interpretative and sometimes strategic process; and "prognostic and motivational frames," which specify dual aspects of <verb> by defining what to do and how to get participants to do it (Snow and Benford 1988). The ongoing framing and reframing of the opponent, the <object>, has not been a major focus of framing research, although it was recognized in Gamson, Fireman, and Rytina's (1982) innovative study of framing.

We have suggested, further, that the usefulness of this method is especially revealed by how it lays bare the internal relatedness and dynamism among these three elements—rather than each being fixed and independent of one another, lifted from a "cultural toolbox" and applied strategically. Thus, there is a fundamental internal dynamic in the keying process by which:

1. Primary frameworks guide but are not deterministic; and
2. For each element, the variable keying of one limits the range of possibilities for the others.

184 *Dynamics of Political Violence*

In this double sense Marx's well-known dictum can be applied to primary frameworks and keying, such that people produce their own meanings, but not in any way they wish.

Finally, our analysis reveals that the keying process itself is a form of contentious politics. Again, this kind of conflict is implicit in the dynamics of contention enterprise, and within the framing perspective. That framing battles occur within movements has been chronicled by several researchers (Snow and Benford 1988; Benford 1993; Ellingson 1995; Ferree, Gamson, Gerhards, and Rucht 2002; Snow 2004), but our approach emphasizes that contention takes place not just over making claims and strategy, the <verb>, but also over identity, the <subject>, and definitions of the <object>, the enemy. While the complexity of interpretative processes is implied by the inherent symbolic interactionism of framing theory, framing research does not capture systematically the dynamism among these basic components. There are ample examples of movements where deep cultural patterns seem to be relevant insofar as they get "keyed" and extended in the fray of political contention. Nationalist movements and ethnic minority movements come immediately to mind, but also, it is a suggestive proposition that culture-war issues that mobilize contending movements over hot-button issues like abortion, public prayer, and the definition of marriage tap primary frameworks and build upon them in the heat of struggle. Another suggestive proposition is that primary cultural frameworks are especially potent in activating emotional responses to political challenge (Taylor and Whittier 1995; Jasper 1997; Polletta 2006).

We cannot close without discussing the implications of our analysis to several of the robust processes and mechanisms offered by the *Dynamics of Contention* research program. We have in mind, most notably, the general process of actor constitution (which itself is a "robust" *interpretative* process—McAdam, Tarrow, and Tilly 2001: 313) and its related mechanisms of identity shift for the <subject>, social appropriation and innovative action for the <verb>, and certification/ decertification and category formation for the <object> which, as recognized by the authors, are still in need of refinement and specification as causal forces. Our analysis offers several proposals in this respect, most notably, demonstrating the persistent role of primary frameworks in the keying process for all three elements. Among Palestinians, the <subject> was keyed in terms of Islamic struggle. This occurred because of primary frameworks, "framing battles" with other contenders over the <subject> owner and because of the influence of outside resources—the keying process in not a closed system.

Second, our analysis has shown that while causal mechanisms work in many directions, there is justification that further research pursues the primacy of some relationships over others. We have in mind the dependency of strategy on collective identity, as mentioned above, it being the predicate of the subject. Paralleling the emphasis that the "new social movements" perspective placed on collective identity but applying it provocatively in a political process analysis, our study suggests that definition of the subject—the movement's collective identity—is a

The Islamization of Palestinian Nationalism 185

hinge on which crucial elements of collective action open and close, most notably, strategic decisions and perceptions of the target and of threat.

Last, while the process of actor constitution captures the dynamic between the collective actor and its object, our tripartite schema is a more parsimonious way of showing how the object's actions affect not just the subject's "actor constitution" but also the keying of "what it must do" and how it keys the object or target. We have seen how Israel's draconian crackdown on Hamas strengthened the Muslim Brotherhood's role in the battle over defining the <subject>. McAdam, Tarrow, and Tilly's formulation of actor constitution captures the dynamic relation of different mechanisms in multiple ways (2001: 315–17), but this "robust process" then needs to be linked with other interpretative/ cultural processes regarding action strategy and perception of opportunity/threat. While presumably the next step in their analysis, these mechanisms are all covered by the umbrella of the semantic triplet.

References

Alimi, E.Y. 2007. *Israeli Politics and the First Palestinian Intifada: Political Opportunities, Framing Processes, and Contentious Politics*. New York and London: Routledge.
Benford, R. 1993. "Frame Disputes in the Nuclear Disarmament Movement. *Social Forces* 71: 409–30.
Benvenisti, M. 1989. *The Shepherds' War*, Jerusalem: Jerusalem Post Press.
Benvenisti, M. 1992. *Mahol Ha'Haradot* [Fatal Embrace], Jerusalem: Maxwell-Macmillan-Keter.
Daqqaq, I. 1983. "Back to Square One: A Study in the Reemergence of the Palestinian Identity in the West Bank 1967–1980," in *Palestinians across Both Sides of the Green Line*, edited by Alexander Schölch. London: Ithaca Press.
Doumani, B.B. 1992. "Rediscovering Ottoman Palestine: Writing Palestinians into History," *Journal of Palestine Studies* 21: 5–28.
Ellingson, S. 1995. "Understanding the Dialectic of Discourse and Collective Action: Public Debate and Rioting in Antebellum Cincinnati." *American Journal of Sociology* 101: 100–144.
Ferree, M. Marx, W.A. Gamson, J. Gerhards, and D. Rucht. 2002. *Shaping Abortion Discourse: Democracy and the Public Sphere in Germany and the United States*. New York: Cambridge University Press.
Franzosi, R. 1999. "The Return of the Actor: Interaction Networks among Social Actors during Periods of High Mobilization in Italy." *Mobilization* 4: 131–49.
Franzosi, R. 2004. *From Words to Numbers: Narrative, Data, and Social Science*. New York: Cambridge University Press.
Gamson, W.A. B. Fireman, and S. Rytina. 1982. *Encounters with Unjust Authority.* Homewood, IL: Dorsey.

Ghanem, A. 2001. *The Palestinian-Arab Minority in Israel, 1948–2000: A Political Study*, Albany: SUNY Press.

Goffman, E. 1974. *Frame Analysis*. New York: Doubleday.

Gunning, J. 2008. *Hamas in Politics*. London: Hurst & Company.

Hatina, M. 2001. *Islam and Salvation in Palestine*, Tel Aviv University: The Moshe Dayan Center for Middle Eastern and African Studies.

Hunt, S, R.D. Benford, and D.A. Snow. 1994. "Identity Fields: Framing Processes and the Social Construction of Movement Identities." Pp. 185–208, in *New Social Movements*, edited by H. Johnston, E. Larana and J.R. Gusfield. Philadelphia: Temple University Press.

Jasper, J.M. 1997. *The Art of Moral Protest*. Chicago: University of Chicago Press.

Jerusalem Media and Communication Center. 1991 *The Stone and the Olive Branch: Four Years of the Intifada–From Jabalia to Madrid*, East Jerusalem: JMCC.

Kaufman, E. 1990. "The Intifada's Limited Violence," *Journal of Arab Affairs*, 9:109–21.

Kimmerling, B. and J.S. Migdal. 1999. *Palestinim: am be'ivatzruto* [Palestinians: the making of a people], Jerusalem: Keter.

Khalidi, R. 1997. *Palestinian Identity: The Construction of Modern National Consciousness*, New York: Columbia University Press.

Kuttab, D. 1988. "A Profile of the Stonethrowers," *Journal of Palestinian Studies*, 17: 4–23.

Levitt, M. 2006. *Hamas: Politics, Charity, and Terrorism in the Service of Jihad*. New Haven: Yale University Press.

Litvak, M. 1991. *Palestinian Leadership in the Occupied Territories*, Tel Aviv: Moshe Dayan Center for Middle East and African Studies.

Litvak, M. 1998. "The Islamization of the Palestinian-Israeli Conflict: The Case of Hamas." *Middle Eastern Studies* 34(1): 148–63.

McAdam, D., S. Tarrow and C. Tilly. *Dynamics of Contention*. New York: Cambridge University Press.

Mishal, S. with Aharoni, R. 1989. *Avanim Ze Lo Hakol* [Speaking Stones], Tel Aviv: Hakibutz Hamehuad.

Mishal, S. and Sela, A. 1999. *Zman Hamas: alimut ve'pshara* [The Hamas Wind: Violence and Coexistence]. Tel Aviv: Miskal.

Morris, A. 2000. "Reflections on Social Movement Theory: Criticisms and Proposals." *Contemporary Sociology*, 29: 445–54.

Morris, B. 1987. *The Birth of the Palestinians Refugee Problem: 1947–1949*, Cambridge, UK: Cambridge University Press.

Noonan, R.K. 1995. "Women Against the State: Political Opportunities and Collective Action Frames in Chile's Transition to Democracy." *Sociological Forum* 10(1): 81–101.

PALGRIC, Survey of Israeli Settlements in the West Bank and the Gaza Strip, 1995.

Paz, R. 1992. "Ha'gorem Ha'islami Ba'intifada" [The Islamic Factor in the Intifada], in *Be'ein Ha'conflict: ha'intifadah* [At the Core of the Conflict: the intifada], edited by G. Gilbar, and A. Susser. Tel Aviv: Hakibutz Hamehuad.

Pearlman, W. 2011. *Violence, Nonviolence, and the Palestinian National Movement*. Cambridge: Cambridge University Press.

Peteet, J. 1994. "Male Gender and Rituals of Resistance in the Palestinian "Intifada": A Cultural Politics of Violence," *American Ethnologist* 21: 31–49.

Polletta, F. 2006. *It Was Like a Fever: Storytelling in Protest and Politics*. Chicago: University Chicago Press.

Robinson, G.E. 1997. *Building a Palestinian State*, Bloomington, Indianapolis: Indiana University Press.

Sa'di, A.H. 2002. "Catastrophe, Memory and Identity: Al-Nakbah as A Component of Palestinian Idenity," *Israel Studies* 7: 175–98.

Said, E. 1986. *After the Last Sky*, New York: Pantheon.

Snow, D. 2004. "Framing Processes, Ideology, and Discursive Fields." pp. 380–412 in *The Blackwell Companion to Social Movements*, edited by D.A. Snow, S.A. Soule, and H. Kriesi. Malden, MA: Blackwell.

Snow, D.A., and R.D. Benford. 1988. "Ideology, Frame Resonance, and Participant Mobilization." Pp. 197–217 in *International Social Movement Research,* edited by B. Klandermans, H. Kriesi, and S. Tarrow. Greenwich, CT: JAI Press.

Snow, D.A., and R.D. Benford. 1992. "Master Frames and Cycles of Protest." Pp. 133–55 in *Frontiers of Social Movement Theory,* edited by A.D. Morris and C. McClurg Mueller. New Haven, London: Yale University Press.

Snow, D.A., E. Burke Rochford Jr., S.K. Worden and R.D. Benford. 1986. "Frame Alignment Processes, Micromobilization, and Movement Participation." *American Sociological Review* 51: 464–81.

Steinberg, M. 1999. "The Talk and Back Talk of Collective Action: A Dialogic Analysis of Repertoires of Discourse among Nineteenth-Century English Cotton Spinners." *American Journal of Sociology*, 105: 736–80.

Swedenburg, T. 1990. "The Palestinian Peasant as National Signifier," *Anthropological Quarterly* 63: 18–30.

Tamimi, A. 2007. *Hamas—A History from Within*. Northampton, MA: Olive Branch Press.

Taylor, V., and N. Whittier. 1995. "Analytical Approaches to Social Movement Culture: the Culture of the Women's Movement." Pp. 163–87 in *Social Movements and Culture*, edited by H. Johnston and B. Klandermans. Minneapolis: University of Minnesota Press.

Tilly, C., and L.J. Wood. 2003. "Contentious Connections in Great Britain, 1828–34." Pp. 147–72 in *Social Movements and Networks: Relational Approaches to Collective Action*, edited by M. Diani, and D. McAdam. Oxford and New York: Oxford University Press.

Wiktorowicz, Q. 2004. (ed.) *Islamic Activism*. Bloomington and Indianapolis: Indiana University Press.

Zuo, J., and R.D. Benford. 1995. "Mobilization Processes and the 1989 Chinese Democracy Movement." *Sociological Quarterly* 14: 178–88.

Chapter 9
Radical or Righteous?
Using Gender to Shape Public Perceptions of Political Violence

Jocelyn Viterna[1]

When describing her sympathies during the 1980s civil war, an elderly woman from rural El Salvador ascribed near deity-like qualities to the Farabundo Marti National Liberation Front (FMLN):

> Yes, (I was) with the guerrillas, because they are the ones who defended us. Because without them, who knows, maybe we would have left fleeing and gone right where the enemy was. But they went in front of us. Yes, the guerrillas. Our guerrillas. Part of us. After God and the Virgin, they defended us. (2002 interview with author)

This woman was not alone in her reverence. I conducted 230 in-depth interviews with Salvadoran men and women, most of whom lived in rural war zones, and my respondents overwhelmingly viewed the FMLN of the 1980s as a righteous, not a radical, organization.[2] Intriguingly, they conveyed the righteousness of

---

1 The author is indebted to James Jasper, Susan Woodward, Robin Wagner-Pacifici, Gilda Zwerman, Louis Esparza, Kathleen Fallon, Sara Shostak, Jason Beckfield, Lorenzo Bosi, Chares Demetriou, Myra Marx Ferree, Nina Namaste, Catherine Turco, members of the Politics and Protest workshop at CUNY Graduate Center, and members of the Radicalization and De-Radicalization conference, for their thoughtful comments on earlier versions of this project. Parts of this chapter were presented at the 2010 *Processes of Radicalization and De-Radicalization* conference, sponsored by the *International Journal for Research on Conflict and Violence*, in Bielefeld, Germany, the 2011 Eastern Sociological Society meetings, and the 2011 American Sociological Association meetings. This project is based in part on data gathered through funding from Harvard University, the Milton Fund, Fulbright-Hays, and the Indiana University department of Sociology. Some segments of this chapter were originally published in *Women in War: The Micro-processes of Mobilization in El Salvador* (2013) by Jocelyn Viterna, and have been reproduced by permission of Oxford University Press, http://ukcatalogue.oup.com/

2 These arguments are based on research completed for *Women in War: The Micro-processes of Mobilization in El Salvador,* 2013, the Oxford University Press. The large majority of the 230 interviews were conducted between 2001 and 2002. They included

the FMLN to me through highly gendered narratives. The FMLN protected the vulnerable—defined explicitly as mothers, their children, and the elderly—while their opponents, the Salvadoran Armed Forces, slaughtered innocent women and children. The FMLN protected women's sexuality—often by recruiting young girls into their guerrilla camps—while the Salvadoran Armed Forces regularly raped young girls and cut babies out of pregnant women's bodies. Even the FMLN's practice of regularly requiring children as young as 12 to join its rebel forces did not taint its righteous image among rural Salvadorans. Respondents, many who themselves had been pressed into the guerrilla army, or who had seen their children obliged to participate in guerrilla camps, explained this practice as an unfortunate necessity of war. The FMLN could only protect "vulnerable" civilians if they required the non-vulnerable—all youth, and all men—to join their ranks. Salvadorans maintained this righteous characterization of the FMLN even when discussing wartime guerrilla actions of which they disapproved, or while noting deep dissatisfaction with the present-day actions of the FMLN political party.

The FMLN, like many violent insurgent organizations, claimed thousands of ideological supporters, both in rural El Salvador and around the globe. Some joined their ranks as combatants. Others collaborated by sharing material resources, military information, or political support. Still others sympathized with the organization's goals while abstaining from any direct supportive action, exemplifying Olson's "free riders" (1965). Yet the reasons why violent political organizations are viewed as "righteous" by varied and dispersed populations remains poorly understood.

This oversight is problematic. At present, most scholarship on political violence focuses on two key questions: Why do some groups (and their individual members) embrace violence to reach their political goals—a process often referred to as *radicalization*? And what might be done to transform a preference for violent politics into an embrace of institutional politics—or *de-radicalization*?[3] These questions are of course important in their own right. Nevertheless, scholars' almost exclusive focus on the actions and ideologies of the political groups themselves leave unanswered equally important questions about how interested parties *perceive* the political groups' actions.

In this chapter, I propose three theoretical modifications to the research agenda on political violence. First, I argue that using the term "radical" as a synonym for all political violence imbues this violence with a normative element that limits scholarly advancement. Interested publics do not always *perceive* political violence as "radical." It also may be considered "righteous"—by those who engage

---

men and women, combatants and non-combatants, living in three different rural zones, each which had been highly contested regions during the war. See Chapter 1 and Appendix A for explanations of my data and methods.

3 For excellent reviews of theoretical causes of political violence and collective violence, see Goodwin 2006; Kalyvas 2006; and Tilly 2003. For an important analysis of the process of de-radicalization, or ideologically giving up violence, please see Bosi 2013.

in it, those who sympathize with its use, and even by those whom it victimizes. Scholars therefore cannot fully understand why people engage in or disengage from violent political groups without also studying public *perceptions* of that group's violence. When a violent group's actions are deemed "righteous" by the publics in which they are embedded, then individuals are more likely to (willingly) join in the first place, and will have a relatively easier time re-integrating into their civilian communities after disengagement. This suggests that even so-called "free riders" may play an important causal role in shaping an organization's survival by shaping the meanings attached to that organization's violent actions in the cultural context within which its participants are embedded. I further argue that violent political groups strategically attempt to control the "radicalness" with which their violent acts are judged to meet their own political goals. Those who seek to create fear among their target populations promote radical perceptions of violence, while those who seek supporters and new recruits seek a righteous public face. Studying public perceptions of political violence therefore allows scholars to better understand the form of political violence that a group may choose, and the consequences of that violence for their political power and influence in a region.

Second, I theorize that *gender* is one of the strongest tools mobilized by political leaders to mitigate the radicalness with which the public perceives their organization's violent acts. There are likely many factors that influence public perceptions of political violence over time and across groups, and I certainly do not mean to imply that gender is the only one.[4] Nevertheless, most societies hold deeply seated cultural understandings of women as essentially peaceful human beings, while men are considered naturally prone to aggression and violence (Alison 2009, Gilligan 1982, Elshtain 1987, Mazurana and McKay 1999, Yuval-Davis 1997). Mobilizing imagery from the existing sexual order is therefore a powerful means by which almost any violent organization can shape its public face. Women's entrance into violent political acts, either as victims or perpetrators, charges those acts with emotion. If men commit political violence against women—and especially against women's sexuality—then most audiences perceive that violence as radical. If men's political violence is committed in the name of protecting women—and especially women's sexuality—it becomes righteous. If women commit violent political acts, the violence is generally seen as radical, especially if they commit those acts in response to, or in collaboration with, a male sexual partner. But if an organization can demonstrate that many women—and especially many mothers—are willing to commit political violence

---

4   For example, I anticipate that groups that engage in quantifiably more violence against civilians are seen as more radical than groups using less violence against civilians; and that some particularly brutal types of violence (beheading, cutting off limbs, etc.) are seen as much more radical than killing with traditional weapons like bombs or guns, even when the outcomes (dismemberment, death) may be relatively similar. My purpose in this chapter, however, is to note that relatively similar forms of violence committed by different groups take on different meanings when imbued with gendered narratives.

on their behalf, then that organization becomes especially righteous. Indeed, the narrative goes, no mother would risk her life or the lives of her children for a cause that was not profoundly just. In short, how groups mobilize gender norms may be critical to solidifying their reputation as either the "good guys" or the "bad guys" in any violent political conflict.

And indeed, it is the "guys" that earn the reputation of righteous or radical. As many scholars have documented, women seldom gain honor, prestige, or political power from their involvement in political violence, regardless of whether they are the victims or the perpetrators. Rather, women who participate in violent movements frequently find that promises of emancipation are abandoned with the return to politics as usual. The reason, I argue, is that women's presence in political violence *always* mobilizes essentialist understandings of women as peacemakers—even, ironically, when women themselves are acting violently.

These insights lead to my third argument: Although gendered framing processes may facilitate the successful movement of political groups away from violent and toward peaceful tactics by facilitating individuals' return to civilian life, these same gendered processes may ironically require a rejection of the so-called "radical" feminist agenda—and its concomitant fight for gender equality—to be successful at mobilizing peace.

In what follows, I first review both the feminist and the political literatures on violence. Next, I build from these literatures to theorize how political groups may use gendered narratives to strategically influence public perceptions of their violent acts. Finally, I apply this theory to the case of the FMLN in El Salvador—an organization that regularly utilized gender narratives to de-radicalize its violent image both as a rebel army during a civil war, and as a political party after the war had ended. I conclude that scholars of political violence—and practitioners working to de-radicalize violent groups—must pay greater attention to the gender narratives surrounding the conflict. Such narratives offer new insight into who joins a violent movement, and how likely they are to leave it. My findings also suggest how (un)likely it is for women to gain political, economic, or societal power from their participation in—and creation of—"righteous" political violence.

Why Examine Public Perceptions of Political Violence?[5]

Scholars of political violence, and especially of civil war, have documented several reasons why individuals join violent groups. Importantly, once violence

---

5 Like many scholars of civil war and political or collective violence, I define violence in this chapter as the physical infliction of harm on a person's body. Other scholars have argued convincingly that violence should be defined along a continuum, noting that threats of physical violence, neglect, withholding of life's basic necessities, among others, are often just as damaging to individual's bodies and psyche's as actual physical blows. I am very sympathetic to these arguments, and especially to the work of scholars like

Radical or Righteous? 193

has begun, many individuals join precisely because they lack other options. Some are forcefully abducted into violent groups, while others believe joining one of the violent parties offers their best chance for survival (McKay and Mazurana 2004; Viterna 2006; Humphreys and Weinstein 2008). Still others may join violent groups to gain material goods or political power (Humphreys and Weinstein 2008, Olson 1965); because they feel pressured to support a cause that their community supports (Taylor 1988; Humphreys and Weinstein 2008); to counter an attack— symbolic or violent—on their perceived collective community (Tilly 2003; White 1989); or because they value the pride they garner from participation (Wood 2003).[6] In still other cases, violence may occur because individuals use warring parties to settle individual scores, without regard for the ideological leanings of either faction (Kalyvas 2006). With the exception of forced abduction, all of these proposed causal factors anticipate that individuals make judgments about the organization they are choosing to join: Will the organization successfully offer protection? Wealth? Retribution? A sense of belonging? Activities of which they can be proud?

Yet scholars struggle to answer the question of *how* individuals judge a group's ability to provide them with participatory benefits—tangible or psychological. Individuals seldom have perfect knowledge of violent groups' actions or ideologies. This is especially true in cases of civil war, where what little infrastructure exists is likely disrupted by violence, where schools or other public gatherings are difficult to convene, and where a climate of distrust discourages open communication about political events more generally. It is also true in cases where violent groups operate illegally in a non-warring society, and must protect their identities and activities in order to escape imprisonment.

Given the lack of full information, I argue that individuals rely on the narratives that an organization tells about itself to judge whether or not they want to join or support one group over the other, or attempt to stay neutral. Their individual-level judgments are by necessity embedded in community life. Individuals discuss the actions and narratives of the violent organizations with trusted others, and through this interaction they create shared definitions of those groups. These shared definitions in turn shape both how likely any one individual is to become an ideological adherent and participant in the first place, and how well-accepted that individual may feel by his or her community after demobilizing from violent actions.

Hume (2009), who clearly articulate how violence takes on many forms as it permeates the lives of individuals in especially violent communities. Nevertheless, in this chapter, I choose to follow Tilly (2003, p. 4) and focus specifically on physical violence, while calling for better terminology to parse out other means of inflicting harm. With greater specification, we can better understand the causes and consequences of the various manifestations of harm (physical and otherwise) and how they may or may not interact with one another.

6   For a discussion of the inadequacy of grievance-based explanations, see Goodwin 2004.

194 *Dynamics of Political Violence*

Just as individuals' must make judgments about political groups, those same political groups must also make judgments about which individuals they will recruit to support their efforts, either as internal group participants or as external supporters.[7] Groups' recruitment strategies are varied. They can choose to forcefully abduct individuals, to offer material incentives for participation, or to motivate individuals to join by arguing that their cause is worthy of activism. Groups are thought especially keen to gain ideological adherents, as these are the people expected to stay committed to the organization over the long term. Opportunistic fighters, in contrast, are more likely to defect when material rewards are not forthcoming (Weinstein 2005).

Yet just as individuals do not have perfect knowledge of groups, groups also do not have perfect knowledge of their target audiences. Who is likely to support the cause if invited? When will violence against civilians attract supporters, and when will it repulse them?[8] Are their ways to coerce an individual's participation while still securing their ideological commitment to the organization? In the absence of this knowledge, I suggest that political groups hedge their bets by using pre-existing, shared cultural meanings about certain identities to match potential recruitment messages to their target audiences. For example, a socialist movement might use narratives promising wealth redistribution to recruit poor individuals,, while narratives promising adventure and fortune might be more effective when recruiting youth (Viterna 2013). Because gender norms—and especially gender norms surrounding violence—are remarkably consistent over time and across social categories (Alison 2009; Enloe 2000a, Goldstein 2001) recruitment messages utilizing gendered narratives may be especially useful for mobilizing recruits and supporters of otherwise unknown intentions into violent organizations.

How Perceptions of Violence are Gendered

Scholars and policy analysts make a clear, if sometimes implicit, argument that violence enacted against civilians is more radical, and more worthy of intervention, than violence enacted against other violent adversaries (Kalyvas 2006). What is

---

7 Although much research focuses on why individuals choose to join a group, the more important question may be, "Why do groups choose to recruit a particular individual?" Being recruited may be one of the most powerful predictors of who joins an organization, such that it is difficult to know if (for example) impoverished individuals join an organization because of the material incentives offered, or rather, because that organization focused on recruiting impoverished individuals (Viterna 2013).

8 Jasper labels this a "naughty or nice" dilemma, where a group's leaders try to decide if others are more likely to do as they want when the group is loved or when it is feared (2004:9, 2006). The answer, Jasper tells us, is dependent on the alternatives available to the group, the audiences targeted, the role of adversaries, and other aspects of the specific arena in which the activities are embedded. See also Kalyvas 2006, for discussion of the rational choices warring parties make about when to use violence against civilians.

Radical or Righteous? 195

seldom discussed, however, is how women—or more commonly, "women and children"—come to signify an even more vulnerable, more righteous category of victims, than "civilians" alone. To illustrate: When I Googled the phrase "many of them women and children," the search engine returned 250 million hits to my computer screen.[9] The first three read as follows (emphases mine):

> http://www.unicef.org/emerg/index_45197.html
> NEW YORK, USA, 15 August 2008—UNICEF remains deeply concerned about the safety and well-being of civilians affected by the hostilities in and around South Ossetia, Georgia. According to the UN High Commissioner for Refugees, 100,000 people, *many of them children and women*, have been displaced as a result of the fighting.

> http://www.wsws.org/articles/2009/may2009/afgh-m06.shtml
> US airstrikes kill scores of civilians in Afghanistan
> *By Bill Van Auken 6 May 2009*
> On the eve of a tripartite summit in Washington which the Obama administration has organized with the presidents of Afghanistan and Pakistan, reports from Afghanistan indicate that US air strikes in western Farah province have killed and wounded scores of civilians, *many of them women and children*.

> http://www.telegraph.co.uk/news/worldnews/africaandindianocean/libya/8335934/
> Libya-protests-140-massacred-as-Gaddafi-sends-in-snipers-to-crush-dissent.html
> Wednesday 05 October 2011
> The Telegraph
> Libya protests: 140 'massacred' as Gaddafi sends in snipers to crush dissent.
> *Women and children* leapt from bridges to their deaths as they tried to escape a ruthless crackdown by Libyan forces loyal to Colonel Muammar Gaddafi.

Activists have long utilized "moral shocks" to generate support for their cause (Jasper 1997). But why is violence against "women and children" more effective than violence against "civilians," or even simply "children," in increasing the radical perception of political violence? Enloe (1993) notes that the phrase "womenandchildren" roles off the tongues of journalists around the world as if it were a single word, simultaneously providing justification for politicians' military plans and validation of soldiers' benevolent masculinity as they commit violent

---

9   Search conducted October 5, 2011. This theme continued to be salient in politics and the media as this chapter heads to press. In making the case for military action against Syria, US President Obama stated on August 30, 2013, that "We cannot accept a world where women and children and innocent civilians are gassed on a terrible scale," while CNN and multiple other news agencies reported that "Rebel officials say more than 1,300 people, including many women and children, died recently as a result of chemical weapons (in Syria)". (http://www.cnn.com/2013/08/27/world/meast/syria-chemical-weapons-red-line/index.html)

acts against others. But even Enloe's sharp analysis does not capture the full extent to which the phrase "women and children" is utilized rhetorically to make clear the particularly brutal nature of an episode of violence. Radical violence is not simply launched against gender-neutral civilians—it is regularly launched against female civilians, mothers, and their children.

There is of course truth to this portrayal. Men are overwhelmingly the perpetrators of violence, and women are the overwhelming majority of adults living in civilian communities within conflict zones (Goldstein 2001, Kumar 2001). Women are often victimized in gender-specific ways during violent conflicts, such as when mass rapes or other forms of sexual torture take place. And women are almost always those tasked with the responsibility of maintaining the security of dependents in their families and their communities, often with few real options for protecting themselves or their loved ones from violent attack, or of providing the basic necessities of life in war-torn economies.

But there is another gendered truth that gets significantly less attention. Men are killed at greater rates than women during most political conflicts.[10] And there is increasingly powerful evidence that men are also regularly sexually assaulted and raped in violent political conflicts (Wood 2009, 2012). In the course of my research in El Salvador, I talked to Catholic nuns who regularly treated sexually-brutalized men in health clinics during the war. The torture of men through rape and castration is also mentioned in war autobiographies (Clements 1984), semi-biographical accounts (Argueta 1991), and in a few scholarly studies (Hume 2009; Turshen 1998). Most recently, Leiby's (2012) analysis of Truth Commissions in El Salvador found that, while the UN-sponsored Truth Commission limited its reports of sexual violence only to acts of rape against women, the lesser studied Tutela Legal report included sexual violence against both men and women. Remarkably, the Tutela Legal study found that 53 per cent of sexual violence victims in the Salvadoran civil war were men. Extensive sexual torture of men has also been documented in the Balkan wars. The Zagreb Medical Centre for Human Rights estimates that 4,000 male Croatian prisoners were sexually tortured in Serb detention camps; 11 per cent of those were fully or partially castrated, and 20 per cent were forced to fellate other prisoners (Littlewood 1997).

Despite increasing awareness of the phenomenon, it remains unclear how often men are sexually assaulted during episodes of political violence. Feminist scholars have demonstrated that sexual violence is always underreported. Given the tremendous threat that sexual assault poses to men's masculinity, and given that men have not benefitted from a global movement calling for the recognition

---

10 See, for example, Viterna (2013), La Mattina (2012). War also kills people in less direct ways through malnutrition, exposure, lack of medical care, and so on. These latter deaths likely weigh much more heavily on women and the dependents for whom they care (Nordstrom 1997), yet they seldom receive media and political attention to the same extent as direct physical infliction of violence. As a result, these deaths are less central to understanding how gendered rhetoric manipulates the *portrayal* of political violence.

and support of male victims of political sexual violence as have women, it is logical to assume that men's sexual assault is underreported at much greater levels than women's. Moreover, whereas my respondents, civil society organizations, and policy makers all regularly cited women's sexual victimization as evidence that the Salvadoran Armed Forces were "radical," I have yet to come across any similar systematic and public condemnation of the Armed Forces—or any other politically violent organization—because of their sexual violence against men.

Violence against Women: Normalized or Aberrant?

Violence against women is a central theme in feminist scholarship. Above, I have argued that political violence against women, and especially against women's sexuality, is perceived by interested publics as an especially radical kind of violence. In sharp contrast, feminist scholars have long argued that violence against women is normalized, invisible, and legitimated by men and women alike (Hume 2009, Dobash and Dobash 1998). Beginning with the radical feminists of the 1970s, scholars such as Pateman (1988) and MacKinnon (1982, 1987, 1989) argued persuasively that men's control over women's sexuality is imbued with violence, and is the foundation of gender inequality more generally. Over the next three decades, feminist scholars documented the extensive violence in which many women live their daily lives. They find that women are most likely to be assaulted by men known to them, and not by strangers (Kelly 2000). The significance of the relationship between the woman and her offender therefore comes to be more relevant in evaluating a violent crime than the actual details of the attack itself (Pateman 1988). Women are thought likely to provoke attacks that are launched by men known to them, and are thought to suffer less when assaulted by a known person than a stranger (MacKinnon 1983). Women's "honor" and actions are still regularly considered as admissible evidence when courts deliberate whether a crime was committed against her (Chant and Craske 2003). And cultural understandings of men as naturally violent, and women as responsible for keeping the peace, underpin the attitudinal and legal tendency to blame women for violence committed against them in their own homes.

These themes resonate with the reality of many Latin American women. In El Salvador, men's masculinity is evaluated in part by how well they control the women in their homes—a control that is in many communities thought to require physical force and sexual virility (Hume 2009). Indeed, almost half of all women who have ever been married or in a relationship reported to a state surveyor that they had suffered some form of abuse at the hands of their partner (FESAL 2008)—a statistic that women's organizations believe reflects extreme underreporting. Some scholars posit that post-conflict societies like El Salvador may experience a surge in domestic violence because men who leave violent organizations suffer a "crisis of masculinity." Giving up their hyper-masculinized violent roles during a conflict, failing to find economic employment or other means of social success after the conflict, and the overabundance of weapons (and familiarity with using them) are the factors thought to account for this increase (Hume 2009, Enloe 2000b). The legal system further re-enforces this normalization of violence against women. The domestic violence law in El Salvador, for example, proscribes no punishment for a man who abuses his family members,[11] and a female police officer that I interviewed in El Salvador readily admitted that police seldom respond to calls about domestic violence because gang violence is always present, and always takes priority, in an organization with limited resources.

This understanding of violence against women as normalized initially appears in stark contrast to my earlier argument that violence against women is seen as especially radical. However, the two phenomena both stem from the same gendered order, and therefore are actually quite compatible. *Political* violence against women may generate especially high levels of outrage precisely because it upsets normalized understandings of *masculinity*, not femininity. Raping or otherwise assaulting a woman emphasizes her subordinated status in society, and therefore emphasizes her femininity. As such, violence against women is relatively normalized in everyday life. Yet when rape and sexual torture against women are used to make political statements it upsets normalized expectations about *which* men have control over women's bodies. It also challenges men's role as protectors of society, and the gender order it encompasses. Political violence against women therefore threatens men's masculinity in much the same way that raping or castrating men themselves threatens masculinity. Whereas sexual violence against men is hidden, sexual violence against women may lead to calls for violent retribution as a way of restoring men's honor. This protective or retributive violence, I argue, is overwhelmingly seen as righteous, not radical.

Violent Women: Righteous or Fiendish?

Sjoberg and Gentry write:

> … women are not supposed to be violent. This is one tenet on which various understandings of gender seem to converge. A conservative interpretation of gender sees women as peaceful and apolitical, a liberal view understands women as a pacifying influence on politics, and feminists who study global politics often critique the masculine violence of interstate relations. Women's violence falls outside of these ideal-typical understandings of what it means to be a woman. (Sjoberg and Gentry 2007, 2)

---

11 The civil code does provide punishment for domestic violence, but women's organizations report that most judges defer to the gender violence law for domestic assault cases, a law which does not specify criminal sentencing. Men seldom spend time in jail for any abuse toward women, including domestic violence, rape, and even femicide (Viterna, unpublished).

When we hear about instances of political violence, we assume that the perpetrators are male. Only when a modifier is added to the subject—female insurgents, women terrorists—do we envision violent actors as women. When women do commit violence, mainstream discourses resist assigning agency to those women (Allison 2009, p. 119–21; Sjoberg and Gentry 2007). Rather, they are explained away as deviants, driven to violent acts by mental illness or irrationality, and often by an unhealthy, overly sexual commitment to a male partner.

Yet when groups of women commit violence, in contrast to individual women, that violence is often described as righteous. Precisely because women are considered peacemakers, and precisely because they are considered the subordinated sector of society, their widespread participation in violent groups adds an aura of legitimacy to the politics of the organization. Armed organizations publicize the role of women in their ranks to portray their cause as so just that *even women* are willing to risk their lives, and the lives of their children, to support it. Sharoni (1995, pp. 44–5), for example, argues that Israeli women's service in the national military is not portrayed as a step forward for women's equality, but rather as a signal that the situation is so grave that even women have to fight. Bayard de Volo (2001) notes how Sandinistas in Nicaragua circulated posters of young mothers carrying a baby in one arm and a gun in the other to promote the righteousness of their organization and shame men into participation. In my own research, FMLN leaders noted that pretty young women in uniform were especially talented at gaining new recruits and new supporters. Their femininity tugged at the heartstrings of civilians, making them more likely to share food and resources with the guerrilla army, while their willingness to fight allowed them to shame young men into participating through threats to their masculinity (Viterna 2013). If we women can fight, recruiters would imply, then surely you are man enough to fight, too.

Resolving Contradictions

Violence, Hume tells us, "is implicitly, if not explicitly, measured by the reaction it generates" (2009, 32). When political violence is committed against women (and their children), it generates outrage, and is perceived as especially "radical." Conversely, when political violence is enacted by women against others, it may signal that the violent group is particularly just, and its violence righteous rather than radical. The symbolic significance that women's participation, as either victims or perpetrators, lends to political violence stands in sharp contrast to the invisibility of women's participation, either as victims or perpetrators, in the more personalized, apolitical violence of so-called "normal" times.

Ironically, each of these perceptions of violence is based on the same traditional gender order. In cases of political violence, both women's rape and women's resistance threaten men's cultural role as public protectors. Men's masculinity is threatened when other men rape their women, and men's masculinity is threatened when women show bravery through participating in violent organizations. Both women's rape and women's resistance may leave men feeling ashamed for not adequately fulfilling their role as protector, and this shame has been rhetorically used by violent groups to recruit men into their ranks. Importantly, defining themselves and their actions as those of a righteous protector allows violent groups to portray themselves as *defenders of the moral social order*, rather than as *radicals seeking societal transformation*.

To recap, I have argued that scholars should pay greater attention to how interested publics perceive a group's political violence. Many violent groups gain adherents and activists by strategically portraying their violent actions as righteous, and not radical. I have further argued that gender narratives are likely to be especially effective in molding public perceptions of political violence, because women's participation in political violence—either as victims or as perpetrators—loads those violent acts with symbolic significance. In the following section, I demonstrate how these insights extend our understanding of the actions of the FMLN militant-insurgency-turned-political-party in El Salvador.

Gender and Political Violence in the FMLN

El Salvador, like most of Central America, has high levels of economic inequality and a long history of political violence. For more than two centuries, the nation was ruled by an authoritarian regime, often in conjunction with the state military. In the 1970s, a period of brief political opening led to a flourish of social movement organizing. The Catholic Church promoted a movement for social justice focused on ending poverty and human rights violations while calling for education and dignified standards of living. Simultaneously, the more traditional leftist organizations (socialist organizations, labor unions) argued for moderate improvements in labor conditions and political freedoms. This liberalization experiment came to a brutal halt at the end of the decade, when the state re-inserted its iron hand by targeting the organizers of both movements for torture, disappearance, and death (see Almeida 2008 for summary). The renewed repression forced activists underground, and, in conjunction with the political maneuverings of Castro in Cuba, facilitated the unification of five different militant factions into one insurgent army. The *"Frente Farbundo Martí para la Liberación Nacional,"* called the FMLN or the *"Frente"* for short, officially declared war on the Salvadoran state in 1980. Over the next 12 years, this violent socialist organization proved to be one of the most successful insurgent armies in modern history (Bracamonte and Spencer 1995), gaining control over more than one-third of the national territory, and successfully winning the hearts and minds of thousands of civilians living in rural war zones.

The FMLN is an especially useful case for examining the relationship between gender, violence, and radicalization. First, Salvadoran women were the perpetrators as well as the victims of political violence. Women comprised approximately one-third of FMLN guerrilla forces (Kampwirth 2002, Luciak 2001), and were also regularly victimized by the Salvadoran Armed Forces. Second, the FMLN is one of several violent insurgent organizations highlighted by scholars for its troops' restraint in *not* committing violent acts—and especially not acts of sexual violence—against civilians (Wood 2006, 2008, 2009, 2012). These factors—women's presence in guerrilla camps, women's victimization by the Armed Forces, and the FMLN's *un*willingness to use rape as a strategy or practice of war—helped the FMLN gain and maintain a righteous reputation among rural Salvadorans in the 1980s. And third, the FMLN has continued to struggle against the label "radical" since it converted to peaceful politics in 1992, a fact that demonstrates how struggles against perceived "radicalism" may continue even after political violence ends. In the next two sections, I review how the FMLN used gender narratives to mitigate the "radical-ness" of its image, first as a militant organization, and then as a political party.

From Radical Insurgents to Righteous Protectors

The FMLN guerrilla army gained civilian supporters through a policy of "protecting," rather than brutalizing, civilians living in war zones. This is objectively measured in the UN Truth and Reconciliation study conducted after the war, through my own interviews with Salvadorans in war zones, and through hundreds of published and unpublished "testimonies," where individuals regularly reported how the Salvadoran state's Armed Forces would attack villages, while the FMLN would strive to evacuate civilians prior to the military arrival and escort them to refugee camps.

Importantly, I find that the FMLN avoided direct violence against civilians in large part through gendered, rhetorical coercion (Viterna 2013). The FMLN seldom forcefully abducted individuals into their ranks. Rather, they used narratives defining who constituted "the vulnerable" to make implicitly clear that those who were *not* defined as vulnerable were expected to join the FMLN guerrillas. This practice began in earnest in the early 1980s, when the Salvadoran Armed Forces increased its indiscriminate killings of rural civilians in what they thought to be guerrilla zones. When possible, the FMLN would warn civilians that the Armed Forces were approaching, and offer to evacuate the "most vulnerable" to a safe location, either alongside a guerrilla camp or, later in the war, to internationally sponsored refugee camps. The sweeping majority of my respondents concurred that the FMLN, as a righteous organization, actively worked to move "the most vulnerable" to refuge, and that the "most vulnerable" were defined explicitly as the very old, the very young, and the mothers of the very young. This was in direct contrast to the Armed Forces, who regularly tortured and killed "women and children."

Yet by explicitly defining who qualified as vulnerable, the FMLN also defined who was *not* vulnerable, and who therefore was expected to join the guerrilla forces. Over and over again, my respondents told me that they "had to" join the FMLN, because refugee camps were "only for the vulnerable." "Youth," defined as girls and boys between the ages of about 12 and 18, and all "men" under the age of about 40 or 45, were *not* vulnerable, and were therefore denied passage to refugee camps. This denial effectively obligated men and youth to join the guerrillas. Ironically, respondents would report that they were "obliged" to join the FMLN while simultaneously rejecting any suggestion that the FMLN had forced them to join. "It was always one's choice" was a statement I heard time and again. Respondents saw little contradiction in arguing that they "had to" join and that joining was "their choice," because they believed the situation, not the FMLN, had constrained their options. As the war progressed, the FMLN began to declare certain areas to be "guerrilla zones" and required all youth and men to join their forces even without the threat of approaching violence from the Salvadoran Armed Forces. Even in these situations, respondents continued to frame FMLN actions as necessary and justified. The fact that the FMLN had moved others in their families—mothers, elderly parents, children, and younger siblings—to safety, also left many feeling indebted to the FMLN.[12]

Importantly, the FMLN regularly used narratives about gender when requiring all youth and all men to join the FMLN forces. Men and young boys regularly reported joining the FMLN because they believed it was better to be a willing joiner of the guerrillas than a forcefully conscripted soldier—or victim—of the Armed Forces. They felt that, as men, they had no choice but to fight. Young women, however, should in theory have been freed from such cultural expectations of becoming soldiers. Nevertheless, the FMLN regularly pressed young women into its ranks by embracing another gendered narrative—the expectation that women protect themselves from rape. This theme was prevalent throughout my interviews. When I asked women why they joined the FMLN, they often provided rationalizations like these:

> Look … during these war years … the soldiers did these things---because when the soldiers would arrive to a place, they would- . I never saw it, but I heard a lot of things about other places. That they would arrive to the houses, and because of this the young girls had to flee with the men, because they would rape the young women. There were young girls that they would rape and after raping them they would kill them.

> So there we were, searching for what little security we could find in the guerrillas. We felt safer there. Because, I mean, we thought that we could defend ourselves there, right. And my mom and dad, well, they were getting old, and they had

---

12   Of note, theses narratives of who "had to" fight, and who was vulnerable and should stay in refuge, continued to mobilize individuals even late in the war when violence was more discriminate, and even when individuals were already living safely in refugee camps. Those who traveled to refugee camps as very young children, upon reaching the age of 12–15, were encouraged by FMLN recruiters to return to the war front because, as "youth," it was their obligation to fight, and leave refugee camp life to the "vulnerable." See Viterna 2013.

little kids, and so perhaps they would be spared, they might capture them but maybe they would just take them away if they captured them, but to us, if they were to capture us, they would do other things with us, rape and all that … because those things happened.

I couldn't go to the refugee camp (located in Honduras) because the Honduran soldiers would rape young girls. (But your sister went, didn't she?) Yes but she already had a child, my niece, in her arms. The baby was about five months old, something like that. (And you thought that it was safer to join the guerrillas than to go to a refugee camp?) Yes! (with conviction). Since the very same guerrillas had taken my mother out of the house and to the refugee camp, since she could no longer live there, then I had to go to live with the guerrilla combatants. I couldn't stay in the house or in any other area that wasn't the guerrillas. (Who said that the Honduran soldiers would rape young girls?) Everyone said so.

Early in the war, young women routinely suggested that they joined the FMLN to protect themselves against rape. The consistency of this narrative across my respondents suggested that FMLN recruiters may have highlighted their ability to protect young women from rape as a key explanation for why young women had to join their army instead of staying in the war zone or traveling to a refugee camp. Of course, the Armed Forces *did* engage in rape and sexual violence against civilians as well as against captured FMLN guerrillas—this aspect of the narrative was most certainly based in reality. As noted above, however, there is now significant evidence that sexual violence was enacted with relatively equal frequency on both men and women. Yet only *women* were recruited with the promise of sexual protection from rape. Only *women's* rape featured prominently in the war narratives of my respondents. Moreover, although there was a shared perception among respondents that young girls would be raped in refugee camps, I struggled to find any evidence that rape actually occurred there, suggesting that the FMLN played the "rape protection" card specifically to keep young women from traveling to refugee camps, even when refugee camps may have by many objective measures provided better protection from violence for them than joining the guerrillas.

Respondents also used gendered narratives of vulnerability to demonize the Salvadoran Armed Forces. The state military's brutality was unquestionable. They committed mass murders against unsuspecting civilians in their homes and fields, as confirmed by forensic evidence and post-war testimonies by victims and perpetrators alike. Nevertheless, when the FMLN and their supporters denounced this violence, they often focused most heavily on the Armed Forces' victimization of women and children. One of the most common themes in war testimonies is that the Armed Forces would cut fetuses out of pregnant women's stomachs. See, for example, Representative Gerry Studds' 1981 Report to the Committee on Foreign Affairs in the U.S. House of Representatives (as cited in Chomsky's *Understanding Power*, 2003; emphases mine):

Dynamics of Political Violence

January 17–18, 1981 – Conversations with refugees from El Salvador (conducted in areas along the Honduras-El Salvador border):

The following is an outline of the statements made by refugees to the [delegation led by Representative Barbara Mikulski], as summarized on the scene by the translator accompanying the group:

Interview – Woman No. 1: "This woman fled in November 1980, and while she was then forced to flee, she was one of the last people from her village to flee. She was 9 months pregnant. She had her little baby, which she is holding in her arms right now, in the mountains on her way out to Honduras. The Army was setting up guns, heavy cannon artillery on the hills around their village, bombing the villages and forcing the people away ... . If people were caught in the village, they would kill them. **Women and children alike. She said that with pregnant women, they would cut open the stomachs and take the babies out. She said she was very afraid because she had seen the result of what a guard had done to a friend of hers. She had been pregnant and they took the child out after they cut open her stomach.** And where she lived they did not leave one house standing. They burned all of them ... ."

Interview – Woman No. 2: Maria: "She say that she would like to tell us the following: That many of her family were killed, so many were killed that she doesn't even remember their names ... . About 7 months ago they killed one of her family and the child was an infant and is now in a hospital in a nearby town close to death. The army threw the baby in the river when they found them, and they took them into the woods and later they were found. She personally saw children around the age of 8 being raped, and then they would take their bayonets and make mincemeat of them. With their guns they would shoot at their faces ... ."
Question: "These were army troops or guards?"
Answer: "Troops. Army."
Question: "Did the left ever do these things?"
Answer: "No. No, they haven't done any of those kinds of things ... but the army would cut people up and put soap and coffee in their stomachs as a mocking. **They would slit the stomach of a pregnant woman and take the child out, as if they were taking eggs out of an iguana.** That is what I saw. That is what I have to say ... ."

Interview – Woman No. 5: "[O]nce she saw [the army] kill six women. First they killed two women and then they burned their bodies with firewood. She said, **one thing she saw was a dog carrying a new born infant in its mouth. The child was dead because it had been taken from the mother's womb after the guard slit open her stomach.**"
Ms. Mikulski: "How were the other two women killed?"

Radical or Righteous?

Answer: "First, they hung them and then they machinegunned them and then they threw them down to the ground. When we arrived the dogs were eating them and the birds were eating them. They didn't have any clothes on. They had decapitated one of the women. They found the head somewhere else. Another woman's arm was sliced off. We saw the killings from a hillside and then when we came back down we saw what had happened. While we were with the bodies we heard another series of gunshots and we fled again. ... [I]t's the military that is doing this. Only the military. The popular organization isn't doing any of this."

Despite the prevalence of this act in war-survivors' testimonies, I have found no direct evidence of cutting fetuses out of pregnant women's bodies in my admittedly limited review of various archival documents. Forensic scientists and other investigators often listed those killed, their ages, and noted if a woman was pregnant. Yet none of the lists I came across that included the death of a pregnant woman also noted that the fetus had been cut from the mother's stomach.

Importantly, I am *not* questioning the veracity of claims that some fetuses were cut from some pregnant women's stomachs during the war. I have no doubt that this practice was utilized by the Armed Forces in their campaign of terror. Rather, my point is that the frequency with which this crime is utilized in narratives appears quite high compared to the likely actual frequency of the act. Logic and evidence suggest, for example, that far more men were sexually tortured in the war than were fetuses cut from their mothers' stomachs, simply given the reality that there were far fewer visibly-pregnant women at any one time than there were men. And yet stories of slicing babies from their mothers' bellies are relatively common in wartime narratives, while stories of men's rape, castration, and other forms of sexual assault are almost completely absent.

In sum, wartime narratives portraying the FMLN as "the good guys" were overwhelmingly gendered. Although it is impossible to pinpoint where these narratives first gained force, it is nevertheless clear that FMLN recruiters promoted these narratives strategically when seeking new recruits and civilian supporters in the war zones (Viterna 2013). By painting a picture of a social order as so thoroughly destroyed by the state military that young women had no choice but to join the FMLN, the FMLN secured women's support—as combatants, spies, medics, radio operators, cooks, and sexual partners—in their guerrilla camps. And by painting a picture of themselves as the protectors of the most vulnerable— women, children, and the elderly—in contrast to the Armed Forces, who brutalized pregnant women and raped young girls, the FMLN also secured their image as righteous protectors with the surrounding civilian population.

This positive image of the FMLN prevailed in rural El Salvador over other proposed narratives. The state, for example, painted the FMLN as communist agitators who kidnapped and killed civilians and forcefully recruited youth into their army—narratives that also had a foot in reality. And this positive image prevailed even late into the war, when the Armed Forces limited its use of indiscriminate violence and enacted a policy of winning the hearts and minds of rural Salvadorans. Most centrally to this chapter, this enduring positive image helped the FMLN gain collaborators and new recruits, from both domestic and international audiences, and appears to account in large part for the success of their violent political actions in the 1980s. This positive image also appears critical to the relatively successful demobilization of FMLN combatants at the end of the conflict, as former guerrillas anticipated a warm return when they re-entered civilian life, especially in rural communities.

From Communist Rebels to Christian Politicians

In 1992, a confluence of factors led to the signing of Peace Accords between the Salvadoran state and the FMLN insurgent army. Most centrally for this chapter, the accords called for the demobilization and disarmament of all FMLN guerrillas and a significant reduction in the size of the state military. They also allowed the FMLN to become a formal, legal political party for the first time in its existence. The first truly democratic elections in the nation's history were held in 1994, and pitted the new FMLN political party against the party of the ruling establishment—ARENA. Although a relatively new party itself (formed in 1981), ARENA's leadership was closely tied to both the military and the para-military death squad activities from the civil war.

Despite tremendous enthusiasm and commitment from their supporters, the FMLN experienced a sound loss in the first elections of 1994, winning only 21 per cent of legislative seats and only 31 per cent of the popular vote for president. Following these disappointing returns, internal FMLN party discussions focused on how they could transform themselves from a militant group to an effective political organization that could maintain its base of support while broadening its overall appeal (Silber and Viterna 2009).

The ARENA party did not make this easy for the FMLN. Across the next 15 years, their campaign strategy focused on portraying the FMLN political party as radical communist insurgents in disguise, bent on turning El Salvador into "another Cuba"—or more recently, "another Venezuela." Through television commercials, radio ads, newspaper articles, and interviews on local news programs, ARENA sought to highlight both the former war exploits and present-day socialist connections of FMLN candidates. They suggested that the FMLN, if elected, would force a return to their previous radical ideologies and violent practices. For example, during one morning news program prior to the 2009 elections—fully 17 years after all insurgent activity had ended—a prominent ARENA supporter continually repeated the question, "What is the FMLN good at?" and then answered his own question by stating that "these people" are only good at blowing up bridges, at kidnaping mayors, at instigating massacres, at burning businesses and crops, at killing livestock, at arming terrorists. Other than terrorism, he concluded, the FMLN had never distinguished itself for anything ("Frente a Frente, Canal 2, 8 July 2008). Another commercial made by ARENA supporters surmised that if the FMLN were to win power, Salvadoran children would be conscripted into war to help Chavez fight for socialism, while showing images of scared young boys being armed and forced into military formation (http://www.youtube.com/watch?v=plGBTupMNx0). Another successful ARENA strategy, particularly in the 2004 elections, argued that a socialist FMLN win would compromise El Salvador's relationship with the United States, and result in the deportation of Salvadorans living abroad and an end to the substantial remittances they sent to back to the nation (Rubin 2004). A final strategy argued that socialists like the FMLN are atheists, and their anti-Christian values, if brought to power, would destroy Salvadoran families and kill innocent unborn children (Arena Propaganda). The overarching message was clear: the FMLN was not a legitimate political party, but rather a radical, violent political organization. If it were to gain political power, it would radically transform the values that good Salvadorans held dear— freedom, peace, and family.

The FMLN, in response, suffered a number of internal divisions. Party leaders argued over whether to stick to their more radical ideological roots or transform themselves into a more mainstream political party. Such divisions are perhaps not surprising given its founding as a coalition of five separate organizations each with a distinct political vision and history. Where the FMLN factions seemed to find the most consensus in rebranding itself was in its slow but consistent backtracking on earlier commitments to gender equality. Early FMLN commitments to always place a woman on the presidential ticket have been foregone. Party-level gender quotas are only loosely enforced. Women's organizations' calls for strengthening legislation against domestic violence, or for enforcing men's payment of child support, have been met with relative apathy from male FMLN legislators. But perhaps most visibly, the FMLN has moved over the past few decades from a militant organization that distributed birth control and utilized abortion in some of its guerrilla camps in the 1980s, to a political party that by 2008 publicly pledged its continuing support for one of the most extreme anti-abortion laws in the world. This move toward increasingly conservative gender values, I argue, helped the FMLN transform its image away from "radicals" intent on changing El Salvador into "another Cuba" toward a righteous, religiously-affiliated organization intent on defending the existing social order (Viterna 2012).

It was not a given that the FMLN political party would eventually adopt a pro-life stance on abortion. When the Peace Accords were signed in 1992, abortion was legal in El Salvador under three circumstances: when the life of the mother was at risk, when the pregnancy was the result of a rape, or when the fetus had abnormalities incompatible with life. In 1995, the postwar legislature began to draft a new criminal code, which initially called for modest expansions in abortion rights. In response to a powerful new pro-life movement, the ARENA party proposed an alternative code that would criminalize abortion in every circumstance. This conservative alternative quickly gained support from the smaller, centrist, Christian Democratic Party. Yet the FMLN initially rejected ARENA's proposal. Some of its representatives made public pro-choice statements (Hipsher 2001). And despite some internal dissent, the party initially voted uniformly for the limited liberalization of abortion rights in the criminal code, and against the total abortion ban. However, the FMLN did not have enough votes to stop the total abortion ban from becoming law in 1997.[13]

The pro-life movement, in conjunction with ARENA, next proposed a constitutional amendment that would commit the Salvadoran state to protect life "from the very moment of conception." The FMLN again voted against this amendment in the first round, but by the second round of voting, when it was clear that they would not have enough votes to block the passage of the amendment, the FMLN leadership allowed its parliamentary representatives to "vote their conscience." The constitutional amendment passed in 1999, with all FMLN deputies either voting in favor, or abstaining.

Party members seldom discussed publicly the FMLN's capitulation to the pro-life movement in the years following the 1999 constitutional amendment. The FMLN made no official statements in favor of or against abortion, and they maintained the official line that abortion was a personal issue that each party member should decide upon individually. However, in 2008, the pro-life movement brought a "Book of Life" to the legislature, asking all deputies to sign it in a symbolic gesture of commitment to the current legislation, making it nigh impossible for the FMLN to continue skirting the issue. In the end, all FMLN representatives signed the book, publicly confirming their commitment to support life from the moment of conception to its natural death, and the complete criminalization of abortion (Accion Mundial 2008).

Although pro-life statements were regularly used by ARENA in presidential campaigns, the FMLN continued to mostly avoid the issue in its campaigning until the 2009 presidential elections. This year, Mauricio Funes won the presidency on an FMLN ticket, marking the first time in the history of the nation that a left-leaning government controlled executive power in El Salvador. Certainly, there were a number of reasons that Funes won in 2009, including his reputation as a centrist candidate with ties to big business; Obama's election in the US; and an increasing disillusionment with ARENA for failing to mediate the economic crisis, lower crime rates, or combat corruption among its officers. Nevertheless, I argue that one of the key ways that Funes successfully de-radicalized the FMLN image in the 2009 election was through moderating the portrayal of the party's policies on gender.

In the 2009 election, ARENA once again utilized its proven tactics of portraying the FMLN candidate as a radical socialist. They publicized pictures of Funes standing side by side with Hugo Chavez. They highlighted the role played by

---

13 Salvadoran abortion laws against abortion result in doctors legally refusing surgery to Salvadoran women with ectopic pregnancies so as not to "kill" an already doomed fetus (Hitt 2006). These laws have also been used to imprison a woman for having a spontaneous miscarriage, because according to the courts, she should have done more to prevent the miscarriage and protect the unborn child in her body (United Nations Human Rights Committee 2010). See Viterna 2012 for additional information.

Funes' wife in organizing world socialist forums in Brazil and in El Salvador. They mobilized US politicians to state that a "socialist" FMLN victory would severely damage El Salvador's political relationship with the United States. Yet Funes seemed relatively impervious to these accusations. Why? Unlike his predecessors, Funes embraced leftist calls for "social justice"—rhetoric affiliated more with the Catholic Church's "liberation theology" than the party's more historic and radical calls for "social revolution." In his campaign appearances, Funes highlighted his education in Catholic schools, his close ties to Catholic priests, and his proven record as a journalist who acted as a watchdog against bad politics by both major political parties. He framed re-distribution programs as the Christian thing to do, not as a means of revolutionizing society. In short, Funes' embrace of the Church succeeded in making long-standing FMLN economic policies appear mainstream, and Christian, not radical and "socialist."

In the end, ARENA's remaining "radical" attack against Funes was that he was pro-abortion, a claim they supported by quoting Funes on the issue in prior years. Despite the FMLN's recent history of supporting pro-life legislation, one campaign commercial asked, "If Funes and the FMLN are in favor of abortion, would you trust the future of your country to them?" (http://www.youtube.com/watch?v=zIidIw0LTOA). The battleground had changed, but once again, the "bad guys" were framed as those who, at least figuratively, cut babies out of women's stomachs.

In response, Funes publicly promised on the campaign trail to support the nation's existing laws penalizing all forms of abortion, including when the life of the mother is in danger. And he has kept his promise. Salvadoran women's organizations were initially heartened when Funes appointed a woman with clear feminist ideals to head the state women's office. However, when this woman signed an international agreement questioning the complete criminalization of abortion in El Salvador, Funes immediately removed her from office, and stripped the organization of much of its autonomy.

In sum, although the FMLN has remained relatively consistent on its economic policies and priorities over the years, they have profoundly changed their position on a woman's rights to control her own body and sexuality. These increasingly conservative changes were by no means inevitable. Other leftist parties in Latin America have recently moved toward the liberalization of abortion rights, and Cuba, one of the FMLN's strongest allies, has long had some of the most liberal abortion laws in the world.

Most importantly, every instance where the FMLN moved toward an increasingly conservative position on abortion occurred in *direct response* to a concerted campaign by the opposition to paint the FMLN as too radical for democratic politics—a campaign that regularly referenced the FMLN's violent start as an insurgent communist organization. The FMLN's desire to succeed in institutional politics, and to counter the political opposition's claims of FMLN radicalism, seems to have been a critical factor pushing the party to embrace increasingly conservative gender policies.

Conclusion

The word "radical" most typically refers to a deviation from what is accepted and traditional. Using violence to achieve political goals may seem radical to some observers, but to others, political violence may seem profoundly acceptable, and not remotely radical. When interested publics believe that the enactors of political violence are defending society's most vulnerable and protecting a morally legitimated social order, then it is especially likely that the shared cultural meanings attached to this group's political violence will include righteousness, not radicalism.

Gender is one of the most profound organizers of social life. Disruptions of the gender order not only threaten public institutions, but also threaten power relations in the most intimate parts of people's lives—the personal relationships of family and community. Actions that threaten the gender order are by definition "radical," whereas actions deemed to protect the vulnerable (typically women and children), and to maintain men's control over [their own] women's sexuality, maintain the existing social order, and resist implications of radicalization.

In this chapter, I have forwarded three arguments. First, I argue that it is inappropriately normative to categorize all political violence as "radical." Political violence is only radical when it deviates from what is acceptable to a specified group. Understanding whether interested publics see violence as radical requires scholars to investigate both how violent organizations strategically frame their violence for certain audiences, and how those audiences in turn evaluate the organizations' actions. Understanding whether and how key audiences understand a group's violence will in turn improve scholars' understandings of why those groups engage in violence in the first place, what kinds of violence they choose (for example, whether or not to engage in sexual violence), and how difficult it will be for individuals to demobilize from violent groups.

Second, I argue that gender narratives may be particularly effective at radicalizing or de-radicalizing public perceptions of political violence over time and across space, because of the extraordinary consistency in cross-cultural (and behavioral) associations between gender and violence. Political violence committed against women is generally considered an outrage, especially when it threatens men's traditional control over their own women's sexuality. In contrast, political violence committed in the name of defending women, and especially women's sexuality, is viewed as righteous, even when committed by non-state groups with otherwise radical political goals. Meanwhile, women's participation in political violence offers groups an aura of legitimacy. Women are thought to be the peacemakers in any society, so when women participate as combatants, it suggests that a cause is so just that *even women* are willing to fight for it.

In the case of the FMLN, narratives of sexual violence against women, and the presence of women combatants, were central to building a public image of the FMLN as a righteous organization. This was true within my interviews, as well as within broader media and archival reports advocating sympathy for the

Radical or Righteous?   211

FMLN cause. In contrast, sexual violence against men, which was also prevalent in the war, was never implicated in rhetorical discussions of good and bad in the Salvadoran civil war, either by my respondents, or by other public reports. Remarkably, the FMLN even used narratives of protecting women from sexual violence as a recruiting tool, suggesting to young women that guerrilla camps were the only places where they would be safe from rape in wartime El Salvador. Thus even when women were taking on radical new roles as guerrilla combatants in wartime El Salvador, the FMLN was still framing these new roles as necessary for protecting women's sexuality from assault by strangers. By defending the "most vulnerable"—women and children—and by protecting women's sexuality, the FMLN in essence portrayed its political violence as rational, not radical, and as a critical factor supporting, not challenging, the existing moral social order.

Third, the utility of gender narratives for mitigating the perceived radicalness of violent political organizations may have real-world implications for peace seekers and feminist activists alike. We know that when an organization's political violence is perceived as especially radical, then the men who participated in that organization have greater difficulty re-integrating into society than those who participated in organizations where violence was perceived as less radical (Humphreys and Weinstein 2007). Because women's participation as both victims and perpetrators in political violence can make an organization's violence seem heroic rather than heinous, it follows that men find it easier to re-integrate into society when exiting a group that utilized gender narratives to prove its righteousness.

Yet the implications for women and feminist progress in post-conflict societies are much less rosy. Despite the symbolic significance that women's participation, as both victims and perpetrators, lends to political violence, women themselves seldom leave political conflicts with righteous reputations. Women who are victims of sexual violence find few resources to support themselves or their children in post-conflict societies that frequently prioritize women's sexual purity. Meanwhile, evidence suggests that women activists have greater difficulty than men re-integrating into civilian society, often because governments and civil society organizations do not pay significant attention to demobilizing women (Denov 2007). This chapter suggests these difficulties may also stem in part from the cultural artifact that women activists are not privy to the honor that men get from their service as "protectors," and in part from the reality that women exiting "righteous" violent groups leave behind a situation where they are encouraged to defend themselves from violence—and even given the tools to do so—and enter a post-conflict situation characterized by an increasing level of private, apolitical violence, with few options for legitimately defending oneself from that violence.

These theoretical conclusions raise important questions about the compatibility of peace processes with goals of gender-egalitarianism in post-conflict societies. Many studies have documented how women who participate in violent political movements are re-subordinated, and how promises of gender equality are often abandoned, with a return to normalcy (See Alison 2009, Chapter 3, for an excellent overview). This "patriarchal backlash" is typically considered an *outcome* of the

212 *Dynamics of Political Violence*

de-mobilization process. In contrast, I suggest that a patriarchal backlash may be a central component of the *process* of de-mobilization. Formerly violent groups aiming to distance themselves from their past radical actions may be strategically inclined to eschew any "radical" agendas. Feminism, as an ideology that seeks to profoundly re-shape social relations between men and women is, by definition, profoundly radical. It is therefore to be expected that any political organization seeking to de-radicalize its public image—a task often required when trading in the use of political violence for peaceful politicking—would also support the re-installation or continuation of conservative, mainstream, normalized gender relations more broadly.

References

Accion Mundial. 2008. Todos los diputados de la asamblea legislative firman el libro de la vida. [Online, June 2008]. Available at: http://www.accionmundial. org/nota.php?seccion=news&archivo=2008–06_sal_diput_firman_libro_vida. [accessed: April 22, 2013].

Alison, M.H. 2009. *Women and Political Violence: Female Combatants in Ethno-National Conflict*. London and New York: Routledge.

Almeida, P. 2008. *Waves of Protest: Popular Struggle in El Salvador, 1925–2005*. Minneapolis: University of Minnesota Press.

Argueta, M. 1991 (1980). *One Day of Life*. New York: Vintage.

Bayard de Volo, L. 2001. *Mothers of Heroes and Martyrs: Gender Identity Politics in Nicaragua, 1979–1999*. Baltimore: Johns Hopkins University Press.

Bosi, L. 2013. Safe Territories and Violent Political Organizations. *Nationalism and Ethnic Politics* 19:80–101.

Bracamonte, J.A.M. and Spencer, D.E. 1995. *Strategy and Tactics of the Salvadoran FMLN Guerrillas: Last Battle of the Cold War, Blueprint for Future Conflicts*. Westport: Praeger.

Chant, S. and Craske, N. 2003. *Gender in Latin America*. London: Latin American Bureau.

Chomsky, N. 2002. *Understanding Power: The Indispensable Chomsky*. 9th edn. New York: The New Press.

Clements, C. 1984. *Witness to War*. New York: Bantam Books.

Denov, M. 2007. Girls in fighting forces: moving beyond victimhood. *Canadian International Development Agency*. [Online]. Available at: http://www.crin. org/docs/CIDA_Beyond_forces.pdf. [accessed: April 23, 2013].

Dobash, R.E. and Dobash R.P. 1998. Violent men and violent contexts, in *Rethinking Violence against Women*, edited by R.E. Dobash and R.P. Dobash. Thousand Oaks: Sage, 141–98.

Elshtain, J. B. 1987. *Women and War*. New York: Basic Books.

Enloe, C. 1993. *The Morning After: Sexual Politics at the End of the Cold War*. Berkeley: University of California Press.

Enloe, C. 2000a. *Maneuvers: The International Politics of Militarizing Women's Lives*. Berkeley: University of California Press.

Enloe, C. 2000b. *Bananas, Beaches, and Bases: Making Feminist Sense of International Politics*. Berkeley: University of California Press.

FESAL. 2008. Encuesta Nacional de Salud Familiar, Asociación Demográfica Salvadoreña. http://www.fesal.org.sv.

Gilligan, C. 1982. *In a Different Voice: Psychological Theory and Women's Development*. Cambridge, MA: Harvard University Press.

Goldstein, J. 2001. *War and Gender: How Gender Shapes the War System and Vice Versa*. Cambridge and New York: The Cambridge University Press.

Goodwin, J. 2004. What must we explain to explain terrorism? *Social Movement Studies* 3, 259–62.

Goodwin, J. 2006. A theory of categorical terrorism. *Social Forces* 84 (4), 2027–46.

Hipsher, P. 2001. Right and left-wing women in post-revolutionary El Salvador: feminist autonomy and cross-political alliance building for gender equality, in *Radical Women in Latin America: Left and Right*, edited by V. González and K. Kampwirth. University Park: Pennsylvania State University Press, 133–64.

Hitt, J. 2006. Pro-life nation. *The New York Times Magazine*. [Online, April 9]. Available at: http://www.nytimes.com/2006/04/09/magazine/09abortion. html?pagewanted=all&_r=0 [accessed: April 20, 2013].

Hume, M. 2009. *The Politics of Violence: Gender, Conflict and Community in El Salvador*. West Sussex: Wiley-Blackwell.

Humphreys, M. and Weinstein, J.M. 2007. Demobilization and reintegration. *The Journal of Conflict Resolution* 51(4), 531–67.

Humphreys, M. and Weinstein, J.M. 2008. Who fights? the determinants of participation in civil war." *American Journal of Political Science* 52(2), 436–55.

Jasper, J. 1997. *The Art of Moral Protest: Culture, Biography, and Creativity in Social Movements*. Chicago: University of Chicago Press.

Jasper, J. 2004. A strategic approach to collective action: looking for agency in social-movement choices. *Mobilization* 9, 1–16.

Jasper, J. 2006. *Getting Your Way: Strategic Dilemmas in the Read World*. Chicago: The University of Chicago Press.

Kalyvas, S. N. 2006. *The Logic of Violence in Civil War*. New York: Cambridge University Press.

Kampwirth, K. 2002. *Women and Guerrilla Movements: Nicaragua, El Salvador, Chiapas, Cuba*. University Park, PA: The Pennsylvania State University Press.

Kelly, L. 2000. Wars against women: sexual violence, sexual politics and the militarised state, in *States of Conflict: Gender, Violence and Resistance*, edited by S. Jacobs, R. Jacobson, and J. Marchbank. London: Zed Books, 34–49.

Kumar, K. 2001. Civil wars, women, and gender relations: an overview, in *Women and Civil War: Impact, Organizations, and Action*, edited by K. Kumar. Boulder, Colorado: Lynne Rienner Publishers, Inc, 5–78.

LaMattina, G. 2012. *When All The Good Men are Gone: Sex Ratio and Domestic Violence in Post-genocide Rwanda*. [Online: Institute for Economic Development

DP223, Boston University]. Available at: http://www.bu.edu/econ/files/2012/11/dp223.pdf. [accessed: April 20, 2013].

Leiby, M. 2012. The promise and peril of primary documents: documenting wartime sexual violence in El Salvador and Peru, in *Understanding and Proving International Sex Crimes*, edited by M. Bergsmo, A. Butenschon, and E.J. Wood. Beijing: Torkel Opsahl Academic EPublisher.

Littlewood, R. 1997. Military rape. *Anthropology Today* 13(2), 7–16.

Luciak, I.A. 2001. *After the Revolution: Gender and Democracy in El Salvador, Nicaragua, and Guatemala*. Baltimore: Johns Hopkins University Press.

McKay, S and Mazurana, D. 2004. *Where are the Girls? Girls in Fighting Forces in Northern Uganda, Sierra Leone, and Mozambique: Their Lives During and After the War*. Montreal, Quebec: Rights and Democracy.

MacKinnon, C. 1982. Feminism, marxism, method, and the state: an agenda for theory. *Signs: Journal of Women in Culture and Society*. 7(3), 515–44.

MacKinnon, C. 1983. Feminism, marxism, method, and the state: toward feminist jurisprudence. *Signs: Journal of Women in Culture and Society*. 8(4), 635–58.

MacKinnon, C. 1987. *Feminism Unmodified: Discourses on Life and Law*. Cambridge, MA: Harvard University Press.

MacKinnon, C. 1989. *Toward a Feminist Theory of the State*. Cambridge, MA: Harvard University Press.

Mazurana, D.E. and McKay, S.R. 1999. *Women and Peacebuilding*. Essays on Human Rights and Democratic Development No. 8. Montreal: International Centre for Human Rights and Democratic Development.

Nash, J. 1973. Resistance as protest: women in the struggle of Bolivian tin miners, in *Women Cross-Culturally: Change and Challenge*, edited by R. Rohrich-Leavitt. The Hague: Mouton, 261–71.

Nordstrom, C. 1997. *A Different Kind of War Story*. Philadelphia: University of Pennsylvania Press.

Olson, M. 1965. *The Logic of Collective Action: Public Goods and the Theory of Groups*. Cambridge, MA: Harvard University Press.

Pateman, C. 1988. *The Sexual Contract*. Stanford, CA: Stanford University Press.

Rubin, J. 2004. El Salvador: payback. *Frontline World*. [Online, 12 October 2004]. Available at: http://www.pbs.org/frontlineworld/elections/elsalvador/. [accessed: April 23, 2013].

Sharon, S. 1995. *Gender and the Israeli-Palestinian Conflict: the Politics of Women's Resistance*. Syracuse, NY: Syracuse University Press.

Silber, I.C. and Viterna, J. 2009. Women in El Salvador: continuing the struggle, in *Women and Politics around the World: A Comparative History and Survey*, edited by Joyce Gelb and Marian Lief Palley. ABC-CLIO, 329–51.

Sjoberg, L. and Gentry, C.E. 2007. *Mothers, Monsters, Whores: Women's Violence in Global Politics*. London and New York: Zed.

Taylor, M. 1988. Rationality and revolutionary collective action, in *Rationality and Revolution*, edited by Michael Taylor. New York: Cambridge University Press, 63–91.

Tilly, C. 2003. *The Politics of Collective Violence*. New York: Cambridge University Press.

Turshen, M. 1998. Women's war stories, in *What Women Do in Wartime*, edited by M. Turshen and C. Twagiramariya. London: Zed, 1–26.

United Nations Human Rights Committee. 2010. *Report on Violations of Women's Human Rights due to the Complete Criminalization of Abortion*. 99th Session. Geneva, Switzerland. [Online] available at: http://www2.ohchr.org/english/bodies/hrc/docs/ngos/JointSubmission_ElSalvador100.pdf. [accessed: April 19, 2013].

Viterna, J. 2006. Pulled, pushed and persuaded: explaining women's mobilization into the Salvadoran guerrilla army. *American Journal of Sociology* 112(1), 1–45.

Viterna, J. 2012. The left and "life": the politics of abortion in El Salvador. *Politics and Gender* 8(2), 248–54.

Viterna, J. 2013. *Women in War: The Micro-processes of Mobilization in El Salvador*. New York: Oxford University Press.

Viterna, J. Unpublished. Expert Testimony Prepared for United States Department of Justice Executive Office for Immigration Review, 2011.

Weinstein, J.M. 2005. Resources and the information problem in rebel recruitment. *Journal of Conflict Resolution*. 49(4), 598–624.

White, R.W. 1989. From peaceful protest to guerrilla war: micromobilization of the Provisional Irish Republican Army." *American Journal of Sociology*. 94(6), 1277–1302.

Wood, E.J. 2003. *Insurgent Collective Action and Civil War in El Salvador*. Cambridge, UK: Cambridge University Press.

Wood, E.J. 2006. Variation in sexual violence during war. *Politics and Society* 34 (3), 307–42.

Wood, E.J. 2008. The social processes of civil war: wartime transformation of social networks. *Annual Review of Political Science*. 11, 539–61.

Wood, E.J. 2009. Armed groups and sexual violence: when is wartime rape rare? *Politics and Society* 37(1), 131–62.

Wood, E.J. 2012. Rape during war is not inevitable: variation in wartime sexual violence, in *Understanding and Proving International Sex Crimes*, edited by M. Bergsmo, A. Butenschon Skre and E.J. Wood. Beijing: Torkel Opsahl Academic EPublisher.

Yuval-Davis, N. 1997. *Gender and Nation*. London: Sage.

Chapter 10

From National Event to Transnational Injustice Symbol: The Three Phases of the Muhammad Cartoon Controversy

Thomas Olesen

Introduction

In an earlier set of works, I analyzed how the Muhammad caricatures published by a Danish newspaper, *Jyllands-Posten*, in 2005 were transformed from a national to a genuinely transnational contentious phenomenon over the course of only three months (Olesen 2007a, b, 2009, 2010). This rapid scale shift (Tarrow 2005) indicates a key aspect of contemporary globalization: that local/national events, due to heightened levels of transnational information and consciousness, are increasingly disembedded (Giddens 1991). This has been a recurring finding in the literature on transnational activism since the mid to late 1990s (e.g. Keck and Sikkink 1998; Khagram et al. 2002; Smith and Johnston 2002; della Porta and Tarrow 2005; Tarrow 2005). What is interesting about the Muhammad cartoon case is that it points to a different and perhaps increasingly important kind of transnational activism: one motivated by religious concerns. However, my motivation for addressing the Muhammad cartoons in the context of this volume is not so much to highlight its religious/cultural character. It is rather to bring out what I consider a neglected aspect in the literature on transnational activism: how some events do not only shift scale, but, in that process, are transformed into *transnational injustice symbols*.

It is thus possible to identify *three phases* in the "career" of the Muhammad cartoons, the most famous caricaturing the prophet Muhammad with a bomb in his turban (for a related, but alternative identification of phases, see Lindekilde et al. 2009: 295). From their publication on 30 September 2005 until late 2005, the cartoons were widely debated in the Danish public sphere (phase 1). In January and February 2006, the debate escalated abruptly and violently to the transnational level, with street protests and attacks against Danish embassies and consulates in several countries in the Arab/ Muslim world (phase 2). The protests waned rather quickly and had largely subsided by early April. Yet the cartoons have continued to appear in cultural and political debates. Of particular interest for this volume on political violence, they have been appropriated by the world's leading jihadist organization, al-Qaeda, and are repeatedly cited as motivation and justification for actual or planned terrorist attacks ideologically anchored in political Islam. This tendency has not gone unnoticed by security analysts. In 2009 the national security and intelligence service of Denmark, PET (2009), published a report documenting the continuing presence of the Muhammad cartoons in al-Qaeda's communications. I take this pattern as a powerful indication that the cartoons have entered a new phase and gradually become established as a major and transnationally available *symbol* of the wider injustices perceived by some individuals and organizations to be systematically committed against Muslims and Islam by the West (phase 3). It is the chapter's primary objective to describe and analyze this third phase in the career of the cartoons controversy. Before doing so I offer a theoretical elaboration of the core concept of the chapter: injustice symbols. This is followed by a background section to the first two phases and a note on methodology.

With this approach I hope to contribute a *political-cultural dimension* to the study of transnational activism in general and to the study of political violence in particular. Despite their extreme and fundamentally anti-democratic nature, jihadist activists, like most forms of activism, do engage in public communication activities aimed at explaining and legitimating their goals and strategies. In this they simultaneously draw on and create cultural-political resources. Injustice symbols, I argue, are central to such processes and a key component in the formation and maintenance of *injustice communities*: networks of individuals and organizations ideologically (but not necessarily physically) connected via shared injustice perceptions and identities. It is one of the foremost expressions of contemporary political globalization that such injustice symbols and communities are increasingly constructed at a transnational scale. The Muhammad cartoons, are thus indicative of a wider dynamic: in the longer historical perspective Palestine has been (and continues to be) a potent injustice symbol in transnational jihadist activism; in 1988 Salman Rushdie's novel *The Satanic Verses* generated transnational contention to an extent where it is now a shared transnational memory; and in recent years the Guantanamo Bay detention center (see Olesen 2011) and the Abu Ghraib violations have become rallying points and injustice symbols for radical Islamists and Jihadist terrorists all over the world.

Injustice Symbols

The concept of "symbol" is a notoriously ambigous and amorfous term. It is constantly used in everyday parlance, in media discourse, and in academia. Rather than engaging in the broad definitional exercise that is required for an in-depth treatment of the concept, I opt for a more direct route in this chapter. Elder and Cobb (1983: 28–9) offer an operational, if also quite inclusive, definition:

> A symbol is any object used by human beings to index meanings that are not inherent in, nor discernible from, the object itself. Literally anything can be a symbol: a word or a phrase, a gesture or an event, a person, a place, or a thing.

Given the empirical context of this chapter, it is useful to narrow concern to the way *events* acquire symbolic meaning. For example, Elder and Cobb (1983) and Alexander (2003) identify "Watergate" as a central event related symbol in American political history. This event—the illegal entry of employees of the Republican party into the Democratic party's headquarters in the Watergate Hotel, Washington, D.C. in 1972—has acquired broader significance, becoming a widely shared symbol of political dirty tricks and scandals, even beyond the United States. This interpretation, as shown by Alexander (2003), did not spring automatically from the event itself, but has evolved over time. The latter observation underlines the social and collective character of symbols (Elder and Cobb 1983: 29): events become symbols only when social and political actors begin reading certain meanings into them, and they maintain symbolic status only to the extent that they continue to be evoked beyond the temporal location of the original event. The My Lai massacre in Vietnam in 1968, for example, became a key injustice symbol for anti-war protestors in the United States and the rest of the world during the Vietnam War, but remains an active and resonant element of American political culture. This was recently evidenced when the 2005 Haditha massacre in Iraq immediately started drawing comparisons with My Lai.[1] Similarly, the 1994 genocide in Rwanda—a still powerful and painful symbol of the West's inadequate attention to human rights violations in Africa—is routinely evoked over ten years later in relation to the humanitarian crisis in Darfur (Olesen 2012).

The My Lai and Rwanda examples indicate how many of our best known event related symbols are in fact *injustice* symbols. The injustice component indicates that *activists* are often key players in processes of symbol construction and maintenance (for related arguments, see Jasper 1997: 159; Williams 1995: 127). Activism, says Eyerman (2006: 193):

> … is a form of acting in public, a political performance which involves representation in dramatic form, as movements engage emotions inside and outside their bounds attempting to communicate their message.

Injustice symbols, I would add, are central to such dramatizing and communicating efforts. At their core injustice symbols contain moral-political claims: they help activists to "perform binaries" (Alexander 2004a: 552–3), identifying wrongdoers considered to commit or having committed injustices towards the activist group and/or its constituency (see also Eyerman 2006: 194). Activists, however, are both

---

1 The comparison, however, was not uncontested. Those arguing against the analogy focused on the facts: many more people (between 300 and 500) were killed at My Lai than at Haditha; the My Lai massacre took place over several hours, while that in Haditha occurred within a few minutes; My Lai was the scene of systematic abuse (rape, torture) of villagers, while none such incidents took place in Haditha. Those making the analogy are less concerned with factual similarities. They see Haditha as just another example of the morally unacceptable consequences of US military engagement (the killing of innocent civilians).

220 *Dynamics of Political Violence*

symbol users and producers in a genuinely dialectical process. It is the systematic and repeated inclusion in activist frames over time that transforms events into injustice symbols. Yet once established as such they enter into political culture; they become a discursive resource available to contemporary and future activists. Becoming established does not imply closure. The meaning of a symbol is never fixed. When a symbol is employed in a new context—geographically or temporally—new meanings are added. Similarly, the salience of injustice symbols is strengthened through systematic usage; conversely, a symbol never or rarely evoked undergoes gradual social weakening.

What marks the passage from event to injustice symbol, however, is not simply that an event can be claimed to entail some kind of injustice. In line with Elder and Cobb's definition, injustice symbolization requires that an event is *interpretively extended* by political actors as an exemplar or symptom of a wider situation of injustice. The local and particular, in other words, must undergo a process of *universalization*. Alexander (2004b) has described a related dynamic. In the postwar decades, he argues, the Holocaust experience was gradually transformed from unjust event to transnationally shared cultural trauma:

> This cultural transformation has been achieved because the originating historical event, traumatic in the extreme for a delimited particular group, has come over the last fifty years to be redefined as a traumatic event for all of humankind. (Alexander 2004b: 197)

Alexander's remarks, moreover, indicate that symbolic processes can and do occur at the transnational level. In relation to the formation of transnational injustice symbols, it means that the background event must be politicized by actors *outside* the original setting, who are willing and able to portray it as a problem that affects and/or ought to concern actors and audiences beyond the immediately affected group(s). The motivation to engage and the opportunities to succeed in interpretive extension and universalization is heigthened under certain conditions. The analysis of transnational injustice symbols consequently needs to take transnational political context into account. Political context is of course a desperately broad term. What I specifically have in mind here are *prominent themes and discourses on the transnational agenda*. For example, the My Lai massacre was immediately interpreted as a symptom of a wider problem: the United States' presence in Vietnam and its Cold War related policies in the Third World in general. Similarly, the violations and humiliations in the Abu Ghraib prison and the Guantanamo detention camp (Olesen 2011) have achieved transnational symbolic status partly because they could be interpretively linked with already existing injustice discourses related to the war on terror and Western aggression towards Muslims and Muslim territories.[2]

---

2   These arguments are not meant to suggest that events cannot become injustice symbols in the absence of already existing transnational discourses and attention. Events

From National Event to Transnational Injustice Symbol   221

Injustice symbols are closely associated with what Jasper and Poulsen (1995) call "moral shocks." Jasper (1997: 161) argues that the most effective moral shocks "are those embodied in, translatable into, and summed up by powerful condensing symbols." While it is not entirely clear what "symbols" means in Jasper's use, I understand it to allude to images and other forms of visual representation. Powerful images, in particular, are central in the formation of transnational injustice symbols. In the modern world images have become central to nurturing perceptions of injustice (Butler 2010; Goldberg 1991; Sontag 2003). Yet the popular saying that "an image says more than a thousand words" may be particularly salient in transnational contexts. This is so because images of suffering and humiliation do not require translation and interpretation in the same way as speech or text; they have the ability to bypass social, cultural, and political layers and barriers and affect emotional responses (for a related argument, see Waters 2001: 19–20). On September 30, 2000, for example, a France 2 freelance cameraman recorded a sequence of live images of a Palestinian father and son (Muhammad al-Durrah) caught in crossfire between Israeli and Palestinian forces. At the end of the footage the boy is seen lying over his father's legs, apparently dead from gunshots. The images were rapidly circulated all over the world, giving rise to widespread condemnation, in the Arab world as well as in the West, of Israel's politics towards the Palestinians (Liebes and First 2003): the image in itself had become a transnational symbol of a much wider situation of injustice.[3]

The First Two Phases of the Muhammad Cartoons Controversy[4]

On September 30, 2005 the right-liberal Danish daily, *Jyllands-Posten*, published 12 satirical cartoons depicting the prophet Muhammad. The cartoons intended to stimulate debate over issues of free speech and self-censorhip. Editors at *Jyllands-Posten* argued that free speech in Denmark was threatened by Muslim groups demanding "special consideration of their religious feeling," and that in a secular democratic society everyone "should be able to stand scorn, mockery and ridicule" (quoted from Lindekilde et al. 2009). The cartoons rapidly drew criticism from Muslim organizations in Denmark, in particular *Det Islamiske Trossamfund* (the Islamic Faith Community), as well as from the ambassadors to Denmark of a number of Muslim countries. Unaware of the explosive potential of the cartoons, both the Danish government and *Jyllands-Posten* intially adopted an unconditional

---

can also help initiate such processes. For example, before the Tiananmen massacre in 1989, human rights issues in China were not high on the transnational agenda, but increasingly became so after the dramatic events of 1989.

3   The moral power of the image was, however, somewhat eroded as it later emerged that the killing bullets might not have been fired by Israeli forces and that the footage was manipulated by France 2 to garner sympathy for the Palestinian cause.

4   This section builds on Olesen (2007a, b; 2009; 2010).

stance to the criticism of this *first phase*—for example, Prime Minister Anders Fogh Rasmussen famously refused to meet with the ambassadors behind the above mentioned critque. For many Muslims and for non-Muslims concerned with inter-religious and inter-cultural respect, this represented a display of arrogance that fuelled further contention. In December 2005, *Det Islamiske Trossamfund* decided to take matters into their own hands, touring parts of the Arab world with material to document what they considered a generally hostile climate for Muslims in Denmark (see *Politiken* 2006a for this material). On their tour the delegation met with Egyptian government and Arab League representatives (Exner 2005). During January, and especially as the conflict escalated, the delegation became the target of criticism in Denmark and accused of contributing to the transnationalization of the conflict (Sørensen 2006; see Lindekilde 2010 for an extended analysis of this aspect). During the escalation phase, spokesmen and leaders of *Det Islamiske Trossamfund* became visible public figures in as well as outside Denmark.

While the delegation from *Det Islamiske Trossamfund* probably paved some of the way towards transnational escalation, the controversy only fully entered this *second phase* during January—and especially late January. Satellite television channels *Al-Jazeera* and *Al-Arabiya* played a pivotal role in the diffusion. On February 1, 2005, as the conflict was gathering full force, Naser Khader, a Syrian born Danish MP and co-founder of the association *Demokratiske Muslimer* (Democratic Muslims), thus remarked that the conflict had escalated when *Al-Jazeera* and *Al-Arabiya* started giving the issue attention on January 26, 2005 (Nielsen and Flensburg 2006). The day after, he said, the cartoons were a major theme in Friday prayers in Egypt, Saudi Arabia and Iraq. Khader's observation is supported by a search in *Al-Jazeera's* archive, which reveals that the issue was reported only twice prior to January 26, 2005 on its website. In the following two weeks, it was reported 36 times.

Arab states and organizations also played a key part in the transnational escalation. The Egyptian government seemed especially bent on transnationalizing the issue. In November it dispatched a number of letters to various international institutions, the UN, the EU, the OSCE, the Arab League and the OIC (Organization of the Islamic Conference), trying to set in motion what the Egyptian foreign minister, Aboul Gheit, called a diplomatic campaign (Hannestad 2005). The campaign was aimed at the cartoons and *Jyllands-Posten*, but also at the Danish government's unwillingness to enter the conflict by meeting the ambassadors or at least expressing regret over the cartoons. Egypt's initiatives created few waves in the EU and the OSCE. Unsurprisingly, the OIC and the Arab League, the two main international bodies in the Arab and Muslim world, proved more fertile ground for their claims. On January 1, 2005, the OIC issued a minute in which the organization called on member states to boycott the Danish funded festival Images of the Middle East (*Politiken* 2006b). The OIC was also behind an initiative in late January to ask the UN to issue a resolution that forbids attacks on religious faith (Ringkøbing 2006).

As anger and frustration began to build up, the Danish government and *Jyllands-Posten* felt forced to change tactics towards at least partial concessions. In late January and early February statements were issued that expressed regret (but not outright apology) over the effect of the cartoons (conciliatory statements directed to the Muslim world were also issued by Danish corporations who were beginning to feel the effects of consumer boycotts). While this dampened some groups, others were infuriated by the lack of an unconditional apology. Protests culminated in early February with arson attacks on the Danish embassy in Damascus (February 4, 2005) and the Danish consulate in Beirut (February 5, 2005). Protests continued for several weeks into February, but by early April the second phase of the cartoons controversy had effectively run its course.

A Methodological Note on the Study of Symbols

When is it reasonable to say that the transnationalization of a local/national injustice event has moved from the scale shift phase to the symbolic phase? What kind of evidence is needed to support such claims? The short answer to these questions, in my view, is the following: an event may be said to have entered a symbolic phase when it is systematically invoked and employed by social and political actors—in this case primarily activists and jihadist activists—to legitimate and explain their actions and ideas. Only when such a pattern can be identified does it make sense to argue that the event has become part of the cultural-political structure that activists draw from in their framing activities. This focus on legitimation and communication indicates that researchers interested in symbolic processes need to direct analytical attention to activist text and speech and to the way certain events are integrated in activist framing activities. Above I emphasized that events need to be systematically invoked to qualify as injustice symbols. This necessarily means that symbolization can only be demonstrated at some temporal remove from the original event. The ground work of symbolization may begin already during or immediately after the original event, but it is only partially completed when the event can be shown to continuously appear as a legitimating discursive resource years after. In the case of the Muhammad cartoons these points are reflected in three methodological choices: first, and in line with the general focus on jihadist political violence in the chapter, evidence is identified in the communiqués of the worlds' leading jihadist organization, al-Qaeda; second, evidence has been gathered from a number of aborted terrorist attacks motivated by the Muhammad cartoons; third, the analysis of this evidence is placed within a temporal frame that seeks to demonstrate the cultural-political anchoring of the controversy.

Symbolization and the Third Phase

The section opens with two tables; the first identifies and reports a selection of key statements by al-Qaeda pertaining to the Muhammad cartoons; the second identifies and reports a selection of successful and unsuccessful/aborted terrorist acts related to the Muhammad cartoons. This is followed by an analysis of the data presented in Tables 10.1 and 10.2.

Dialectics and Action in Symbol Development

From Table 10.1 it is notable that two years have passed from al-Qaeda's initial appropriation of the cartoons and what might be seen as the second wave of cartoon-related communication in 2008. A closer look at the background for the second wave reveals an interesting finding. The renewed verbal attacks by bin Laden and al-Zawahiri in March and April 2008 came as a response to a reprinting of the cartoons in a number of Danish newspapers earlier that year. This reprinting, in turn, was a response to the arrest of a group of Danish Muslims suspected to have plotted to murder cartoonist Kurt Westergaard (see Table 10.2, incident 1). This relation suggests that the formation of the Muhammad cartoons as a transnational injustice symbol did not take place in isolation from the original setting, but rather in a dialectical interplay. The original event and its initial construction as an injustice against all Muslims was undoubtedly a motivating factor behind the aborted assasination plans (recall bin Laden's 2006 justification of attacks on the cartoonists; see Table 10.1, quote 2). At the same time, the reprinting of the cartoons that followed in the wake of the arrests contributed strongly to the growth of the injustice symbol, further increasing its transnational salience, visibility, and contentious potential. As demonstrated by Table 10.2, the majority of aborted or successful terrorist attacks in Denmark have occurred after 2008. Establishing whether or not there are direct or indirect links between al-Qaeda's employment of the cartoons and the incidents reported in Table 10.2 is not the purpose here. Rather, I wish to emphasize how attacks or aborted attacks, in a manner similar to statements, are ingredients in the dialectical and continuously developing character of injustice symbols. As discussed in the theoretical section, injustice symbols evolve through social and political usage. Statements and frames involving the original event is one route; actions are another. Metaphorically, an injustice symbol can be thought of as an event that grows another layer of meaning every time it is employed in framing activities and when actions are conducted that are either immediately or retrospectively legitimated with reference to the injustices of the original event. There is a potentially reinforcing and dialectical dynamic at play here. Every statement and act increases the social and political visibility of the event and convinces (some) audiences of its unjust nature (see the discussion in the concluding section on the contestedness of the symbol). In the context of political violence this may, additionally, involve an increase in the status of specific targets/perpetrators associated with the event.

Table 10.1   Al-Qaeda communiqués related to the Muhammad cartoons

Incident	Quote
1. Ayman al-Zawahiri,[a] video first broadcast on *al-Jazeera*, March 4, 2006	"They did it on purpose and they continue to do it without apologizing, even though no-one dares to harm Jews or to challenge Jewish claims about the Holocaust nor even to insult homosexuals" (cited from BBC 2006).
2. Osama bin Laden, audiocasette speech April 23, 2006	"This speech comes to further urge you and prompt you to [come to] the aid of the Prophet and punish those responsible for the vile crime being committed by some journalists from amongst the Crusaders and the apostate heretics, who have insulted the Prophet Muhammad" (bin Laden 2006).
3. Osama bin Laden, audio recording released by as-Sahab[b] on March 19, 2008	"In closing, I tell you: if there is no check on the freedom of your words, then let your hearts be open to the freedom of our actions.And it is amazing and to make light of others that you talk about tolerance and peace at a time when your soldiers perpetrate murder even against the weak and oppressed in our countries.Then came your publishing of these drawings, which came in the framework of a new Crusade ... (bin Laden 2008).
4. Ayman al-Zawahiri, audio questions and answers session released April 17, 2008	"Denmark has done her utmost to demonstrate her hostility towards the Muslims by repeatedly dishonoring our Prophet ... I admonish and incite every Muslim who is able to do so to cause damage to Denmark in order to show your support for our Prophet" (al-Zawahiri 2008).
5. Mustafa Abu al-Yazid, communiqué related to bombing of the Danish embassy in Pakistan, June 2, 2008	See quotes in Table 10.2, incident 2.
6. Adam Gadahn,[c] video titled "Let's Continue Our Jihad and Sacrifice," released on as-Sahab June 13, 2009	"Had the malicious Crusader Rasmussen defended insulting of the Jews—for example—or casting of doubt of the statistics of what is called the Jewish Holocaust, would he be secretary-general of NATO today? Obviously not" (Gadahn 2009).
7. Ayman al-Zawahiri, video titled "The Facts of Jihad and the Lies of the Hypocrites," released on as-Sahab August 5, 2009	"The publicized crusader campaign did not stop [criticizing] Hijab only, and before that there was the offensive cartoons of the prophet Muhammad, prayer and peace upon him, and before that was insulting the Holy Qur'an in Guantanamo Bay and in Iraq" (al-Zawahiri 2009).

a   At the time of the quote al-Zawahiri was considered second-in-command of al-Qaeda. After the killing of Osama bin Laden in 2011 he was appointed as the new leader of al-Qaeda.
b   As-Sahab is considered to be al-Qaeda's public relations branch; see, for example, Rogan (2007).
c   Adam Gadahn is an American citizen who became affiliated with al-Qaeda in his early twenties. He has a senior position within the network and has been centrally involved in al-Qaeda's communication efforts.

226 *Dynamics of Political Violence*

Table 10.2   Successful and unsuccessful/aborted attacks motivated by the cartoons

Incident	Quote
1. Planned attack on Kurt Westergaard, 2008	On February 12, 2008 three persons (all residents of Denmark) were arrested under suspicion of planning to murder Kurt Westergaard, author of perhaps the best known and most publicized of the 12 cartoons: the prophet Muhammad with a bomb in his turban. One of the arestees was released immediately after, while the remaining two were adminstratively expelled from Denmark, a decision that was later revoked for fears that the arestees would be subject to torture in their country of origin, Tunisia. The decisions were followed by a lengthy legal aftermath that shed some doubt over the quality of some of the evidence presented by the police.
2. Bombing of Danish embassy in Pakistan, 2008	On June 2, 2008 the Danish embassy in Pakistan was struck by a powerful car bomb, killing eight people. That this was a symbolic and long-distance punishment motivated by the Muhammed cartoons was made evident shortly after in a June 3 communiqué by a senior al-Qaeda commander, Mustafa Abu al-Yazid (2008): "And this comes in retaliation for what the infidels from the so-called state of Denmark have published: the insulting cartoons of the prophet Mohammed." This, al-Yazid goes on, "should serve as a warning to the infidel countries … They must apologize immediately, or else this will only be the first step in our struggle." Later in the same year on September 4, al-Qaeda posted a video on the Internet, which showed images and speech of the suicide bomber as well as a computer animated rendition of the attack. In the video the suicide bomber cites the Muhammad cartoons as the reason for the attack and threatens future acts of retaliation (for part of the video, see Live Leak 2008).
3. The Headley/ Rana case, 2009	In October 2009, American authorities arrested two men, David Coleman Headley (formerly Daood Sayed Gilani) and Tahawwur Hussain Rana for alleged terror plots against *Jyllands-Posten*. During the trial in Chicago Headley has told judges that the plans were developed in association with Lashkar-e-Taiba, a Pakistan based Islamic terrorist organization responsible for the 2008 terrorist attacks in Mumbai (Headley also cooperated with Lashkar-e-Taiba in the planning of the Mumbai attacks). At Headley's arrest police found a return ticket from Atlanta to Copenhagen, indicating that an attack was imminent, and discovered several videos of key sites recorded by Headley in Copenhagen before his arrest. In the trial hearings in 2011, it emerged that he had planned attacks on Flemming Rose (the *Jyllands-Posten* editor who commissioned the cartoons) and Kurt Westergaard (see above). Apparently a larger attack had been plotted, but when this was scaled down by Lashkar-e-Taiba, Headley proceeded to carry out a "plan B" in association with Rana (Rana received a guilty verdict for his role lot in May 2011).

Incident	Quote
4. Attack on Kurt Westergaard, 2010	In early January 2010 a Somali man and long-time resident in Denmark, Muhudiin Mohamed Geles, entered the house of Kurt Westergaard (see also incident 1). Westergaard fled to a safe room in the house and avoided injury. The attacker was arrested by police at the scene. It later emerged that he had been loosely affiliated with the Somali terrorist organization al-Shabaab and with al-Qaeda in Kenya. Immediately following the attack a spokesman for al-Shabaab denied direct affiliation, but strongly supported the attack and called on all Somalis in Denmark to carry out new attacks (Astrup and Strudsholm 2010). During the trial, the attacker explained that he had been offended by the cartoons and by the conduct of Westergaard. In 2011 he was found guilty of terrorism and convicted to 9 years in prison.
5. Lors Doukaiev, 2010	Lors Doukaiev, a Chechenian living in Belgium, was arrested on September 10, 2010 in Copenhagen after a bomb had accidentally detonated in a hostel where he stayed. During the subsequent trial evidence was presented to support allegations that the bomb had been intended for *Jyllands-Posten's* headquarters in Aarhus. Doukaievs background and organizational affiliations remain unclear and is believed to have acted as a so-called lone wolf. He was convicted to 12 years in prison in 2011.
6. Aborted attack on Jyllands-Posten, 2010	On December 29, 2010 three men were arrested in an apartment in a Copenhagen suburb (subsequently two other men were arrested in Denmark and Sweden, respectively). In their possession police found a machine gun and a handgun. The men are currently in prison for having planned to attack *Jyllands-Posten's* Copenhagen offices with the intent of killing as many employees as possible. Four of the men are either residents or citizens of Sweden and have various national backgrounds (including Tunisia and Lebanon). The arrests came after Danish intelligence police had observed the group for a longer period.

What is notable in Table 10.2 is how all the incidents (with the exception of incident 2) were either aborted or unsuccessful. In a peculiar twist on the dialectical process it might be speculated that every time a terrorist attempt fails, it becomes potentially more prestigious to conduct a *successful* attack.

A Hierarchy of Perpetrators

Injustice symbols evolve in tandem with the identification of individuals or collectives considered to bear some element of guilt for the injustices committed. In the case of the cartoons, a certain hierarchy or ensemble of perpetrators and potential targets of attacks may be identified. At the micro level we find two persons in particular: Flemming Rose, the commissioning editor at *Jyllands-Posten*, but, as evidenced by Table 10.2, predominantly the "bomb in the turban" cartoonist Kurt Westergaard. At the meso-level *Jyllands-Posten* as a collective is

228 *Dynamics of Political Violence*

considered to bear responsibility. Table 10.2 thus shows how some of the aborted attacks were directed at *Jyllands-Posten* as a whole (for example incidents 5 and 6). At the macro-level "Denmark" is portrayed as as perpetrator (consider for example quote 4 in Table 10.1)—sometimes represented by the Prime minister Anders Fogh Rasmussen ("Crusader Rasmussen"; see quote 6, Table 10.1). The car bomb attack on the Danish embassy in Pakistan similarly demonstrated this construction of collective guilt.

Universalization

There is a rising level of symbolic identification evident in this hierarchy. Rose and Westergaard are responsible in a very direct way due to their editor and author roles. *Jyllands-Posten* and Denmark, on the other hand, are symbolic targets in the sense that the actions of some individuals are extended to broader collectives of which these indviduals are "members." In most instances where the cartoons are mentioned in al-Qaeda statements they are placed in an even broader structural context. The cartoons are, in other words, universalized and presented as a symptom or exemplar of a much wider situation of injustice: the West's systematic oppression of and disrespect for Muslims all over the world. Consider, for example, quote 7 in Table 10.1 where al-Zawahiri locates the cartoons in the context of a string of other unjust occurences such as the Hijab ban in France and Guantanamo Bay. Similarly, in quote 6 the former Danish Prime Minister Anders Fogh Rasmussen's ascendance to the post of NATO general secretary is offered as evidence of a systematic disregard for Muslims and Islam. The growth and resonance of the Muhammad cartoons has consequently been facilitated by the relative ease with they could be fitted into and appropriated by existing injustice discourses and communities at the transnational level (for a discussion of injustice communities in relation to the Guantanamo Bay detention center, see Olesen 2011). These discourses, which exist at a structural level, are dialectically related to injustice symbols. On the one hand, as argued, the transformation from unjust event to injustice symbol is energized and shaped by already available injustice discourses. On the other hand, injustice discourses are themselves constantly evolving social and political forms, which feed on and require a steady flow of injustice symbols to maintain strength and visibility.

The Diversity of Symbol Constructors

For an event to be considered a *transnational* injustice symbol it must be documented that it is interpreted and employed as such by organizations and individuals in a variety of geographical settings. Table 10.2 is evidence of such variety: the Pakistan bomb was planned by al-Qaeda and carried out by what appears to be a Pakistani suicide bomber; in the Headley and Rana case the defendants had Pakistani backgrounds but planned their acts based in Chicago; Lors Doukaiev travelled from Belgium to Denmark to (apparently) attack *Jyllands-Posten*; and the two attacks on Kurt Westergaard were committed or planned by people and groups residing in Denmark. Also, Table 10.1 demonstrates how the cartoons have been appropriated by an organization, al-Qaeda, which is transnational in both its composition and its intended audiences. Admittedly, a good deal of the terrorist incidents reported in Table 10.2 (incidents 1, 4, 6) have origins in Denmark or Sweden. This observation is not incompatible with the transnational argument. As discussed earlier, the national setting of the background event does not become irrelevant as transnational processes escalate, but is rather involved in a dialectical interplay with them. It is not surprising that motivations are more pronounced in milieus and individuals with proximity to the original issue. Yet as it has emerged in several of the trials involving Danish citizens or residents who have committed or planned to commit cartoon-related terrorist acts, these acts and/or plans typically have had several transnational aspects: first, the acts were planned and conceived in tandem with the extensive use of jihadist websites; second, at least some of the individuals and cells involved had received support from individuals and groups outside of Denmark and engaged in terror related travel activity.

The Visual Dimension

The transformation from injustice event to injustice symbol cannot be separated from the visual dimension: the fact that contestation revolved around images/cartoons rather than oral or written statements (for a visual analysis of the Muhammad Cartoons, see Müller et al. 2009). It would be an obvious exaggeration to attempt to explain the cartoons' transformation to injustice symbol with reference to the visual dimension. After all, Salman Rushdie's Satanic Verses achieved injustice symbol status without being visually driven. Furthermore, as the remark on the prohibition of depiction suggests, the character of the images set certain limits on its diffusion potential, at least in the Muslim parts of the world. Notwithstanding these reservations there are at least two image related arguments that require special attention in analyzing the cartoons' transformation to transnational injustice symbol. First, the conflict related not only to the satirical/insulting character of the cartoons, but to the fact that Islam forbids any depiction of the prophet Muhammad. Perceptions of injustice, then, developed at two levels that fuelled each other to become a very powerful focal point for expressions of anger: the character of the images conveyed certain Western stereotypical conceptions of Islam (as perceived from a Muslim point of view) while the depiction in and by itself constituted an instance of Western aggression and insensitivity towards Muslims and Islam. Second, images have a transnational diffusion potential that is greater and works through different, more emotionally charged, mechanisms than oral and written statements. Images have symbolic qualities in the sense that they condense a certain set of meanings in a singular visual expression. This set of meanings can be amplified through textual contextualization, but it also has autonomy in the sense that the image to some extent speaks for itself. This condensing quality makes images highly effective in communication efforts. Of course, as is also

230   *Dynamics of Political Violence*

shown by Müller et al. (2009) in their visual analysis of the cartoons, images are always interpreted through cultural lenses; that is, their meanings are never fixed. This should caution us against exaggerating the transnational diffusion potential of images; at least if by transnational diffusion we understand more or less equal distribution and similar patterns of interpretation on a transnational scale. Yet, and with due reservations that this involves an element of simplification, it may make sense to speak about a transnational Muslim interpretive community. Within this community, and partly as a result of the double insulting nature of the cartoons described above, the Muhammad Cartoons had a strong diffusion potential that in turn has facilitated their transformation to transnational injustice symbol.

Symbols and Cultural-political Consequences

As is well-known within the literature on social movements, measuring and analyzing the effects and consequences of activism is fraught with theoretical and methodological difficulties. Yet it remains essential for political sociologists to at least probe these aspects of the phenomena they study. In the case of the Muhammad Cartoons' injustice symbol, I think it useful to outline two complementing routes to approaching the issue. This is all the more important as it helps to underline the overarching theoretical idea of the chapter; that activists are both producers and users of injustice symbols. First, the Muhammad Cartoons injustice symbol can be viewed as an outcome of activism. The literature on social movement effects and outcomes has been preoccupied with political effects; above all, can activism be shown to have had an effect on policy? It remains less well-researched how activists through their activities also create artifacts such as, for example, symbols. As noted in the introduction the overall objective of the chapter has been to offer a cultural-political contribution to the study of transnational activism and political violence and radicalism. Political violence and radicalism are in many ways prolific producers of symbols in that their actions, as a result of an almost perfect compatibility with news criteria such as drama, conflict, and sensation (Dowling 1986: 14; Laqueur 1987: 121; Schmid and de Graaf 1982: ch. 2) receive wide public attention, thus increasing their social visibility and facilitating entry into political and popular culture. Departing somewhat from the case of the Muhammad Cartoons it is evident, for example, how major terrorist events like 9/11, the 2004 Madrid bombs, and the 2005 London bombs have attained symbolic status and become active elements in both national and transnational political memory.

Yet, and this leads me to the second route, symbols cannot simply be regarded as outcomes; they also have effects. Johnston captures the dialectical sensitivity needed to appreciate this aspect:

> Artifacts are the results of performances, the products that—usually intentionally, but sometimes unintentionally—become available as the foci and/or the raw materials for subsequent performances. (Johnston 2009: 15)

This is a different way of saying what has been underlined repeatedly throughout the chapter: that injustice symbols enter into (transnational) society's cultural-political structure. It is when such a development has occurred that we can begin to consider the effects of injustice symbols. What I have in mind is effect, not in a linear or strictly causal, but rather dialectical manner. When an event is transformed into an injustice symbol, it becomes a potential cultural-political resource for contemporary and future activists (or "subsequent performances" in Johnston's terminology). The case of the Muhammad Cartoons offers important pointers in that direction. As discussed above, the cartoons have, especially since 2008, played a crucial role as a legitimizing and motivating reference for successful or planned terrorist attempts. This is not by any means a mechanical effect: symbols should rather be seen as part of Swidler's (1986) well-known cultural toolbox. Whether and to what extent they are actually employed by political actors depends on context and strategic calculations. What the dialectical approach enables us to appreciate is that symbols and activism are closely intertwined: activism produces symbols, but symbols also produce activism.

Concluding Remarks on the Contestedness of Injustice Symbols

The discussions have so far placed emphasis on the Muhammad cartoons as a transnational injustice symbol in radical Islam and jihadist terrorism, and the way it has evolved within that specific political/ideological framework. This has been done at the price of somewhat downplaying the essentially *contested* nature of the Muhammad cartoons' injustice symbol. Terrorists do by no means enjoy a monopoly over the interpretation of the cartoons. There are at least two aspects of this observation that deserve mention in this concluding section of the chapter. First, while most Muslims felt the cartoons to be an offence against their beliefs, only a minority has considered them to be legitimate ground for violent actions and terror. Thus even among those who share an injustice symbol at a general level, we often find considerable difference in strategies to counter and/or ameliorate the perceived injustice. It underlines what has been emphasized throughout the chapter: that injustice symbols are not fixed social and political entities. Because injustice symbols evolve in the process of social and political action they are under constant negotiation: what should the symbol be taken to mean; and what kind of actions can be legitimated with reference to it? Second, in most European countries, including Denmark, opinions have been divided as to whether the publication of the cartoons should or should not have taken place. Free speech hardliners believe that public critique and commentary should never take social, political, and cultural sensibilities into account (as shown in the background section this was the rationale behind *Jyllands-Posten's* publication of the cartoons). Free speech softliners, in contrast, argue that in a global world and in multicultural societies free speech should be administered in ways that do not deliberately provoke the beliefs and values of certain groups (see Lægaard 2009 for an extended discussion).

232   *Dynamics of Political Violence*

For the hardliners the heated response to the cartoons largely served as proof of their original point. From their perspective, it might be suggested, the reaction rather than the cartoons has become an injustice symbol. For the softliners the cartoons do have elements of an injustice symbol. Their interpretation, however, does not derive from the religious/cultural sources of Muslim criticism, but is based on *political* concerns with tolerance and respect in a globalized world and in multicultural societies. These observations call for a certain qualification of the way the term transnational has been applied in the chapter. The variation within Islam over the interpretation of the cartoons and the opposing interpretations in the West point to a highly heterogeneous transnationalization. Within Islam the cartoons are widely known and accepted as an injustice symbol, but the meanings attached to them are by no means homogenous. In some quarters of the West the cartoons do enjoy an injustice symbol status (although for different reasons that in the Muslim world), while in others it is rather the reactions to the cartoons that have become an injustice symbol. It is a task for future research to investigate, disentangle, and compare this transnational variety of interpretations of the cartoons and to analyze its implications for theoretical concepts and empirical realities such as globalization, the transnational public sphere, and transnational civil society.

References

Alexander, J.C. 2003. Watergate as democratic ritual, in *The Meanings of Social Life: A Cultural Sociology*, edited by J. C. Alexander. Oxford: Oxford University Press, 155–77.
Alexander, J.C. 2004a. Cultural pragmatics: social performances between ritual and strategy. *Sociological Theory*, 22(4), 527–73.
Alexander, J.C. 2004b. On the social construction of moral universals: the "Holocaust" from war crime to trauma drama, in *Cultural Trauma and Collective Identity*, edited by J.C. Alexander, R. Eyerman, B. Giesen, N.J. Smelser, and P. Sztompka. Berkeley: University of California Press, 196–263.
al-Yazid, M. A. (2008). [Online]. Available at: http://www.nefafoundation.org/miscellaneous/ FeaturedDocs/nefadenmarkpakistan0608.pdf [accessed: June 10, 2011).
al-Zawahiri, A. 2008. [Online]. Available at: http://www.nefafoundation.org/miscellaneous/ FeaturedDocs/nefazawahiri0508–2.pdf [accessed: May 22, 2011].
al-Zawahiri, A. 2009. [Online]. Available at: http://www.scribd.com/doc/59358589/The-Facts-of-Jihad-and-Lies-of-Hypocrites-Al-Zawahri [accessed: August 10, 2011].
Astrup, S. and Strudsholm, J. 2010. Al-Shabaab roser angreb mod muhammedtegner. *Politiken*, January 2.
BBC 2006. [Online]. Available at: http://news.bbc.co.uk/2/hi/middle_east/4775222.stm [accessed: June 10, 2010].

Bin Laden, O. 2006. [Online]. Available at: http://www.memri.org/report/en/%20 0/0/0/0/0/ 0/1677.htm#_ednref3 [accessed: June 4, 2010].

Bin Laden, O. 2008. [Online]. Available at: http://www1.nefafoundation.org/ miscellaneous/ FeaturedDocs/nefabinladen0308.pdf [accessed: June 23, 2010].

Butler, J. 2010. *Frames of War: When is Life Grievable?* London: Verso.

della Porta, D. and Tarrow, S., eds, 2005. *Transnational Protest and Global Activism*. Lanham: Rowman and Littlefield.

Dowling, R.E. 1986. Terrorism and the Media: A Rhetorical Genre. *Journal of Communication*, 36(1), 12–24.

Elder, C.D. and Cobb, R.W. 1983. *The Political Uses of Symbols*. New York and London: Longman.

Exner, P. 2005. Danske muslimer opfordrer til global protest. *Politiken*, 10 December.

Eyerman, R. 2006. Performing opposition or, how social movements move, in *Social Performance: Symbolic Action, Cultural Pragmatics, and Ritual*, edited by J.C. Alexander, B. Giesen, and J.L. Mast. Cambridge: Cambridge University Press, 193–217.

Gadahn, A. 2009. [Online]. Available at: http://www.nefafoundation.org/ miscellaneous/ FeaturedDocs/nefa_gadahn0609.pdf [accessed: July 5, 2011).

Giddens, A. 1991. *Modernity and Self-Identity*. Cambridge: Polity.

Goldberg, V. 1991. *The Power of Photography: How Photographs Changed Our Lives*. New York: Abbeville Publishing group.

Hannestad, A. 2005. Egypten føler sig forsmået af Fogh. *Politiken*, November., 18.

Jasper, J. 1997. *The Art of Moral Protest: Culture, Biography, and Creativity in Social Movements*. Chicago: The University of Chicago Press.

Jasper, J.M. and Poulsen, J.D. 1995. Recruiting strangers and friends: moral shocks and social networks in animal rights and anti-nuclear protests. *Social Problems*, 42(4), 493–512.

Johnston, H. 2009. Protest Cultures: Performances, Artifacts, and Ideations, in *Culture, Social Movements, and Protest*, edited by H. Johnston. Farnham: Ashgate.

Keck, M. and Sikkink, K. 1998. *Activists beyond Borders: Advocacy Networks in International Politics*. Ithaca: Cornell University Press.

Khagram, S., Riker, J.V. and Sikkink, K., editors, 2002. *Restructring World Politics: Transnational Social Movements, Networks, and Norms*. Minneapolis: Minnesota University Press.

Laqueur, W. 1987. *The Age of Terrorism*. London: Weidenfeld and Nicolson.

Liebes, T. and First, A. 2003. Framing the Palestinian-Israeli conflict, in *Framing Terrorism: The News Media, the Government and the Public*, edited by P. Norris, M. Kern, and M. Just. New York: Routledge, 59–74.

Lindekilde, L. 2010. Soft repression and mobilization: the case of transnational activism of Danish Muslims during the cartoons controversy. *International Journal of Middle East Studies*, 42(3), 451–69.

Lindekilde, L., Mouritsen, P. and Zapata-Barrero, R. 2009. The Muhammad cartoons controversy in comparative perspective. *Ethnicities*, 9(3), 291–313.

Live Leak (2008). [Online]. Available at: http://www.liveleak.com/view?i=948_ 1220775584 [accessed: August 9, 2011].

Lægaard, S. 2009. Normative interpretations of diversity. *Ethnicities*, 9(3), 314–33.

Müller, M.G, Özcan, E. and O. Seizov 2009. Dangerous Depictions: A Visual Case Study of Contemporary Cartoons Controversies. *Popular Communication* 7(1), 28–39.

Nielsen, H.F. and Flensburg, T. 2006. Khader i fortrolige samtaler med Statsministeren. *Politiken*, February 1.

Olesen, T. 2007a. Contentious cartoons: elite and media driven mobilization. *Mobilization*, 12(1), 37–52.

Olesen, T. 2007b. The porous public and the transnational dialectic. *Acta Sociologica*, 50(3), 295–308.

Olesen, T. 2009. The Muhammad cartoons conflict and transnational activism. *Ethnicities*, 9(3), 409–26.

Olesen, T. 2010. Porous publics and transnational mobilization, in *Transnational Challengers*, edited by S. Teune. Oxford: Berghahn Books, 129–45.

Olesen, T. 2011. Transnational injustice symbols and communities: the case of al-Qaeda and the Guantanamo Bay Detention Camp. *Current Sociology* 59(6): 717–34.

Olesen, T. 2012. Global injustice memories: the case of the 1994 Rwanda genocide. *International Political Sociology* 6(4): 373–89.

PET 2009. Tegningesagen i al-Qaida's ideologiske perspektiv. [Online]. Available at: http://www.pet.dk/upload/aq_tegninger.pdf [accessed: August 4, 2011].

Politiken. 2006a. Delegationens mappe. *Politiken*, February 26.

Politiken. 2006b. Islamisk boykot: forslag om boykot. *Politiken*, January 4.

Ringkøbing, J. (2006). Massivt had mod Danmark. *Politiken*, January 30.

Rogan, H. 2007. Abu Reuter and the E-Jihad: Virtual Battlefronts from Iraq to the Horn of Africa. *Georgetown Journal of International Affairs*, Summer/Fall, 89–96.

Schmid, A.P. and de Graaf, J. 1982. *Violence as Communication: Insurgent Terrorism and the Western News Media*. London: Sage.

Smith, J. and Johnston. H., eds, 2002. *Globalization and Resistance: Transnational Dimensions of Social Movements*. Lanham: Rowman and Littlefield.

Sontag, S. 2003. *At betragte andres lidelser*. København: Tiderne Skifter.

Swidler, A. 1986. Culture in Action: Symbols and Strategies. *American Sociological Review*, 51(2), 273–86.

Sørensen, A.M. 2006. Politisk flertal truer imamerne. *Politiken*, February 4.

Tarrow, S. 2005. *The New Transnational Activism*. Cambridge: Cambridge University Press.

Waters, M. 2001. *Globalization*. London: Routledge.

Williams, R.H. 1995. Constructing the public good: social movements and cultural Resources. *Social Problems*, 42(1), 124–44.

PART IV
Dynamics of (Transnational) Diffusion

Chapter 11
Radicalization from Outside: The Role of the Anarchist Diaspora in Coordinating Armed Actions in Franco's Spain

Eduardo Romanos

The classical difference between moderates and radicals in social movements had a strong geographic component in the case of postwar Spanish anarchism. The clandestine movement in Spain employed notably moderate tactics in its struggle against the Franco regime (1939–1975) while a significant part of the diaspora community defended more radical ones. However, in neither case was adherence to these positions unanimous. On both sides of the border dissident groups were formed which defied the predominant line on tactics. In Spain some of these groups participated in the anarchist insurgency. This chapter examines the process of radicalization which led to the carrying out of armed actions against the Franco regime on the basis of the exchanges that took place between groups and organizations in the homeland and in the diaspora. My hypothesis is that the anarchist diaspora played a central role in the coordination of the armed actions and the transfer of violent tactics to the movement inside Spain.

The study of the radicalization of postwar Spanish anarchism connects two usually separate literatures; that dealing with diasporas and social movement studies (Ellis and Van Kessel 2009, Sökefeld 2006). Within the literature on diasporas I will focus on that part that deals with interactions between diaspora and homeland communities in relation to conflict in the homeland. The role of the diaspora as an agent of radicalization or moderation in homeland conflicts has been the subject of extensive research. Koinova (2010) has recently reviewed major theoretical accounts of this question and identified three major clusters of arguments. The predominant idea in the scholarship is that "diasporas often perpetuate conflicts by way of their traumatic identities, myth of return, attachment to territory and various practices such as fund-raising for radical causes and taking up arms to fight for the homeland" (Koinova 2010: 163). This is supposedly what we find in the intra-state wars of disintegration of former Yugoslavia during the 1990s, the Tamil Tigers and the conflicts in Sri Lanka, the Albanians and the conflict in Kosovo in the 1990s, the Kurds and the conflict in Iraq, and many other cases. However, some scholars find this view biased arguing that certain diasporas (even among those just mentioned) could also be engaged in moderate politics and in peace-building and democratization activities. There is also a third position which holds that diasporas may relate differently to different phases of a conflict cycle in the homeland. As Smith (2007: 10) points out, they can be both peace-maker and peace-wrecker in the same conflict at different periods.

Within the literature on social movements I will here focus on studies of the dynamics of diffusion. The concept of diffusion was imported into social science from physics, more specifically from research into the diffusion of certain types of waves from one system to another (della Porta and Diani 2006). When social movement scholars speak of diffusion they mean "some element of a social movement (e.g. tactic, frame, ideology, protest, repertoire, campaign) is spreading across some set of actors (e.g. organizations, networks, groups, people, communities, states) in a social system either through direct or indirect networks of communication" (Soule 2013). Narrower definitions focus on the idea that the item to be spread must be an innovation (e.g. Rogers 1995, Soule 2004, Givan, Roberts and Soule 2010). Is it possible to speak of innovations in the case of the transfer of violent acts within Spanish anarchism? Political violence was a known and previously used tactic (though to a limited degree) in the repertoire of action of the anarchists (Herrerín 2011, Avilés and Herrerín 2008). "Propaganda by the deed" is a classical form of anarchist action defined as dramatic interventions in the form of violent attacks on property and persons in order to make a major impact on public opinion and denounce a situation of misery and exploitation. Although only sporadically employed, it has contributed to a negative image of anarchists as 'bomb-throwers,' down to the present day (Romanos 2013). It may be worth reminding ourselves here that the activists we are dealing with in this chapter, a significant number of them at any rate, had lived through a bloody armed conflict, the Spanish Civil War (1936–1939) which, according to the latest figures produced half a million fatal victims (Preston 2012, Ledesma 2010).

It might thus be argued that the transfer of violent acts in postwar Spanish anarchism was not diffusion in the strictest sense of the word. However, the innovation may also reside in the employment of violent tactics in a different context from that previously known and the inclusion of new nuances that make the tactic of violence relatively innovative. In any case the transfer does not seem to have been a typical organizational process. The radicalization of Spanish anarchism in the post-war period was a complex process involving groups and organizations within the same social movement, but operating in (and exerting control of, in terms of activist influence) very different spaces (homeland and diaspora), with specific characteristics. It thus seems to me that the discoveries and theoretical debates related to the process of diffusion with social movements may be of assistance in providing a better understanding of the process of radicalization within Spanish anarchism.

The study of the radicalization of Spanish anarchism in this chapter consists of a comparison across time of two of the main processes of diffusion of violent tactics in the movement, those that took place in the late 1940s and the early 1960s. The comparison is focused on four questions: the identity of the transmitters and their position within the social movement, the content of the item being diffused, the kinds of links established between the transmitter and adopter and the form in which the actors become involved in the process. The identification of differences and similarities between the two cases seeks to throw light on the kind of diffusion of radicalization which may prevail in contexts of repression. At the same time this examination of the connection between the dynamics of diffusion (as it is generally understood) and organizational linkages across settings (geographical and national) aims at achieving greater understanding of the processes of radicalization in transnational movements.

The chapter opens with a brief discussion of transnationality in post-war Spanish anarchism. It then turns to a panoramic view of the moderate tactics employed by the homeland community, a brief introduction mainly based on my own previous work. This is followed by a comparison of the two processes of diffusion of violent tactics with four sections dealing with each of the four questions mentioned above. The chapter closes with some final conclusions which summarize its main findings as well as offering some tentative ideas on factors facilitating the relatively low rate of adoption of violence and the relatively limited impact of the armed actions carried out in two cases. The data used for the comparison comes mainly from memoirs written by activists (Alberola and Gransac 1975, Téllez 1996, 1992, 1974, Paz 2001, Christie 2003, Andrés 2006, Gurucharri and Ibáñez 2010).

Spanish Anarchism: A Transnational Movement?

Transnational social movements (TSM) are defined by their ability to mobilize people across national boundaries around a shared aim (Smith 2013). To a large degree research into them has focused on organizational issues, specifically, the emergence and development of transnational social movement organizations (TSMOs), that subgroup of transnationally organized advocacy groups that were founded to promote some form of social or political change (Smith, Wiest and Eterovi 2004, cited in Tarrow 2012: 187). Their existence is not new. Research has shown that they were already present in the second half of the nineteenth century and the first half of the twentieth century (see, for example, Hanagan 1998). However, the number of TSMOs has increased exponentially in recent decades, from the end of the Second World War up to today. This growth has been accompanied by various global trends such as "the growth and increasing bureaucratization of states, the proliferation of intergovernmental institutions, and the expansion of the world economy" (Smith and Wiest 2012: 45). We can thus speak of a bi-directional relationship between global integration and TSMOs. While globalization has undoubtedly had effects on the organizational character of social movements, TSMOs have themselves promoted changes in global economic and political integration.

Was postwar Spanish anarchism a transnational movement? Let us briefly examine the organizational situation of the movement during the Spanish Civil War

240 *Dynamics of Political Violence*

and what the end of that war meant for the movement. The three main movements were: the anarcho-syndicalist trade union *Confederación Nacional del Trabajo* (CNT), the "specific" anarchist organization *Federación Anarquista Ibérica* (FAI) and the youth organization *Federación Ibérica de Juventudes Libertarias* (FIJL), set up in 1910, 1927, and 1932 respectively.[1] The relationship between them was always close and sometimes involved conflict (see Romanos 2009a, 2009b). Towards the end of the Civil War in October 1938, the three organizations came together to set up the *Movimiento Libertario* in the shape of a liaison committee which was to serve as an "organism of cooperation and political consultation" for the anarchist movement as a whole. However, the existence of this body turned out to be more symbolic than real. The end of the war led to hundreds of thousands of Spanish people fleeing into exile, many of them anarchists. The majority went to France.[2] There they reconstructed their networks of activists and created the CNT, FAI and FIJL in exile, which maintained contact with their sister organizations inside Spain. In exile and perhaps even more so inside Spain the CNT was the central organization. Around it gathered the rest of the traditional anarchist organizations and newly created groups as well.

We can thus state that postwar Spanish anarchism was a TSM, though of a special type; one which arose in the context of a war which forced part of the movement's activists to leave their native country and go into exile while other activists remained inside the country. Postwar Spanish anarchism can thus be understood as a TSM of deterritorialized migrants (Hanagan 1998), in this case related to a violent conflict. This is not an isolated phenomenon, quite the contrary. Armed conflicts such as that in Northern Ireland (Maney 2000) and others that took place in other parts of the world, have transformed social movements which were originally local or national in nature into TSMs able to mobilize activists in various countries in search of either a solution to the conflict in question (Almeida 2013) or its radicalization. In the case of Spanish anarchism we are not just talking about a simple TSMO but rather a network of groups and organizations which shared, both in exile and inside Spain, a common collective anarchist identity.

The Moderate Tactics of the Homeland Community

Armed struggle did not represent an effective option for the solution of the "Spanish problem," in the view of the main committees of the CNT, as well as that of the majority of anarchists inside Spain. The "Spanish problem" was General Francisco Franco and his dictatorship, which ruled the country from the end of the

---

1   An additional organization was the female branch of the movement *Mujeres Libres* (Free Women), founded in 1936, although the National Federation was created only in August 1937.

2   About half a million crossed into France in the first three months of 1939, about two hundred thousand returned in the following months.

Radicalization from Outside

Spanish Civil War. The repression organized by the Francoist state decimated the political opposition, including the anarchists. Their organizations were declared illegal and their members were persecuted and suffered reprisals, not only for trying to rebuild these organizations in clandestine form but also for having belonged to them in the past (Álvaro 2006).

Instead of violence, the postwar anarchist movement opted for the creation of and participation in opposition platforms aimed at gathering together mass support from Spanish people and the help of the victorious powers in the Second World War (Romanos 2011a). The most significant of these initiatives were:

1. The *Alianza Nacional de Fuerzas Democráticas*, created in October 1944 by the anarchists along with the socialists and republicans; and
2. The government of the Republic in exile, which the anarchists joined on September 21, 1945 with responsibility for the ministries of Public Works and Agriculture.

Neither of these initiatives achieved their objectives. Furthermore, the second of them had dramatic consequences for the anarchist diaspora as it was the trigger for its division. From that point on there existed two rival groups: those who supported the pro-alliance position of the activists in Spain and those who regarded this policy as alien to the methods and goals of anarchism. This latter group controlled the official bodies of the Spanish anarchist movement in exile (see Romanos 2011b).

After a long period of practically no activity the clandestine anarchists became active again at the start of the 1960s. Once more the main initiatives were moderate and alliance focused and were drawn up by small affinity groups formed by friends or acquaintances whose small-sized and more closed nature helped protect them from police infiltration. Two of these groups formed alliances with dissident elements within other trade unions: with dissidents from the *Unión General de Trabajadores* (UGT) the *Alianza Sindical Obrera* (ASO), based in Barcelona, and with falangist dissidents the trade union initiative known as "*cincopuntismo*," with its base in Madrid. Both initiatives, while relatively important because they represented a boost for the anarchist movement had a rather limited impact and continuity.

Who Coordinated the Violence?

There are four elements involved every diffusion process: a transmitter, an adopter, an item to be diffused, and a channel along which the item may be transmitted. My comparison of diffusion processes in Spanish anarchism focuses in the first place on the transmitters and, more specifically, on their position within the movement. The question of the status of the transmitter seems to be important; is located on the periphery of the movement or, by contrast, occupies a position of power within it with privileged access to the other actors in the social system. The position of the transmitter may affect the identification of the adopter with the transmitter, and, as a result, the quality of the diffusion (Wood 2007, Chabot and Duyvendak 2002, McAdam and Rucht 1993, Strang and Meyer 1993).

During the second half of the 1940s the armed struggle in Spain was coordinated by the main organizations of the anarchist movement in exile in France. Between 1945 and 1947, the diaspora community underwent a process of radicalization or "ideological recovery" (Montseny 1978: 231) which framed the conflict in the homeland in categorical and uncompromising terms (see Lyons 2006). It was proposed that "the nuclei of uprising and rebellion" be encouraged and "resistance and direct action, sabotage" promoted in order to "strike effective blows against the enemy on all fronts" (MLE-CNT 1947: 34). Radicalization meant "opting exclusively for insurrection as the only method for expelling Franco from power" (Herrerín 2004: 99). In this case the anarchist diaspora provided not only financial assistance, which is the most common form of support that migrants provide to insurgent groups (Byman et al. 2001), but also arms and personnel. A *Comisión de Defensa* was formed to coordinate the armed struggle and it was responsible for recruiting "*militantes de acción*" among the diaspora community who were supposed to smuggle arms and explosives across the frontier into Spain and there form resistance groups. The armed actions were financed by the *Fondos Pro-España* collected directly from contributions from exiled activists, cultural activities and membership fees. However, this funding proved to be insufficient. Furthermore, the development of the *Comisión de Defensa* was not without its problems, derived in large measure from the committee proliferation and internal competition which held back the Spanish anarchist movement in exile as a whole throughout its existence.

As well as coordinating and funding armed actions inside Spain, the exiled organizations sought to supervise those groups that carried them out as closely as possible. If these groups acted independently the exiled organizations automatically disavowed them. This was the case of the *Movimiento Libertario de Resistencia* (MLR), which had originally been known as the *Movimiento Ibérico de Resistencia* (MIR) and which was one of the organizations responsible for carrying out armed struggle inside Spain in the 1940s. The name change was the work of Liberto Sarrau, the MLE's representative in Spain and it seems that it irritated those in charge of the exiled anarchist organizations which saw in it the emergence of an autonomous organization which would try to take over the functions of the movement related to the armed struggle. As a result, the organization in exile removed Sarrau from his position and disowned the MLR (Téllez 1992). The control exerted by the exile community over the armed struggle is so clear that when the exiled organizations cut off the supply of resources allocated to violent actions the number of these was drastically reduced (see Herrerín 2004). This cutting off of funding was related to the fear that the Spanish anarchist organizations in France might be banned.[3]

---

3   A turning point in this regard was the consequences of a robbery in Lyon on January 18, 1951. The robbers were allegedly former members of the FAI and the assault left three people dead and various others wounded. The robbery outraged the French public opinion

Radicalization from Outside 243

The situation in the 1960s was different with regard to the position of the transmitters inside the movement in that during this second period armed actions were not coordinated by the movement in exile as a whole but rather by a small group of young people inside it through their own organization: FIJL in exile. The organism specifically founded to coordinate armed actions—*Defensa Interior* (DI)—was formally subordinate to a commission made up of the CNT, the FAI and the FIJL in exile, but the evidence from activists shows that

> ... it was always the FIJL which drove the strategy of armed struggle, which promoted the operations that were carried out and which provided, either from its own ranks or through the contacts it had with young anarchists from other countries, the activists to carry them out. (Gurucharri and Ibáñez 2010: 198)

These young people maintained a considerable distance from their elders, to the extent of feeling "disgusted by the immobility imposed by [the CNT and the FAI]" (Alberola and Gransac 1975: 54). This distance had developed during the second half of the 1950s. In the social world of exiled Spanish anarchism (see Alted and Domergue 2003), the young carried out certain specific activities such as summer "*concentraciones*" at which the armed actions carried out by remains of the guerilla movement inside Spain and the subsequent police repression were discussed. In the view of these young people news of these activities was silenced in the official press of the anarchist organizations in exile. However, the young lacked the economic resources necessary to autonomously organize the armed struggle and so remained to some extent dependent on the CNT. As was the case in the 1940s armed actions were financed by a special fee paid by members, a fund-raising strategy which again failed to raise the amount of money expected (Gurucharri and Ibáñez 2010).

The dependence of the young on the rest of the movement can also be seen in the development of the DI. Its origin and activities coincided with a change in the leadership of highest ranking organism of exiled Spanish anarchism—the *Secretariado Intercontinental*. After this change the return of the former leadership meant the end of the DI's activities inside Spain. The DI was finally shut down in 1965. However, some young people continued with the armed struggle using as a justification a clause in the document that founded the DI which granted freedom of action to militants in cases where other branches of the movement sabotaged or weakened the armed struggle, which is what finally happened. From then on, however, the armed actions were mainly carried out outside Spain, and hence outside the remit of this chapter, which has its focus on armed actions inside Spain.

---

and with it there began a campaign to discredit the CNT in France, a campaign which ended with the arrest of a number of its leaders (Sánchez 2006). From that point on the support and help for armed actions in Spain declined significantly.

What Kind of Violence?

As has already been noted, what was transmitted from the diaspora community to the community of origin was violence in the form of armed actions. This tactic has certain specific characteristics related to the process of diffusion, for example the fact that "collective violent events are very much influenced by previous events" (Soule 2004, Pitcher et al. 1978). The participants in a given movement will be more inclined to use violence if they themselves or other participants in the same movement have used it before. Another peculiarity of this political violence has to do with the difference between the behavioral and ideational types of diffusion with the former involving the transmission of tactics or collective action repertories, and the latter the transmission of collective action frames (see Givan, Roberts and Soule 2010). However, given its dramatic consequences violence seems to be a tactic that will be adopted only if social movement activists in some way have previously shared the ideational process which legitimates it as a form of action. As a result, the difference between behavior and ideas does not seem so clear when it comes to violent tactics inside social movements. Both peculiarities can be seen in some form in the case of Spanish anarchism.

The document produced by the congress of the anarchist movement in exile in 1947 which approved the creation of the *Comisión de Defensa* stated that,

> ... clandestine activities will be carried out in Spain with the aim of crushing the regime of Franco and the Falange [the sole legal political party under Francoism] and achieving the complete liberation of the Spanish people, revaluing and applying direct action methods and encouraging the Spanish revolution in accordance with the objectives of our ideals. (MLE-CNT 1947: 34)

The "direct action" referred to here is the "propaganda of the deed," which consisted of violent attacks on property and persons in order to denounce a situation of misery, exploitation, and/or repression (Romanos 2013). The members of the urban guerrilla movement and the previously mentioned *Movimiento Libertario de Resistencia* (MLR) employed this form of dramatic and direct political violence in the 1940s. The urban guerilla movement was one of the most significant armed initiatives of this period and it focused its activities mainly on the principal cities of Catalonia and especially in Barcelona. Its actions included the sabotage of lines of communication and energy infrastructure, robberies of individuals and businesses and the assassination of informers and regime sympathizers and activists (Paz 2001, Téllez 1992, 1974). The MLR was officially constituted at the *Pleno Regional* of the *Juventudes Libertarias de Cataluña y Baleares* on July 6, 1947. A short time later, members of the MLR assassinated Eliseo Melis, who was thought to be a police informer. Other actions of the MLR included the dissemination of anti-Franco propaganda, robberies of businesses (in search of funding for other actions) and the placing of a bomb in some communication towers in Barcelona, though it was discovered before it went off (Téllez 1992). Some of the guerilla

Radicalization from Outside 245

leaders managed to remain active during the 1950s, but they were only able to do so on a sporadic basis, while the MLR dissolved itself on February 21, 1948.

In this period armed actions were legitimated on the basis that they were a reaction against the repression organized by the Francoist state. Thus the "Details of the organization and functioning of the 'MLR'," define it as a "terrorist type organization" the objective of which was "to use terrorist methods against the terror imposed by fascism the Spanish people."[4] The difference with the radicalization that occurred in the 1960s consisted of a change to a violence that was more symbolic or expressive in nature and that did not include violence against people, except in the case of tyrannicide. *Defensa Interior* (DI) began to take action in 1962 with a series of attacks the most famous of which was the placing of a bomb in the *Basílica del Valle de los Caídos* on August 12, and its activities were carried on by the *Consejo Ibérico de Liberación* (CIL) in 1963. Their members wanted to assassinate the dictator but except in this case the bombs planted in attacks on the regime and its allies (Banks, Opus Dei, the Falange, and so on) were intended to only damage property.[5] The objective of the attacks was to gain international solidarity for activities in opposition to the dictatorship and the dissemination of the lack of freedom in Spain and so damage, in so far as possible, the Europeanist aspirations of the regime and its desire to attract tourists (an important source of income). Into the latter category fall many of the actions of the anarchists, especially those against tourism trade targets, such as the sabotage of aircraft at Spanish airports, or others that were to fly to Spain, which occurred in the spring of 1963.

The call for solidarity found a response in the actions of anarchist groups in other countries. The Italian group *Giovanile Libertario*, for example kidnapped the Spanish Vice Consul in Milan in September 1962 and passed on the information to the DI in order to facilitate its international dissemination (Andrés 2006, Sacchetti 2005, Téllez 1996).[6] The call also attracted the participation of activists from these groups in the diffusion of the armed struggle in Spain (see following section) as well as the participation of other activists on an individual basis. An example of the latter is Stuart Christie, a young Scottish anarchist who came into contact with members of the DI in Paris. In his memoirs he speaks of the new focus given to the use of violence by the young activists. The direct damage of the instrumental violence used by the urban guerilla movement and the MLR in the 1940s was substituted in the 1960s for a violence which sought to raise awareness and capture headlines through actions with a high symbolic impact (Christie 2003).

---

4   Document dated on September 24, 1947 in Spain (deposited in the International Institute of Social History, Liberto Sarrau Archive, 20).

5   However, on at least two occasions these attacks produced victims (Herrerín 2004: 241–5).

6   The action was justified as a response to the death penalty sought for Jordi Conill, an anarchist student accused of planting bombs in Barcelona. Once this sentence was commuted to life imprisonment, the diplomat was released.

Type of Links

In a highly influential and widely cited study, Tarrow (2005: ch. 6), distinguishes three types of diffusion according to the mechanisms that underlie each of them: *direct* (or *relational*) diffusion, which depends on interpersonal ties between initiators and adopters of innovations; *indirect* (or *nonrelational*) diffusion, which relies on impersonal ties through the media or word-of-mouth; and *mediated* diffusion, which relies on the intermediation of third parties acting as translators or brokers among actors who might otherwise have no contact with one another or recognize their mutual interests (see also Tarrow 2012: 174). What kind of links was established in the diffusion processes of the Spanish anarchist movement? In order to answer that question we will have to examine how insurgency and its supporting groups were formed in Spain.

In the 1940s the clandestine anarchist groups supporting the armed struggle were founded in large measure due to personal contacts between activists inside Spain and others in exile. Earlier, young exiled activists had taken part in the creation of a youth organization in France and its first meeting had taken place at Toulouse on 8–9 April, 1945. Later some of these activists cooperated with young militants inside Spain in the reorganization of the FIJL, mainly in the area closest to the border and especially in Catalonia. By the end of 1945 a *Comité Regional* of the FIJL had been created in Barcelona. Later an exiled activist accompanied by another based inside Spain visited various Spanish cities (among others Valencia, Granada, Malaga, Seville, and Madrid) and contacted organized groups of young people (Téllez 1974: 66). This type of tour continued to be carried out for some years and they proved useful for checking the state of the insurgent movement and for supplying both material and symbolic resources (Paz 2001: 215).

Direct, personal relationships were also the link by which groups responsible for carrying out armed operations were formed. For example, the urban guerilla movement in Catalonia had its origin in the support groups which accompanied the delegations sent from France to liaise with groups inside Spain (Téllez 1992: 61–2). Furthermore, a document drafted by the MLR in September 1947 illustrates the role played by interpersonal networks of trust in the formation of the committee which was to coordinate the activities of this organization: the representative in Spain of the *Comisión de Defensa* in exile "charged one of the comrades with whom he collaborated with the preliminary work for start of the MLR's activities. This comrade in turn looked for a second comrade and when he found him the two together looked for a third, so constituting the *Comité revolucionario.*"[7] At another level, the *Comisión de Defensa* in exile was composed of five members representing the organizations that were members of the anarchist movement with four representing the movement in exile and with one representing the movement inside Spain. The latter either travelled now and again to France or lived there and maintained contact with Spain by way of activists carrying out liason functions.

---

7   Document cited in note 4.

In the 1960s interpersonal relations also played a fundamental role in the reactivation of the armed struggle. In this context it is worth highlighting the contacts made by Quico Sabaté, one of the most famous anti-Franco guerrillas, with various groups of young exiles, especially from the Paris area. Furthermore, the youth meetings at which the activities of Sabaté and other guerrillas were discussed were often held, and not by chance, in parts of France adjacent to the routes used by the *maquis*. Some of the young people who later participated in the DI had experience contacting activists inside Spain as they had carried out liason activities for the CNT in exile. They were, thus, familiar with the border posts and the false papers necessary to cross them (Gurucharri and Ibañez 2010).

In order to re-organize the radical groups inside Spain the young activists in exile used personal contacts established with foreign activists who were in favor of the use of violence against in the struggle against the Francoist regime. They probably thought the police would be less suspicious of foreigners. The participation of foreigners also internationalized the conflict in the homeland (see Byman et al. 2001: 96). The memoirs of Gurucharri and Ibáñez (2010) mention some of these journeys which were used for transporting orders, material and propaganda for the mounting of armed attacks. Among them was that of the Italian anarchists from the *Gruppo Giovanile Libertario* in Milan who in June 1962 set out on a motorbike from Toulouse and visited several cities in Spain, that of a "young French comrade who spoke Spanish pretty well" and at the end of 1962 contacted some groups in Catalonia, as well as that of Stuart Christie who in 1964 acted as a "Sherpa" to carry a consignment of explosives across the border (see also Christie 2003).

To summarize, the personal contacts between the homeland and diaspora communities seem to have played a vital role in the creation and functioning of the insurgency and its support groups within the clandestine movement. The available sources do not provide the necessary information to develop network analysis, but interpersonal communication can be inferred through the routes employed by the transmitters, membership of the same groups, and geographic proximity or adjacency between the transmitter and the adopter (Givan, Roberts and Soule 2010). The accounts of some participants suggest that the processes of diffusion of radicalization occurred fundamentally by way of personal contacts. Participants in the groups and organizations that made up the diaspora community established interpersonal communication with participants in the insurgency and their support groups in the homeland community, disseminating through these contacts the necessity to practice a particular form of violence against the Francoist regime and transferring to them the resources necessary to carry it out. This type of direct diffusion may be partly explained by the political context. The limits on other kinds of communication established by the Francoist dictatorship left little margin for communication by other channels. Moreover, the objective of the diffusion was violence (more instrumental; more expressive) and it must be remembered that the process of diffusion took place inside a clandestine movement that for the most part rejected the radicalization. The reasons for adopting such a dangerous

248   *Dynamics of Political Violence*

tactic and the instructions for carrying it out were better explained by way of face to face contact. It is thus reasonable to think that interpersonal links served to convince those that finally accepted the risks associated with the use of violence or its logistical support.

Role of Participants

Snow and Benford (1999) identify four possible types of diffusion based on the existence of two types of agent (transmitter and adopter) and the two general roles these can adopt in the process (active and passive). The four types are: reciprocation, in which both agents show a mutual interest in the object of diffusion; adaptation, in which an active adopter strategically selects an item or items to import from the transmitter; accommodation, in which the transmitter promotes the diffusion of a relatively alien practice by tailoring the innovation to the targeted socio-cultural context; and contagion, in which both agents have no interest in the item being diffused. The comparison of the two processes of diffusion that occurred within Spanish anarchism provides an opportunity to empirically examine this typology. The results of the comparison will also provide more information on which to base an answer to one of the question asked by Soule (2004) in this regard: are certain types of diffusion more or less likely to occur in repressive regimes?

As was seen in the first section of this comparison (identity and status of the transmitter), the activists in exile that supported the use of violence played an active role in the transmission of this form of struggle to certain groups inside Spain. We will now focus on the role of the receivers. The first thing that can be said is that in some cases they played a fairly active role in the design of the insurgency. In fact, this is shown by the experience of the MLR, the previous incarnation of which (the *Movimiento Ibérico de Resistencia*, MIR) seems to have been planned inside Spain. In the summer of 1946 *the Comité Regional* of the FIJL in Catalonia (reconstituted after the war with the support of activists in exile) discussed the strategy of armed struggle with the *Federación Local* of Barcelona being put in charge of drawing up a specific project of this nature which finally became the MIR (Téllez 1974: 68).[8]

However, the activists inside Spain did not confine themselves to questions of organizational design but rather swelled the ranks of the groups responsible for carrying out violent activities. This is what can be seen, for example, from the testimony of Antonio Téllez (1974) with regard to the MLR. The committees of the main clandestine anarchist organizations had the power to propose the names of activists they considered suitable for membership of the MLR. Furthermore, and

---

8   The Catalan initiative did not, however, enjoy the support of all the FIJL inside Spain. The national meeting of the FIJL held in Madrid on July 12, 1947 rejected the existence of the MLR on the same day that members of that organization assassinated Eliseo Melis in Barcelona (Paz 2001: 218). Cfr. Téllez (1992: 101).

again according to Téllez, it seems that there was no shortage of young anarchists who wanted to spread the armed struggle against Franco. Among these surely the best known is José Luis Facerías, a postwar anarchist activist in Catalonia who in April 1946 became the responsible of *Secretaría de Defensa* within the FIJL in this region. After a period in prison, from which he was released in June 1947, he soon joined the MLR, which had recently been created with the help of activists that had come from France. After the MLR was wound up, Facerías continued to carry out armed activities and become one of the most active urban guerillas in Catalonia.

The clandestine activists inside Spain also showed themselves to be active in attempts to solve some of the problems that arose in the anarchist movement in exile because of the armed struggle in Spain. This was the motivation for example, for the visit to the 1947 congress of the CNT in exile by a delegation representing the MLR, FIJL and FAI, with activists from Madrid and Barcelona, to put across its point of view with regard to the disowning of the MLR by the anarchist movement in exile. However, the delegates were refused permission to participate in the congress (Téllez 1992: 102ff). After the congress, some of the delegates returned to Spain where they continued to participate in armed activities without the support of the movement in exile and without being able to make the same kind of impact as in previous years.

During the 1960s the involvement of activists from inside Spain was also active and important, for example, in the process of legitimizing and operating of the DI. The FIJL in exile—which was in charge of getting DI under way- received an important delegation from inside Spain at an internal meeting held in the autumn of 1961 (Gurucharri and Ibáñez 2010: 65). The delegation was led by a young man from Madrid (Jacinto Guerrero Lucas), who some activists had put in contact with the secretary of the FIJL in exile. The two together had contacted some groups of young people in Madrid, Barcelona and Zaragoza. After having been identified by the Francoist police Guerrero Lucas decided to stay in France and cooperate with the young exiles in the funding, coordination and legitimation of armed actions inside Spain.

The relatively active role of the adopters of the diffusion wanted to play even came to cause certain problems for the transmitters. The organizations in exile usually confined activists inside Spain to a backseat role and on certain occasions these activists requested a more direct role in the armed struggle. Thus in 1962 the groups that the FIJL had in Madrid, Barcelona and Zaragoza were supposed to form themselves into an "organization and propaganda front," without any involvement in armed actions carried out by activists originating from abroad. In the light of this situation the representative of the Barcelona group vehemently demanded that the movement abroad supply his group with weapons so that it could carry out its own armed actions. The weapons were never supplied, among other things because the police arrested the representative in question a few days later (Gurucharri and Ibáñez 2010: 101).

Conclusion

This chapter has examined the cross-national transfer of radical tactics in conflict-generated transnational social movements between diaspora communities and their communities of origin. It did this through a comparison across time of two processes of diffusion of radicalization in the Spanish anarchist movement. The processes examined here took place in the late 1940s and the early 1960s. In both cases, the transmitter of diffusion was the diaspora community in France, some of whom coordinated armed actions against Franco's regime in Spain. The comparison shows some differences and similarities between the two cases. Processes differed in terms of the logic of the armed actions and in the status of the transmitter within the movement: in the 1940s a more instrumental type of violence was coordinated with the support of the official organization in exile while in the 1960s a more expressive kind of violence was organized by a dissident group of exiled youth. On the other hand, in the two cases the roles of transmitter and adopter were both active, and diffusion used network ties, with groups of activists crossing the border in order to collaborate with others in Spain.

To what extent may this type of direct, reciprocal diffusion of radicalization prevail in highly repressive contexts? This chapter shows that this type of diffusion predominated in Spanish anarchism during the Franco regime. However the comparison of these two cases does not allow the results obtained to be extrapolated beyond this particular movement in this particular context. In order to achieve this a broader comparison including other similar cases would be necessary. However, certain elements can be identified which would support such a hypothesis. First, it seems reasonable to think that in highly repressive contexts in which the state controls the media and other methods of communication then diffusion will require alternative communication channels such as direct interpersonal relations. The development of computer mediated communication which states (including some strongly repressive ones) currently find difficult to control may change this scenario. However, even in these cases the trust and influence facilitated by face to face contact would seem to continue to be of importance. Furthermore, the dramatic consequences of violence make it a tactic that seems to be suitable for diffusion only between actors who share strong motivations and direct involvement in the process. Receptors would be unlikely to adopt violence if they had not somehow previously participated in the process of its legitimation as a form of action. Thus the diffusion of violent tactics in social movements seems to be not only a behavioral process but an ideational one too.

The two cases compared here also show a low level of reception of radicalization. The plans for the insurgency made in the diaspora did not receive sufficient support in the homeland community. The adopters were highly motivated but in both cases there were few of them, they were confined to a specific area (close to the border with France) and they remained marginal by comparison with the moderate line defended by the bulk of the anarchist movement in Spain. How can the low rate of adoption of violence in the two cases be explained? A full discussion of this question would exceed the scope of this chapter. Nevertheless some hypotheses can be advanced, specifically with reference to mobilizing frames, the structural situation and available resources. Firstly, social movements frames removed from the social realities and cultural meanings of their period are unlikely to resonate with their audiences (see Snow and Benford 1988). In the case studied here the transfer of violence took place in a context in which the dramatic consequences of an extreme violent armed conflict—the Spanish Civil War—which was still predominantly thought of (within the anarchist movement too) as a collective tragedy that there was no wish to repeat. Furthermore, the radicalization of the Spanish anarchists took place in a European context in which the valued political virtues were moderation and integration. Secondly the structural situations of the transmitters and potential adopters were very different which may have made diffusion difficult (see Wood 2012, Strang and Soule 1998). Those who decided on and organized the decision to use violent tactics lived in the democratic context of the Fourth and Fifth Republics in France while the armed actions had actually to be to be carried out under the conditions imposed by Franco's dictatorship. Finally, the resources available for the coordinators of the armed struggle were very limited in relation to those of their competitors, both inside and outside the movement. The imbalance with regard to the use of force by the Franco regime was enormous. At the internal level, the few resources which the clandestine movement had were controlled by moderate groups who opted for other tactics in the struggle against Francoism. The human and material resources necessary to carry out armed actions came in large measure from abroad. It is to be expected that an insurgency of this type would only achieve occasional and very limited success, as indeed happened in the case of Spanish anarchism. This is what is stated in the literature on diasporas and homeland conflicts but there are few case studies which support this view and still fewer comparative ones. The comparison over time included in this chapter provides new evidence for the debate.

References

Alberola, O., and Gransac, A. 1975. *El Anarquismo Español y la Acción Revolucionaria, 1961–1974*. Paris: Ruedo Ibérico.

Almeida, P.D. 2013. War and social movements, in *The Wiley-Blackwell Encyclopedia of Social and Political Movements*, edited by D.A. Snow et al. Malden, MA: Blackwell.

Alted Vigil, A., and Domergue, L. 2003. *El Exilio Republicano Español en Toulouse, 1939–1999*. Madrid: UNED—PUM.

Álvaro, M. 2006. *'Por Ministerio de la Ley y Voluntad del Caudillo.' La Jurisdicción Especial de Responsabilidades Políticas (1939–1945)*. Madrid: CEPC.

Andrés, L. 2006. *La CNT en la Encrucijada. Aventuras de un Heterodoxo*. Barcelona: Flor del Viento.

Avilés, J., and Herrerín, Á., eds. 2008. *El Nacimiento del Terrorismo en Occidente: Anarquía, Nihilismo y Violencia Revolucionaria*. Madrid: Siglo XXI.

Byman, D., Chalk, P., Hoffman, B., Rosenau, W. and Brannan, D. 2001. *Trends in Outside Support for Insurgent Movements*. Santa Monica: RAND.

Chabot, S., and Duyvendak, J.W. 2002. Globalization and transnational diffusion between social movements: Reconceptualizing the dissemination of the Ghandian repertoire and the 'coming out' routine. *Theory and Society* 31, 697–740.

Christie, S. 2003. *General Franco Made Me a 'Terrorist*. Hastings: Christiebooks.

della Porta, D., and Diani, M. 2006. *Social Movements: An Introduction*. 2nd edn. Malden, MA: Blackwell.

Ellis, S., and van Kessel, I. 2009. Introduction: African social movements or social movements in Africa, in *Movers and Shakers: Social Movements in Africa*, edited by S. Ellis and I. van Kessel. Leiden—Boston: Brill, 1–16.

Givan, R.K., Roberts, K.M., and Soule, S.A. 2010. Introduction: the dimensions of diffusion, in *The Diffusion of Social Movements: Actors, Mechanisms, and Political Effects*, edited by R.K. Givan, K.M. Roberts and S.A. Soule. Cambridge: Cambridge University Press, 1–15.

Gurucharri, S., and Ibáñez, T. 2010. *Insurgencia Libertaria: Las Juventudes Libertarias en la Lucha Contra el Franquismo*. Barcelona: Virus.

Hanagan, M. 1998. Irish transnational social movement, deterritorialized migrants, and the state system: The last one hundred and forty years. *Mobilization* 3(1), 107–26.

Herrerín, Á. 2004. *La CNT Durante el Franquismo: Exilio y Clandestinidad*. Madrid: Siglo XXI.

Herrerín, Á. 2011. *Anarquía, Dinamita y Revolución Social: Violencia y Represión en la España de Entre Siglos (1868–1909)*. Madrid: Catarata.

Koinova, M. 2010. Diasporas and international politics: utilising the universalistic creed of liberalism for particularistic and nationalist purposes, in *Diaspora and Transnationalism: Concepts, Theories and Methods*, edited by R. Bauböck and T. Faist. Amsterdam: Amsterdam University Press, 149–66.

Ledesma, J.L. 2010. Una retaguardia al rojo: las violencias en la zona republicana, in *Violencia azul y roja. España, 1936–1945*, edited by F. Espinosa et al. Barcelona: Crítica, 152–250.

Lyons, T. 2006. Diasporas and homeland conflict, in *Territoriality and Conflict in an Era of Globalization,* edited by M. Kahler and B. Walter. Cambridge: Cambridge University Press, 111–32

Maney, G. 2000. Transnational mobilization and civil rights in Northern Ireland. *Social Problems* 47(2), 153–79.

McAdam, D., and Rucht, D. 1993. The cross-national diffusion of movement ideas. *Annals of the American Academy of Political and Social Sciences* 528, 56–74.

MLE-CNT. 1947. *Dictámenes y Resoluciones del II Congreso del MLE-CNT en Francia*. Toulouse: MLE-CNT en Francia.

Montseny, F. 1978. *Seis Años de mi Vida, 1939–1945*. Barcelona: Galba.

Paz, A. 2001. *CNT 1939–1951: El Anarquismo Contra el Estado franquista*. Madrid: FAL.

Pitcher, B.L., Hamblin, R.L., and Miller, J.L.L. 1978. Diffusion of collective violence. *American Sociological Review* 43, 23–35.

Preston, P. 2012. *The Spanish Holocaust: Inquisition and Extermination in Twentieth-Century Spain.* London: HarperPress.

Rogers, E.M. 1995. *Diffusion of Innovations*. 4th edn. New York: Free Press.

Romanos, E. 2009a. Confederación Nacional del Trabajo (CNT), in *The International Encyclopedia of Revolution and Protest: 1500 to the Present*, edited by Immanuel Ness. Oxford: Blackwell, 847–50.

Romanos, E. 2009b. Federación Anarquista Ibérica (FAI), in *The International Encyclopedia of Revolution and Protest: 1500 to the Present*, edited by Immanuel Ness. Oxford: Blackwell, 1187–9.

Romanos, E. 2011a. Emociones, identidad y represión: el activismo anarquista durante el franquismo. *Revista Española de Investigaciones Sociológicas* 134, 87–106.

Romanos, E. 2011b. Factionalism in transition: a comparison of ruptures in the Spanish anarchist movement. *Journal of Historical Sociology* 24, 355–80.

Romanos, E. 2013. Anarchism, in *The Wiley-Blackwell Encyclopedia of Social and Political Movements,* edited by David A. Snow et al. Malden, MA: Blackwell.

Sacchetti, G. 2005. *Senza Frontiere. Pensiero e Azione dell'Anarchico Umberto Marzocchi (1900–1986)*. Milano: Zero in condotta.

Sánchez, F. 2006. *El Maquis Anarquista: de Toulouse a Barcelona por los Pirineos*. Lleida: Milenio.

Smith, H. 2007. Diasporas in international conflict, in *Diaspora in Conflict: Peace-makers or Peace-wreckers?*, edited by H. Smith and P. Stares. New York: United Nations University Press, 3–16.

Smith, J. 2013. Transnational social movements, in *The Wiley-Blackwell Encyclopedia of Social and Political Movements,* edited by David A. Snow et al. Malden, MA: Blackwell.

Smith, J. and Wiest, D. 2012. *Social Movements in the World-System: The Politics of Crisis and Transformation.* New York: Russell Sage Foundation.

Smith, J., Wiest, D. and Eterovi, I. 2004. Uneven globalization: Understanding variable participation in transnational social movement organizations. Department of Sociology, Unpublished Paper, SUNY Stony Brook, New York.

Snow, D.A., and Benford, R.D. 1988. Ideology, frame resonance, and participant mobilization, in *From Structure to Action: Comparing Social Movement Research across Cultures*, edited by B. Klandermans, H. Kriesi and S. Tarrow. Greenwich, CT: JAI, 197–217.

Snow, D.A., and Benford, R.D. 1999. Alternative types of cross-national diffusion in the social movement arena, in *Social Movements in a Globalizing World*, edited by D. della Porta, H. Kriesi and D. Rucht. London: Macmillan, 23–39.

Sökefeld, M. 2006. Mobilizing in transnational space: a social movement approach to the formation of diaspora. *Global Networks* 6(3), 265–84.

Soule, S.A. 2004. Diffusion processes within and across movements, in *The Blackwell Companion to Social Movements*, edited by D.A. Snow, S.A. Soule and H. Kriesi. Malden, MA: Blackwell, 294–310.

Soule, S.A. 2013. Diffusion and scale shift, in *The Wiley-Blackwell Encyclopedia of Social and Political Movements,* edited by David A. Snow et al. Malden, MA: Blackwell.

Strang, D. and Soule, S.A. 1998. Diffusion in organizations and social movements: From hybrid corn to poison pills. *Annual Review of Sociology* 24, 265–90.

Strang, D., and Meyer, J.W. 1993. Institutional conditions for diffusion. *Theory and Society* 22, 487–511.

Tarrow, S. 2005. *The New Transnational Activism.* Cambridge: Cambridge University Press.

Tarrow, S. 2012: *Strangers at the Gates: Movements and States in Contentious Politics,* Cambridge: Cambridge University Press.

Téllez, A. 1974. *La Guerrilla Urbana. 1: Facerías.* Paris: Ruedo Ibérico.

Téllez, A. 1992. *Sabaté, Guerrilla Urbana en España (1945–1960).* Barcelona: Virus.

Téllez, A. 1996. *La Red de Evasión del Grupo Ponzán. Anarquistas en la Guerra Secreta Contra el Franquismo y el Nazismo (1936–1944).* Barcelona: Virus.

Wood, L.J. 2007. Breaking the wave: repression, identity, and Seattle tactics. *Mobilization* 12, 377–88.

Wood, L.J. 2012. *Direct Action, Deliberation, and Diffusion: Collective Action after the WTO Protests in Seattle.* Cambridge: Cambridge University Press.

Chapter 12

Protest Diffusion and Rising Political Violence in the Turkish '68 Movement: The Arab-Israeli War, "Paris May" and The Hot Summer of 1968

Emin Alper

The Turkish student movement, which became very powerful in 1968 and strongly influenced the course of Turkish politics, especially between 1968 and 1971, was unquestionably part of the global student movement. The Turkish student movement first came to the agenda in 1960 as the most important oppositional movement to the governing Democratic Party and its authoritarian measures. Student militancy and the repressive measures of the government prepared the pretext for the military coup on 27 May 1960. Therefore, the Turkish student movement had independent and autonomous roots from its Western equivalents from the beginning. However, especially after 1967, the course of the Turkish and Western student movements revealed significant parallels: First, the anti-imperialist demonstrations in 1967, then massive campus mobilizations in 1968, increasing political violence and rapid radicalization between 1968 and 1970 and finally the rise of guerilla units in 1971–72.

Despite the proximity of the timing of similar events, many activists of the period did not consider the influence of the global student movement, especially the Western one, decisive for the Turkish one and continued emphasizing the local roots of the Turkish movement.[1] According to them, the Turkish student movement cannot be understood as simply the diffusion of the Western student movement to Turkey. Actually, such a consideration involved an understandable reaction to the right-wing ideas which tried to degrade the Turkish student movement as a simple imitation of the Western one, or to depict it as an extension of a world-wide fashion that swept the country as well. However, since the history of the Turkish student movement was written by the very activists of the period, or written according to their testimonies, the autonomous character of the Turkish student

---

1   Several interviews with the ex-activists of the period reveal these views. Some of the books that collected these interviews are Baykam (1999a, 1999b) and Feyizoğlu (2004).

movement was overstressed in time.[2] Although the political content of the Turkish student movement was quite different from its global equivalents, the similarities in the timing of certain turning points in particular and the action repertoires of the activists reveal that the Turkish case was not an isolated one and although it had completely local and autonomous roots it re-created and re-organized itself in the second half of the sixties with the diffusion of frames, repertoires and tactics from the Western student movement.

Defining the Concepts and Framework

As Strang and Meyer (1993: 488) define it, diffusion means the "flow of social practices among actors within some larger system." When we talk about diffusion of protest movement, we generally refer to the spread of certain ideas, action repertoires, tactics, strategies, slogans and any kind of innovative practices regarding social movements, from one site to the others. The discussions of diffusion generally involve the following four elements: "a transmitter, an adopter, an innovation that is being diffused, and a channel along which the item may be transmitted" (Soule 2007; 295). However, diffusion does not simply mean that the social practices are emulated and mimicked in whole cloth from one site to another, but "creative borrowing, adaptation, and political learning are often vital to its success." (Givan, Roberts and Soule 2010: 2). In the following pages, I will stress the creative part of borrowing and political conditions of adaptation for the Turkish student movement, in relation to the Western student movement.

Diffusion linkages and channels can be categorized as *direct* or *indirect*. While direct diffusion refers to the transmission through channels which involve direct, personal and frequent contact between the movement actors belonging to different sites, indirect diffusion takes place between the actors that are not directly connected (Soule 2007, della Porta and Diani, 2006: 182–84). In the latter case, a minimal identification between adopter and transmitter, who share similar social positions situated in similar social structures and broadcasting of practices and information through media channels generally provide the conditions of diffusion without direct contact. Therefore, the diffusion does not have to proceed through formal and direct ties, but indirect and informal interaction between agents through media or common cultural understandings can create the necessary basis for diffusion (Givan, Roberts and Soule 2010: 11).

In this chapter, I will show that indirect diffusion is at play regarding the Turkish case, since there were hardly direct and organizational connections

---

2   The major source of history writing of Turkish 1968 is the eighth volume of the *Encyclopedia of Socialism and Social Struggles (Sosyalizm ve Toplumsal Mücadeleler Ansiklopedisi)* which is mostly written by the ex-activist, leftist intellectuals (STMA, 1986). The articles in this encyclopedia generally ignore the diffusive effects of the Western '68 to the Turkish '68.

between Turkish and Western students in the sixties. I want to highlight more indirect and invisible ties between the movement actors.

I also want to employ two other categories of diffusion to analyze the mechanisms of diffusion in the Turkish case: Behavioral and ideational diffusion. The behavioral dimension involves the diffusion of action repertoires, like sit-ins, boycotts, strikes, occupations and so on. Ideational diffusion mostly refers to "the spread of collective action frames that define issues, goals and targets" (Givan, Roberts and Soule 2010: 4). With regard to the diffusion of anti-imperialist demonstrations in Turkey, I will discuss how ideational diffusion preceded behavioral diffusion, and the way Turkish left-nationalist students first adapted anti-imperialist discourse as a re-formulation and re-framing of their nationalist and developmentalist claims, and then took to the streets under the indirect influence of the Vietnam protests of their counterparts.

Although the whole history of the Turkish '68 protests needs to be re-written from the perspective of the diffusion of the global student movement, in this chapter, I intend to highlight just two cases of indirect diffusion of protest and the case of subsequent increasing political violence (that took place almost at the same time as the Western equivalents), which significantly contributed to rendering the Turkish '68 protests part of a global protest movement. The first of these two cases is the diffusion of anti-imperialist demonstrations to Turkey, following the Arab-Israeli War of June 1967. The second case pertains to the diffusion of mass protests and action repertoirs of European students to Turkey after the May '68 protests in Paris. Finally, I will analyze the initial phase of rising political violence and radicalization in the Turkish student movement, not simply as an outcome of diffusion mechanisms but as a product of similar action and counter-action mechanisms, which were at work in many Western countries at the time.

Regarding the first case, I will emphasize the role of the Arab-Israeli War in the diffusion of anti-imperialist demonstrations. Particularly, my aim is to focus on the role of agency and selective adoption of anti-imperialist demonstrations by Turkish students. While anti-imperialist views and support for the Vietnamese people had already been a common cause among radical leftist activists in Turkey, the latter had refrained from massive demonstrations in order to support the Vietnamese resistance, as 'Vietnam' itself was not a popular cause in Turkish public opinion overall. However, with the Arab-Israeli War, Turkish students seized the opportunity to popularize anti-imperialism and consequently organized the first massive anti-imperialist demonstration, which could be considered equivalent to the Vietnam protests organized by Western students. Moreover, they managed to create a very popular symbolic target during the course of the events, that is, the Sixth Fleet of the US Navy, which became the key reference point of American military existence in the Eastern Mediterranean.

The second case concerns the immediate diffusion of the events of May 1968 from Paris to Turkey and the almost simultaneous eruption of university occupations in June in Istanbul and Ankara. Parallel to the existing literature of diffusion, I will emphasize the role of the media coverage of the "Paris May," which reinforced a common identity of "students" between the Turkish and the Western European ones, and created thus "a sense of shared identification between activists," that facilitated the diffusion (McAdam and Rucht 1993: 60). Moreover, the media significantly increased the self-confidence of students in their ability to bring about political change, by warning the public of the coming of a new wave, which would be almost impossible to resist and which would be initiated and carried out by a new social actor, namely the students.

Besides stressing the role of agency and selective adaption in the diffusion processes, by focusing on these two cases, I will investigate the interaction between local political dynamics and the diffusion mechanisms. Regarding the first case, I will show that nationalist, anti-American feelings among Turkish students, that arose as a result of the Cyprus crisis of 1964, were reframed by a universal anti-imperialist discourse in 1967, mainly because of the increasing opposition around the Vietnam War. With respect to the second case, I will show how dispersed and isolated campus protests regarding university regulations and administration were amplified and turned into a massive uprising under the influence of "Paris May." Therefore, overcoming the dichotomy between "local dynamics" and "diffusion from outside," I will show how local demands and themes turned into universal ones and resonated with the global movement and how otherwise weak and sporadic protests became massive ones with the demonstration affect and the diffusion of frames, tactics and repertoires of the global student movement.

Finally, focusing on increasing political violence in the summer of 1968, I will explain the simultaneity of events in Turkey and the Western world by emphasizing the operation of similar action and counteraction mechanisms rather than diffusive mechanisms (although the diffusion processes played crucial roles in triggering these mechanisms). The escalation of violence between students and police forces and right-wing groups, following the massive 1968 occupations, took place almost at the same time as the movement radicalization in Western countries. However, simultaniety of events does not automatically imply the existence of diffusion. The display of similar causal mechanisms in different parts of the world can be the reason for striking similarities and simultaneities. I will explain the following radicalization of the student movement just after the major campus occupations of June 1968 not as a result of a simple diffusion mechanism, but the triggering of similar action and counteraction mechanisms between the students, state and right-wing groups, which is more-or-less at stake in many countries at the same time.

The initial radicalization of students in the immediate aftermath of the campus occupations of 1968 was mostly a product of the action-counteraction dynamic between opposing actors, as we will discuss in detail below. This dynamic started only after a significant number of students were mobilized, a fully-fledged movement was formed, the self-confidence of movement actors increased and the disruptive capacity of the movement signalled a threat to the police forces. The counteraction of police forces to stop and punish the disruptive activities of the students, developed in the anti-Sixth Fleet demonstrations and campus mobilizations of 1968, would lead to a spiral of violence, as would happen in many Western countries.

Simultaniety of events does not automatically imply the existence of diffusion but can show the process of similar local mechanisms at similar times. In this chapter, I will consider the simultanous rise of political violence in the Turkish context after the summer of 1968, not merely as a result of diffusion but as the operation of similar mechanisms triggered by similar protest movements shaped by diffusive mechanisms.

From the Arab-Israeli War to the Anti-Sixth Fleet Demonstrations

The anti-imperialist, pro-Vietnam demonstrations escalated significantly within the US student movement after 1965. European students also started organizing anti-imperialist demonstrations in the following years. The first major anti-Vietnam war demonstrations in West Germany were held in Berlin in 1966. In the same and following years anti-Vietnam war demonstrations spread to Italy, France and Japan (Staggenborg 2008: 50).

The protests of the US students intensified during the spring of 1967, due to mounting military casualties in Vietnam in that year, which found significant repercussion in the Turkish media.[3] European students organized massive pro-Vietnam demonstrations in coordination with each other in October 1967 (Ali 1995: 214–16). On the other hand, the equivalent of anti-imperialist demonstrations in Turkey started in the summer of 1967, although with a less-articulated stress on Vietnam. The gradual intensification of anti-imperialist demonstrations in Turkey (which targeted the very existence of the Sixth Fleet of the US Navy in the Mediterranean) throughout the second half of 1967 and into 1968, parallel to the escalating demonstrations in the West, provides us with a significant case to investigate the diffusion of anti-imperialist demonstrations from the West to Turkey.

The close relationship between German, English, Italian and American students, as seen especially during the anti-Vietnam campaigns at the end of 1967, were absent in the case of Turkey (Ali 1995: 217–55). While coordinated campaigns or panels and discussions, organized with the participation of major student leaders from different countries, were the usual forums of European students, Turkish students were definitely outside this network. Therefore, the diffusion could only be indirect in the Turkish case.

Anti-imperialist views in Turkey started to be circulated after 1962, the year that the influential, leftist magazine *Yön* (The Direction) was first published. The magazine was the ideological founder of a Third Worldist socialism, which promoted an independent, anti-imperialist, nationalist, state-led industrialization as the only viable direction for Turkey. According to the magazine, market capitalism did not serve in any way the interests of the country, which needed

---

3   See major Turkish newspapers, especially *Cumhuriyet* of 15 and 16 April of 1967.

260   *Dynamics of Political Violence*

rapid industrialization, but on the contrary, the interests of US imperialism. The prevailing mode of market economy, therefore, was the product of an alliance of pro-business right-wing parties and the US, which had a certain interest in blocking Turkish development. The left-nationalist forces should purge the US imperialism to bring about economic prosperity and income equality (Atılgan 2002).

These anti-imperialist views were limited to a small circle of intellectuals in the first half of the sixties. However, these views started to resonate in the wider public opinion with the Cyprus Crisis in 1964. The Cyprus Crisis and the "Johnson letter" which followed provided an opportunity for anti-imperialist, leftist intellectuals to reformulate the "national interests" in terms of left-wing nationalism. The Johnson letter was a secret letter sent to Prime Minister İsmet İnönü by US President Lyndon Johnson to prevent any possible military intervention by the Turkish Navy in Cyprus in order to solve the Cyprus Crisis on behalf of Turkey. This letter, which involved implicit threatening phrases, was leaked to the press and infuriated the public (Alper 2009: 251–66). For the first time, Turkey's cold war ally, the US, appeared as an obstacle for Turkish people to Turkey's aim of preserving the rights of Turks on the island. Anti-Greek and anti-US feelings suddenly swept the country, galvanizing street protests.

Left-wing intellectuals successfully seized the opportunity created by the Johnson letter and effectively presented the membership of Turkey to NATO as inhibiting the pursuing of an independent policy for the interests of the country. The climax of the Cyprus issue really helped the spread of anti-imperialist thought, especially among students. However, the prevailing atmosphere in the street demonstrations was overwhelmingly chauvinist, rather than being consistently anti-imperialist.

In the following years, left-nationalist and anti-imperialist views slowly gained momentum among intellectual circles and students. Major Turkish student organizations, which were officially recognized by the state, and their confederation, TMTF (The National Federation of Turkish Students), were dominated by left-nationalist students. Their political views were more-or-less in line with the Third Worldist socialism of *Yön* magazine. Along with these organizations there were more independent and socialist-oriented student groups, gathered under the Federation of Opinion Clubs, close to the more radical Turkish Labor Party (Alper 2009: 319–323). The latter would gain prominence in 1968.

The anti-imperialist stance of these organizations was revealed by their press declarations made between 1965 and 1967.[4] The head of these organizations occasionally issued press releases or organized small symbolic demonstrations denouncing the military adventures of US imperialism. Vietnam was especially

---

4   One of the first clear anti-imperialist declaration of the students was from the TMTF. The second head of the TMTF, Cavit Savcı, protested the Vietnam occupation of the US forces with a press declaration. *Akşam*, 8.7.1966. A few days later, the representative of Egyptian Socialist Youth Organization visited the Turkish Student leaders. The student representatives commonly declared to fight imperialism. *Cumhuriyet*, 26.9.1966.

Protest Diffusion & Rising Political Violence in the Turkish '68 Movement   261

stressed in a few declarations that underlined the solidarity of Turkish youth with the Vietnamese people. However, there were no massive anti-imperialist gatherings or demonstrations until the summer of 1967.

The awareness of the public towards the Vietnam issue should have significantly risen in 1967, since the media coverage of the war in Vietnam obviously mounted in this year due to the escalation of the war. During April 1967, some important newspapers gave special place to the massive anti-Vietnam war demonstrations organized by US students.[5] However, these demonstrations did not show any immediate diffusive effect among Turkish students. Probably, activist students did not think that Vietnam was an issue hot enough to galvanize public opinion and mobilize the students.

There were two main reasons to think like that. First, Vietnam was located in a geographically far area and there was no cultural similarity or affinity between Turkish and Vietnamese people to help Turkish people identify with the cause of the Vietnamese Independence War. Secondly and more importantly, the Vietnam issue was not a cause that students felt very strongly about to support it politically, since it was considered by public opinion as a fight between the two Cold War Blocs. Unsurprisingly, the right-wing newspapers were blatantly accusing the leftist intellectuals supporting the Vietnamese resistance with supporting Soviet expansionism, which was also considered a threat to Turkey. Vietnam was not, therefore, the best issue to stress for the leftist students, who insisted on an independent way oriented neither to the US nor to the Soviet Union.

Therefore, a strong mobilization against US imperialism should have waited for the eruption of another spectacular event, which could resonate in Turkish public opinion, namely the Arab-Israeli war.

The first demonstration over the mounting tension between the Arab world and Israel was organized by a few Arab students studying in Turkish universities. Approximately 30 Arab students, claiming that they represented the 1,500 Arab students in Turkey, gathered in front of the Consulate of the United Arab Republics and denounced the US, England and France since they supported Israel, which deported two million Palestinians. Parallel to that, a couple of Turkish student organizations released a declaration denouncing imperialist countries which were anxious about a united and powerful Arab existence in the region.[6]

The frequency of declarations of student organizations rose with the start of the war on 5 June 1967. On the 7 June 1967 major student organizations demanded that Turkey openly support the Arabic countries against their war with imperialism. Students, without dropping a chauvinistic stance, did not forget to make the remark that Turkey should be the pioneer of Arab countries in this anti-imperialist struggle.[7] One of the biggest confederations of youth organizations declared that

---

5   See *Cumhuriyet*, April, 1967.

6   *Cumhuriyet*, 28.5.1967.

7   *Cumhuriyet*, 8.6.1967.

262   *Dynamics of Political Violence*

the Arab countries should fight to preserve their natural resources against the US and Israel, as the latter "was founded by American Jewish millionaires."[8]

A few days later the representatives of the largest student confederation walked to Taksim Square and burnt the wreath which had been put by the commanders of the US Sixth Fleet to the statue of Atatürk.[9] This was the first activity targeting the US Sixth Fleet, which was a significant part of the American Navy in the Mediterranean. The routine visit of the Sixth Fleet to Istanbul had this time provoked the anger of students, taking place as it did just after the Arab-Israeli war.

The following day the first massive anti-imperialist demonstration was organized by the students. According to reporters, 4,000 students came together to protest against the US military existence in the Eastern Mediterranean. The target of the demonstrators was Dolmabahçe Port, where the US soldiers disembarked. Angry students cracked the barricade of the Turkish soldiers in Dolmabahçe, however, with slogans praising the Turkish Army and its "anti-imperialist" character, took down the American flag at the port and raised the Turkish flag.[10] They shouted slogans like "Yankee go home" and "the US is the killer of Muslims." The representative of the students read a declaration blaming US imperialist aims in the Middle East and added that they did not want to see the fleet which, at the same time, cut off the Turkish navy on its way to Cyprus.[11] The students, therefore, tried to merge a nationalist cause, namely the Cyprus one, with a more universal anti-imperialist stance in solidarity with the Arab people. Following this major demonstration, the Sixth Fleet and its regular visits to Turkey became one of the symbolic targets of leftist students and every visit provoked significant anti-imperialist activities.

When the Sixth Fleet decided to visit Turkey again in October, the demonstrations escalated further. This time the students were determined to prevent the disembarking of the US soldiers to Istanbul. Students were using quite a macho discourse and stating in their declarations that Turkey is not a place for the US soldiers to sleep with Turkish girls.[12] On 7 October, student organizations organized a sit-in in Dolmabahçe port to prevent the disembarking of US soldiers.

---

8   *Cumhuriyet*, 16.6.1967.

9   *Akşam,* 23.6.1967.

10   The Turkish left split into two major lines after long discussions between 1966 and 1968. The discussion was about whether the socialist left should coalesce with the army and progressive wing of the bureaucracy or not. The line represented by the Turkish Labor Party definitely opposed to a strategic alliance with the army. However, some communists who were close to the illegal Turkish Communist party, believed that the Turkish army played a progressive role against the reactionary forces in the near past, therefore the communists should build a national front with them. The student movement was dominated by the second line of thought in the 1968. So, they shouted pro-army slogans in the demonstrations. The honey-moon between the students and the army continued until the martial law declared in the second half of 1970 (Alper, 2009).

11   *Cumhuriyet*, 25.6.1967.

12   *Milliyet*, 7.10.1967.

Protest Diffusion & Rising Political Violence in the Turkish '68 Movement   263

The Fleet Admiral was able to land in Istanbul by helicopter since the port was occupied by the protestors. During this successful demonstration, students read a press release which denounced American imperialism and its military intervention in every corner of the world, as well as in Vietnam.[13] Students started consistently uniting Turkish nationalist sentiments with those of the Third World, by defining a common interest among the peoples of the Third World from Vietnam to Egypt.

A few days later students from the more radical Opinion Clubs started a hunger strike to protest against the Sixth Fleet. Students accused the US Army of spending thousands of dollars to kill people in Vietnam and expressed their shame due to the welcoming attitudes of the Turkish government to the US soldiers.[14] In the following days, students sporadically harassed the US soldiers who wanted to visit the night clubs of Istanbul and a few street fights erupted between soldiers and students. The American flag in Taksim Square was taken down and burnt by two students.[15] The demonstrations spread to Izmir when the Sixth Fleet visited there.[16]

Just after the waning of anti-Sixth Fleet demonstrations, a new crisis erupted in Cyprus. When Greek Cypriot paramilitaries attacked some Turkish villages in November huge demonstrations were organized in Turkey.[17] The Cyprus protests in the fall of 1967 were short, but strong, however, the differences between the protests of 1964 and 1967 were significant: The 1964 protests which were led by the students were merely nationalist and chauvinistic but in 1967 protestors were clearly differentiated. Alongside the right-wing, nationalist students, left-wing students took to the streets with anti-imperialist slogans and avoided directly targeting the Greek people. In three years, with the increasing influence of the leftist intellectuals of *Yön*, and the world-wide diffusion of the anti-imperialist frame, the anti-imperialist discourse became popular among Turkish students. The claims of Turkish nationalism were re-framed with the new anti-imperialist discourse.[18]

The new Cyprus crisis helped Turkish students to remind the Turkish people of the role of the US Navy as the barrier against Turkish interests in the island. The Sixth Fleet appeared now as a more concrete symbol and the opposition against the Sixth Fleet found much stronger ground.

Protests against the Sixth Fleet continued in the summer of 1968, during the next visit of the Fleet, albeit in a much more massive and harsh way. These protests would be a threshold for student activism and radicalization, since during the

---

13   *Cumhuriyet*, 8.10.1967.

14   *Akşam*, 11.10.1967.

15   *Cumhuriyet*, 17.10.1967.

16   *Cumhuriyet*, 16.10.1967.

17   *Cumhuriyet,* 16, 17, 23.11.1967.

18   The military coup of 1967 in Greece also facilitated the re-formulation of the Turkish cause in Cyprus with anti-imperialist terms. Since the coup was planned and implemented by the US government, according to the left-nationalists, to fight against the Greek thesis in Cyprus was equal to fight against imperialism. For a typical left-nationalist argument supporting the Turkish intervention to Cyprus (Selçuk 1967).

clashes between police and students, the first killing by a policeman took place—Vedat Demircioğlu, a student from Istanbul Technical University, died during a police raid on a dormitory. The repercussion of this incident on the students was similar to that created by the killing of Benno Ohnesorg or the shooting of Rudi Dutschke on the German student movement. Indeed, student militancy sharpened after his death, and became more radicalized both against the police and the American symbols in the country.

Protesting American imperialism through the symbol of the Sixth Fleet was one of the major innovations of the Turkish students. Around this very concrete symbol of US military existence, they seized the opportunity of criticizing the US long-distance operations in Vietnam, its support of Israel and animosity to "our Muslim brothers" in the Middle East and its "negative" attitude to the possible Turkish landing on Cyprus. Students successfully integrated these popular nationalist feelings into a world-wide criticism of imperialism. The Arab-Israeli war, in this sense, functioned like a bridge that connected the particularistic anti-US feelings of nationalist students to the more universalistic anti-imperialist cause. Turkish activists overcame the difficulty of mobilizing masses of students on a less sympathetic issue, like Vietnam, by first stressing Muslim solidarity in the Middle East against US imperialism (although these students were clearly and militantly secularist) and then reminding people of the role of the US in the Cyprus issue. The anti-Sixth Fleet demonstrations were a kind of equivalent of the anti-Vietnam demonstrations that took place in the US and Europe throughout 1967, since the militancy in these demonstrations and violent repression of these (often with casualties) started a new phase of radicalization in these countries as well as Turkey.

The diffusion of an anti-imperialist frame and the action repertoires of anti-imperialist demonstrations to Turkey was not an outcome of a natural, inevitable and direct diffusion process. The local dynamics mattered and the interaction of local dynamics with the influence of the outside world determined the character of the Turkish protests. The frame of anti-imperialism fell on fertile ground in Turkey mostly because of the Cyprus crisis and the mounting suspicion in public opinion of the US, beginning with the Johnson letter. While once criticizing the US was equal to being communist and a traitor, in the mid-sixties it became commonplace among Turkish citizens. However, only a small minority of Turkish intellectuals formulated anti-American feelings with an anti-imperialist discourse in 1964. In a few years, this frame started getting popular among students, mostly with the influence of a world-wide opposition to the US imperialist aims in Vietnam and with the sensational events such as the Russel tribunal. The ideational diffusion was followed by a behavioral one, when the first anti-imperialist demonstrations of Turkey started in the summer of 1967, after the anti-Vietnam war demonstrations of the spring in the US.

The Campus Occupations of 1968

June 1968 witnessed a massive uprising of students all over the country. Without any plan or decision, student protests spontaneously started in the Ankara Language-History and Geography Faculty and spread to major universities in a few days. The extent of participation in the incidents was much beyond the imagination of the student activists. The June events were a kind of turning point for student politics. The massive boycotts and occupations increased the politicization of students and added new militants to the socialist students' movement. Indeed, it was the first and one of the most important steps in the radicalization of the student movement.

The timing of the June occupations clearly revealed that it was a kind of diffusion of European student protests, mainly the Paris events of May, to Turkey. However, stressing the diffusion in the summer of 1968 does not mean that there was no opposition or protests on the campuses before then or that it suddenly erupted with the inspiration of "Paris May." In contrast, the Turkish student movement was already powerful from 1960 on, as mentioned above. Besides the directly political ones, there were many campus protests throughout the sixties criticizing the university regulations and administrations. These protests were mainly organized by highly active student organizations and the rate of participation was quite high. However, these activities were sporadic and mostly limited to a single campus or university. What was quite different and significant in the June protests was that they took place in almost all campus and universities, spontaneous in the beginning, but coordinated in the following days, massive in an unprecedented way and innovative in introducing new repertoires. This was possible with the diffusive effect of the protests by European students that swept Europe in the spring of 1968.

As mentioned above, it is hard to mention a direct diffusion in the Turkish case. Although there were no direct connections between the students of Europe and Turkey, Turkish students were aware of the importance of what was happening in Europe (Zileli 2000: 293), mostly through the media

The most important indirect tie between Turkish and European students was the cultural understanding that they belong to a common social category (Strand and Meyer 1993: 490). This understanding was unquestionably reinforced by the intense media coverage of European student protests in April and May of 1968 in Turkey. Turkish students, who were already politically active, recognized once again that the category of "the youth," of which they were a part, started being a significant actor in politics.

The media coverage not only reinforced a common identity between Turkish and European students, but also created a self-fulfilling prophecy by depicting the recent student movement like a natural flood which was impossible to resist. Such a depiction increased the students' self-confidence and created an expectation in the eyes of politicians and even the students that the spread of the protests to Turkey was just a matter of time. Unsurprisingly then, a spark in Ankara University on June 11 was enough to make it a vast fire expanding to all other universities.

The media coverage and the interest of intellectuals in the subject also highlighted some student grievances which had been formulated before and created indirect pressure for university reform. This indirect pressure might have created a significant opportunity for students to voice their grievances about university regulations, since they probably thought that it was just the right time to press for certain changes.

The key role, therefore, in the Turkish '68 was played mainly by newspapers, since TV broadcasts had not yet started widely in Turkey. The newspapers gave significant room to the student uprising and published "scientific evaluations" of the reasons for this uprising. The Turkish press was closely watching the events that started from the shooting of Rudi Dutschke in Germany, followed by the student protests in April against Springer Press, the protests of Italian students, and finally the massive protests which erupted in Paris in May and the political turmoil which brought the French government to the brink of collapse.

Cumhuriyet (a center-left newspaper) published a serial report entitled "The Political Earthquake in European Universities" prepared by Gül Işık (1968) on 3 May to analyze the reasons for these events.[19] The same day, student protests broke out in Paris. The events of 3 May were reported on the front page by many Turkish newspapers. In the first week of protests, *Cumhuriyet* gave a lot of room to the events on the front page, stressing the endemic character of student uprisings.[20] *Milliyet* (a more centrist newspaper) also closely followed the Paris events and also stressed the endemic character of student movements, by referring to the uprisings in Spain and Sweden that had started after the Paris events.[21] After the massive strikes began at the end of May, France became regular front page news in almost all Turkish newspapers.[22]

At the beginning of June, *Cumhuriyet* stated that the English government was afraid of possible events in their country and was taking precautions to prevent them.[23] *Milliyet* and especially its chief editor Abdi İpekçi insistently warned the Turkish government against the threat of the spread of student events to Turkey. According to him, the complaints of the students in the West and Turkey were similar, and because of that the diffusion of boycotts and occupations in Turkish universities would not be a surprise unless the necessary reforms in the university system were initiated (İpekçi, 1968a, 1968b). *Milliyet* published many articles written by professors, intellectuals and student leaders in May, to shed light on the reasons for the student uprisings. Two serial interviews were also published, one about the hippy movement,[24] the other about the German student movement by

---

19   *Cumhuriyet*, 3.5.1968.

20   *Cumhuriye*, 4.5.1968.

21   *Milliyet*, 20–21.5.1968.

22   Rightist newspapers also stressed the importance of Paris events with their headlines. See especially, *Tercüman*, 19.5.1968.

23   *Cumhuriyet*, 2.6.1968.

24   *Milliyet*, 12–17.5.1968.

Haldun Taner.[25] Abdi İpekçi (1968a, 1968b) consciously highlighted the importance of the universal uprising of students to warn the rulers, in order to convince them to make reforms before the inevitable explosion of the students' movement in Turkey.

Most probably, ministers and security forces in Turkey had also been expecting similar events and trying to take precautions. The rector of İstanbul University, Ekrem Şerif Egeli, when answering some questions by journalists about whether there were any conspirators among university students who were preparing to create chaos, declared that there were no such students and there were no reasons to witness student events in Turkey, since the university administrations were working to solve the problems of students.[26] Harun Karadeniz (one of the significant student leaders of the period) on the other hand, notes in his memoirs that at the beginning of June there was a political atmosphere in which the government, public opinion and students were as if waiting for the uprising (Karadeniz 1969: 91), for the inevitable "flood."

The socialist students also watched the student protests all over the world closely and planned to initiate a wave of student protests, questioning the educational problems of students and demanding a "revolution in education" (Karadeniz 1969: 91). The activist students did not seriously think that such massive mobilizations as in Europe could be achieved: Their target was modest. They planned to start the campaign and protests in the fall, during the opening of the universities but the spontaneous protests did not wait that long.

It is interesting that the occupation started not through the initiatives of the student organizations, but through a bunch of non-militant students who pressured the official student organization for an occupation in Ankara University (Zileli 2000: 288–9). Although in the spread of protests to other universities the organizations played a more significant role, the initiation of the protests in Ankara University shows that formal organization may not play a significant role in the diffusion process, since most of the formal student organizations in Turkey had decided to wait for the autumn, while the push of ordinary students was decisive in the June protests.

Indeed, the media coverage of the student events fashioned the image of an unavoidable wave that would possibly sweep the country, as students already had strong organizations in Turkey. Unquestionably, such an image enhanced the students' confidence, since it underlined that a collective action organized by them could bring about important political changes, even to the extent of threatening a government. Furthermore, the media coverage of the Paris events highlighted the student grievances prevailing in Turkey, thereby creating indirect pressure for university reform. The way in which the Paris events were covered in the media created a self-fulfilling prophecy by warning the university administrations and the government to deal with the students' accumulated problems. The loud

---

25 *Milliyet*, 5–10.6.1968.
26 *Milliyet*, 25.5.1968.

legitimization and publicization of the students' grievances, and the expectations and pressures for university reform created a significant opportunity for students to use their collective power.

In June 1968 a spontaneous boycott protesting the examination system at Ankara University, which could have remained a local incident as had been previously the case, suddenly evolved into a massive wave of university occupations (a new practice for Turkish students, adopted from France).[27] The declaration of one of the student leaders –"Turkey will be a second France, unless our demands are satisfied"—reveals how Turkish students realized and used the opportunity created by May '68.[28] The occupations spread to the universities of Istanbul, Izmir and even Erzurum in a few days. Besides the local demands related to the regulations of each faculty and university, students demanded a sweeping university reform which would initiate student participation in university administrations. The following month, July, would witness a re-eruption of the anti-Sixth Fleet demonstration. This time a much more numerous and confident student mass took the streets to protest US imperialism and the existence of the US Navy in the Mediterranean. The summer of 1968 would be a turning point in the history of the Turkish student movement, which would rapidly radicalize in a few years and finally lead to the emergence of guerilla units at the end of 1970.

Political Violence and Radicalization of the Movement

The summer of 1968 was a threshold in the radicalization process of the Turkish student movement, which went hand in hand with increasing level of political violence. However, the initial phases of escalating violence cannot be seen as the result of diffusion or simple imitation of more violent tactics. The radicalization mechanism was mostly related to the action-counteraction dynamic between the students, police forces and right-wing groups. The above-mentioned effects of diffusion helped the creation of a more unified, consistent and strong movement, which eventually encouraged the students in more daring and disruptive actions that would trigger an escalating spiral of violence between the students and their opponents. It is interesting to see that the radicalization mechanism in Turkey started to proceed mostly at similar times to countries like USA, Italy, Germany and Northern Ireland. However, this time, more than diffusion of violent repertoires it may be more accurate to mention the working of similar causal mechanisms in Turkey and other countries. The diffusion of violent practices would be a case in 1969 and 1970 in Turkey, especially during the formation of armed groups. However, in the initial phases of political violence, action-counteraction dynamic

---

27   According to an eyewitness, one of the initiators of the first spontaneous occupation at Ankara University shouted "we should do what the European students did," in order to convince the students to begin an occupation. (Zileli 2000: 288)

28   *Tercüman,* 12 June 1968.

Protest Diffusion & Rising Political Violence in the Turkish '68 Movement   269

between opposing groups was more decisive. Since the diffusion mechanism can go hand in hand with the local mechanism of action-counteraction, just after and during the radicalization of the Turkish student movement, the diffusion of tactics, actions and means between radical or armed groups would continue and shape the character of the movement after 1968. However, the later diffusion of violent tactics is out of the scope of this chapter.

The radicalization process of social movements should be discussed in a relational framework, which refuses to attribute fixed and static positions to the social actors, but emphasizes relational causal mechanisms, as the studies of contentious politics proposed (McAdam, Tarrow, Tilly 2001). The studies of contentious politics, at the same time, aim to underline the recurrent causal mechanisms that shape the political trajectory of the contention. Rather than deriving universal rules about contentious politics, it first defines the causal mechanism which plays a crucial role in the development of contentious politics, and then identifies the recurrent and repeating ones in different cases, times and locations. As Alimi noted, some relational causal mechanisms like "competition for power between movement actors" or "action-counteraction between movement actors" were stressed by many authors as common or recurrent causal ones which can be detected in many different cases as the cause of radicalization of movements.[29] "Action-counteraction mechanism between movement actors," which is more relevant for our case, simply concerns the incremental steps in the escalating dynamics between activists and state forces which occurs when each side raises the stake in response to the other's action (Alimi 2011: 100). The initial radicalization of the Turkish student movement should also be considered as the changing attitude of students, state forces and right-wing groups to each other in the course of events and be understood as the outcome of a common relational mechanism of "action-counteraction escalation," which is at work in many cases of movement radicalization.

The anti-Sixth Fleet demonstrations in the summer of 1968 were in many ways different from the ones of 1967. The summer demonstrations were more massive, harsher and more disruptive in terms of harassing the US soldiers in the street. When the US soldiers disembarked in July of 1968 students decided to prevent them passing to Taksim by blocking the main roads. Since one of the campuses of Istanbul Technical University was in one of the main roads to Taksim, students based in the campus were easily able to block the way. Moreover, students from the campus occasionally went out to throw stones at one of the hotels near the campus which hosted US soldiers (Karadeniz, 1969: 107–10).

During a minor scuffle between a plainclothes policeman and a student in front of the campus, students went out from the campus and took the policeman hostage. This action suddenly increased the tension and the police forces, provoked by the

---

29 For the formulation of "action-counteraction escalation" mechanism and implementation of it to the cases of the Weathermen, Fatah-Tanzim and al-Qaeda see Alimi (2011).

highly illegal attempt of the students, launched a massive attack on the student dormitory in the campus to save the hostage.[30]

The police forces were visibly tolerant of the students during the campus occupations of June, unlike the case in many Western countries. Most probably having learned some lessons from the Paris May, the government refrained from harsh treatments of students, trying not to provoke more massive mobilizations as the French government did. The government was respectful of campus autonomy and did not intrude on the campuses during the occupations. The university administrators, who were mostly sympathetic to the left-leaning Kemalist Peoples Republican Party, did not let the police in and tried to end the occupation by negotiating with students. Therefore, campus occupations did not mark a beginning of political violence in Turkey, unlike many Western countries.

However, in a few weeks the situation has changed, mostly because of the physical attacks of students on US soldiers. The police forces were probably more cautious and tense during the anti-Sixth Fleet demonstrations in July—they were determined to prevent any disruption by the students, to prevent any physical attack on the US soldiers that would probably lead to a kind of diplomatic crisis. So, the policemen were no longer tolerant towards the students. The determination of the police probably made the students more determined and started a competition between them which eventually led to the students taking a policeman hostage.

The attack on the dormitory was so harsh that many students were injured and one of them, Vedat Demircioğlu, fell (or was thrown according to some testimonies) from the second floor of the dormitory. Demircioğlu was in a coma when he was transferred to the hospital. The harsh treatment of students by the police provoked the students further. Next day, when the students gathered in Taksim Square to protest the Sixth Fleet as planned before, a significant cleavage took place among students, in which the pro-violence group would gain a minor victory.

In the summer of 1968, socialist Opinion Clubs gained significant power, while semi-official student organization power gradually faded away. However, the socialist students involved two opposing groups. The dominant group was close to the Turkish Labor Party and held the Opinion Clubs. These students supported legal and peaceful demonstrations and believed that socialism would be the outcome of a long, mainly parliamentary struggle depending on the working class. A minority group in the Opinion Clubs, which was influenced by some members of the illegal Turkish Communist Party, believed that the working class was not powerful enough in Turkey, so socialism must be brought about by a coalition of left-wing officers, intellectuals and students. This group, called National Democratic Revolution (NDR), supported a high level of militancy, violent protests and disruptive tactics. Their model of seizure of power was to raise the level of street violence and create political turmoil to prepare the ground for left-wing army officers to stage a coup (Samim, 1981).

---

30   *Cumhuriyet*, 18.7.1968.

The first symbolic victory of the NDR group took place in the protest following the dormitory raid. The organizers of the protests did not want to escalate the level of violence just after the dormitory raid and refrained from any provocation of police forces which could lead to harsh treatment and eventually harm the popularity of the movement (Karadeniz, 1969: 113). However, in the demonstration, the members of NDR successfully galvanized the bitter feelings of students and convinced them to attack the US soldiers waiting in Dolmabahçe port. Meanwhile, the government, which was heavily criticized for the dormitory raid, ordered the police to sit back, not to trigger a new violent clash. So the angry students coming from Taksim Square walked to Dolmabahçe port with no opposition by police forces and threw a few US soldiers already disembarked, into the sea. This event suddenly became a symbol of the students' anti-imperialist fight and was used by the NDR as the victory of radical tactics (Karadeniz, 1969: 116). It was the beginning of the rise of minority radical groups among students.

A few days later, Demircioğlu died in the hospital. His death angered and provoked the students further and agitated students clashed with the police throughout the day in Beyazit Square.[31] This was the most massive, violent and long clash between the police and students ever seen. The Beyazit clash marked the start of a spiral of escalating violence between the students and the police. From that time on most of the demonstrations ended up with clashes with police forces. In such a violent environment, the students supporting peaceful demonstrations started gradually losing the initiative, while the NDR became the leading force by the end of 1968.

In the last part of 1968, right-wing reactionary groups (mostly Islamist and proto-fascist students) also increased their attacks on the leftist students as an answer to growing impact of leftist students in politics. Commando camps were organized by the extreme Nationalist Action Party in the summer of 1968 to train right-wing students for student clashes.[32] As a result, demonstrations started to become more violent. Almost every demonstration after the summer of 1968 was attacked by small gangs of right-wing and fascist groups. These groups did not refrain from using guns to terrorize the demonstrators. The result was a rapid radicalization of the student movement which would lead to them resorting to arms, first as an effective medium of self-defense. In 1969, the clashes became deadly and students were killed with bullets (Alper 2009: 390–487).

The diffusion process of action repertoires and ideologies to the Turkish students maybe did not directly lead to the radicalization of students and mounting political violence in the initial stages of the movement. However, the diffusion process helped the re-creation of the movement around a more solid target of imperialism, namely the Sixth Fleet, and the unification and amplification of different campus activities in a massive occupation campaign in June 1968. The immense self-confidence of the students that they gained in the anti-Sixth Fleet

---

31 *Cumhuriyet*, 26.7.1968.
32 *Cumhuriyet*, 1.8.1968.

272   *Dynamics of Political Violence*

campaigns and especially in the June occupations encouraged them to resort to more disruptive actions. The stiff actions of students against the Sixth Fleet soldiers in July was unthinkable before they realized their power as one of the important political actors of the new times, not only in Turkey but in the world as well. The increasing threat of student actions backed by such self-confidence alarmed the state forces and right-wing groups. The escalation spiral of police and student violence that started in the summer of 1968 marked the initial stage of the radicalization of the student movement. The radical wing of the student movement, which was in the minority before, suddenly gained the upper hand. Once the leadership was held by this radical wing, political violence escalated more in line with their conscious tactics. The spiral of escalating violence would eventually lead to the organization of guerilla units. Although the dynamics of escalation was determined by the local configuration of right-wing student groups, and the police forces in the Turkish context, what was at play was mostly a universal mechanism of action and counteraction and rising escalation of violence between opposing groups as in many Western countries.

Conclusion

In this chapter, I examined the reasons behind the similarity and spontaneity of Turkish student movement with that of Western countries, especially focusing on the events in 1967 and 1968. I put the diffusion mechanism of ideas, action repertoires and so on, and almost the universal mechanism of escalating political violence due to action and counteraction of opposing groups as the explanatory concepts. I highlighted different aspects and mechanisms of the diffusion process of global movements by investigating two cases from Turkey in 1967 and 1968 and the succeeding escalation of political violence in the immediate aftermath. In the first case, I highlighted the selective and innovative adoption of anti-imperialist demonstrations in Turkey. Unlike the anti-imperialist demonstrations in the West, Turkish anti-imperialist demonstrations emphasized the Vietnam issue less. Turkish students managed to seize the opportunity of organizing massive demonstrations after the Arab-Israeli War, which symbolized imperialist pressure over a Muslim country. Simultaneously they innovatively found a popular target during these demonstrations, the US Sixth Fleet, which would be an important symbol of US imperialism in the Turkish '68. Then, immediately after the Arab-Israeli war, the eruption of the second Cyprus Crisis gave another chance to the left-wing students to popularize their anti-imperialist views. Different than the chauvinistic 1964 demonstrations, these demonstrations were clearly anti-imperialist—the symbol of the Sixth Fleet was getting more concrete. The anti-imperialist demonstrations became stronger in 1968, triggering new tensions in the street. The interaction between the local dynamics and the diffusive effects of anti-imperialist demonstrations, especially from the West, created the unique aspects of the Turkish anti-imperialist demonstrations with the innovative tactics of the local agents.

In addition, I showed how the diffusive effect of the protests can magnify and connect otherwise separate claims of local campus protests into a massive campaign. The influence of the Paris May did the same thing for the Turkish '68 by connecting and amplifying the scattered protests that were not rare in Turkish campuses through the sixties in one massive uprising in the June of 1968. In this process I highlighted the importance of self-fulfilling prophecies of media coverage in protest diffusion and the significant opportunities provided to the protesters by this coverage. I showed that stressing the endemic character of student protests facilitates the diffusion of the protests by underlining the common political identity of students all around the world and by increasing their self-confidence in their capacity and resources by representing these demonstrations as inevitable floods and showing the deep political influences of this flood. I also emphasized that the media coverage of the events created an opportunity for students to loudly pronounce their grievances, since the media created indirect pressure on administrators. This opportunity was quickly seized, however, not by organized students, but by ordinary students who forced the student organizations into an occupation.

Finally, I stressed that unified and amplified student protests (created with the help of diffusion mechanisms) generated a disruptive social force, against which first the state forces then the right-wing groups reacted. The diffusion mechanism between the Western student movement and Turkey helped the creation of massive mobilization of students in the summer of 1968. The mobilization sparked a harsh clash between students and the police, which triggered rapid escalation of action and counteraction between a more self-confident student movement and its opponents. The initial radicalization of the movement, which took place as a result of similar causal mechanisms with many Western countries, would gain momentum after the radicals grasped the initiative in the student movement in an environment of escalating violence. When the right-wing groups took to the streets to answer leftist militancy, the political violence would mark every kind of political protest. Alongside the escalation of political violence, however, the diffusion mechanism would not stop and the diffusion of more violent means, tactics and actions would start proceeding parallel with the action and counteraction of opposing forces. The almost simultaneous arming of student activists to start the vanguard war against the state in 1970 and 1971 should also be investigated from the perspective of diffusion mechanisms, which could be the subject of another chapter.

References

Ali, T. 1995. *Sokak Savaşı Yılları*. Istanbul: İletişim Yayınları.
Alimi, E.Y. 2011. Relational Dynamics in Factional Adoption of Terrorist Tactics: A Comparative Perspective. *Theory and Society*, 40, 95–118.

Alper, E. 2009. *Student Movement in Turkey, 1960–1971*. Bogaziçi University: Unpublished PhD Thesis.

Atılgan, G. *Yön-Devrim Hareketi*. Istanbul: TÜSTAV, 2002.

Baykam, B. 1999a. *68'li Yıllar: Tanıklar*. Istanbul: Imge Yayınları.

Baykam, B. 1999b. *68'li Yıllar: Eylemciler*. Istanbul: Imge yayınları.

della Porta, D. and Diani, M. 2006. *Social Movements: An Introduction*. Blackwell Publishing.

Feyizoğlu, Turhan. 2004. *Fırtınalı Yılların Gençlik Liderleri Konusuyor.* Istanbul: Ozan Yayıncılık.

Givan, R.K., Roberts, K.M. and Soule, S. A. 2010. Introduction: The Dimensions of Diffusion, in *The Diffusion of Social Movements: Actors, Mechanisms and Political Effects*, edited by Givan, R.K. et al. Cambridge University Press, 1–18.

İpekçi, A. 1968a. Editorials. *Milliyet*, 14 May, 1.

İpekçi, A. 1968b. Editorials. *Milliyet*, 19 May, 1.

Işık, G. 1968. Avrupa Üniversitelerinde Siyasi Deprem (The Political Earthquake in European Universities). *Cumhuriyet*. 3 May, 7.

Karadeniz, H. 1969. *Olaylı Yıllar ve Gençlik.* Istanbul: May Yayınları.

McAdam, D. and Rucht, D. 1993. Cross-National Diffusion of Movement Ideas. *Annals of the American Academy of the Political and Social Sciences,* 528: 56–74.

McAdam, D., Tarrow, S. and Tilly, C. 2001. *Dynamics of Contention.* Cambridge University Press.

Samim, A. (Murat Belge). 1981. The Tragedy of Turkish Left. *New Left Review*, 126(1), 60–85.

Selçuk, İ. 1967. Barış için Savaş (War for Peace). *Cumhuriyet,* 23 November, 2.

Sosyalizm ve Toplumsal Mücadeleler Ansiklopedisi. 1986. vol. 8, Istanbul: Iletişim Yayınları.

Soule, S.A. 2007. Diffusion Processes within and across Movements in *The Blackwell Companion to Social Movements*, edited by S.A. Soule, D.A. Snow and H. Kriesi. Blackwell, 294–311.

Staggenborg, S. 2008. *Social Movements.* Oxford University Press.

Strand, D. and Meyer, J.W. 1993. Intsitutional Conditions for Diffusion. *Theory and Society*, 22, 487–511.

Zileli, G. 2000. *Yarılma (1954–1972)*. Istanbul: İletişim Yayınları.

Chapter 13

The Evolution of the al-Qaeda-type Terrorism: Networks and Beyond

Ekaterina Stepanova

In theory, ten years after the terrorist attacks of September 11, 2001, unprecedented in scale and in their information and political effect, it is time to come up with a clear verdict on what we know about modern transnational terrorism and the effectiveness of the fight against terrorism. The reality, however, does not easily fit into any single linear scheme: the way to understand the dominant patterns of terrorism, especially on a global scale, is not through fixing some established, durable and static phenomenon, but through the study of a set of interconnected, dynamic—and non-linear—processes. Among these *non-linear processes* are:

1. The continuing transnationalization of terrorism at different levels of the world politics and the further blurring of the boundary between traditional categories of "domestic" and "international" terrorism;
2. Constantly emerging new local-regional contexts for flare-ups of terrorist activity;
3. Further evolution and transformation of dominant ideological forms of terrorism;
4. The dynamic formation of hybrid, network, and post-network organizational models of armed actors employing terrorist means; and
5. The upgrade of logistical, financial and, most importantly, information and communication tactics, means, and methods, as well as the widening range of targets.

These processes evolve against the background of broader and more fundamental trends in world politics. They include the emergence of the increasingly dense "glocal" (global–local) information and political space and the new possibilities for manipulating this space, the lack of decline in one-sided—direct and intentional—violence against civilians in contrast to significant decline of major conventional wars and battle-related deaths, the general rise in asymmetrical violence—both in the form of "new interventionism" generated by the world's lead states and their blocs (especially from the Euro-Atlantic community) and in the form of insurgent and terrorist activity by the multiplying and increasingly assertive non-state actors at different levels of world politics. Furthermore, while throughout the 2000s terrorism posed as the most dynamic form of contemporary armed violence, in the

276   *Dynamics of Political Violence*

2010s that role may shift to the less organized, but incomparably more mass-based forms of semi-spontaneous social protest (as illustrated by a tide of socio-political revolutions that flooded the Middle East in 2011).

As noted above, the use of terrorist means at any level of world politics and the process of radicalization that leads to the group's resort to terrorism are *dynamic processes*. Methodologies centered on identifying more-or-less static causes and explanations are not particularly well-suited to understanding dynamic processes, as they tend to portray terrorists as little but obedient, passive objects to persistent socio-political, economic and psychological forces outside their reach (Bjorgo: 3). A more useful framework for understanding dynamic processes is an *actor-oriented approach*, according to which terrorists are intentional actors that develop willful strategies to achieve political objectives, a resort to terrorism is a multicausal and multi-dimensional process, and a certain variety of terrorism may emerge due to one set of causes, and continue to function for different reasons.

Terrorism: Organizational Asymmetry and Transnationalization

Terrorism is premeditated use of or threat to use violence against soft—civilian and other non-combatant—targets to create broader intimidation and destabilization effects in order to achieve political goals by exercising pressure on the state and society. Thus, terrorist means are employed in the context of asymmetrical confrontation at a (sub)national or transnational level between a non-state actor and its ultimate state-based protagonist (the state, a group of states, international organization). This implies *status asymmetry*: state-based actors enjoy a formally recognized international status within the world system. In most cases, states also remain more powerful than non-state actors in terms of military, political and socio-economic potential (*power asymmetry*).

In violent asymmetrical confrontation between state-based and non-state actors the former do not, however, simply overwhelm the latter. Rather, the protagonists differ in their strengths and weaknesses. Violent non-state actors challenging individual states or the global order altogether rely on comparative strengths other than status or conventionally understood power, such as the high mobilizing potential of *extremist ideologies* and the specifics of *organizational systems* (Stepanova 2008). It is the critical, mutually reinforcing link between ideological and organizational aspects of terrorism that turns them into the main comparative advantages of terrorist actors at levels from local to global. The starting assumption is that the more organizational patterns of a violent non-state actor, especially at the transnational level, are different from the organizational system of its state-based protagonists, that is, the stronger is the organizational asymmetry between the two—the stronger are the former's comparative advantages in asymmetrical confrontation that involves the use of terrorist means. Hence, this chapter's central focus is on network-based hybrid and "post-network" organizational forms.

In the early twenty-first century, it has become commonplace to talk about the high degree and speed of transnationalization of terrorism. What is often ignored is that transnationalization of terrorism primarily manifests itself in *qualitative* rather than quantitative terms. In quantitative terms, incidents of so-called "domestic terrorism" still outnumber acts of "international terrorism" by a large margin (should one choose to stick to the outdated strict dichotomy between "domestic" and "international" terrorism). As even terrorists whose goals do not go beyond localized contexts tend to increasingly transnationalize at least some aspects of their activity, the line between domestic and international terrorism has become increasingly blurred. In a globalized world, all terrorism becomes transnationalized to some degree. This makes it critical to distinguish between different levels, stages and qualities of transnationalization. Of decisive importance is no longer in how many countries a group raises funds or whether or not its members attended a terrorist training camp abroad. The main criterion to establish the level of transnationalization is the overall level of a group's *ultimate goals and agenda*—local, regional or global (Saikia and Stepanova 2009: xvii–xxi, xxiii). A self-generating, homegrown cell that has limited or no direct contact with counterparts abroad, but engages in terrorist activity in the name of a markedly transnational agenda and sees itself as integral part of a global network with shared ideology, should be seen as manifestation of an advanced form of transnational terrorism.

The diversity of modern terrorism notwithstanding, in the early twenty-first century international attention was primarily focused on a particular ideological and organizational variety of transnational terrorism catalyzed by the September 11, 2001 terrorist attacks. For brevity's sake, this al-Qaeda-inspired transnational movement is referred to in this chapter as the "global jihad" movement.

The focus of this chapter on organizational patterns of terrorism at the highest—global—level of transnationalization and, more specifically, on the "global jihad" movement with its unlimited, universalist goals, outreach, and agenda is also merited by other considerations. There are very few terrorist groups and movements at this level, that is, groups whose ultimate goals and agenda are unlimited, global in their outreach and non-negotiable (examples other than al-Qaeda and al-Qaeda-linked/inspired cells and networks include totalitarian apocalyptic sects such as Aum Shinrikyo). In contrast, the more local you go, the more context-specific, concrete and geographically limited are terrorist groups' goals, the greater the variety of their organizational patterns and the harder it is to generalize beyond individual case studies or the limits of comparative analysis. Also, for terrorist actors pursuing unlimited goals at the global level—such as al-Qaeda or Aum Shinrikyo—terrorism *is* the dominant violent tactic. In contrast, many groups at the more localized levels, particularly those that are engaged in armed conflicts, tend to combine terrorist means with other violent tactics (such as guerrilla-style combat targeting military and security forces and objects) and sometimes with non-violent protest as well.

Networks: Advantages and Drawbacks for Terrorist Actors

Since September 11, 2001, al-Qaeda and the subsequent modifications of "global jihad," including the broader and looser movement comprised of self-generating cells (the post-al-Qaeda movement), have been commonly described as "model" networks. As time passes, analysts find it harder to keep pace with the rapid changes in organizational forms of this movement. It is no longer sufficient to refer to the post-al-Qaeda movement as a standard network, described in the most general terms.

Analysis of organizational patterns of terrorist actors has been dominated by *organizational network theory* according to which a network is a specific, separate organizational form that has gained force and displays important advantages over other organizational forms in an age of rapid development of information and communication technologies (Arquilla and Ronfeldt 2001, 2002). For a certain system to function as a network it does not suffice for its elements to be linked by horizontal ties (as opposed to dominant vertical ties in hierarchies). All of its elements must view themselves as parts of a broader network and be ready to act as a network. From the point of organizational network theory, the main characteristic of a network is its non-hierarchical, decentralized character, which explains the primary focus of this theory on the relations and conflicts between networks and hierarchies. Compared to hierarchies, networks are more flexible, mobile, adaptive to change and more stable during crises and system shocks. Non-state socio-political actors that display key network features gain considerable advantages in asymmetrical confrontation against the more hierarchical state structures. The lack of a strict hierarchy and of central leadership exercising direct control over subordinate units complicates the task of destroying these movements.

However, when it comes to organized political violence, especially in the form of terrorism, there is a tendency to overemphasize its network advantages and characteristics. Excessive or exclusive focus on the use of network forms by militant/terrorist and other underground structures distorts the general picture by underestimating the positive social mobilization potential of networks in the information age. The spread of networks is not limited to non-state protest actors, in the first place, and when it comes to the latter, network features can be traced in protest groups of different types: in fact, environmental and civil society networks, including ICT-based social networks, are more widespread and more clearly display network features than militant-terrorist or criminal networks. This fully applies to transnational movements such as anti-globalists or movement against the use of landmines.

In practice neither the contrast between networks and hierarchies nor the distinctions between informal decentralized networks and formal organizations are strict dichotomies. There is a broad range of intermediate structures between the two extremes of a pure network and a pure hierarchy and most modern organizational models are hybrids and display both network and hierarchical elements, sometimes in combination with elements of other organizational forms, such as clans. In a dynamic process of organizational development, a more coherent organization balancing hierarchical and network features, such as al-Qaeda, may evolve into the more decentralized post-al-Qaeda movement dominated by network forms.

In terrorism studies, general shift towards networks is often interpreted as a sharp contrast between the "old" terrorism by hierarchical nationalist, leftwing or other terrorist groups and the "new" transnational terrorist networks (Gunaratna 2002: 54–8, 95–101). This interpretation is hardly merited, as network characteristics had long been part of organizational design for several militant/terrorist groups active at a more localized level (Irish Republican Army (IRA), Sendero Luminoso, Hamas, Al-Aqsa Martyrs Brigades). While for much of the second half of the twentieth century, terrorist means were primarily employed by leftist, nationalist or mixed groups (such as the Palestinian Liberation Organization) that favored more centralized structures, some of these groups (such as the IRA) started to employ network elements as early as the 1970s. By that time, the first concept of segmented network-type resistance—Carlos Marighella's "urban guerrilla" concept—was already in place (Marighella 1975). The asymmetrical organizational solution offered by Marighella is to avoid excessive centralization through creation of autonomous groups connected to one another and to the center by shared ideology and direct action rather than through strict vertical command links and able to generate "free initiative." The key condition for such a network to be effectively coordinated by the strategic command is the extremely general nature and simplicity of its political/ideological goals. To be part of the network, it is not sufficient to share the movement's ideology—a cell can only become networked through direct militant action. Surprisingly few present accounts of the al-Qaeda-inspired transnational terrorism have been as accurate in summarizing the main strengths and characteristics of its organizational forms as Marighella's urban guerrilla concept.

In the following decades, the spread of network features has increasingly affected both non-violent and violent non-state actors at levels from the local to the global producing a variety of hybrids that combine features associated with more than one organizational form. In this sense, organizational differences between modern terrorism at the transnational and the more localized levels are more gradual than substantial (with more centralized models more widespread in the localized contexts). Typical network resistance tactics, such as swarming, are no less popular among the localized groups combining guerrilla attacks against military targets with terrorist means, than among the cells of the post-al-Qaeda type. Nor is the terrorism with a markedly global, universalist agenda exclusively dominated by network forms: Aum Shinrikyo—as most other totalitarian apocalyptic sects—was structured as a strict hierarchy.

The final reservation concerns the need to keep in mind not only advantages of networks as violent actors in asymmetrical confrontation against the less flexible state structures, but also some of their serious drawbacks. Networks can experience difficulties when faced with the need to make strategic political–military decisions and to put them into effect. They lack purely organizational mechanisms to ensure that these decisions are followed by the main elements within the network and to exercise control over the implementation process. The informal (latent) nature of links between network elements allows the system to function effectively only under certain conditions. The mere fact that multiple cells form a network and even their ideological proximity may not suffice to impose upon them strong and stable mutual obligations to engage in violent activity, especially in the form of terrorism against civilians.

Against this background, the evolution of the al-Qaeda-inspired movement stands out as a shift from a more centralized network to one of the loosest ones. It has no strict vertical chain of command and displays informal leadership patterns at the macro level and multiple and diverse cell patterns at the micro level. Why then, despite all these characteristics, does this movement manage to act effectively and as the one, however loose, movement? How does a structural model that displays the main network characteristics neutralize its inherent weaknesses?

Evolution of al-Qaeda: The Main Approaches

The analytical approaches to the process of evolution of the "global jihadi" terrorism can be grouped into three broad categories:

1. The al-Qaedaization approach;
2. The emphasis on regionalization of al-Qaeda; and
3. The approach promoted in this chapter—the "post-Qaeda" interpretation of the main direction of the movement's transformation.

The respective approaches differ in the way they assess the scale and substance of al-Qaeda's transformation, the speed of this process and the key factors that affected this process.

The al-Qaedaization Approach

The al-Qaedaization approach was prevalent in the aftermath of September 11, and is still held by those in political and expert circles who tend to see al-Qaeda everywhere, most of the time and behind any act of Islamist/Islamicized terrorism in any regional context (Gunaratna 2002). As the one based on evidence of poor, mostly speculative nature, this approach would hardly merit serious discussion, had it not been used in the early- to mid-2000s to guide and justify policies of the world's lead powers, with dramatic consequences for and counterproductive impact on international politics and security, particularly in Iraq and Afghanistan, where terrorist activity was most sharply on the rise over the 2000s.

Needless to say, this approach is the least actor- or process-oriented one. While it acknowledges a degree of evolution of al-Qaeda in the post-September 11 decade, its interpretation of this evolution is not substantive and can be best summed up as mechanic "expansion," including automatic "penetration" into most local-regional armed conflict areas in Muslim-populated regions of the world. While this approach routinely refers to "al-Qaeda networks," it is the only one that refuses to acknowledge the scale and degree of the movement's decentralization and still recognizes the critical vertical command and control role for "al-Qaeda Central" depicted as a consolidated and territorially-based "master headquarters."

The Regionalization Approach

The approach that has been gaining prominence more recently—and in the early 2010s may have become prevalent in the mainstream US and Western academic and security analysis—describes the main direction of al-Qaeda evolution as the process of regionalization. This process can be disaggregated into three organizational/strategic levels.

First, it still leaves some direct strategic and command role for the "core al-Qaeda" based in Pakistan and Afghanistan, but acknowledges its relatively declining role.

Second, according to the regionalization approach, the main level and the most perilous variety of al-Qaeda-type terrorism has been shifting towards several organizationally coherent "regional affiliates," based and primarily active in Muslim countries: al-Qaeda in the Arabian peninsula, al-Qaeda in the Lands of the Islamic Maghreb, or al-Qaeda in East Africa (Rollins et al. 2011a, 2011b). This thesis is a major step forward, as compared to primitive "al-Qaedaization," as it at least tries to distinguish between these "regional affiliates" and other genuine, locally based militant Islamist groups (such as Hamas or Hizbullah) that have become integral parts of respective national political contexts.

The third—and, according to this interpretation, less important—level is formed by al-Qaeda's "ideological adherents"—small cells and even individuals active, by some accounts, in over 70 countries. However, these adherents "who know the group only through its ideology to carry out violence in its name" are interpreted as a sign of al-Qaeda's weakness and organizational degradation explained primarily as a direct result of counterterrorist pressure from the United States and its allies (White House 2011: 3, 19; Rollins et al. 2011a: 30).

The regionalization approach to al-Qaeda evolution needs to be placed in a specific political and analytical context that emerged in the follow-up of the clear failures and counterproductive effects of the Bush administration's "war on terrorism," especially in the way it was projected to Iraq and Afghanistan, and led to the review of this counterterrorism campaign under the Obama administration. The resulting emphasis on "regionalization" reflects some greater nuance and adequacy in grasping changes in the al-Qaeda-linked networks, but stops short of acknowledging the full scale, speed and degree of the movement's more radical and far-reaching transformation. For instance, an attempt to hint at al-Qaeda Central's loss of any practical meaning beyond symbolic and ideological significance would

282   *Dynamics of Political Violence*

hardly be feasible within this political context, as it would have deprived the US military and security presence in Afghanistan in the late 2000s—early 2010s of much of its declared political rationale and would have contradicted efforts to explain away US/NATO counterinsurgency failures in Afghanistan primarily by the interference of al-Qaeda from the Pakistani territory. Markedly, the idea of degradation of the al-Qaeda core and activity in Afghanistan ("naturally," as a result of efficient US counterterrorist operations) and of the shift of the main terrorist threat to the United States to the "al-Qaeda core in Pakistan" (Rollins et al. 2011a: 1, 11, 13) emerged right at the time when the US administration was in a bad need of the public-relations justification and cover-up for its decision to withdraw the bulk of US forces from Afghanistan. Likewise, a certain underestimation of the significance and threat posed by the third, micro-level of small radical "jihadi" terrorist cells, as compared to larger "regional affiliates," may reflect the reluctance to recognize—and political embarrassment about—the fact that the overwhelming majority of such mini-cells emerge and function not in far-away conflict zones deep inside the Muslim world, but in the Western states themselves.

Unsurprisingly, the regionalization approach has become the mainstream analytical framework in the West (especially since it became the main direction of revising the US national counterterrorism strategy under the administration of Barack Obama). It is also gradually gaining international prominence, including in the UN circles.

The Post-Qaeda Approach

The approach put forward in this chapter goes further in assessing the degree and scale of the transformation of "original al-Qaeda" over a dozen years since 9/11. It denies any serious residual strategic/command role for the historical "al-Qaeda core" by the late 2000s—early 2010s, beyond its symbolic role of an ideological catalyst for the broader movement.

In contrast to regionalization-centered interpretation, the approach taken in this chapter questions the role of "regional affiliates" as al-Qaeda's main successors and new centers of gravity. With the possible exception of al-Qaeda in the Arabian peninsula, all other so-called "affiliates," be it in Iraq, Maghreb, the Horn of Africa, or Southeast Asia, have had deep homegrown roots (sometimes activated or aggravated by external interventions) and have emerged as essentially authentic movements. Their real agenda has been and remains inextricably tied to respective regional/local conflicts and issues, while any declared links or pledges of loyalty to al-Qaeda are at best nominal and no solid or verifiable evidence has been provided to prove any operational links (Rollins et al. 2011b: 5).

Instead, it is the looser, *ideology-driven networks* of much smaller and more elitist radical cells, with more explicitly transnational, globalist agenda not tied specifically to any single local/regional context, that form the cutting edge and the main driving force of what has long transformed into post-al-Qaeda movement. In contrast to armed groups tied to specific local/regional contexts in the Middle

East, Asia or Africa, cells of this type are truly "exterritorial" in their outlook and goals and have most commonly emerged in Western countries themselves. In Europe, the most affected countries have been the UK, Spain, France, Germany, the Netherlands, and Denmark (Neumann 2008). In the late 2000s, the emergence of this type of cell and of terrorist plots of "global jihadi" type sharply increased in the United States: out of 40 committed or prevented terrorist attack over a decade since September 11, 2001, over half occurred in 2009–2010 (Bjelopera and Randol 2010: 1). These cells display diverse radicalization paths and organizational patterns, are hardly linked to one another in any formal way and are mostly united by the shared ideological discourse of "global jihad." Still, together they form—and see themselves as part of—an adaptive and resilient transnational network-type movement that, despite its marginality, can pose a serious terrorist threat to international security.

The post-Qaeda approach is also distinct from other interpretations of al-Qaeda's evolution after September 11, 2001 in that it does not view the US-led "war on terrorism" as the single decisive factor in al-Qaeda evolution, suggesting a more complex, multidimensional and actor-oriented explanation outlined below.

Evolution of the "Global Jihad": From a Hybrid Network to a Post-network?

Al-Qaeda's organizational pattern evolved from a more formalized organization to a more amorphous, decentralized network of cells that spread and multiplied in a way that resembled franchise business schemes. These cells share the movement's markedly transnational version of radical Islamism (the ideology of "global jihad"), follow general strategic guidelines formulated by its leaders and ideologues and use the name of "al-Qaeda" as a brand but are not formally linked to the "core al-Qaeda" in organizational terms. This creeping network displays the main characteristics of a segmented polycentric integrated network, or SPIN structure (Gerlach and Hine 1970, Gerlach 1987, Gerlach 2001). The main integrating force for a standard modern network that approximates the SPIN structure is its shared ideology. Using modern means of communication, shared ideology helps connect the fragmented, dispersed, isolated or informally interlinked elements of a network. To emphasize this connection, the term used in this chapter to refer to both violent and non-violent networks of this type is *ideological–functional network*. For modern ideological–functional networks, common ideological beliefs and values play a higher role as the main connecting and binding principle than they do for more traditional organizational types of anti-system group.

At first sight, transnational post-al-Qaeda movement resembles a standard ideological–functional network. It is even seen sometimes as nothing else but a network embodiment of the ideology of "global Salafi jihad." The movement's cells emerge in different political contexts and are dispersed in many parts of the world. If they are tied into a broader decentralized network, it is through some latent, hidden links. However, these characteristics do not appear to match the active, resilient and seemingly well-coordinated manner in which post-al-Qaeda cells carry out terrorist activities. The scope and frequency of these activities require a higher level of intra-organizational coherence and trust than the one that can be provided by shared religious/ideological beliefs or ICT-based links alone. In other words, in terms of coordination, the post-al-Qaeda movement is too effective for a modern network.

Social Network Explanation: A Critique

Even some of the lead network warfare theorists have come to realize that the organizational dynamics of al-Qaeda-type transnational terrorism cannot be reduced to a standard evolution or fragmentation of an impersonalized ideological–functional network. The search for alternative explanations has largely been conducted within the framework of the (psycho)sociological *social network theory* that explores all sorts of interlinkages between social actors and the social structures that stem from and are based on these links (Scott 2000). It views networks not as a specific, separate organizational form, but as a system of interrelations in society that characterize all forms of social life. Accordingly, the distinction between an informal network and a formal organization is more important than the contrast between network and hierarchical organizational forms. While any organization requires at least a minimal set of hierarchical features, a network of interconnected, but autonomous elements in principle lacks central leadership and strict hierarchy.

Addressing the problem from the social network-centered angle has both advantages and drawbacks. The main advantage is the specific attention that this approach pays to the (psycho)sociological aspects of the radicalization process, especially to the radicalization of Muslims into potential members of radical al-Qaeda-style Islamist cells in Western states and to further radicalization of these cells through intragroup social dynamics. Indeed, the cells of the post-al-Qaeda movement are united not only by ideological proximity, the feeling of being a part of the same network of semi- or fully-autonomous units or informal network-type links. The best available psycho-sociological accounts of modern transnational violent Islamist networks show that cells and members of the same cell are also linked by close personal and intragroup relations (Sageman 2004, 2007a). In order to function effectively as segments of larger networks, such cells require and display a very high level of interpersonal trust and mutual obligations. These close social and personal ties are often established before a radicalized cell joins the transnational movement. These links are not primarily of the clan or family type and are often based on friendship, shared regional or national background, or common professional, educational and other experience. According to analysis by Marc Sageman, who was the first to put together the available information on the psycho-sociological characteristics and personal background (first for 150 and later for 500 active "jihadists"), friendship played an important role in joining a radical Islamist cell—or the one that gradually became such through a process of intra-group radicalization—for 68 per cent of them. Kinship and family links played the same role for no more than 14 per cent (Sageman 2004a: 111–13).

There is no need to reproduce in detail the specific mechanisms of cell formation of the transnational Islamist movement. They are context specific, do not conform to a single pattern and have been addressed in other studies (Taarnby 2007, Bokhari et al. 2006: 7–21, Neumann 2008). Specific radicalization and cell-formation mechanisms may be significantly nuanced even for different kinds of diaspora Muslims in the West. Islamist cell members range from visitors and first-generation immigrants to second- and third-generation European-born citizens or even, in some cases, Western converts. A group of Muslims (that may range from childhood friends and people originating from the same area in their home countries to Western-born people of the same neighborhood, university friends or colleagues) get together, establish close friendly relations and form a tightly integrated group. This relatively narrow brotherhood of like-minded friends and comrades gradually becomes increasingly politicized and radicalized under a combination of external political, psychological or socio-cultural pressures and internal group dynamics, and finds natural guidance and ready answers too many of its concerns in the radical Islamist ideology. At some point, group members realize the futility of mere talk and the need to turn to active "propaganda by deed." The group is then ready to become an integral part of the "global jihad" movement, often joining it as a cell. For some cells the direct link to "jihad" through a contact with an active, preferably veteran "jihadist" had been necessary (Sageman 2004: 120–121). However, there is no one single pattern and the accessibility of the direct link to jihad has lost much of its earlier role as the critical element in the entire chain. More cells now appear to see direct action itself as the quickest and most accessible way to become part of the broader movement, find ways and means to organize terrorist activity on their own, and carry out terrorist acts. While earlier analyses described it as a long and gradual process requiring personal intercommunication (Sageman 2004: 108, Taarnby 2007: 181), more recent sources point to an increasingly rapid process facilitated by the growing role of online communication through electronic information providers and Internet blogs and forums (Sageman 2007b: 4; Europol 2009: 13–14, 20).

However, the excessive focus on sociological aspects of "jihadi" radicalization in the West and on social alienation and group dynamics as the main explanation of the formation of the post-al-Qaeda terrorist cells also has its drawbacks. For instance, Sageman, on a basis of his extremely useful data on the role social bonds in al-Qaeda-style cell formation, makes a far more problematic conclusion: that the role of religious extremism—and political/religious ideology in general—is effectively superseded by friendship ties and social integration problems and reinforced by dynamics of intra-group radicalization and other sociological and psychological factors (such as young men's drive for "glory"). This neglect of the role of radical ideology as a major driving force and organizational glue for the post-al-Qaeda movement is typical for many social network theorists.

It partly stems of their genuine disappointment as (psycho)-sociologists with the formalistic, rationalist concepts of ideology or religious extremism and especially the failure of such concepts to properly account for ethical/psychological issues and radicalization factors. Also, by prioritizing the role of social networks and of social integration issues in the process of radicalization, this approach *artificially de-politicizes and de-ideologizes terrorism*. It ignores the fact that the main driving factors of cell formation may have little to do with personal problems of socialization, lack of social integration, immediate social circumstances of radicalizing individuals or social group dynamics.

The social-network-centric approach downgrades the importance of an extremist religious/ideological discourse of "global jihad" for multiple, seeming disparate post-Qaeda cells. The "god farther" of this distinct tradition in Islamist thought was Sayyed Qutb, the radical Egyptian theorist of the 1950s–1960s. This ideology combines strong religious imperative (reflected in the primacy of the category of "faith"—an ethical contract with God at the individual and collective level—over all other categories, including "jihad") with quasi-religious features (it incorporates elements of genuine socio-political protest). The social network-centric approach also neglects the powerful mobilization and radicalization impact of both national, but especially broader international *political* developments on the formation of the post-al-Qaeda cells. These cells primarily frame their action in highly politicized, anti-neo-imperialist discourse driven by what they see happening in Iraq, in Afghanistan and elsewhere. The impact of these events which are interpreted as injustices and crimes "against all Muslims" is reinforced by and reinterpreted through the prism of the ideology of "global jihad."

Unsurprisingly, the later versions of Sageman's social bonds concept boil down to an upgraded and modernized version of the leaderless resistance concept (Sageman 2007b). The original concept was developed in the 1980s and 1990s by the US right-wing white-power extremist Louis Beam (Beam 1992). Leaderless resistance is actively employed by many right-wing extremists and radical environmentalists, but remains a quite unstable and not necessarily effective organizational principle, as it may easily degrade to sporadic, semi-anarchist violence (Garfinkel 2003). How can unity of action and strict implementation of generally formulated goals be ensured in a fragmented, dispersed transnational structure whose different level and multiple micro-cells are not directly linked? How can such a network movement function in the absence of a centralized system of direct control and subordination and in a way that prevents them from slipping into meaningless, sporadic and diffuse violence?

Ideological-strategic Guidelines at Macro-level and Brotherhoods at Micro-level

The movement that emerged in the process of al-Qaeda-linked networks' evolution in the early twenty-first century is not a pure network. Like most structures, it also displays some elements of hierarchy. For instance, it has some leaders—even if these are more ideological inspirers than leaders in the traditional sense. It also displays both informal horizontal links between its cells and some vertical links (within cells and between ideological-strategic and operational micro-cell levels). This hybrid structure allows network and hierarchical elements to reinforce their comparative strengths and compensate for their mutual weaknesses. In addition, certain elements of other organizational forms, especially at the micro-level of individual cells, such as associations, play a role. Even elements of clan-based organization—or the ones imitating it—cannot be discounted altogether, given both the origin of the historical al-Qaeda (networks with a strong presence and impact of Gulf Arab radicals) and the importance of a specifically interpreted ethical imperative ("honor") for transnational "jihadists." However, the hybrid structure of the post-Qaeda movement cannot fully explain why autonomous cells manage to act in line with the general strategic guidelines formulated by the movement's leaders and ideologues.

Some of the organizational characteristics of this type of transnational terrorism appear to be untypical of either pure networks or pure hierarchical organizational forms. One of such characteristics is the movement's ability to ensure effective coordination of actions undertaken by autonomous lower-level cells. Coordination is carried out neither by means of centralized control as in hierarchies, nor through compromises and consultations as in networks (Mayntz 2004, Stepanova 2008: 141). Rather, the movement's activities are coordinated directly by means of strategic guidelines formulated by its ideologues in the most general way. Another related characteristic is that, despite the ulterior nature of both horizontal and vertical links at different levels of the system, these links appear to be effectively and promptly operationalized when required—for instance, to carry out a terrorist attack by several cells.

Such coordination is only possible if the movement's segments not only support its ideological goals but fully identify themselves with these goals and if the ideology that ties the system together meets certain conditions. The first condition is the unity of ideology and strategy. This may only be achieved if the ideology itself serves as a set of direct strategic guidelines and if these ideological/strategic guidelines already contain specific tactical instructions or recommendations. To put it simply, ideological goals should be formulated in such a way that they may be implemented through various means and in different contexts—in fact, whenever an opportunity to undertake violent activities in the name of these goals presents itself. Regardless of the context of action, it would then still qualify as the one directed towards the achievement of the overall movement's ultimate goals. The second condition is the need for a relatively consolidated basic ideological/ strategic discourse, despite the multiplicity of leaders/ideologues, varying ideological guidance and diversity of organizational forms and contexts.

Violent Islamist extremism in its most ambitious and transnationalized form and its main ideological pillar—the concept of "global jihad" as the necessary strategy towards the achievement of the new global order ("global caliphate")—are unique in that they manage to meet both of the above requirements. The ideology of "global jihad" already contains detailed recommendations for practical action.

One example is provided by Qutb's detailed recommendations on the formation and activities of the vanguard, elitist Islamic revolutionary groups that have to first undergo the process of "purification" or, using the modern wording, radicalization (Qutb 1980: 20, 47)—recommendations that are, knowingly or instinctively, closely followed by the emerging cells of the post-al-Qaeda movement. The more vulgar popularizers of this ideology, such as bin Laden, have further emphasized its encouragement and advance blessing for any context-specific violent actions, explicitly including terrorist attacks. For instance, the notorious 1998 al-Qaeda fatwa prescribed a course of action that, regardless of the exact context, circumstance or pretext, would qualify as being directed towards the same "general goal." In it, bin Laden stressed the need "to kill Americans and their allies" as "an individual duty for every Muslim who can do it in any country in which it is possible to do it" (Laden 1998).

The second requirement for the consolidation of ideology and strategy to the point where they can serve as an effective coordination mechanism for a loosely structured network movement is the standardization and unification of strategic discourse. For the post-al-Qaeda movement, with its multiple leaders, ideologues and hybrid, diverse and multi-level organizational patterns, the key role in meeting this requirement has been played by information and propaganda activities. These activities built on and developed the original al-Qaeda ideology. They have been increasingly conducted through electronic information and communications systems. Since the mid-2000s, the information providers associated with the al-Qaeda-linked or al-Qaeda-inspired networks (ranging from the Al-Fajr Media Center, the Al-Sahab Foundation for Islamic Media Publication or the Global Islamic Media Front to personal websites of the leading radical Islamist clerics and the affiliated Internet blogs and forums) have qualitatively upgraded and intensified their activities in an increasingly coordinated way. By the early 2010s, intensive online discussions and propaganda have become the main means for ideological–strategic unification for the "Internet scholars." They may include some first-generation al-Qaeda-linked preachers, such as the anti-Soviet Afghan jihad veterans Abu Yahya al-Libi and Abu Musab al-Suri, but are increasingly dominated by the "Internet-generation" clerics, such as the Kuwaiti Hamed bin Abdallah al-Ali who made one of the first attempts to speak as a voice of the new consolidated collective discourse of "global jihad" and to reinforce the movement's doctrinal unity, by publishing the Covenant of the Supreme Council of Jihad Groups in January 2007 (al-Ali 2007).

This system of coordination through ideological/strategic guidelines at macro-level, however, does not yet explain coordination mechanisms within individual micro-cells. A network, especially the transnational one engaged in systematic organized violence in the form of terrorism, needs to display a higher level of interpersonal trust at the micro level of its units than a hierarchy or a less loose and less transnationalized network. It is here where Sageman's "social bond" theory comes back into play, but only if it is treated not as a strict alternative to the ideologically-integrated network concept, but as an explanation that *supplements* the ideology-centered perspective as it is modified above. The integration of elements of organizational network and social network theories is facilitated by certain similarities between an organizational form known as "association," or "brotherhood," and the "social network" category. In sum, the missing link at the micro-level of individual cells is provided by effective coordination and group cohesion through higher level of inter-personal trust and stronger mutual personal obligations, more typical to "brotherhoods" than to the more impersonalized networks. This stems from the specifics of micro-cells' formation and radicalization processes—largely as they are described by social network theorists.

While exact mechanisms of cell formation are context specific and do not conform to a single pattern, one pattern common to most cells appears to be that the most favorable environment for breeding potential volunteers is in areas of the closest and most intensive contact with "aliens"—both in the regions of extended Western economic, military, political and cultural presence and influence in the Muslim world and particularly in parts of Muslim diasporas and communities in the West. It is unlikely that the leaders/ideologues of the post-al-Qaeda movement deliberately masterminded an organizational model that would allow them to make up for the structural weaknesses of a network without undermining its main strengths. Instead, it was a combination of an organic process of organizational evolution and pro-active adjustment. As a result, a dynamic system evolved. It both displays a high degree of ideological indoctrination and is characterized by much stronger intra-cell social cohesion, interpersonal trust, commitment and obligations at the micro level than any standard impersonalized ideological–functional network.

Conclusion

The choice of one or another analytical approach to the process of al-Qaeda's evolution and transformation in the years since 9/11 determines both how the actual threat posed by al-Qaeda-inspired transnational terrorism is assessed and how the effectiveness of prevention and suppression of this type of terrorism is interpreted.

Take, for instance, the perception formulated within the framework of the dominant regionalization approach (the official approach taken by the US Obama administration) that the old leadership of the "core al-Qaeda" still retained some important direct strategic command and control functions ten years after the attacks of September 11, 2001. Among other thing, this approach allowed the Obama administration to declare "decisive progress" in the war with "al-Qaeda as organization" at any politically convenient moment: for instance, to present the May 2011 liquidation of the long defunct bin Laden by US special forces as "the most important strategic milestone in … effort to defeat al-Qa'ida" (White House 2011: 3). In contrast, from the viewpoint of the post-al-Qaeda approach promoted in this chapter, the anti-terrorism meaning of bin Laden's death and its significance for the "global jihad" movement have been relatively limited. The main strength of this movement has been the dynamic interaction of its specific, truly globalist vein of ideological/religious extremism (that will outlive bin Laden as its rather vulgar popularizer, with a younger, Internet-based generation of ideologues well in place) with adaptive and innovative organizational patterns. The latter go beyond network-type structure and involve direct coordination role of ideological/ strategic discourse for its multiple and otherwise fragmented elements—and that discourse is alive, well and undergoing a process of further adaptation, refinement and consolidation.

The striking and dynamic *interdependence of mutually reinforcing ideological and organizational patterns* is indispensable in the analysis of the evolution process of al-Qaeda-inspired movement. Furthermore, the central role of extremist ideology, especially the one with a strong religious imperative—both as a mobilizing factor and as a direct organizational principle—makes it futile to design ways to weaken organizational asymmetry separate from the need to address the ideological asymmetry. An ideology whose "subject matter … is mankind and sphere of activity is entire universe" (Qutb 2000: 242) is not merely *inter*nationalist or *trans*national, but *supra*national. It does not simply aspire to get control of existing states, but pretends to exist in another dimension which lies outside the (inter)state framework altogether, in the imagined borderless world where people are characterized not by their ethnicity or citizenship, but by whether or not they share the faith in one God. Its adepts fight for a mode of existence, a way of life, an all-embracing global system through the establishment of the "direct rule of God on earth" which, as they genuinely believe, would guarantee the freedom of human beings from any form of unjust governance by other people. In contrast to territorially based actors that may display certain ideological proximity, but are inseparably and primarily tied to local political agenda and armed struggle, the multiple cells of supranational ideologically-integrated post-al-Qaeda network movement do not defend territory, nation, or the state. As such, their existential ideology—and the organizational system linked to and dependent on this ideology—are unlikely to be moderated or neutralized. Thus, the main attention should be concentrated on preventive counter-radicalization work with a potential pool of volunteers who are not yet radicalized enough to form this type of terrorist cell.

References

al-Ali, H. bin A. 2007. [*Covenant of the Supreme Council of Jihad Groups*]. [Online]. Available in Arabic at http://www.h-alali.net/m_open.php?id=991da3ae-f492–1029-a701–0010dc91cf69 [accessed: August 31, 2011].

Arquilla, J. and Ronfeldt, D. 2002. Netwar revisited: the fight for the future continues. *Low Intensity Conflict & Law Enforcement*, 11(2–3), 178–89.

Arquilla, J. and Ronfeldt, D. (eds). 2001. *Networks and Netwars: The Future of Terror, Crime, and Militancy.* Santa Monica (Calif.): RAND.

Beam, L. 1992. Leaderless resistance. *The Seditionist*, 12, 1–7.

Bjelopera, J. and Randol, M. 2010. *American Jihadist Terrorism: Combating a Complex Threat*. Congressional Research Service (CRS) Report for Congress no. R41416. Washington D.C.: CRS, 2010.

Bjorgo, T. (ed.). 2005. *Root Causes of Terrorism*. London: Routledge.

Bokhari, L. et al. 2006. *Paths to Global Jihad: Radicalisation and Recruitment to Terror Networks*. Kjeller: Norwegian Defence Research Establishment (FFI).

Europol. 2009. *EU Terrorism Situation and Trend Report 2009*. The Hague: Europol.

Garfinkel, S. 2003. Leaderless resistance today. *First Monday* [Online], 8(3). Available at http://firstmonday.org/htbin/cgiwrap/bin/ojs/index.php/fm/article/view/1040 [accessed: August 31, 2011].

Gerlach, L.P. 1987. Protest movements and the construction of risk, in *The Social and Cultural Construction of Risk: Essays on Risk Selection and Perception*, edited by B.B. Johnson and V.T. Covello. Boston (Mass.): D. Reidel, 103–45.

Gerlach, L.P. 2001. The structure of social movements: environmental activism and its opponents, in *Networks and Netwars: The Future of Terror, Crime, and Militancy*, edited by J. Arquilla and D. Ronfeldt. Santa Monica: RAND, 289–310.

Gerlach, L.P. and Hine, V.H. 1970. *People, Power, Change: Movements of Social Transformation*. New York: Bobbs-Merril.

Gunaratna, R. 2002. *Inside Al Qaeda: Global Network of Terror*. New York: Columbia University Press.

Internet World Statistics: Usage and Population Statistics. 2010. [Online]. Available at: http://www.internetworldstats.com/africa.htm; http://www.internetworldstats.com/stats1.htm; http://www.internetworldstats.com/middle.htm; http://www.internetworldstats.com/stats5.htm [accessed: August 31, 2011].

Laden, O. bin. 1998. [World Islamic Front for jihad against Jews and crusaders: initial 'fatwa' statement]. *al-Quds al-Arabi* [Online], 23 February. Available in Arabic at http://www.library.cornell.edu/colldev/mideast/fatw2.htm [accessed: August 31, 2011]; in English at http://www.pbs.org/newshour/terrorism/international/fatwa_1998.html [accessed: August 31, 2011].

Marighella, C. 1975. *Minimanual of the Urban Guerrilla*. Boulder (Col.): Paladin Press.

Mayntz, R. 2004. *Organizational Forms of Terrorism: Hierarchy, Network, or a Type Sui Generis?* Max Planck Institute for the Study of Societies (MPIfG) Discussion Paper no. 04/4. Cologne: MPIfG.

Neumann, P. 2008. *Joining al-Qaeda: Jihadist Recruitment in Europe*, Adelphi Paper no. 399. London: Routledge.

Ouchi, W. 1980. Markets, bureaucracies and clans. *Administrative Science Quarterly*, 25(1), 129–41.

Qutb, S. 1980. *Milestones*. Cedar Rapids (Iowa): Unity Publishing Co.

Qutb, S. 2000. War, peace, and Islamic Jihad, in *Contemporary Debates in Islam: An Anthology of Modernist and Fundamentalist Thought*, edited by M. Moaddel and K. Talatoff. Basingstoke: Macmillan, 223–45.

Rollins, J. et al. 2011a. *Al Qaeda and Affiliates: Historical Perspective, Global Presence, and Implications for U.S. Policy.* CRS Report for Congress no. R41070. Washington D.C.: CRS.

Rollins, J. et al. 2011b. *Osama Bin Laden's Death: Implications and Considerations.* CRS Report for Congress no. R41809. Washington D.C.: CRS.

Ronfeldt, D. 2005. Al Qaeda and its affiliates: a global tribe waging segmental warfare? *First Monday* [Online], 10(3). Available at http://firstmonday.org/htbin/cgiwrap/bin/ojs/index.php/fm/article/view/1214/1134 [accessed: August 31, 2011].

Sageman, M. 2004. *Understanding Terror Networks.* Philadelphia: University of Pennsylvania Press.

Sageman, M. 2007a. *Leaderless Jihad: Terror Networks in the Twenty-First Century.* Philadelphia: University of Pennsylvania Press.

Sageman, M. 2007b. Radicalization of global Islamist terrorists. Testimony before the US Senate Committee on Homeland Security and Governmental Affairs. Washington DC, 27 June.

Saikia, J. and Stepanova, E. 2009. *Terrorism: Patterns of Internationalization.* New Delhi, London, Los Angeles: Sage.

Scott, J. 2000. *Social Network Analysis: A Handbook.* 2nd edn. London: Sage.

Stepanova, E. 2008. *Terrorism in Asymmetrical Conflict: Ideological and Structural Aspects.* Oxford: Oxford University Press.

Taarnby, M. 2007. Understanding recruitment of Islamist terrorists in Europe, in *Mapping Terrorism Research: State of the Art, Gaps and Future Direction*, edited by M. Ranstorp. London: Routledge, 164–86.

The White House. 2011. *National Strategy for Counterterrorism.* Washington D.C.: The White House.

Chapter 14

Conclusion

Martha Crenshaw

The chapters in this volume offer intriguing findings about the processes by which controversy and conflict evolve into violence, which many scholars have come to describe as "radicalization." As the editors explain in the introduction, the book is organized in terms of four areas: how the state relates to its challengers, how the challengers relate to each other, how meaning and interpretation are contested, and how patterns of violence are diffused across national borders. In this conclusion I identify some of the common themes that emerge from the discussions of these topics and in doing so raise some questions for future research. These themes relate to the meaning of radicalization itself, the centrality of context and contingency in radicalization processes, the nature of outbidding in extremism, the powerful contribution of emotions to conflict dynamics, unintended consequences of policies and actions, and agency in the dynamics of transnational diffusion. I also draw out some of the policy implications of the analyses presented here.

The Meaning of Radicalization

The volume sheds considerable light on the meaning of the concept of radicalization. First, what is "radical" is highly context-dependent, a matter of perspective on the part of both perpetrator and audience. Behavior that is routine in one setting and at one time may be regarded as exceptional and extreme in others—even violence can be normal and accepted. For example, in her chapter on gender and violence, Viterna says that relevant publics can see violence not as radical but as righteous. She argues that categorizing all violence as "radical" is inappropriately normative. We must understand the perceptions of audiences, which will be relative and subjective; we should not base our conception of radicalization only on an abstract theoretical perspective. Alimi and Johnston's argument that we need to bring culture into the discussion of radicalization is pertinent here. Culture, however, is not determining. The novel tactic of suicide missions has diffused across many different quite varied cultures, with its adoption facilitated by reframing it as martyrdom or a demonstration that "we do not fear death." The geographical diffusion of the tactic has been widespread and rapid. It has now become a hallmark of the al-Qaeda and affiliates brand, but its origins lie in Lebanon in the early 1980s, and the Sri Lankan Liberation Tigers of Tamil Eelam were avid practitioners who perfected the miniaturization of explosives that could be worn on the body of the perpetrator. Before it became a mainstay of the wars in Iraq and Afghanistan, Palestinians figured prominently in the tactic of suicide missions.

As this example suggests, we need to disaggregate and refine the definition of the dependent variable if we seek to explain radicalization generally as escalation toward sustained political violence. The problem of explaining radicalization is more complex than simply explicating a shift from non-violence to violence in general or across the board, although this shift is important. We need to answer the more specific question of the adoption of particular forms or repertoires of violence directed against specific categories of targets. The type of violence employed and the symbols it evokes matter. Viterna argues that the sexual victimization of women is frequently cited as a way of condemning violence as "radical" but that the victimization of men is not. In her view, violence is perceived as "radical" when it is committed by women or against women and children. But it is men who are mobilized, often by emotionally compelling narratives that may or may not be empirically substantiated.

The individual and group choices among types of escalatory violence depend on factors that are not yet well understood. For example, despite an abundance of scholarly attention to the issue we still do not understand decisions to employ suicide missions in preference to other forms of terrorism (Crenshaw 2007). Is the resort to this tactic the result of indoctrination into an ideology of martyrdom or an organization's strategic calculus based on the expectation that suicide attacks are more effective than other forms of terrorism? As a consequence of this differentiation among forms of violence, the process of radicalization is also about legitimizing selected repertoires of contention, not just legitimizing the resort to violence in itself as a means of diminishing the power of the state or expressing the demands of a social movement. Thus an important driver of radicalization is the ability of users and supporters to justify the choice of a specific form of violence. Possibly violence must be successfully framed as legitimate resistance to oppression in order for radicalization to occur. Supporters of violent resistance often reject some methods while accepting others. For example, within the global jihadist movement, disputes are intense over whether or not killing civilians, especially Muslim civilians, is morally justifiable according to the tenets of Islam. In Iraq the brutal tactics of the al-Qaeda affiliated groups alienated other Sunni resistance organizations.

Alimi and Johnston propose a different conception of radicalization, seeing the transition of Palestinian opposition to the Israeli state from nationalism to political Islamism as one of its forms. Radicalization for them is a shift in direction or ideology rather than a shift in method and levels of violence. They argue that cultural patterns are constitutive elements of the process of transition. We could look at this causal mechanism in reverse, however. Possibly the change was actually more about the utility of violence—groups that preferred escalation for strategic reasons sought moral legitimacy and thus adopted a new and compelling justificatory narrative, such as the emphasis on martyrdom. Stepanova's focus on ideology is compatible with this interpretation.

Context and Contingency

The evidence and arguments presented here demonstrate repeatedly and convincingly that strategies and outcomes are contingent on context and the behavior of other actors, as the editors intended and emphasized. Taken together, the chapters constitute a powerful argument against determinism and over-simplification. The admittedly complex environment in which radicalization occurs is important. The chapters also underscore the dangers of prediction in this field, which is a salutary caution for all social scientists and policy analysts. As Stepanova points out, the processes of radicalization are essentially non-linear. Outcomes are likely to be unexpected. Surprise is predictable.

The role of contingency and circumstance is stressed throughout this volume. Conflict does not automatically lead to violence because of innate predispositions, particular belief systems (religious or otherwise), or generalized conditions such as official oppression. These factors may matter but not in the same way at every time in every place. The prison setting, for example, may or may not lead to individual propensity for violence or conversion to radical beliefs. There are too many mediating variables to permit easy causal inferences.

It is thus essential for analysts to trace the unfolding of events and to accommodate timing and sequence. As the editors observe, accounting for how processes unfold is a type of explanation, and the order in which things happen is critical to outcomes. As political actors make choices they are themselves transformed, and their future choices are thus shaped by past decisions. Radicalization arises from multiple interactions that change over time. These processes are extremely fluid and volatile. Change is constant. As Gupta notes in analyzing South Africa, triggers of radicalization produce different results depending on contexts and actors. Actors align and realign themselves according to what others are doing as well as their expectations about the future of the conflict, particularly whether or not it is escalating or de-escalating.

Outbidding in Extremism

The most prevalent theory of how relationships among multiple challenging groups produce radicalization is that of outbidding in extremism. Competition is thought to spur escalation as rivals strive to outdo each other in order to win the support of a shared constituency, in the absence of authoritative institutions that can adjudicate the contest for power. For example, della Porta stresses the importance of competitive interactions during protest cycles. Such rivalries can lead to the formation of conspiratorial underground organizations that resort to terrorism, although escalation in this direction is by no means inevitable.

The underlying assumption behind the theory of outbidding in extremism, often implicit, is that it is violence, not non-violence, that is valued by the critical public and that thus elicits popular support and arouses enthusiasm. More moderate groups operating in the same social movement sector as violent groups presumably seem timid or even collaborationist by comparison and as a consequence lose out in the game. If they do not learn and adapt, they will presumably lose power within the movement.

The process of outbidding can be fueled by anger, especially when the state takes actions that cause the population to feel that it needs to be represented by armed defenders and avengers. Outbidding in extremism can thus be seen as a response to a popular demand, often stimulated by repression that is resented as unjust. The origins of theories of outbidding lie in studies of ethnic conflict, but constituencies can be linked by political affiliation rather than ethnic identity, as De Fazio claims. A feeling of community need not be based on ethnicity.

Rivalries are an integral part of a web of relationships linking challengers to each other, the public, and the state, but we need to investigate more closely what is at stake in intra-movement competition. Rivalry is not just about power and control over the movement and the right to represent a community but about a struggle over collective identity, meaning, and authenticity (as suggested by Alimi and Johnston with regard to the Palestinian resistance movement). There can be intense competition among actors over how the struggle is to be framed and interpreted. There can also be rivalry over interpretation of the past and memory, such as the determination of who is the legitimate heir to the reputation of a historic and heroic resistance to oppression.

There is ample historical evidence of the operation of the outbidding phenomenon, as the chapters by della Porta and De Fazio demonstrate, but it is also important to remember that outbidding does not always occur (notwithstanding De Fazio's claim that radicalization is almost inevitable and universal within a social movement). If it does occur, it is not automatically successful in advancing the fortunes of the most extreme group in the constellation of challengers. Gupta's chapter on South Africa, for example, explains that after an initial period of escalation radicalization faded, even though the presumed drivers of violence such as state repression and intra-movement competition remained relatively constant. She suggests that it is not just the existence of competitive relationships but who the competitors are that matters. In the case of South Africa, relative power, credibility, and organizational culture led to stalled radicalization, as the more violent activities of the Pan Africanist Congress were not imitated by the African National Congress. Similarly, Alimi and Johnston point to the effect of relative power position within a movement on preferences about specific repertoires of contention.

We need to ask more questions about the conditions under which outbidding is likely, to compare cases where it is present to where it is absent, and to evaluate the outcomes of competition carefully. What causes movement fragmentation in the first place? Is organizational splintering under stress inevitable? Under what general circumstances do perceived moderates appear more attractive than extreme rivals? When do audiences reward violence and when do they reward negotiation or compromise? When does competition among likeminded groups lead to differentiation and when to imitation? If outbidding dominated interactions among militant groups, all would eventually be equally radical as rivals converged, but this is not the case. Even after lengthy experience with violence some actors are more radical than others (for example, Hamas and Palestinian Islamic Jihad would be considered more violent than Fatah). Violence proneness is uneven among participants in collective action, as Johnston points out in his discussion of emotion and protest. Gupta argues that positioning oneself along the tactical spectrum is a process of constant adjustment to changing circumstances, in many ways a result of observation and learning. It is not uncommon for the adoption of violence (especially indiscriminate violence against civilians) to alienate previously sympathetic audiences (the case of the jihadist movement has been mentioned previously). Sometimes groups learn from their mistakes, but sometimes they persist in the path of escalation despite popular disapproval. Zarqawi's organization in Iraq is a case in point. The brutal tactics of al-Qaeda in Iraq (AQI) contributed to the emergence of the "Awakening" movements that reconciled with the government.

Donatella della Porta's suggestion that state repression encourages imitation of radical tactics because it enhances solidarity within a movement is an intriguing proposition that warrants further empirical investigation. Does the repression-solidarity-imitation hypothesis, for example, contradict the basic premises of the outbidding in extremism theory, which stresses rivalry and competition? What is the role of emotion in competitive outbidding processes?

Paying attention to the mechanisms that enhance solidarity and cohesion also points to the fact that outbidding does not represent the entire picture of interactions among challengers. A more comprehensive analysis is needed.

First, processes of radicalization are also driven by antagonistic relationships between non-state actors or social movements that do not seek the support of the same constituency. The interactions between Protestants and Catholics in Northern Ireland and Sunni and Shia militants in Iraq are a case in point. Both della Porta and De Fazio mention the competition between left and right in Italy. Alper notes that the dynamics of relationships with right-wing groups reinforced radicalization in the leftist student protest movement in Turkey. Groups may turn purposefully to violence in order to defend a community against violence from other non-state actors, especially in circumstances where they believe that the state will not or cannot protect them. Terrorism, for example, is often associated with sectarianism (in Pakistan, for example, where the most extreme jihadist groups are often the most sectarian). Groups that are ostensibly pro-state may still threaten and undermine its authority. Protestant loyalist resistance to British government efforts to reach a settlement in Northern Ireland is an example.

298   *Dynamics of Political Violence*

Second, cooperation among groups is also frequent and can also produce higher levels of violence. The formation of larger more powerful groups or alliances that consolidate the space of violent opposition and dominate the production of resources can permit more extensive and sustained challenges to state authority as well as credibly enter into a negotiated peace process. On this subject many questions remain open for further research. At what points in a conflict do challengers unite, as opposed to fragmentation and competition, and what are the consequences of collaboration? What forms of cooperation are likely to result, under what circumstances? When do groups merge, for example, or merely cooperate occasionally on tactics and operations? Does ideological solidarity promote cooperation? Are more cohesive and unified groups more likely to succeed in pressing their claims against the state?

Emotions

Johnston's chapter emphasizes that emotions are essential to the generation of processes of radicalization. Anger is often a trigger for escalation. For example, an action taken by the state (typically involving the excessive use of force) becomes a catalyst not just because it is deadly but because it is interpreted or framed as particularly unjust and unprovoked (e.g., the deaths of protestors during political demonstrations, such as the death of Benno Ohnesorg at the hands of the German police in 1967). At other times, the process can be less abrupt; anger can build gradually until it is shared by a critical mass.

Anger is often linked to perceptions of injustice, and both mass and social media can play a key role in spreading knowledge and awareness of narratives and symbols that affront a population's sensibilities and may consequently motivate small numbers of people to the use of violence. Anger is closely related to demands for vengeance. In addition, it is not necessarily spontaneous. The arousal of anger can be even more directed, in fact exploited, by actors who seek to use events to mobilize support for their cause (e.g., the Danish "Cartoons" controversy).

Johnston reminds us that another important contribution of anger is in overcoming fear, an emotion that we do not often think of as relevant to the psychology of radicalization. Anger enables ordinary people to cease to fear reprisals for their actions, for example. Formerly compliant subjects become willing to accept higher risks; they are emboldened by outrage as well as by the sense that they are not alone. Johnston refers to this shift in attitude as "fear abatement."

The fact that emotions can drive escalation toward violence reinforces the importance of contingency. Crowds can get out of hand, protest policing can become undisciplined, and in the heat of the moment both opposition and authorities can make mistakes. Loss of control can occur on both sides, although it is hard to predict when and where it will happen. The beginning of the "Arab Spring" in Tunisia is a case in point. A single event led to a cascade of reactions that overturned regimes in Tunisia and Egypt and precipitated a civil war in Syria.

Because anger is such a potent force, challengers may seek to use violence to provoke the state to over-reaction. Such provocation is thought to be a preferred tactic of "spoilers" in peace processes, for example (Kydd and Walter 2002). However, we do not know when and how this strategy is chosen, when it is effective, or who among multiple challengers is likely to employ it. Spoilers are not always the weaker parties who stand to lose out in a peace agreement. In Colombia, for example, it was the largest group, the FARC, that held out against government offers to join a negotiated settlement in the 1980s. Instead a smaller group, M-19, joined the political process.

In this area of inquiry there is a serious need to introduce comparisons: are there cases when extremely provocative state actions did not have radicalizing effects? Why? We also need to look at the other side: when do states succumb to the temptation to respond to provocation? Under what circumstances will they exhibit restraint when faced with an escalatory spiral? What are the consequences of threats and coercive retaliation in terms of adversary behavior and public opinion?

Emotions other than anger and fear also contribute to outcomes. Alper refers to the self-confidence that the Turkish student movement gained through successful campaigns of protest as a driver of escalation toward violence. They were not thwarted or frustrated but emboldened. Instead their assertiveness alarmed the authorities and far-right groups, who responded harshly, which in turn gave the radical minority of the student movement the ascendancy. Social psychology points to love for the in-group rather than hate for the out-group as a motivator of violence (McCauley and Moskalenko 2011).

Unintended Consequences

The question of unintended consequences is usually addressed to the actions of states as they confront challengers, but it is also relevant to the actions of oppositional forces. As discussed earlier, we are accustomed to the idea that repression can stimulate rather than quell dissent and violence. Repression legitimizes violent opposition in addition to arousing the strong emotions that propel passive bystanders into action and move peaceful protesters to violence, including terrorism. The chapters in this volume provide numerous examples (see also Crenshaw ed. 2010).

Law enforcement can backfire. De Vito argues that the sources of prison radicalization may be outside rather than inside the prison space, since jailed militants maintain contacts with the external organization and are influenced by events outside the prison walls. For instance, judicial trials, typically thought of by the state and its defenders as testaments to the appropriate and fair implementation of democratic principles and the rule of law, may unexpectedly impel radicalization as they mobilize outside support for the accused prisoners. As de Graaf (2011) argues, terrorism trials are not only a demonstration of the rule of law but a theatre for the terrorists. Their impact on radicalization depends on audience perceptions.

At the same time, internally, prisons provide individuals the space and time for ideological indoctrination into militancy.

What is less commonly analyzed is how soft or conciliatory policies may also backfire. Clumsy efforts by the state to prevent violence may instead fuel perceptions of discrimination, as those social elements identified as likely to be "radicalized" and thus in need of remediation are stigmatized and alienated from mainstream society (e.g., Muslim youth in the United States or Europe). According to Lindekilde, such countermeasures may even increase rather than diminish the threat of terrorism. His account indicates that the long term consequences of policies may be counterproductive even if short term effects are positive. As he concludes, we need to know more about how governments manage unintended adverse consequences of their actions. Are policy makers, for example, misled by the appearance of short term advantage?

Scholarship has generally neglected the unintended consequences of decisions made by challengers. Non-state actors are certainly not more omniscient than governments. It is not clear that Bin Laden anticipated the American reaction to the 9/11 attacks. Certainly some leaders of the Taliban seriously underestimated American and NATO military potential and willingness to use force. Nor did the Italian Red Brigades appear to anticipate the negative effects (for their cause) of the kidnapping and murder of Aldo Moro. What are the effects of these miscalculations?

Transnationalism

It is scarcely novel to point out the importance of the transnational dimensions of protest, terrorism, and rebellion, but exactly how these dimensions contribute to radicalization is not well understood. Several types of diffusion of ideas and repertoires are relevant to the escalation of violence.

First, local events can motivate violence in distant audiences. Alper's discussion of the Turkish student movement and its receptiveness to outside influences shows that indirect diffusion can have a powerful impact in the absence of direct or organizational connections between protesters in different countries. Even in the absence of brokers, some events have the intrinsic potential to spark transnational diffusion and imitation while others do not. Part of the appeal of the catalysts resides in the symbols themselves, their quality of resonance with the experience and attitudes of the receptive audience, their evocative power, and their appeal in particular political and cultural circumstances or cultures. Visual images are particularly important in an electronic age, as Olesen explains. Images condense a set of meanings in a singular visual expression. However, is it important to remember, as Olesen also points out, that not all those who respond emotionally to an injustice symbol will resort to violence. It is difficult to predict or explain who will react in what way.

Alper argues that ideas precede behavior in diffusion processes. Discourses emanating from outside can reframe the meaning of local contention and thus provide the bridge that links the event to external audiences. Communications as well as "bridging events" can connect the particular to the universal experience. Media coverage is especially important in the diffusion process. Once ideas have transferred, action may follow. But when does action follow ideas, and when is that action violence? What is the role of ideology (as Stepanova would surely ask)?

A critical element of the process of transnational diffusion can also be direct agency. Actors, who themselves may be transnational or local, seize on or create symbols, brands, and ideas and then promote them for their own strategic purposes. Frames and references are deliberately borrowed and adapted in order to be persuasive with audiences. The popular reaction to events is thus not entirely spontaneous; it is generated or brokered. There is a development, cultivation, and mediation process. As the editors note in the introduction, we need to understand more about these pivotal actors—their composition, location in the movement, sources of authority, and relationship to the actors who adopt new techniques, brands, or ideological frames.

Second, some organizational entities in themselves transcend borders (al-Qaeda being an excellent contemporary example), and these actors are directly at the center of the explanation of some processes of diffusion. They can be an outside branch of a local movement—for example, a diaspora—or a genuinely transnational organization that tries to manipulate or incorporate local actors into a global frame and a global movement, such as al-Qaeda, the subject of Stepanova's chapter. In focusing on agency, Stepanova argues that the level of transnationalism is determined by a group's goals and agenda rather than organizational structure or physical location. In fact, she describes al-Qaeda as representing a supranational ideology that lies outside the state framework entirely. Ideology, which forms the prism through which events are interpreted as unjust, is the source of radicalization, not social networks per se or specific catalyzing events or cultures. Strategic actors like al-Qaeda do not merely take advantage of events (e.g., in Olesen's terms transforming events into transnational injustice symbols); on their own initiative they can create compelling events complete with dramatic visual effects (such as the 9/11 attacks on New York and Washington with the unforgettable images of smoke and flames pouring from the collapsing World Trade Center towers and the Pentagon). Such organizations are skilled in what the American government calls strategic communication, otherwise known as propaganda. Al-Qaeda's video capabilities are one of its most important assets, and the English language *Inspire* magazine is another case in point. As Olesen points out, the salience of symbols is further reinforced through systematic usage. Repetition deepens their impact. Perhaps because of their supranational ideological orientation, actors such as al-Qaeda are adept at portraying local events as problems that are of general concern to a much broader constituency spread across many settings.

Romanos refers to the central role that the anarchist diaspora played in violence within Spain. Exiled organizations were transmitters of innovation, although not all were equally influential. The means of transmission was (not surprisingly) through personal contact and social networks, not news media. His chapter suggests several questions for further research: what outside actors are good transmitters? What are the channels of diffusion of innovation? When does tactical innovation involve escalation? When does it involve de-radicalization (as the editors ask in the introduction)?

A review of the historical examples cited in these chapters shows that the transnational diffusion of justifications for violence and awareness of repertoires is scarcely new. Technology has facilitated communication, hastened diffusion, and extended outreach, but the elements of transmission are basically the same.

Concluding Thoughts

Our efforts to understand the highly complicated processes of radicalization should be aimed not just at explaining the phenomenon but at discovering how violent conflict can be avoided as an outcome of contentious politics or, if it cannot be averted, to bring violence quickly and fairly to an end once escalation has occurred. As scholars we tend to avoid prescription, but in this case we have an obligation to offer what ideas we can about the peaceful settlement or resolution of political disputes. We need to inform sensible and restrained public policy.

A basic principle is that the leaders of states need to understand that their actions can be catalysts for radicalization. Anything the state does that justifies and legitimizes violence on the part of an opposition is dangerous (unless the state seeks escalation). Even well-meant policies intended to prevent or conciliate can backfire. And in an age of instantaneous communication what appear to be purely local events can have global resonance and provoke violence far beyond national borders.

Government decision makers also need to recognize that control of radicalization processes is impossible, especially when transnational influences and actors are involved. "Counter-radicalization" sounds like a reasonable policy goal, but the state is not well placed to convince individuals or communities that violence is not an appropriate course of action or that certain repertoires are illegitimate. The unexpected is likely to happen. Policy makers also need to maintain awareness of the constantly shifting dynamics of a struggle. Prior assumptions should always be questioned.

The implications of facing multiple challengers within an overall oppositional movement may not be well understood. Policy makers often appear to be indifferent to the distinctions and relationships among challengers and to lump together diverse organizations and even constituencies. Over-simplification is always a temptation. The range of relationships among groups within a movement is both broad and fluid, as allies can become rivals and enemies become friends in rapid reversals of position. What is at stake in an internecine struggle for power is an equally complex problem. Although outbidding in extremism is by no means inevitable, governments should be cautious about taking actions that will encourage escalation toward violence by encouraging groups to believe that their supporters will reward violent extremism. Encouraging "moderates" is a risky course, but it is not a foregone conclusion that the most intransigent groups will drive the process of contention.

References

Crenshaw, M. 2007. Explaining Suicide Terrorism: A Review Essay. *Security Studies*, 6(1), 133–62.

Crenshaw, M. ed. 2010. *The Consequences of Counterterrorism.* New York: Russell Sage Foundation.

De Graaf, B. 2011. *Evaluating counterterrorism performance: A Comparative Study.* London and New York: Routledge.

Kydd, A. and B.F. Walter. 2002. Sabotaging the Peace: The Politics of Extremist Violence. *International Organization*, 56(2), 263–96.

McCauley, C., and Moskalenko, S. 2011. *Friction: How Radicalization Happens to Them and Us.* New York: Oxford University Press.

Index

abortion 84, 207–9
activism 14–15, 34–5, 62, 103, 119, 126,
    144, 149, 183, 194, 217–19,
    230–31, 263
adoption 2, 10, 16, 97, 117, 140, 239, 250,
    257, 272, 293–4, 297
affinity group 241
Afghanistan 65, 105, 109, 195, 280–82,
    286, 294
African National Congress (ANC) 10,
    137–41, 143, 145–60
agency 2, 7, 16–17, 74–5, 77, 94, 182–3,
    199, 257–8, 293, 301
Al-Ali, Hamed bin Abdallah 288
Al-Assad regime 28–9, 31, 40, 43
Al-Jamaa al-Islamiyya 106–9
Al-Jihad 106–9
Al-Qaeda 17, 59–60, 104, 106, 108,
    217–18, 223–9, 269, 275, 277–90,
    293–4, 297, 301
Al-Zawahiri, Ayman 109, 225
alliance 57, 61, 108, 147, 160, 241, 260,
    262, 298
anarchism 237–41, 243–4, 248, 250–51
antiterrorism 75–6, 82–3, 85
apartheid 17, 137–8, 147, 151, 153–4, 158, 160
Arafat, Yasser 13, 176–7, 180, 182
arena 206–9
attacks 9, 28, 32, 33, 51, 56, 59, 97, 99,
    100, 106–7, 110, 125, 128–9,
    149–60, 181, 197, 217–18, 222–4,
    226–9, 238, 244–5, 247, 270–71,
    275, 277, 279, 288, 294, 300–301
audiences 2, 8–11, 12, 14, 37, 86, 142–7, 153,
    159, 161, 191, 194, 206, 210, 220,
    224, 229, 251, 293, 297, 299–301

backfire management 64–6, 67
backfire mechanism 7, 51–5, 57–8, 62, 66
behavioral 170, 210, 244, 250, 257, 264

Bin Laden, Osama 225
bombing 55, 99, 177, 182, 204, 225–6
border 15, 16, 29, 94, 142, 204, 237, 246,
    247, 250, 290, 293, 301, 302
Bourdieu, Pierre 11, 15
Brigate Rosse (Red Brigades) 82, 101–3
broken negotiations 32–4

cartoons 1, 14, 64, 217–18, 221–31
civilians 150–51, 153, 160, 190–91, 194–6,
    199–201, 203, 205, 219, 275, 280,
    294, 297
Civil Rights Movement 10, 33, 115, 122,
    124, 125
civil war 1, 3, 11–12, 28–9, 31–2, 44, 115,
    129, 189, 192–3, 196, 206, 211,
    238–41, 251, 298
Chile 41, 44, 173
Christie, Stuart 245, 247
clandestine political violence 93
collective action 94, 96–8, 120, 140, 170–
    73, 183, 185, 244, 257, 267, 297
collective violence 27, 31–4, 40
competitive escalation 93–5, 103, 110
Confederación Nacional del Trabajo (CNT)
    240, 242–4, 247, 249, 251
Conill, Jordi 245
Consejo Ibérico de Liberación (CIL) 245–6
consequences 16, 56, 61, 78, 80, 105, 159,
    191, 193, 219, 230, 241, 244, 250,
    251, 288, 293, 298–300
constituencies 7–10, 109, 117–18, 142,
    146, 148, 296, 302
contentious politics 1, 3, 31, 44, 52, 54, 71,
    84, 86, 115, 116, 119, 184, 269, 302
contestation 9, 229
controversy 217, 218, 221–3, 293, 298
coordinated destruction 32
counter-radicalization 290, 302

306 *Dynamics of Political Violence*

counterterrorism 6, 7, 51–60, 62, 64–67, 281, 282
critical terrorism studies 5

death squads 6, 206
demobilization 95, 96, 206
democracy 27, 28, 56, 93
Denmark 59, 60, 61, 64, 218, 221, 222, 224–9, 231, 283
deprivation 45, 148
de-radicalization 7, 51, 71–3, 75, 7 6, 80–86, 138, 189, 190, 302
diaspora 6, 237, 238, 241, 242, 244, 247, 250, 251, 285, 289, 301
dictatorship 240, 245, 247, 251
diffusion 3, 5, 14, 15–17, 28, 58. 59, 77, 87, 94–5, 222, 229–30, 238–9, 241–2, 244–50, 255–9, 264–9, 271–3, 293–5, 302
direct action 96, 127, 130, 146, 149, 242, 244, 279, 285
dynamics of contention 31, 37, 40, 45, 116, 169, 171

economy 8, 94, 239, 260
Egypt 29, 35, 39, 106–9, 176, 222, 260, 263, 286, 298
El Salvador 1, 12, 14, 189–190, 192, 196–8, 200, 204, 206, 208, 209, 211
Elias, Norbert 11, 74
emotional management mechanisms 27, 45
emotions and mobilization 6, 30, 33, 34, 40, 41, 42, 45, 219, 293, 298–9
escalation 3, 17, 32, 33, 72, 84, 93, 94, 95, 100, 103, 110–11, 122, 137–9, 222, 258, 261, 269, 272–3, 294–300, 302, 303
exile 108, 141, 147, 240–44, 246–50

factionalism 8, 9, 140
fear abatement 27, 34–7, 39, 40, 298
Federación Anarquista Ibérica (FAI) 240, 242, 243, 248, 249
Federación Ibérica de Juventudes Libertarias (FIJL) 240, 243, 246, 248, 249
Federal Republic of Germany 80, 82, 102, 259, 266, 268, 283

feminist 33, 192, 196–8, 209, 211
Ferabundo Marti National Liberation Front (FMLN) 12, 13, 189, 190, 199–203, 205–10
Foucault, Michel 74, 80
frame analysis 11–13, 15, 183,
framing 40, 57–60, 86, 116, 140, 169–74, 182–5, 192, 211, 223–4, 257, 293
France 6, 16, 77, 81, 85, 221, 228
Franco, General Francisco 16, 36, 37, 237–51
free riders 190, 191
fundamentalism 95, 104, 105

gender 12, 13, 96, 118, 189– 212, 293
Germany 6, 9, 80, 82, 102, 259, 266, 268, 283
global jihad 17, 277, 278, 282–8, 294
movement 277, 289
Goffman, Erving 11–15, 74, 170–71, 174, 183
Greece 27–30, 263
grievance 28, 35, 41, 59, 116, 143, 144, 266–8, 273
guerrilla 3, 100, 189–212, 244, 247, 277, 279

Hamas 175–85, 279, 281, 297
hard repression 62, 111
Horn of Africa 282
hybrid structures 287

identity 2, 7, 13, 16, 33, 37, 39, 52, 54, 55, 57, 62–6, 99, 126, 140, 143, 153, 169, 174–7, 183, 184, 238, 240, 248, 258, 265, 273, 296
ideological-functional network 17, 283, 284, 289
injustice 14, 41, 45, 53, 57, 60, 217–32, 286, 298, 300, 301
insurrection 32, 156, 242
insurgency 3, 59, 115, 200, 237, 246–51
intifada 11, 13, 171, 174, 175, 177, 179, 180, 181, 182
intra-movement dynamics/competition 3, 5, 7–10, 16, 73, 82, 114–20, 122–6, 128, 131, 138, 141–8, 152–61, 296
Ireland 27, 28
Islam 14, 60, 103–8, 173, 175, 218, 228, 229, 231, 232, 294
Islamic Jihad 13, 175, 179, 182, 297
Israel 107, 173–85, 221, 261, 262, 264

Index

Italy 6, 9, 27, 61, 77, 79–85, 95, 98, 101, 102, 259, 268, 297

kidnapping 83, 101, 300

legitimation 77, 79, 80, 85, 119, 223, 249, 250
Liberation Movement 85, 137– 61
London 16, 44, 55, 59, 230
long-term anger 41, 43, 45
loyalist 122–30, 298

marxism 105, 175
massacre 52, 137, 141, 147, 160, 176, 181, 182, 195, 206, 219–21
media 30, 35, 44, 53, 74, 76, 82, 108, 117–20, 147, 169, 181, 195, 210, 218, 248, 250, 256– 61, 266, 268, 273, 288, 298, 301, 302
Middle East 9, 27, 28, 103–5, 109, 264, 276, 283
military 28–33, 105, 108, 178, 181, 190, 199–207, 257, 259, 260, 262–4, 277, 279, 282, 289, 300
moderates 33, 119, 122, 123, 126, 129, 131, 237, 297, 303
Movimiento Ibérica de Resistencia (MIR) 242, 249
Movimiento Libertario de Resistencia (MLR) 242, 244–9
murder 82, 203, 224–6, 300
Muslim 13, 14, 52, 59– 63, 103–10, 174–80, 185, 217–18, 220–32, 262, 264, 272
Muslim Brotherhood 103, 106, 108, 175, 179, 185, 285, 287, 289

narrative 13, 14, 54, 58, 74, 105, 121, 122, 171, 178, 182, 190, 192–4, 200–205, 210, 211, 294, 295, 298
nationalism 13, 104, 148, 160, 169–85, 260, 263, 294
network 7, 14–16, 33, 56, 57, 61, 78, 79, 82, 84, 93, 98, 99, 103, 105, 106, 118, 121–3, 126, 127, 130, 151, 155, 156, 174, 177, 218, 225, 238, 240, 246, 247, 250, 259, 275–90, 301, 302
network analysis 126
new social movement approach 184

NICRA 123–31
Northern Ireland 8, 10, 17, 82, 83, 115–17, 119–32, 240, 268, 297

organizational asymmetry 276, 290

Pakistan 62, 104, 105, 109, 195, 225, 226, 228, 281, 282, 297
Palestine 8, 169, 174, 176, 178, 180, 218
Palestinian Liberation Organization (PLO) 175–9, 181
Pan African Congress (PAC) 10, 137–9, 143, 145
police 7, 8, 28–45, 52, 59, 62, 94, 96, 97, 102, 106–10, 115, 116, 120, 122–30, 137, 150, 151, 156, 173, 198, 227, 241, 244–9, 258, 264, 268–73, 298
police infiltration 241
policing 30, 39, 51, 94, 120, 142, 157, 298
political outbidding 10, 115–19, 128–31
political process approach 2, 8, 97, 115, 117, 125, 169, 170
politicization 77, 85, 106, 265
Poqo 149–53, 157
post-network forms 276, 283, 290
Prima Linea (Front Line) 83, 101
primary framework 170–74, 180–84
prison 7, 73–87, 141, 182, 196, 220, 227, 249, 295, 299, 300
prisoners 7, 74– 87, 109, 152, 196, 299
propaganda 55, 56, 122, 151, 207, 238, 244, 247, 249, 285, 288, 301
property damage 30, 245
protest 3, 5–12, 15–16, 27–45, 51–2, 56–7, 76–9, 93–111, 115, 120, 122–32, 137, 138, 141, 146–52, 170–72, 182, 195, 217, 219, 223, 238, 256–73, 276–8, 286, 295–300
protest movement 256, 257, 297
protest policing 51, 298
protest violence 27, 32–4, 43–5

quantitative narrative analysis 121
Qutb, Sayyed 286, 288, 290

radicalization process 3, 16, 56, 139, 144, 145, 159, 268, 269, 284

radicals 57, 60, 63, 101, 119, 126, 140, 148, 200, 207, 237, 273, 287
rape 39, 190, 196, 198–211, 219
recruitment 12, 13, 52, 57, 59–62, 100, 103, 194
reflexive anger 41, 44–5
reflexive emotions 32, 41, 42
relational field 2
relational mechanism 55, 57, 58, 73, 131, 139, 269
relational perspective 31, 45
religion 103, 107, 180
religious violence 103
repertoire of action 2, 57, 82, 94, 102, 111, 119, 169, 257, 271
repression 6–10, 28–31, 34–44, 51, 57, 61, 62, 65, 74, 76, 80–87, 94, 97, 98, 106–11, 115, 120, 122–3, 128–32, 138, 144, 152, 181, 200, 239, 241–5, 265, 296–9
resource mobilization approach 8
revolution 31–3, 105, 107, 129, 154, 174, 209, 244, 267, 276
right-wing 99, 107, 110, 181, 182, 255, 258, 260, 261, 263, 268–73, 286, 297
riot 28, 31, 41, 74, 109, 115, 129, 137
risky shift 38
robbery 242
RUC 124, 128

sabotage 149, 151, 242, 244, 245
Salafi 104, 105, 283
Salafist 62
scattered attacks 32, 33, 273
secret police 31
semantic Triplets 121, 122, 172, 185
September 11, 2001 15, 275, 277, 278, 280, 283, 289
social movement organizations 12, 93, 99, 105, 117
social movement studies 1, 11, 12, 14, 15, 51, 93, 237
social movements 3, 5–10, 12, 27, 30, 32, 34, 41, 42, 71, 78, 93–9, 103, 105, 110, 111, 115–20, 127, 128, 142, 154, 169, 171, 182, 200, 230, 237–40, 244, 250, 251, 256, 269, 294, 297

South Africa 3, 10, 17, 137–43, 147, 149–53, 156, 160–61, 295–6
Spain 16, 27, 28, 35, 44, 82, 237, 240–50, 266, 283, 301
Spanish Civil War 241, 251
SPIN structure 283
stalled radicalization 139, 296
state violence 29
strategies of contention 120, 128
structure 2, 6, 11–13, 17, 45, 66, 74, 76, 99, 119, 154, 156, 160, 170–73, 223, 231, 256, 278, 284–90
suicide Terrorism 104, 117
Sweden 227, 229, 266
symbols 15, 153, 172, 177, 217–24, 227–31, 264, 294, 298, 300, 301
Syria 28–35, 39, 43, 44, 105, 195, 298

tactics 2, 8, 15–17, 28–32, 41–3, 94–6, 102, 111, 119, 120, 123, 126, 132, 138, 140–44, 148–50, 157–61, 170, 177–9, 192, 208, 223, 237–40, 244, 250, 251, 256, 258, 268–73, 275, 277, 279, 294, 297, 298
Three Mile Island 34
Tilly, Charles 30–34, 37, 45, 121
transformative event 4
transgressive tactics 119, 138, 140
transnational 5, 14, 15, 79, 83, 116, 175, 217–32, 239, 250, 275–9, 282–90, 293, 300–302
triggering 38, 39, 44, 110, 120, 145, 258, 272
Turkey 255–73
typology 6, 7, 32, 51–4, 56, 58, 66, 67, 248
tyrannicide 245

underground organizations 9, 98–100, 296
United Kingdom, UK 39, 123, 283
United States of America (USA) 6, 79, 143, 195, 207, 209, 219, 220, 264, 268, 281–3, 300

violent conflict 1, 130, 196, 240, 302

Weber, Max 43
women 12, 13, 33, 108, 137, 150, 173, 179, 189–212, 240, 294